THE PUBLICATIONS

OF THE

𝕾𝔢𝔩𝔡𝔢𝔫 𝕾𝔬𝔠𝔦𝔢𝔱𝔶

περὶ παντὸς τήν ἐλευθερίαν

VOLUME LXXXIX

FOR THE YEAR 1972

Selden Society

FLETA

VOLUME III

BOOK III AND BOOK IV

EDITED

WITH A TRANSLATION

by

H. G. RICHARDSON

and

G. O. SAYLES

LONDON

THE SELDEN SOCIETY

1972

Printed in Great Britain by
William Clowes & Sons, Limited
London, Beccles and Colchester

CONTENTS

ACKNOWLEDGMENT

The Selden Society is indebted to the British Academy, the Max Rayne Foundation, the Ames Foundation, and Professor A. L. Goodhart for grants which have enabled this second part of the Society's edition of *Fleta* to be published as an additional volume for the year 1972.

PREFACE

Books I and II of *Fleta* were published in 1955 but further work was interrupted by other projects and not resumed until 1970. The interruption was unfortunately too long: and it should be said that neither the final MS. sent to the printers nor the proofs had the benefit of Mr. Richardson's erudite scrutiny, and he cannot therefore be held responsible for any errors that may have escaped notice.

While this volume was going through the press it was vetted by Professor S. E. Thorne when he was coping with the corresponding passages in Bracton, and a wealth of legal scholarship was thus made available to me. And Professor S. F. C. Milsom placed every word under minute examination and gave invaluable help in ensuring that the translation provides, as far as any translation can do so, the exact interpretation of the legal technicalities of the Latin text: to him I am truly grateful. It should perhaps be added that some, though happily not many, parts of *Fleta* defy satisfactory translation. The author has succeeded too well in the work of compression and squeezed out the sense: in Horace's phrase, *brevis esse laboro, obscurus fio*.

As well as the generous grants made to the Selden Society for the publication of this volume, which are acknowledged on another page, the Carnegie Trust for the Universities of Scotland most kindly made a grant to me in aid of the research required in completing the Text and Translation. It is hoped that the efforts made to justify the trust of all these benefactors will prove to have been not unsuccessful.

G. O. S.

Warren Hill,
Crowborough,
Sussex.

FLETA

Book III and Book IV

LIBER TERTIUS

CAP. I. DE RERUM ADQUISICIONIBUS

Superioribus libris expositum est de personis et earum accionibus, modo dicendum est de rebus et rerum accionibus que in patrimonio nostro vel extra habentur vel neutro.   In patrimonio nostro sunt terre, tenementa et hereditates,
5 extra patrimonium vero res sacre et communes.   In neutro sunt iura, seruitutes, aduocaciones ecclesiarum et abbathiarum que sine fundo alienari non possunt. Rursus prediales seruitutes per se non censentur ideoque in bonis esse non videntur vel extincte esse si per se censeantur.   Nam et manica videtur extincta cum non accedat vestimento, et tignum non videtur possideri cum non
10 accedat edificio.   Iste tamen seruitutes non dicuntur esse extra bona, cum possidentes excepcionem et non possidentes habeant accionem.

Rerum autem alie sunt corporales, vt que tangi possunt, alie incorporales, vt iura et seruitutes, alie communes vt aer, mare et litus maris, alie publice vt ius piscandi et applicandi flumina et portus.   Riparum eciam vsus publicus est de
15 iure gencium sicut ipsius fluminis ad plus vero se habet commune quam publicum eo quod vnum ad omne animatum et aliud ad omnem populum se extendit. Alie vniuersitatis vt theatra, stadia et ea que sunt ciuitatibus communia dominio et vsu, set alia communia dicuntur esse vniuersitatis dominio tantum et fructu, vt fundi et serui ciuitatum qui ita sunt omnium hominum ciuitatis quod nullius
20 per se.   Alie nullius vt res Deo rite per pontifices dedicate, quod enim diuini iuris est et in nullius hominis bonis est.   Sacra enim sunt, vt cimiteria, ecclesie, sacre capelle, edes sacre religiosorum que si diruantur adhuc manet locus sacer. Sacra eciam sunt dona que ad Dei ministerium sunt dedicata, vt calices, cruces et turribula, que alienari prohibentur excepta causa redempcionis captiuorum.
25 Quasi sacra sunt muri et porte ciuitatum, quia pena capitalis in tales est consti-

9. tignum] lignum, J.; possideri] possidere, J.   19. vt *om.* J.   21. et] id, J.; vt] ad, J.

BOOK III

CHAPTER 1. OF ACQUIRING PROPERTY

In the preceding books we have treated of persons and actions concerning them; now we must speak of things and actions concerning things which are deemed to be within our patrimony or outside it or are in neither category. Included in our patrimony are lands, tenements and inheritances: excluded are things that are sacred or owned in common. In neither category are rights, servitudes, the advowsons of churches and abbeys, which cannot be alienated apart from the land. On the other hand predial servitudes are not considered to have an existence on their own and therefore do not seem to be property or, if considered separately, are non-existent, just as a sleeve does not seem to exist as such when it is not attached to a garment and a beam does not seem to be possessed when it is not part of a building. So such servitudes are not regarded as existing apart from property, since those who possess them have an exception and those who do not possess them have a right of action.

Some things, again, are corporeal in that they may be touched; others are incorporeal, such as rights and servitudes; others are common, such as the air, the sea and the sea shore; others are public, such as the right to fish and to moor on river banks or at ports. By the law of nations the use of river banks is public just as is the use of the river itself; yet it may be regarded as more common than public because what is common is available to all living things and what is public is available to all people. Some things belong to the community, like theatres, stadia and those things which are the common property of cities in ownership and use; but other things are said to belong to the community but only in ownership and profit, such as the lands and the slaves of cities, which so belong to all citizens that they belong to none individually. Other things belong to nobody, such as things solemnly dedicated to God by priests, because they are subject to divine right and are no man's property. These things are sacred: cemeteries, churches, dedicated chapels, the dedicated buildings of religious, the site of which remains still sacred even if they become ruins. These also are sacred; gifts dedicated to the service of God, like chalices, crosses and censers, which it is forbidden to alienate except for the sake of ransoming captives. The walls and gates of cities are quasi-sacred, because capital punishment has been decreed for

tuta qui scalis adhibitis huiusmodi muros transcenderint vel aliquid violando
inmiserint. Hostile namque est et abhominabile alias ingredi quam per portas.
Et inde est quod lex specialiter dicitur sanccio quod iniuriosis penam inponit.
Nec liceat cuiuis ad priuatum comodum muros municipales communi vtilitati
5 confectos reficere. Item res nullius esse dicuntur pluribus modis, natura
scilicet siue iure naturali, vt volucres, fere bestie et pisces, censura vt diuina et
casu, vt hereditas iacens ante adicionem et vt liberi homines et habitum pro [175]
derelicto et serui egrotantes eiecti a dominis suis quos lex facit liberos.

CAP. II. DE ACCESSIONIBUS

10 Iure autem gencium siue naturali dominia rerum adquiruntur multis modis, f. 69
quandoque per occupacionem eorum que non sunt in bonis alicuius et que nunc
non fiunt ipsius regis de iure ciuili et non communia vt olim, sicut sunt fere
bestiarum, volucres, pisces et animalia que nunquam fuerunt domestica que in
terra, mari et aere nascuntur, que cum capiuntur captoris fiunt, que eciam cum
15 euaserint et naturalem ceperint libertatem vt vana fit eorum prosecucio captoris
esse desinunt et rursus noui fiunt occupantis. Continet eciam occupacio piscacio-
nem, venacionem, inclusionem et apprehensionem, nec sola prosecucio facit rem
esse meam, nam etsi feram bestiam vulnerauerim its vt capi possit, non tamen est
mea nisi ipsam ceperim set occupantis. Inclusionem, vt patet de apibus, quarum
20 fera est natura, si in arbore namque mea consederint non propter hoc mee erunt
antequam a meo alueo includantur, non magis quam volucres nidum in arbore
mea facientes, set si alius incluserit earum dominus erit. Agmen eciam apium
quod ex alueo meo euolauerit quamdiu in conspectu meo fuerit meum esse dici
poterit dum tamen possibilis sit eius deprehensio, alioquin fit occupantis nisi
25 sciuerit ipsum meum et quo casu furtum facit nisi animum habeat restituendi.
De volucribus autem et feris bestiis factis mansuetis, que ex consuetudine
eunt et redeunt, volant et reuolant, vt sunt cerui, falcones, grues et huiusmodi
secus erit, quia semper nostre esse dicuntur quamdiu de eis intelligi poterit quod
animum habuerint reuertendi, que licet conspectum nostrum effugerint, quo-
30 cumque tamen loco fuerint, nostre esse intelliguntur, et furtum facit qui eas animo
lucrandi retinuerit, dum tamen noticiam habuerit veri possessoris. Et con-
similiter dici poterit de hominibus liberis qui in seruitutem nostram deducti
fuerint: cum extra potestatem nostram euaserint, pristinum statum receperint.
Apprehensionem vt in hiis que communia sunt sicut in mari et litore maris in

---

4. vtilitati] vtilitate, J. 6. *posterius* vt] et, J. 12. *prius* non *addidimus.* 20. con-
cederint, J. 21. *post* alueo *add.* vel amne, J. 22. mea *om.* J. 23. alueo meo] eo
minime, J. 24. eius] ei, J. 29. animum] animam, J. 34. et *om* J.

those who bring ladders and scale over these walls or throw anything against them to breach them, for it is a hostile and detestable act to enter a city elsewhere than by its gates.   And hence it is that the law is specifically called a sanction which imposes a penalty upon wrongdoers.   Nor is anyone permitted to rebuild for private profit town-walls constructed for the public welfare.   Things are said to belong to no one in various ways: for example, by nature or by natural law, like birds and wild animals and fish; by public opinion as regards sacred things; by accident, as in the case of an inheritance lying vacant before the arrival of the heir.   In this category are free men, and anything regarded as derelict, and sick slaves, turned out by their masters, whom the law makes free.

Bracton,
f. 8*b*

CHAPTER 2.   OF ACCESSIONS

Bracton,
f. 8*b*

By the law of nations or by natural law the ownership of things is acquired in many ways, sometimes by taking possession of things that are not the property of anyone else and which now do not belong to the king by civil law and are not common property as once they were.   Such are wild beasts, birds, fish and animals which have never been domesticated and which are born on the earth, in the sea or in the air.   These, when they are captured, become the captor's, but if they should escape and recover their natural freedom so that their pursuit is in vain, they cease to be their captor's and belong, on the contrary, to him who again takes possession of them.   The taking of possession also comprises fishing, hunting, confining, and seizing.   But pursuit alone does not make a thing mine; for even though I should wound a wild beast so that it is possible for me to capture it, nevertheless it is not mine unless I do so, but belongs to him who takes possession of it.   An example of confining is that of bees, which are wild by nature and which, if they should settle in my tree, are not on that account mine until they are shut up in my hive, any more than birds nesting in my tree, for if another cages them he will be their owner.   A swarm of bees, moreover, which flies out of my hive may be said to be mine so long as it is in my sight, provided its capture is possible, but otherwise it becomes the property of him who takes possession, unless he knows it to be mine, in which case he commits theft unless he has the intention of restoring it.

Bracton,
f. 9

The position is different, however, with birds and wild beasts which have been tamed and which are accustomed to come and go, to fly away and fly back, such as deer, falcons, cranes and the like, because they are said to be always our property so long as they can be deemed to have an intention to return.   And although they may flee from our sight, nevertheless in whatsoever place they may be they are understood to be ours, and he commits theft who retains them with a mind to profit thereby, provided he has knowledge of the true possessor.   Similarly it may be said of free men who have been brought into slavery under us, that if they should escape out of our control they would recover their former status.   An example of seizing is seen in those things that are common property like

lapillis, gemmis et aliis in litore maris inuentis, et similiter in insulis in mari natis et in similibus.

    Adquiritur autem nobis iure gencium dominium rerum per accessionem, diuina natura operante, vt que ex animalibus dominio nostro subiectis nata sunt
5 nobis adquiruntur. Et quod per alluvionem agro nostro flumen adiecerit id iure gencium nobis adquiritur. Est autem alluuio latens incrementum. Per alluuionem autem adici dicitur quod tam paulatim adicitur quod percipi non possit quo momento temporis adicitur. Secus vero si incrementum non sit latens set manifestum, vt si vis fluminis partem aliquam ex predio tuo detraxerit et
10 vicini predium ampliauerit certum est eam tuam permanere, et si longiori tempore fundo vicini adheserit et arbores forte fundo vicini atraxerit que radicauerint extunc videntur fundo vicini adquisite. Opinio quorundam tamen est quod vtilis rei vendicacio in persona prioris domini obseruatur, quorundam vero quod cessat rei vendicacio quia alterius facta est. Habet eciam locum eadem species   [176]
15 accessionis in insula in flumine nata que si in medio fluminis fuerit orta communis erit eorum dominorum qui ab vtraque parte fluminis prope ripam predia possident pro modo latitudinis prope ripam existentis cuiusque fundi. Quod si alteri parti proximior sit eius erit tantum vel eorum qui ab illa parte prope ripam predia possident. Si autem in mari nascatur insula que non sit virgultis susten-
20 tata occupanti concedatur dum tamen alius ius exigere non poterit in eadem, vt si flumen circuiens agrum alicuius insulam redigat, et quo casu non minus propter hoc erit insula illius cuius ager prius erat. In mecienda autem vicinitate huiusmodi insularum ponatur punctus in medio vtriusque agri et si insula sit citra punctum tunc huius tantum vel illius tantum erit. Si autem sit citra punc-
25 tum et in ipso puncto et vltra, tunc pro indiuiso comunis erit vt tantum michi de ipsa cedat quantum continetur a medietate puncti vsque ad agrum meum et sic fiat in persona vicini quo ad diuisionem. Et videtur quod vicinitas et remocio insule considerari debent secundum principium natiuitatis sue, et inde est quod si inter insulam que michi proximior est et contrariam ripam vicini, que est vltra
30 flumen, alia insula sit nata, tunc fiet mensura a mea insula et non ab agro meo. Si autem insula rotunda fuerit tunc omne quod michi est propinquius michi cedat et similiter vicino cedat quod ei vicinius est. Set hec que dicta sunt locum f. 69b habent in agris non limitatis, nam in limitatis non habet locum ius alluuionis. Sunt autem agri limitati qui assignantur alicui certis locis et terminis vt sciatur
35 quod et cui datum sit et quid retentum et quid relictum. Preterea agris limitatis non cedit insula racione vicinitatis in flumine publico, immo concedatur occu-

    1. *posterius* in *om.* J.   5. adquiruntur] adquiritur, J.   16. dominorum] dominis, J.; prope ripam] propinam ipsam, J.   17. existentis] existens, J.; Quod] que, J.   29. contrariam] contraria, J.   34. sciatur] sciant, J.   36. concedatur] contendatur, J.

the sea and the sea shore, with respect to precious stones, gems and other things found on the sea shore and, similarly, to islands arising in the sea, and the like.

By the law of nations, moreover, we acquire the ownership of things by accession, through the working of Providence: for example, the progeny born to animals subject to our ownership is acquired by us. And what a river may add by alluvion to our land is, by the law of nations, acquired by us. Alluvion means an imperceptible increment, and that is said to be added by alluvion which is so gradually added that it cannot be perceived at what moment of time the addition is made. It is otherwise if the addition is not imperceptible but plain to see: for example, if the violence of a river should remove some part of your land and enlarge your neighbour's with it, then certainly it would remain yours; but if for a very long time it remained fast to your neighbour's land and it happened to bear with it trees that rooted in that neighbour's land, thenceforth they are regarded as an accession to your neighbour's land. Some, however, are of the opinion that a beneficial interest in the thing remains in the person of the first owner, but others maintain that any recovery of it is at an end because the thing has become the property of the other. The same kind of accession also takes place when an island arises in a river, for, if it should arise in the middle of the stream, it will be the common property of those owners who possess lands on each side of the river next to the bank, in proportion to the frontage of each property lying next to the bank. But if the island is nearer to one side, it will belong solely to him or them who possess lands next to the bank on that side.

Bracton,
f. 9b

If, however, an island arises in the sea, not held in place by vegetation, it belongs to the [first] occupant, provided that no one else can enforce his right to it: as, for example, if a river flows round someone's field and turns it into an island, for in such a case the island will on this account be none the less the property of him whose field it formerly was. In measuring the nearness of such islands a point is fixed midway between the two fields, and if the island is to one side of the point, then it will belong solely to this man or solely to the other; but if the island is within the point and on the point and beyond the point, then it will be the common property of both so long as it is undivided so that on division there will fall to me as much of it as is contained from the mid-point up to my field, and similarly with respect to my neighbour. And it seems that the nearness to and remoteness from an island ought to be reckoned according to the moment it begins to exist, and hence it is that, if between the island that is closer to me and the opposite bank across the river belonging to my neighbour another island comes into existence, then the measurement should be made from my island and not from my field. If, however, the island should be round, then all that is nearest to me will fall to me and similarly all that is nearest my neighbour will fall to him. But what has been said does not apply to fields with defined boundaries, for in such the right of alluvion has no place. Fields with defined boundaries are such as are assigned to someone in definite places and with definite boundaries so that it may be known what is given and to whom and what is retained and what is left. Furthermore, an island in a public waterway does not belong to fields with defined boundaries because they are closest, rather does it

panti vel regi propter suum priuilegium.   Habet eciam locum species accessionis
in alueo fluminis a flumine derelicto.   Cedit enim eis qui prope ripam fluminis
predia possident pro modo scilicet latitudinis cuiusque agri.   Nouus autem
alueus eius iuris incipit esse cuius et ipsum flumen, id est publicum.   Flumen
5   enim sibi alueum constituendo agrum priuatum facit publicum et e conuerso, et
sic dicuntur flumina vice censitorum id est iudicum vel principum fungi.   Iudex
enim vel imperator sepe quod vnius est alteri adiudicat, iuste vel iniuste, bona fide
vel mala, et vbi flumen michi abstulerit meum predium per aluei constitucionem
et deinde redierit ad alueum antiquum, in predio quondam meo de iure stricto
10   nichil possum vendicare, cedit enim hiis qui prope ripam predia habent.   De
equitate tamen nullo modo hoc optinet.   Vbi autem flumen alueum sibi non
constituerit in agrum meum set illum inundauerit, non mutatur species eius quantum ad proprietatem.

     Est autem alia accessio que fit humana natura operante, per adiunccionem
15   vnius speciei ad aliam per applumbaturam vel ferruminacionem, secundum quod
in Institutis legitur, vbi dicitur que pars alteri accrescere debet, nam si per
applumbaturam minor cedit maiori vel preciosiori set si neutra preciosior
quilibet suum vendicabit.   Vendicat eciam sibi locum ius accessionis in edificiis
per humane nature laborem, vt si quis in solo suo alienam materiam edificauerit
20   ipse dominus intelligitur edificii, quia omne quod inedificatur solo cedit, nec   [*177*]
tamen is qui materie dominus fuerit dominus esse desinit nec suum eximere
potest, set pro eo duplum consequi solebat, modo precium tantum consequetur.
Qui autem in fundo alieno de suo construxerit mala fide materiam presumitur
donasse et cum domino soli merito debeat materia remanere, eo quod edificia
25   solo cedunt et pro possessore soli iudicabitur propter duplex beneficium possidendi, quamuis obscura fuerit vtriusque iura.   Eadem autem species accessionis
in fructuariis et vsuariis circa fructuum obuencionem potest assignari.

     Alia autem accessio est diuina natura operante et humana et queritur ex ea
dominium, vt ecce.   Si Ticius alienam plantam in solo suo posuerit Ticii erit plan-
30   ta.   Si autem Ticius suam plantam in Meuii solo posuerit Meuii erit planta,
dum tamen in vtroque casu radicata fuerit planta.   Secus autem ante radi-
cacionem.   Et sic fiat de semine seminato.

     Adquiruntur eciam res nobis per specificacionem, vt si quis de aliena materia
speciem aliquam sibi fecerit, factor dominus erit speciei.
35   Est eciam alius modus adquirendi per confusionem.   Confunduntur enim
liquida vt mel, oleum, vinum.   Confunduntur eciam solida sicut aurum,
argentum, plumbum et ferrum.   Et quod ex hiis redigitur inter eos commune

---

     1. accessionis] accionis, J.   3. predia . . . latitudinis, Br., *om.* J.   3. Nouus]
Ficus, J.   6. censitorum] centorium, J.; principum] principium, J.   9. quondam] quo-
dam, J.   12. in *om.* J.   15. aplumbaturam, J.; ferriminacionem, J.   16. in *om,* J.
20. inedificatur] inedificicatur, J.   22. modo] modum, J.   27. vsuariis] vsurariis, J.;
circa] contra, J.   35. eciam] et, J.

belong to the [first] occupant or to the king by virtue of his privilege.   A kind of accession takes place also in the bed of a river when deserted by the stream: the bed falls to them who possess estates next to the bank, that is to say, in proportion to the frontage of each field.   The new river bed begins to have the same legal character as the river itself, namely, a public character, for the stream in forming its bed makes private land public and conversely.   And so rivers are said to act as though they were magistrates, that is, judges or princes.   For a judge or emperor often adjudges the property of one man to another, rightly or wrongly, in good faith or bad.   And where a river has taken my land from me by forming a river-bed and thereafter returns to its old bed, in strict law I can claim nothing in what was formerly my land, for it belongs to those who have lands next to the bank.   In equity, however, this does not by any means hold good.   Where, however, the river does not form a bed for itself in my field but floods it, its identity is not changed so far as ownership is concerned.

There is another kind of accession which is produced through human activity by joining one kind of thing to another by soldering or welding, as we read in the *Institutes*,[1] where it is said which part ought to accrue to the other, for, if it is by soldering, the lesser falls to the greater or the more valuable, but if neither is more valuable, each owner may claim his own.   The right of accession also claims a place for itself in buildings constructed by human labour: for example, if someone should build with another man's material on his own soil, he is understood to be the owner of the building because all that is erected on it accrues to that soil. He who owned the material, however, does not cease to be the owner of it but he cannot regain it but formerly used to sue for double its value, though he now

sues for the value only.   He, however, who in bad faith has built with his own material on the soil of another, is presumed to have given him the material and it ought rightly to remain with the owner of the soil, since buildings accrue to the soil and are adjudged to the possessor of the soil because possession gives a two-fold advantage, especially where the right of each may be obscure.   The same kind of accession, moreover, may be observed with usufructuaries and usuaries in connexion with forthcoming profits.

Another form of accession is by the operation of divine and human forces, and thence arises a question of ownership: as, for example, if Titius should put a plant belonging to another in the soil belonging to himself, the plant will belong to Titius.   If, however, Titius should put a plant of his in soil belonging to Maevius, the plant will belong to Maevius, provided that in each case the plant takes root, for it is otherwise before it has rooted.   And the case is similar with seed that is sown.

Things are also acquired by us through specification: for example, if someone should make for himself any article out of another man's material, then the maker will be the owner of the object.

There is another manner of acquisition by confusion.   For liquids, like honey, oil and wine, are confused, as are also solids, like gold, silver, lead and

---

[1] Institutes, II. i. 25

erit, siue separari possit siue non, de quorum facultatibus corpora siue species confunduntur. Et idem erit cum casu fortuito confundantur si separari non possint materie. Set si possint separari vnusquisque partem ponderis quam habuit in rudi materia habebit et mensure. Cum autem frumentum alicuius
5 cum frumento alterius mixtum fuerit non propter hoc erit frumentum inter eos commune set quisque de aceruo pro quantitate sui frumenti partem suam vendicabit. Sicuti non essent pecora tua et mea mixta nobis communia. Et differt confusio a mixtione, nam species dicuntur misceri et materie confundi, et species mixte in eadem remanent substancia, confuse vero in aliam materiam
10 transferuntur.

Item adquiritur nobis dominium iure ciuili ex causa donacionis, ex causa successionis, reuersionis, testamentaria et aliis modis diuersis. Item adquiruntur nobis corporalia per tradicionem: res enim corporales tradicionem paciuntur. Secus vero de incorporalibus, vt sunt iura, aduocaciones ecclesiarum, vsufructus,
15 obligaciones, acciones, hereditas, que ipsum ius est, seruitus, qua subicitur predium predio, et huiusmodi, que nichilominus nobis adquiruntur per adquisicionem fundi et aliis pluribus modis. Gleba proprie est solum datum cui aduocacio ecclesie est annexa, quia incorporalis est nec in donacione tangi potest manu, et ideo solo debet quis seysiri cum aduocacione pertinente.

20 ## CAP. III. DE DONACIONIBUS

Donacio est quedam institucio que ex mera liberalitate, nullo iure cogente,   f. 70
procedit, vt rem a vero eius possessore ad alium transferat. Dare autem est rem accipientis facere cum effectu, alioquin inutilis erit donacio cum irritari valeat et reuocari, vt si facta fuerit de re aliena. De vendicione secus erit quia vendicio
25 de re aliena quo ad accipientem valebit eo quod, etsi postea per verum dominum a feoffato tollatur, donatarius tamen escambium quandoque consequi poterit a venditore, nisi iure suo male vsus fuerit. Donacionum alia simplex et pura   [178]
que nullo iure ciuili vel naturali cogente nullo precedente metu vel vi interueniente ex mera gratuitaque liberalitate donantis procedit et vbi nullo casu velit
30 donator ad se reuerti quod dedit. Alia sub modo, condicione vel ob causam in quibus casibus non proprie fit donacio cum donator id ad se reuerti velit, set quedam pocius feodalis dimissio. Alia absoluta et larga et alia stricta et coartata sicut certis heredibus quibusdam a successione exclusis vel si ab inicio larga fuerit et postea ex conuencione coartata ita quod donatarius rem sibi datam

13. corporalia] temporalia, J.   22. transferat] transferatur, J.   28. precedenti] procedenti, J.; vi *om.* J.

iron. And what is constituted from these, whether it can be resolved into its constituents or not, will be the common property of those by whose authority the masses or objects are confused.   And this will be the case where they are confused

Bracton,
f. 10*b*

by accident if it is not possible to separate the materials; but if the materials can be separated, each owner will have as much in weight and measure as he had of the raw material.   Where, however, one man's wheat has become mixed with another's, the wheat will not on this account be held in common between them, but each will claim from the heap a portion equivalent to the wheat he had. Similarly, when your beasts are mixed with mine, we do not have them in common.   There is a difference between confusion and mixing, for objects are said to be mixed and materials to be confused, and objects that are mixed remain the same in substance, while those things that are confused are transformed into another material.

By the civil law we acquire ownership also by cause of gift, succession, reversion, legacy and in sundry other ways.   We acquire corporeal things by livery, for corporeal things are capable of livery; but it is otherwise with incorporeal things, like rights, the advowsons of churches, usufructs, obligations, actions, inheritance (which is itself a right), servitude (by which land is subjected to land) and the like, which nevertheless are acquired by us when we acquire lands and in many other ways.   Strictly speaking, glebe is the land given [to a church], to which the advowson of the church is annexed, and because the advowson is incorporeal and cannot be touched with the hand when it is given, therefore one ought to be given seisin of the soil with the advowson as appurtenant.

CHAPTER 3.   OF GIFTS

Bracton,
f. 11

A gift is a disposition which proceeds out of pure generosity and without legal compulsion, which transfers property from the true possessor to another. To give, therefore, is to cause property to belong effectively to the recipient: otherwise the gift will be useless since it can be invalidated and revoked: for example, if the gift is made of property belonging to someone else.   In selling it will be otherwise; for the sale of another's property will hold good as regards the recipient because, even if it is afterwards taken from the feoffee by the true owner, nevertheless the donee can sometimes sue the vendor for an exchange, provided he has not abused his right.   Some gifts are simple and absolute which, without any compulsion of civil or natural law, without any threat beforehand or the intervention of violence, proceed out of the pure and free generosity of the donor and in which he does not wish that what he gives shall in any case revert to him. Other gifts are subject to a mode or condition or dependent on the cause [of

Bracton,
f. 11*b*

the gift being fulfilled] and in such cases there is, strictly speaking, no gift where the donor wishes it to revert to himself, but rather a sort of feudal demise.   Some gifts are absolute and unrestricted and others are restricted and limited: for example, to certain heirs, others being excluded from the succession, or again at the beginning the gift may be unrestricted and afterwards by agreement circumscribed so that the donee cannot sell or alienate the property given to him to

vendere non possit vel alienare certis personis vel non nisi certis vel nullis.   Alia
perfecta et alia incepta et non perfecta vt si donacio lecta fuerit et concessa et
homagium captum ac tradicio non dum fuerit subsecuta.   Alia incepta et de-
fectiua et post tempus confirmata.   Confirmacio enim omnem suplet defectum.
5 Poterit eciam esse in pendenti donec per ratihabicionem heredis cum ad etatem
venerit roboretur.

   Quidam autem dare poterunt, quidam vero non.   Dare namque poterit
omnis dominus et non dominus seysitus, sane mentis et sui iuris, senex et
valitudinarius, masculus et femina, liber et seruus aliquando, legitimus et bastard-
10 us in suo casu, maior et minor, furiosus et quandoque fatuus, dum tamen donum
ex post facto confirmauerint cum etatem, discrecionem recuperauerint et sani-
tatem.   Inhibetur tamen in carta de libertatibus ne quis det alicui vel vendat
amplius de terra sua quam de residuo terre sue possit sufficienter facere domino
feodi seruicium ei debitum quod ad feodum illum pertinuerit.   Dare autem non
15 poterunt illi qui generalem rerum suarum non habent administracionem, sicut
sunt minores, incarcerati, surdi et muti et naturaliter furiosi et mente capti, nisi
dilucidis gaudeant interuallis, serui, leprosi a communione gencium interdicti,
reges in casu, archiepiscopi, episcopi, abbates, priores, religiosi et hospitalium
rectores et ecclesiarum.   Ea precipue que possident nomine corone et ecclesiarum
20 suarum dare non poterunt, nisi per hoc fuerit earum condicio meliorata, set
ad clericorum alienaciones requiritur aliorum confirmacio, alioquin poterunt
iura ecclesie alienata reuocari.   Preterea dari non poterunt sine regio assensu
tenementa que de rege tenentur.   Rursus nec bastardi dare poterunt nisi heredes
sibi legitime procreauerint cum assignatos per modum donacionis sibi facere
25 non possint, nec eciam de aliquo crimine capitali accusati post feloniam perpetratam dum tamen condempnacio mortis vel vtlagarie subsequatur.   Dare eciam
non poterunt viri suis vxoribus nec e conuerso constante matrimonio, quia
omnino hoc prohibetur in lege, precipue post fidem interdictam ne fiant propter
libidinem vel alterius eorum inmoderatam egestatem.   Si autem viri hoc fecerint
30 et vxores ab huiusmodi tenementis post mortem virorum fuerint eiecte, per assisam
noue disseisine non recuperabunt nec heredes eorum per consequens per assisam
mortis antecessoris de morte earum.   Si autem vir extranee persone donacionem fecerit ea mente vt eam sue det vxori non valebit donacio, quia pro fraude
facta inhibicioni reputabitur, quia non refert an quid fiat per simile quando
35 tantumdem valeat.   Simplices autem donaciones vxoribus a viris suis non sunt   [179]
faciende in ipso matrimonio ante nec post.   Fieri tamen poterunt propter nupcias pro dotis constitucione ita tamen quod racionabilem dotis quantitatem non
excedant.   Verba autem legis sunt hec:
   Si in nomine et substancia nichil distat a dote ante nupcias donacio facta a

7. Nota. De hiis qui dare [possunt] et qui non, J. *in margine*.   20. earum] eorum, J.
39. distat] distet, J.

certain persons or only to certain persons or to none.   Some gifts are completed
and others begun and not completed: for example, if the gift has been read and
acknowledged and homage taken but livery has not yet followed.   Other gifts
are begun and are defective, but, after a time, confirmed: confirmation, indeed,
makes up for every defect.   A gift may also be in suspense until it is validated
by the ratification of the heir when he comes of age.

Some persons are able to make a gift and some persons are not.   For every
one, owner or not, who is in seisin may make a gift if he is of sound mind and
legally competent: old and sick, male and female, free and (sometimes) bond,
legitimate and bastard (in certain cases), of full age and minor, insane and (sometimes) imbecile, provided that they afterwards confirm the gift when they are of
full age or recover wisdom and sanity.   It is forbidden, however, by the Charter
of Liberties that a man shall give or sell to anyone more of his land than leaves
him with land sufficient to enable him to do the lord of the fee the service due
to him which pertains to that fee.   They, however, will not be able to make a gift
who do not have the general administration of their affairs, such as minors,
prisoners, the deaf and dumb, those insane by nature and mentally retarded (save
when they enjoy lucid intervals), villeins, lepers forbidden the society of men,
kings (in certain cases), archbishops, bishops, abbots, priors, religious and the
rectors of hospitals and churches.   In particular, they may not give those things
they possess in right of the Crown and of their churches, unless their condition
should be improved thereby; but to alienations by the clergy the confirmation of
others is required, otherwise the rights of the church that have been alienated may be recalled.   Further, tenements which are held of the king cannot be
given without his assent.   Again, bastards cannot make a gift unless, where they
cannot by terms of the gift appoint their assigns, they have begotten legitimate
heirs.   Neither can those accused of any capital crime make a gift after the felony
has been committed, provided it is followed by sentence of death or outlawry.
Neither can husbands make gifts to their wives, nor the reverse, while the marriage
subsists, because this is absolutely prohibited in law; especially is this so after
troth has been plighted, lest the gifts should be made for the sake of lust or result
in the excessive impoverishment of one of them.   If, indeed, husbands should
do this and after their death the wives should be ejected from the tenements so
given, they will not recover by an assize of novel disseisin, nor shall their heirs
consequently recover by an assize of mort d'ancestor on their death.   If, moreover, a husband should make a gift to a third party with the intention that the
latter shall give it to the wife, the gift will not be valid, for it will be considered to
be a fraud against this prohibition, because it does not matter whether what is
done is precisely the same when it amounts to the same thing.   Simple gifts,
indeed, must not be made by husbands to wives, whether during the marriage or
before or after marriage.   Gifts may, however, be made because of marriage to
constitute the dower, provided that they do not exceed the reasonable amount of
a dower.   The wording of the law is as follows:[1]

---

[1] Codex, 5. 3. 20. 4.

Bracton,
f. 12

Magna Carta,
c. 32

Bracton,
f. 12

Bracton,
f. 12 b

Bracton,
ff. 12b, 29

Bracton,
ff. 12b, 29

Bracton,
f. 29b

viro, quare non eciam simili modo et in matrimonio contracto dabitur? Sanci-
mus itaque omnes licenciam habere, siue priusquam matrimonia contraxerint
siue postea, mulieribus donaciones facere propter dotis donaciones vt tamen non
simplices donaciones intelligantur set propter dotem et propter nupcias facte.
5   Simplices et enim donaciones non propter nupcias fiant, set propter nupcias
vetite sint, non tamen propter ipsarum nupciarum affeccionem efficiantur, nam
si tales fieri possent donaciones ob amorem habitum inter virum et vxorem, sic
posset alter ipsorum egestate et inopia constringi, quod non est sustinendum.
     Cum autem minori facta fuerit donacio et curator assignatus alius a donatore
10 curatorque nomine minoris seysinam habuerit, si donator postea se ponat in seysinam quamuis inde obierit seysitus, nunquam propter hoc mutabitur status f. 70b
minoris quin retineat contra quoscumque: secus vero si idem sit donator et
tutor et quo casu non valet donacio.   Recipere autem poterit minor tutore auc-
tore ac consentire donacioni sibi facte.   Donacioni vero a se faciende vel iterum
15 donatorem admittendi ad seysinam alicuius auctoritate consentire non potest et
sic suam condicionem meliorare set non deteriorare.   Valebit tamen cautela
disseisine cum conuiccione pro donatore, dum tamen assensus minoris et eius
tutoris interuenerint.

CAP. IV.   DE DONACIONE FACTA PLURIBUS

20   Dari autem poterit tam masculo quam femine, libero quam seruo, maiori
quam minori, surdo quam muto, viro quam vxori, legitimo quam bastardo, vni
quam pluribus, semel quam pluries et pluribus quam vni.   Cum autem pluribus
fiat donacio vt concubine et pueris suis natis et nascituris et eorum heredibus
nullus alteri succedit cum omnes pariter feoffati tenuerint in communi set dece-
25 dente vno pars eius per ius accrescendi superstitibus eius accrescit et eorum
heredibus a pluribus vsque ad vnum et ad donatorem non reuertetur quamdiu
vnus fuerit superstes vel heredes habuerit.   Si autem facta fuerit donacio concubine tantum et heredibus suis, si legittima fuerit et heredes habuerit, fratrem vel
sororem vel remotiores, bene poterit ipsa suos pueros feoffare quamdiu heredes
30 extiterint qui donum suum warantizare possint, secundum quod fit de terra data
in maritagium, que si heredes non habuerit non valebit donacio ab ea facta set ad
donatorem reuertetur.   Cum autem concubina et pueri sui simul feoffati fuerint
et omnes vel quidam illorum ab extraneo vel vno participum suorum eiecti
fuerint omnes per assisam noue disseisine recuperabunt.   Et cum quidam eorum

3–5. vt tamen . . . Simplices, Br., *om.* J.

If in name and substance a gift made by a husband does not differ from dower before marriage, why shall it not also be given in like manner after a marriage has been contracted? We decree therefore that all shall have leave, either before or after they contract marriage, to make gifts to their wives on account of dower, provided that simple gifts are not understood but gifts made on account of dower and on account of marriage. For simple gifts are not made on account of marriage but are forbidden because of marriage, because they are not effective by reason of the affection arising out of marriage. For if such [simple] gifts could be made because of the love between husband and wife, it *Bracton, f. 13b* could be that one of them might be brought into straightened circumstances through poverty and want, which cannot be tolerated.

When, however, a gift is made to a minor and a guardian assigned other than the donor and the guardian has seisin in the name of the minor, if the donor afterwards puts himself in seisin, although he should die seised thereof the position of the minor shall nevertheless not be altered to prevent him from retaining the gift against anyone whomsoever. But on the other hand, if the donor and *Bracton, f. 12b* guardian are one and the same, in that case the gift is not valid. However, with his guardian's authority a minor may receive and consent to a gift made to him. But he may not, however, by anyone's authority consent to the making of a gift by himself or to the admission of a donor to seisin again. And thus he is able to better his condition but not to worsen it. But the device of a disseisin with verdict for the donor will be effective, provided the assent of the minor and his guardian are obtained[1].

CHAPTER 4. OF A GIFT MADE TO SEVERAL PERSONS

Bracton, f. 12b

Bracton, f. 13

A gift may be made as well to a man as to a woman, to a free man as to a villein, to one of full age as to a minor, to deaf as to dumb, to husband as to wife, to legitimate as to bastard, to one as to several, at the one time as well as on successive occasions, and to several persons as well as to one. Should, however, a gift be made to several, as, for example, to a concubine and her children, born and to be born, and to their heirs, none succeeds to another since, all being equally enfeoffed, they hold in common; but if one dies, his part accrues by right of accretion to his survivors and their heirs, from several such down to one, and the gift does not revert to the donor so long as there is one survivor or one of them has heirs. If, however, the gift were made to the concubine only and her heirs, if she is legitimate and has heirs, a brother or a sister or some remote heirs, she can well enfeoff her children so long as there are heirs who can warrant her gift, just as is done with land given as a marriage portion. But if she should have no heirs, a gift made by her will not be valid but will revert to the donor. If, however, the concubine and her children should be enfeoffed together, and all (or some of them) should be ejected by a third party or by one of their parceners, all will recover by an assize of novel disseisin. And if some of them die seised of

---

[1] Cf. Britton, II. c. 3, § 12 for the details of this collusive action to provide a donor with a life-interest.

decesserint de partibus suis seysiti heredes eorum versus extraneum deforci-
atorem per assisam mortis antecessoris partes illas recuperabunt. Cum
autem mater eorum que nomine eorum extitit in seysina primo decesserit et
extraneus se statim intrudat qui petentibus pueris seysinam restituere noluerit   [*180*]
5   succurritur eis per assisam noue disseisine, racione matris que nomine eorum fuit
in seysina die quo obiit vt procuratrix, siue pueri prius in seysina extiterint cum
adquisita sit eis possessio per matrem siue non, et non per assisam mortis antecessoris.   Pluribus eciam pueris concubine fieri poterit donacio in communi
pura et simplex, nullos coarcando heredes, habendo et tenendo sibi et heredibus
10   suis et cum omnes possessionem receperint per se vel per procuratores vt per
concubinam matrem eorum nullus ex morte alterius assisam habebit quia omnes
feoffati sunt simul habendo et tenendo non totum nec partem per se set vt
quilibet eorum totum habeat cum aliis in communi, et cum vnus moriatur non
descendit aliqua pars heredi morientis separatim nec in communi ante mortem
15   omnium set pars illa communis per ius accrescendi accrescit superstitibus de
persona ad personam vsque ad vltimum superstitem, et cum ille obierit tunc
primo locum habebit assisa mortis antecessoris in personis heredum et ad
vltimam seysinam cuiuscumque talium premoriatur erit recurrendum et si
nullos heredes habuerint reuertatur terra ad donatorem.   Item fieri poterit don-
20   acio pluribus simul quorum quibusdam valebit donacio quibusdam non vt si vir
vxori sue et pueris eorum communibus vel ex alio viro progenitis donacionem
fecerit pro pueris valebit pro vxore vero minime valebit constante matrimonio.
Fieri eciam poterunt donaciones pluribus, legitimis et bastardis, maioribus et
minoribus simul et vicissim, quamuis minor consentire non possit nisi tutore auc-
25   tore.   Si autem donacio fiat duobus fratribus maiori et minori maior minoris
poterit esses tutor et cum vterque legitimus extiterit descendit eorum alteri et non
reuertetur pars morientis donatori nec fratri suo superstiti accrescit per ius
accrescendi set iure successionis: secus tamen esset si vnus alterius heres esse non
posset.   Et si donator seysinam caperet post mortem sui tenentis, statim com-
30   petit fratri superstiti remedium per assisam noue disseisine nec obstabit excepcio
si dominus dicat quod partem defuncti seisiuit nomine custodie si defunctus heredem procreatum reliquerit infra etatem, cum neuter alterius partem ab alia sciuit
distinguere.   Item fieri poterit donacio pluribus pueris nominatis et non nominatis, presentibus et absentibus, natis et nascituris, per tutores tamen.   Ipse enim
35   possidet cuius nomine possidetur eciam si nomen a baptismo nondum recepit.
Seruus eciam domino adquirit quamuis ipso ignorante.   Vero eciam heredi
quamuis absenti adquiritur liberum tenementum per custodem cum veri

4. noluerit] voluerit, J.   18. cuiuscumque] quicumque, J.   26. *posterius* et *addidimus*.
33. pueris, Br., *om* J.

their portions, their heirs will recover the said portions against a deforciant third party by an assize of mort d'ancestor. If, however, their mother, who is in seisin in the name of all of them, dies first and a third party immediately intrudes himself and refuses to restore seisin to the children at their request, they have a remedy by an assize of novel disseisin and not by an assize of mort d'ancestor, and the reason is that the mother was in seisin on the day she died as procuratrix in their name, whether or not the children were previously in seisin when possession was acquired for them by the mother. To several children of a concubine a gift may also be made in common, absolute and simple, not limited to any particular heirs, to have and to hold to them and their heirs; and if all obtain possession by themselves or by procurators—for example by the concubine, their mother—none through the death of another will have an assize because all are enfeoffed together to have and to hold, not the whole nor a part in severalty but so that each of them shall have the whole in common with the others. And when one of them dies, no part descends to the heir of the deceased, in severalty or in common, before the death of all; but that common part by right of accretion accrues to the survivors, from one to another, until the last survivor. And when he dies, then, for the first time, will there be an occasion for an assize of mort d'ancestor regarding the persons of the heirs, and it will be necessary to go back to the last seisin of whichever of them dies first; and if they have no heirs, the

Bracton,
f. 13b

land will revert to the donor. Again, a gift may be made to several persons together, and it will be valid for some of them and not for others: for example, if a husband makes a gift to his wife and their own children or the children begotten by another husband, the gift will be valid for the children but it will not be valid

Bracton,
f. 28

for the wife while the marriage subsists. Gifts may also be made to several, to those who are legitimate and those who are bastard, to those of full age and those who are minors, together or successively, although a minor may not consent [to a gift] without his guardian's authority. If, however, a gift is made to two brothers, one of whom is of full age and the other a minor, the one of full age may be guardian of the minor, and, if both are legitimate, the gift descends to the one of them [who survives] and the portion of the deceased does not revert to the donor, nor does it accrue to the surviving brother by right of accretion but by right of succession: it would be otherwise if one of them could not be the heir of the other. And if the donor should take seisin after the death of his tenant, immediately the surviving brother has a remedy available to him by an assize of novel disseisin, and if the lord says that he seized the portion of the deceased by way of wardship, this exception will not stand in the way, should the deceased have left an heir of his body under age, since neither [of the brothers] knew how

Bracton,
f. 28b

to distinguish the portion of one from the portion of the other. Further, a gift may be made to several children, named and unnamed, present and absent, born and unborn, acquired by guardians in this case, for he possesses in whose name something is possessed, even if he has not yet received a name in baptism. A villein also acquires for his master even though the latter is in ignorance, and a free tenement is acquired by a guardian for a true heir, although he be absent, if the guardian is in possession in the name of the true heir. Possession is ac-

heredis nomine fuerit in possessione. Per procuratorem vero adquiritur possessio tam absenti quam presenti et retinetur sicut corpore proprio.

CAP. V. QUIBUS DARI INHIBETUR

Religiosis autem et aliis ecclesiasticis personis terras aut possessiones sibi   f. 71
5 appropriare aliisque alienare ea mente vt in manum mortuam remaneant concorditer inhibetur cum dominis feodorum et regni defensioni per consequens in dampnum cedant et debilitatem ideoque sic statutum est:

Nullus religiosus vel alius terras vel tenementa aliqua emere, vendere vel sub   [181]
colore donacionis vel termini aut alterius tituli cuiuscumque ab aliquo recipere
10 aut arte vel ingenio vel alio quouis modo sibi et ecclesie sue appropriare presumat
vel aliter per quod terre vel tenementa huiusmodi ad manum mortuam quoquo
modo deueniant sub forisfactura eorundem tenementorum. Et si quis contraire
temere presumpserit extunc liceat inmediato capitali domino feodi perquisiti
infra annum a tempore alienacionis inpune ingredi et tenere sibi et heredibus
15 suis in dominico quod prius habuit in dominio, quod quidem si infra annum non
fecerit extunc statim post annum finitum capitali domino superiori oriatur eadem
accio per dimidium annum duratura et sic vlterius de domino ad dominum vsque
ad regem, dum tamen plene fuerint etatis, infra regnum Anglie et extra prisonam,
et si aliquis dominorum sui iuris non fuerit vel extra regnum saluabitur ei tamen
20 accio expellendi cum venerit, dum tamen ei negligencia non possit inponi, vel competet ei remedium per supplicacionem si rex inde seysinam ceperit. Et si omnes
capitales domini tepidi extiterint negligentes et remissi in hac parte terras et tenementa huiusmodi capiet rex in manum suam de quibus alios promisit per
seruicia ad defensionem regni facienda saluis tamen dominis feodorum wardis,
25 eschaetis et aliis ad ipsos pertinentibus necnon eciam seruiciis inde debitis et consuetis feoffare, nec competet eiectis in hoc casu remedium recuperandi per assisam
noue disseisine.

Et in carta de libertatibus inhibetur ne quis terram suam det alicui domui religiose ea mente vt eam postea de domo tenendam resumat nec liceat alicui domui
30 religiose terram alicuius sic accipere ita quod tradat illam ei a quo ipsam recepit.
Et quis terram suam sic dederit donum cassetur et terra domino feodi incurratur.

Et si qui religiosi in fraudem harum constitucionum aliquem cuius terram habere affectant inplacitent qui per collusionem prelocutam defaltam facere
voluerit in curia regis post defaltam ob quam huiusmodi tenementa sic sibi ad-

6. defensioni] defensionem, J.   23. rex *addidimus*.   30. quod tradat] protradat, J.
31. quis] qui, J.   32. in *addidimus*.   34. quam] que, J.

quired by a procurator for one who is absent as well as one who is present and is retained as though by the principal in person.

CHAPTER 5. TO WHOM IT IS FORBIDDEN TO MAKE A GIFT

Bracton,
f. 12

By agreement it is forbidden to religious and other ecclesiastical persons to appropriate to themselves and to alienate to others lands and possessions with the intention that they should remain in mortmain, since as a consequence this would result in loss to the lords of fees and in weakening the defence of the realm, and therefore it is enacted as follows:

St. de viris
religiosis

No person, religious or other, shall presume to buy or sell any lands or tenements or to receive them from anyone under pretence of a gift or a lease or any other title whatsoever, or by any craft or device or in any other manner to appropriate them to himself or his church, or otherwise so that such lands or tenements come in any way into mortmain, on pain of forfeiture of the same.   And if anyone should presume hardily to offend against [this statute], thereupon it shall be lawful for the immediate chief lord of the fee so acquired, within a year from the time of alienation, to enter with impunity and to hold to himself and his heirs in demesne what he previously had in service, but if within a year he does not do this, then immediately after the expiry of the year the same action shall be open for the space of half a year to the superior chief lord, and so forth from lord to lord up to the king, provided that [in each case] the lords are of full age, within the realm of England, and out of prison; and if any of the lords should not be legally competent or be out of the kingdom, nevertheless the action for expulsion shall be reserved for him when he comes, provided that negligence cannot be imputed to him; or if the king should have taken seisin of the land, a remedy by petition shall be available to him.   And if all the chief lords shall be indifferent, negligent and remiss in this matter, the king shall take into his own hands such lands and tenements, with which he has promised to enfeoff others in consideration of services to be rendered for the defence of the realm, saving, however, to the lords of the fees the wardships, escheats and other things appertaining to them as well as the services due and accustomed therefrom, nor in this case shall there be a remedy available to those ejected for recovering [their lands] by means of an assize of novel disseisin.

Magna Carta,
c. 36

And in the Charter of Liberties it is forbidden to anyone to give his land to any house of religion with the intention of afterwards resuming it and holding it from that house, nor shall it be lawful for any religious house to accept anyone's land on condition that it transfers it back to him from whom it received it.   And if anyone should give his land in this fashion, the grant shall be quashed and the land shall accrue to the lord of the fee.

And if to defeat these enactments fraudulently any religious shall implead anyone whose land they are seeking to obtain and he, by pre-arranged collusion, should be willing to make default after default in the king's court whereby they

quirant prouisum est quod statim post defaltam ante iudicium reddendum inquiratur vtrum petens ius habeat in sua peticione vel non. Et si compertum
fuerit quod ius habuerit procedatur ad iudicium pro petente, qui si ius non habuerit res petita proximo domino feodi incurratur si infra annum a tempore
5 inquisicionis capte illam petat alioquin superiori domino infra dimidium annum
primum sequentem hanc petenti et sic habeat quilibet dominus post proximum
dominum spacium dimidii anni post annum primum domini inmediati ad petendum successiue vel expellendum huiusmodi clericos quousque perueniatur ad
regem cui tunc demum pro defectu aliorum dominorum tenementum incurratur.
10 Et in omnibus iuratis aramiatis super premissis admittantur domini feodorum ad
iuratores calumpniandos et pro rege admittantur quilibet de populo cum solus
vbique presencialiter esse non poterit. Et quamuis iudicium clarum existat
remaneat tamen terra in manu domini regis quousque tenementa per petentem vel
per aliquem dominum feodi disracionetur et vicecomes loci de exitibus interim
15 prouenientibus regi respondeat. Ex beneuolencia tamen regis conceditur
religiosis quandoque quod feoda propria ingrediantur dum tamen ad nullius
iniuriam vel nocumentum inquisicione tamen solempni procedente quorum per   [182]
cartas suas ratificat et confirmat.

Et sicut inhibentur eis plurium terrarum amplexus et incrementa, ita de di-
20 minucionibus et alienacionibus terrarum suarum faciendis est eis interdictum
secundum formam huius constitucionis:

Prouisum est eciam quod abbates, priores, custodes hospitalium et aliarum
domorum religiosarum tenementa domibus suis collata de cetero alienare non
presumant quod si fecerint statim capiatur terra alienata in manum regis dum
25 tamen per regem vel per suos predecessores illi domui extitit collata et quo casu
emptor de terra vel pecunia proinde soluta nullum habeat recuperare. Et si ab
alio facta fuerit collacio quam a rege vel suis predecessoribus tunc habeat ille a
quo vel a cuius antecessore tenementum alienatum collatum fuit breue ad f. 71b
recuperandum tenementum illud in dominico, quod tale est:

30 Precipe A. quod reddat B. tale tenementum quod tali domui fuit collatum
per predictum B. vel antecessores suos et quod ad predictum B. reuerti debet
per alienacionem quam talis abbas fecit predicto A. de predicto tenemento
contra formam collacionis predicte vt dicit.

Et eodem modo de tenementis datis pro cantaria sustentanda alienatis. Et si
35 tenementum aliquod datum fuerit pro capella, luminari, potura pauperum vel
alia elemosina facienda que quidem seruicia vel elemosine per biennium sint
substracte quamuis huiusmodi tenementa non fuerint alienata, extunc eo ipso
competit accio donatori aut eius heredi ad petendum tenementum in dominico

7. *post* inmediati *add.* spacium, J.   8. successiue] successionem, J; vel . . . clericos,
om. in statuto.   9. tenementum *addidimus ex statuto*.   11. admittantur] admittatur, J.
18. ratificat] pacificat, J.   23. religiosarum] religiosorum, J.   34. sustentanda]
sustentenda, J.

may thus acquire such tenements for themselves, it has been provided that, immediately after the default and before judgement is rendered, inquiry shall be
made whether the demandant has right in his claim or not.   And if it should be
found that he has right, judgement will be passed for the demandant, but if he
has no right, the property demanded will accrue to the next lord of the fee if he
demands it within a year from the taking of the inquisition, but otherwise it
accrues to his superior lord if he demands it within the half year next following.
And so, subsequent to the first year of the immediate lord, each lord has a period
of half a year after the last lord to make successive claims or expel the said clerks
until the king is reached, to whom at last [the land] then accrues by reason of
default by the other lords.   And in all juries held to enquire into the aforegoing
matters, the lords of the fees shall be admitted to challenge the jurors, and there
shall be admitted on behalf of the king any of the people, since he cannot by himself be present everywhere.   And although the judgement is clear, nevertheless
the land shall remain in the king's hand until the tenements are deraigned by the
demandant or by some lord of the fee, and the sheriff of the place shall answer
to the king for the issues forthcoming in the meantime.   Out of the king's ben-
evolence, however, it is sometimes conceded to the religious that, provided this
is not to the damage or grievance of another, they may, while the inquest is
following its solemn course, enter their own fees whose possession he ratifies and
confirms by his charters.

And just as it is forbidden to them to increase and embrace more lands, so
also is it forbidden them to diminish or alienate their lands, according to the
terms of this enactment:

It is also provided that abbots, priors, wardens of hospitals and other houses
of religion shall not presume henceforth to alienate tenements bestowed upon
their houses, and if they should do so the land alienated shall be forthwith taken
into the hand of the king, provided that it was by the king or by his predecessors
that the land was bestowed upon such a house, in which case the purchaser shall
not have recovery either of the land or of the money paid for it.   And if the
endowment were made by any other than the king or his predecessors, then
shall he, by whom or by whose ancestor the alienated tenement was bestowed, have a writ to recover that tenement in demesne, in the following
form:

Command A. that he surrenders to B. such-and-such a tenement which was
bestowed by the aforesaid B. (or by his ancestors) upon such-and-such a house
and which should revert to the aforesaid B. on account of the alienation which
such-and-such an abbot has made of the aforesaid tenement to the aforesaid A.
against the terms of the aforesaid endowment, as he says.

And in the same way with respect to tenements given for the maintenance of
a chantry, which have been alienated.   And if any tenement has been given for
a chapel or a lamp or for food for the poor or to provide some other charity, and
the said services or charities have been withdrawn for two years although such
tenements may not have been alienated, thereupon an action is available on that
account to the donor or his heir to demand the tenement in demesne which had

quod pro huiusmodi seruiciis vel elemosinis faciendis fuit collatum per breue de
seruicio per biennium retento.

　　Et ne huiusmodi religiosi per oneraciones indebitas superueniencium
depauperentur, per quod huiusmodi seruicia et elemosinas subtrahere cogantur
5　vel terras suas vendere vel alienare, ex principis constitucione inhibitum est quod
nullus hospitari presumat in domibus religiosorum de aliena aduocacione nisi
specialiter rogatus nec sumptibus domus nec suis propriis contra tutorum
domuum voluntatem. 　Nec eciam presumat quis temere illicenciatus currere in
parco alieno aut in alterius viuario piscari. 　Verumptamen si contingat aliquem
10　in huiusmodi domibus per licenciam magistri domus vel eius balliui hospitari
quod non aperiat fenestras inhibitas vel cum vi sua aliquas frangat serruras et
victualia vel alia bona violenter capiat vel extrahat sub colore empcionis aut
aliter quoquo modo. 　Equos eciam huiusmodi religiosorum vel personarum ec-
clesiasticarum, militum et dominarum, boues, carros vel carectas, naues, batellos
15　vel huiusmodi nullus capere presumat ad cariagium inde faciendum nisi de
voluntate eorum quorum fuerint quorum voluntati statim satisfaciat prout
conuenit. 　Et si quis in premissis deliquerit per prisonam voluntariam punietur
et grauem redempcionem et quo casu si grauati sequi velint dampna in duplo
recuperabunt. 　Et in premissis habebit rex sectam suam de huiusmodi transgres-
20　soribus inquirendi quando voluerit et vnde talis ordinatur processus quod indic-
tati distringantur statim per magnam districcionem quod veniant ad diem
continentem spacium vij. ebdomadum, ad quem diem si non venerint pro
conuictis habeantur et per sectam regis restituant dampna in duplo grauatis et
grauiter puniantur per prisonam et redempcionem. 　Item nec grauenter viri　［183］
25　religiosi, persone ecclesiastice vel alii pro eo quod vetuerunt hospicium vel
victualia alicui vel pro eo quod questi fuerint forte de aliquo grauamine eis illato
in predictis articulis contento, quod si quis fecerit et inde conuincatur puniatur
per penam supradictam nec excipientur in premissis consiliarii domini regis,
iusticiarii de foresta vel alii quicumque iusticiarii vel ministri regis non magis
30　quam mediocres vel minores. 　Inhibetur eciam religiosis et aliis personis ecclesiasticis ne ipsi vel balliui sui equos alicuius aut canes de perhendinando in domibus
vel maneriis suis recipiant. 　De vicecomitibus prouisum est quod non hospitentur
alicubi nisi propriis sumptibus, verumtamen concessum est quod in domubus
religiosorum vicissim per vnam noctem tantum cum sex equis et non pluribus
35　sumptibus alienis in suis balliuis hospitentur dum tamen frequenter non venerint.

　　10. hospitari *addidimus ex statuto*.　　　　　15. Nota pro cariagio, J. *in margine*.
　　20. inquirendi] inquirat, J.

been bestowed for the performance of such services or charities, by a writ
concerning service withheld for two years.

And lest such religious should be impoverished by the undue burden of chance
visitors, whereby they may be compelled to withdraw such services and charities
or sell or alienate their lands, by the prince's enactment it is forbidden that anyone shall presume to be entertained in religious houses in the advowson of others,
unless he is specially invited, either at the expense of the house or his own
against the will of the rulers of the houses.   Nor also shall anyone rashly presume to course without leave in the park of another or to fish in another's stew.
And, indeed, if it should happen that anyone is entertained in such houses by
leave of the master of the house or his bailiff, he shall not open forbidden win-
dows or forcibly break any locks and take or carry off by force victuals or other
goods under the pretence of buying them or in any other way whatsoever.   Nor
also shall anyone presume to take the horses, oxen, wagons or carts, ships, boats
or the like belonging to such religious or ecclesiastical persons, knights and ladies,
to provide transport therewith except by the good will of those to whom they
belong, and then he shall straightway satisfy their demands as agreed.   And if
anyone should offend in the foregoing matters, he shall be punished by imprisonment at pleasure and a heavy ransom, and in this case, if those aggrieved wish
to sue for damages, they shall recover double the amount.   And the king shall
have his suit, when he will, to make enquiry regarding such transgressors in the
foregoing matters, and for this purpose the following procedure is appointed,
namely, that those indicted shall be forthwith distrained by the grand distress to
appear on a day within the space of seven weeks, on which day, if they do not
appear, they shall be held to be guilty, and at the suit of the king they shall pay
double damages to those aggrieved and shall be severely punished by imprisonment and ransom.   Nor shall men of religion, ecclesiastical persons or
others be harassed because they deny lodging or victuals to anyone or because
they happen to have complained of some grievance done to them, as set out in the
aforesaid articles.   And if anyone should do this and be convicted thereof, he
shall be punished by the penalty aforesaid, nor shall there be excepted from the
foregoing provisions king's counsellors, justices of the forest or any other justices
whatsoever or king's ministers, any more than those of middling and lower rank.
It is also forbidden to religious and other ecclesiastical persons to receive, by
themselves or their bailiffs, the horses or dogs of any other person to stay in
their houses or manors.   As regards sheriffs, it is provided that they shall not be
given hospitality anywhere except at their own expense, although it has been conceded that from time to time they may be entertained in the houses of men of
religion for one night only with six horses, and no more, at the expense of others
in their bailiwicks, provided they do not come with any frequency.

CAP. VI.   QUE DARI POTERUNT ET QUE NON

Dare autem poterit quis iuste omnino quod suum est et iniuste quod omnino
alienum et tam terram quam sibi accidere poterit per mortem alicuius antecessoris
vel alterius tenentis de eo ad vitam tantum vt fidelitas et seruicium tali donatario
5 attornentur quam terram habet et qualitercumque tenuerit per se vel in communi
cum alio.   Accio autem, res sacra, res corone, liber homo, iurisdiccio, pax, muri
et porte ciuitatis a nullo dari debent vt valida sit donacio.

Res quidem corone sunt antiqua maneria regis, homagia, libertates et huiusmodi que, cum alienentur, tenetur rex ea reuocare, secundum prouisionem
10 omnium regum christianorum apud Montem Pessoloniam anno regni regis
Edwardi filii regis Henrici quarto habitam, et si de escaetis suis proinde satisfacere
debent ad valenciam.   Nec valebit deforciantibus· longi temporis prescripcio.
Diuturnitas enim temporis tantum in hoc casu magis iniuriam auget quam
minuit, cum constare debeat singulis quod huiusmodi libertates de iure naturali
15 vel gencium ad coronam tantum pertineant.   De terris et tenementis regis secus
erit.   Refert vtrum ille terre fuerint dominice terre regis ex antiquo corone annexe
vel de eschaeta vel perquisito, quia de antiquis maneriis per predecessores regis   f. 72
alienatis non currit tempus contra regem sicut contra alium.   Terras vero suas
de eschaeta vel perquisito dare poterit rex et licite alienare, et de huiusmodi
20 terris tenetur rex ad escambium vel warantizare si per predecessores suos
expresse fuerit obligatus: alias vero terras alienatas non tenetur warantizare set
pocius reuocare.   Ex gracia tamen principis et pro pacis conseruacione vt popu-
lus regi subditus eo amplius in pace existat et quiete, conceditur aliquibus baronibus quod curias suas habeant, warennas in dominicis terris, feireas, furcas, mer-
25 cata et huiusmodi minutas libertates, que magis cedunt populo ad comodum
quam ad grauamen, vt populum sibi iudicialem iusticiabilem in suis curiis in
tramite iuris foueant et protegant.

CAP. VII.   QUE SUNT NECESSARIA IN DONACIONIBUS   [184]

Ad hoc autem quod donacio sit valida plura occurrunt.   Oportet enim quod
30 donator sit plene etatis, nomine suo seysitus in feodo per bonum ingressum, sane
mentis et bone memorie, quamuis inpotens sui et in egritudine et in lecto mortali
constitutus, et quod sit mera, pura, libera, gratuita et non coacta, nec per vim vel

---

4. donatario] donatori, J.   15. pertineant] pertineat, J.   16. vtrum ille] ille vtrum, J.
17. escheta, J.   18. non *addidimus*.   31. *ulterius* et, *om*. J.

CHAPTER 6. WHAT MAY BE GIVEN AND WHAT NOT

Bracton,
f. 13b

Anyone may lawfully make a gift of what is wholly his, and unlawfully of what is wholly another's, and he may make a gift of land that may fall to him by the death of some ancestor or of someone else who is his tenant for life only, so that fealty and service will be attorned to such donee, as well as of land he has and howsoever he holds it, whether alone or in common with another. But a

Bracton,
f. 14

right of action, sacred property, property of the Crown, a free man, jurisdiction, peace, the walls and gates of a city may be given by no one so that the gift is valid.

The property of the Crown consists of the king's ancient manors, homages, franchises and the like which, if alienated, the king is bound to resume, according to the enactment of all Christian kings made at Montpellier in the fourth year of the reign of King Edward, the son of King Henry, and, if [alienated] from his escheats, the [king] ought to make satisfaction for the value thereof. Nor does prescription for a long time avail the deforciants [of a franchise]: indeed, in this case the length of time increases the injury all the more rather than diminishes it, since it ought to be known to everybody that franchises of this kind by natural law or the law of nations belong solely to the Crown. It will be different with the king's lands and tenements. Here it is a question whether these lands were royal demesne annexed to the Crown of old time or [have accrued] as an escheat or acquisition, because in the case of ancient manors alienated by the king's predecessors time does not run against the king as it does against another. But his lands accruing from escheat or acquisition the king may give and lawfully alienate, and in respect of such lands the king is bound to make an exchange or to warrant, if he has been expressly bound to do so by his predecessors: he is not, however, bound to warrant other alienated lands, but rather

Bracton,
ff. 55b, 56

to resume them. By grace, however, of the prince and for the preservation of peace so that the people subject to the king may live the more completely and quietly in peace, it is conceded to some barons that they have their courts, warrens in their demesne lands, fairs, gallows, markets and the like minor franchises, which tend rather to the advantage of the people than to their grievance, so that they may foster and protect in the course of the law the people within their jurisdiction who are justiciable in their courts.

CHAPTER 7. WHAT THINGS ARE NECESSARY IN GIFTS

Bracton,
f. 14, 14b

In order, however, that a gift may be valid several things must concur, for it is necessary that the donor shall be of full age, seised in his own name in fee by means of a good entry, of sound mind and good memory even if infirm and sick and lying on his death-bed, and that the gift shall be genuine, absolute, free,

metum extorta. Est autem metus presentis vel futuri periculi causa mentis trepi-
dacio et presertim viri constantis et non cuiuslibet vani hominis vel meticulosi,
et talis debet esse metus qui in se contineat mortis periculum vel corporis
cruciatum. Refert tamen vtrum metus preueniat donacioni vel subsequatur,
5 quia si primo coactus et per metum compulsus promisero et postea gratis tradidero
talis metus non excusat, set si gratis promisero et postea conpulsus tradidero, tunc
excusat metus propter violenciam et compulsionem, velut hominis detencio in
prisona cuius nulla valebit donacio, nam qui potestatem sui non habet nec
eorum que sua esse debent quomodo potestatem donandi habebit. Et pro lege
10 habetur qui ab aliis possidetur ipse nichil poterit possidere, quod eciam dici
poterit, vt videtur, de captis ab hostibus et seruis sub potestate dominorum
constitutis terram dominorum suorum alienantibus ad dampnum ipsorum
dominorum. Set si detenti donatores pristinam receperint libertatem et effecti
fuerint sue potestatis, res ita gestas mere inde poterunt reuocare, nisi alienacion-
15 em probauerint per dissimulacionem vel ratificacionem.

Oportet eciam quod res certa in donacionem deducatur, quamuis incertus sit
rei euentus, quia rei incerte nulla tenet donacio et quod certa res redonatur vel re-
promittatur sicut homagium vel aliud certum seruicium. Si autem exprimatur sic
'faciendo inde donatori vel capitali domino tantum seruicii pro tenemento illo
20 quantum facit tantum tenementum eiusdem feodi' et de seruicio contencio
habeatur, recurrendum erit ad inquisicionem patrie vel ad magnam assisam.
Item oportet quod certa verba interueniant donacioni congrua, sicut et stipulaci-
oni, et instrumenta et testes: scripture enim pro perpetua memoria doni neces-
sarie sunt. Oportet quod inter dantem et accipientem concurrat mutuus consen-
25 sus et eadem voluntas et quod error de re data non habeatur neque dissensus in
numero, genere vel quantitate. Item in quibusdam donacionibus exigitur
alterius consensus necessario quam donatoris et donatarii, sicut in donis eorum
qui non tantum suo nomine tenuerint vbi requirendus est consensus omnium
eorum quorum interfuerint. Et nota quod conuenciones et pacta, condiciones
30 et modi diuersi donacionum, incidunt donacionibus, que si statim apponantur
legem dant donacioni et ipsam informant et excepcionem dant donatori et
personas ligant contrahencium et ipsam rem datam obligant et cum ipsa re trans-
eunt de persona in personam, que si ex interuallo adiciantur non insunt omnino
donacionibus, set quandoque pariunt accionem et quandoque excepcionem.
35 Et ita contrahitur donacio vt si dicam: 'Do tibi vt facias.' Sex enim donacioni
concurrunt: res, verba, scriptum, consensus, tradicio, iunctura.

Item in coaccionibus oportet quod coactus statim cum euaserit clamorem,
strepitum et hutesium faciat et leuet et ad villatas et coronatores ad comitatum [185]

2. *prius* et] est, J.   6. postea, Br., *om.* J.   9. quomodo] qui modo, J.   14. gestas,
Br., *om.* J.   25. dissensus] discensus, J.   31. *ulterius* et] in, J.   34. pariunt]
perimunt, J; accionem] accioni, J; excepcionem] excepcioni, J.   36. res . . . iunctura,
Br. *mutatis mutandis, om.* J.   37. coaccionibus] coacconibus, J.

voluntary and not made under duress, nor extorted by force or fear.   And fear is

Bracton,
f. 16b

a mental agitation, caused by danger in the present or in the future, especially in a man of strong will and not merely some weak or timid fellow; and the fear ought to be such as to constitute danger of death or bodily torture.   It depends, however, whether the fear precedes the gift or follows it; for if, having first been coerced and constrained by fear, I should make a promise and thereafter I should freely give delivery, such fear does not excuse.   But if I should freely promise and thereafter give delivery under compulsion, then, because of the violence and compulsion, fear does excuse, as in the case of a man detained in prison whose

Bracton,
f. 17

gift will not be valid; for how will he, who is not master of himself or of the things which ought to be his, have any power to make a gift?   And it is held as law that he who is possessed by others can possess nothing himself, which also might be said, it seems, of those taken by the enemy and of villeins, living under the authority of their masters, who alienate their master's land to the injury of their masters.   But if donors under detention should recover their former liberty and become their own masters, they can completely revoke what has thus been done unless they approve the alienation by indifference or by ratification.

Bracton,
f. 15b

It is also necessary that what is included in the gift shall be precisely defined, although it may be uncertain when the gift is to take effect, for the gift of something undefined does not hold good; and it is necessary for some certain thing to be given or promised in return, for example, homage or some other certain service.   If, however, it is expressed thus, 'doing therefor to the donor or chief lord as much service for that tenement as such a tenement of the said fee provides' and a dispute arises concerning the service, recourse must be had to an inquest by a jury or to a grand assize.   Furthermore, it is necessary that precise words be used as suitable to a gift as to a stipulation, and that there shall be instruments and witnesses, for writings are necessary as a perpetual memorial of the gift.   It is necessary that between the donor and the donee there shall be mutual agreement and the same intentions and that there shall be no mistake

Bracton,
f. 16

regarding the thing given nor any disagreement regarding number, kind or quantity.   Further, in some gifts the agreement of someone other than the donor or donee must needs be required, as, for example, in gifts by those who do not hold solely in their own name, where the agreement of all those who have an in-

Bracton,
f. 16b

terest must be sought.   And note that agreements and pacts, conditions and divers modes of giving, become parts of gifts and, if they are immediately put into them, give legal effect to the gift and shape it, give an exception to the donor, bind the persons of the contracting parties, burden the thing that is given, and pass with the thing itself from person to person; but if these are added after an interval of time they are no part whatsoever of the gifts, although they sometimes give rise to an action and sometimes an exception.   And a gift is contracted in this way: for example, if I say, 'I give to you that you may do'.   Six things, indeed, are associated in a gift—a thing, words, writing, consent, delivery, conjunction.

Further regarding coercion.   It is necessary that, immediately he escapes, he who is coerced shall make a clamour and raise the hue and cry and show openly

vim, metum, violenciam et coaccionem sibi factam palam ostendat et sic saluabitur sibi accio, alioquin consentire videbitur propter dissimulacionem. Et non
solum excusatur quis et excepcionem habet si sibi ipsi inferatur vis et metus, verum
eciam si suis, vt filio vel filie, patri vel fratri vel sorori et aliis domesticis et
5 propinquis.

CAP. VIII. DE DONACIONE SIMPLICI

Simplex donacio et pura est vbi nulla adiecta est condicio neque modus.
Simpliciter enim datur quod nullo additamento datur vt ecce 'Do tibi tantam
terram cum pertinenciis in tali villa pro homagio et seruicio tuo habendam et f. 72*b*
10 tenendam tibi et heredibus tuis de capitali domino feodi et heredibus suis per
seruicia inde debita et consueta, reddendo inde michi et heredibus meis tu et
heredes tui per annum tantum ad tales terminos pro omni seruicio, consuetudine
et demanda seculari', ita quod certa sit res que datur et certa seruicia in scriptis
sint expressa donatori saltem facienda quamuis incerta fuerint alia que tacite
15 remittuntur. 'Et ego et heres mei warantizabimus, acquietabimus et defendemus
predictam terram tibi et heredibus tuis contra omnes gentes per predicta
seruicia'. Et sic acquiris rei dominium ex causa donacionis et heres tuus post
te ex causa successionis. Heres enim tuus licet in donacione comprehendatur
non tamen aliquid sibi adquirit in donacione eo quod tibi soli facta est donacio
20 tibi tenenda et heredibus tuis sub cuius vocabulo omnes heredes propinqui conprehenduntur et remoti, nati et nascituri.

CAP. IX. DE DONACIONE CONDICIONALI

Vt sicut ampliari poterunt heredes per modum donacionis ita poterunt
coartari quod omnes heredes ad successionem non vocabuntur hereditatis ante-
25 cessoris. Modus enim legem dat donacioni et tenendus est eciam contra ius
commune quia modus et conuencio vincunt legem vt si alicui cum vxore fiat
donacio habenda et tenenda sibi et heredibus quos inter se legitime procreabunt,
ecce quod donator vult quod tales heredes in hereditate paterna et materna succedant aliis heredibus eorum remocioribus penitus exclusis. Et quod voluntas
30 donatoris obseruari debeat manifeste apparet per hec statuta:

4. suis] vis, J.   30. statuta, J. *in margine.*

to the [nearest] townships and the coroners at the county court the force, fear, violence and coercion done to him, and in this way a right of action will be preserved for him, otherwise he will seem to consent by reason of his indifference. And not only will anyone be excused and have an exception if force or fear should be brought to bear upon himself, but also if it is brought to bear against any of his family, like a son or daughter, father or brother or sister, and others of his household and relatives.

Bracton,
f. 17

CHAPTER 8.　OF A SIMPLE GIFT

A simple and absolute gift is one where no condition or mode is attached. A simple gift is that which is given with no qualification: as, for example, 'I give you such-and-such an amount of land with appurtenances in such-and-such a township for your homage and service, to have and to hold to you and your heirs of the chief lord of the fee and his heirs by the services due and accustomed therefor, you and your heirs rendering therefor to me and my heirs so much a year at such-and-such terms for every service, custom and secular demand' (so that the thing that is given may be certain and the services, set down in the deeds as to be done at least to the donor, may be certain, although others which are tacitly remitted may be uncertain) 'and I and my heirs will warrant, acquit and defend the land aforesaid for you and your heirs against all men in consideration of the services aforesaid'. And in this way you acquire ownership by cause of the gift, and after you your heir by cause of succession. For your heir, although he is included in the gift, does not, however, acquire anything for himself as regards the gift because the gift is made to you alone, to be held to you and your heirs, under which word are included all heirs, near and remote, born and to be born.

CHAPTER 9.　OF A CONDITIONAL GIFT

Bracton,
f. 18

And just as the [number of] heirs can be increased by the mode of gift, so the [number] can be limited, with the result that all heirs will not be called to the succession of the inheritance of an ancestor. The mode indeed imposes law upon the gift and it must be observed even though it is contrary to common right, because the mode and the agreement defeat law, as, for example, if a gift should be made to someone, with his wife, 'to have and to hold, to him and the heirs whom they lawfully beget between them', it follows that the donor wishes such heirs to succeed as are within [both] paternal and maternal inheritance, to the entire exclusion of their other heirs more remote. And that the intention of the donor should be observed appears clearly by this statute:

Quia autem dudum regi durum videbatur quod in casibus in quibus tenementum etc.

Modus autem et condicio multiplex esse poterit quandoque ad comodum donatarii ne det vel ne faciat quandoque vero ad eius incomodum quod det vel
5 faciat. Quatuor autem sunt genera contractuum que in donacione incidere poterunt, scilicet 'Do vt des,' 'Facio vt facias,' 'Facio vt des,' 'Do vt facias.' Isti autem sunt modi donacionum et obligant contrahentes ita quod si vnus dederit vel fecerit alius tenetur ad dandum vel faciendum secundum quod conuenit. Repetere non tamen poterit statim quod dedit quamuis alius non fecerit quod
10 promisit nisi super hoc ab inicio conuenerit. Hec autem diccio 'vt' modum denotat, 'si' condicionem, 'quia' causam. Si autem dicas, 'Do tibi tantam [186] terram vt michi necessaria inuenias' vel 'vt michi des tantum,' quamuis non sit omnino gratuita simplex tamen est et pura, dum tamen inde debita sequatur tradicio. Et ne huiusmodi dona donatoribus sint preiudicialia constitutum est
15 quod si quis terram suam alicui dimiserit ad feodi firmam vt faciat ei seruicium proinde ad valenciam veri valoris vel saltem quarte partis per annum et tenens cessauerit de seruicio et permittat terram iacere incultam vel alio modo custodiatur quominus distringi possit in eadem, extunc oritur donatori vel heredi suo accio ad petendum tenementum illud in dominico dum tamen solucio seruicii
20 per biennium cessauerit per breue sequens:

Precipe A. quod iuste etc. reddat B. tale tenementum quod A. de eo tenuit per tale seruicium et quod ad predictum B. reuerti debeat eo quod predictus A. in faciendo predictum seruicium per biennium cessauit, vt dicit.

Verumtamen si tenens ante iudicium contra ipsum redditum in curia venerit et
25 arreragia et dampna reddere sit paratus et offerat securitatem inuenire prout curia considerabit ad faciendum vel reddendum deinceps quod in carta continetur, tunc remaneat tenementum ei qui si iudicium expectet ab accione in perpetuum sit exclusus.

Si autem sic dicas, 'Do tantam terram cum pertinenciis habendam et tenend
30 am tibi et heredibus tuis si heredes de corpore tuo habueris,' si tales heredes michi procreauero quamuis defecerint, succedent tamen michi alii heredes mei remociores in infinitum quia satisfactum est condicioni set ante procreacionem tantum erit res michi data liberum tenementum et post meum decessum tibi reuertetur tanquam ad donatorem pro adiunccione cum modo.
35 Fiunt eciam quandoque donaciones ex causa precedente vt si dicam, 'Do tibi hanc rem quia michi bene seruiuisti' et quo casu, licet tu non bene seruieris, valet tamen donacio quia falsa causa adiecta non perimit donacionem non magis quam legatum. Item ex causa subsequente vt sic 'Do tibi hanc rem vt michi bene

---

4. ne] nec, J.   6. *prius* vt] et, J.   15. seruicium, *om.* J.   17. permittat] permittit, J.
21–23. Precipe . . . dicit, *ex statuto, om.* J.   25. *posterius* et *addidimus.*   34. adiunccione]
adiniunccione, J.   36. *post* rem *add.* vt, J.   38. vt] quia, J.

St. Westminster, II. c. 1

Bracton, f. 18

Bracton, f. 19

Bracton. f. 18*b*

Bracton, f. 18

St. Gloucester, c. 4

St. Westminster, II. c. 21

St. Gloucester, c. 4

Bracton, f. 18

Bracton. f. 19*b*

Because lately it seemed to the king that it was hard in cases in which a tenement etc.[1]

Mode and condition may be manifold, sometimes to the advantage of the donee (that he do not give or do not do) and sometimes, indeed, to his disadvantage (that he give or do). There are, moreover, four kinds of [innominate] contracts which may enter into a gift, namely: 'I give that you shall give'; 'I do that you shall do'; 'I do that you shall give'; 'I give that you shall do'. These are the modes of gifts and they bind the contracting parties so that, if one should give or do, the other is bound to give or do, according to what is agreed. But although one of them does not do what he has promised, the other cannot straightway demand back what he has given, unless this has been agreed from the beginning. The word *ut*, be it remarked, denotes a mode, *si* a condition, *quia* a cause. If, however, you say: 'I give you such-and-such an amount of land so that you shall find me in necessaries' or 'so that you shall give me so much', although the gift is not altogether free it is nevertheless simple and absolute, provided that due livery thereof follows. And, lest this kind of gift should be prejudicial to donors, it has been enacted that, if a man shall demise his land at fee farm to anyone so that he shall render him as service therefor the amount of the true yearly value or at least a fourth part thereof, and the tenant shall cease to render the service and permits the land to lie uncultivated or [if the land] is otherwise so kept that he cannot be distrained therein, thereupon, provided the service has ceased to be rendered for two years, an action shall be available to the donor or his heir to demand that tenement in demesne by the following writ:

Command A. that lawfully etc. he shall render to B. such-and-such a tenement which A. held of him by such-and-such service and which ought to revert to B. because the aforesaid A. has ceased to render the aforesaid service for two years, as B. says.

Nevertheless, if before judgement is given against him the tenant shall come into court, prepared to render arrears and damages, and shall offer to find security, as the court shall adjudge, to perform or render thenceforward what is contained in the charter, then the tenement shall remain his, but if he waits for judgement, then he shall be barred from an action for ever.

If, however, you say thus, 'I give such-and-such an amount of land with appurtenances to have and to hold to you and your heirs, if you shall have heirs of your body', and if I should beget such heirs, even though they should fail, nevertheless other heirs of mine, however remote, will succeed me *ad infinitum*, because the condition has been satisfied. But before they are begotten the property given to me will be simply a freehold and after my death it will revert to you as the donor, because of the [condition] joined to the mode.

Gifts are also sometimes made for a precedent cause: for example, if I say 'I give this thing to you because you have served me well', in which case, although you may not have served well, yet the gift is valid, since the addition of a fictitious cause does not destroy a gift any more than it does a legacy. And, again, gifts

---

[1] The provision of writs of formedon in the descender to ensure that the donor's intention was observed.

seruies,' valida erit donacio.   Si autem addatur condicio in causa subsequenti
erit donacio in pendenti, vt ecce 'Do tibi hanc rem si michi bene seruieris,' adhuc
pura et perfecta erit donacio resoluitur tamen sub condicione et in pendenti erit
donec sciatur vtrum existat condicio vel non.

5   Fieri eciam poterit donacio viro et vxori sue simul et heredibus utriusque com-   f. 73
munibus vel inter se procreatis vel procreandis vel eorum alterius tantum vel
heredibus eius qui alium superuixerit.   Item pluribus fieri poterit donacio per
modum simul et successiue vt ecce 'Do A. filio meo primogenito tantam terram
tenendam sibi et heredibus suis de corpore suo progenitis qui si tales sibi non
10   genuerit vel si habuerit et defecerint tunc volo quod terra illa ad B. filium meum
postnatum reuertatur tenenda sibi et propriis heredibus suis, vt supra, qui si
nullos tales habuerit vel si habuerit et defecerint tunc volo et concedo pro me et
heredibus meis quod predicta terra reuertatur ad C. tercium filium meum habenda
et tenenda sibi et heredibus suis de corpore suo progenitis' et sic de pluribus filiis
15   parentibus vel extraneis, 'et si predicti A. B. C. sine heredibus de corporibus suis
progenitis decesserint tunc volo quod predicta terra reuertatur ad me at ad
alios heredes meos.'

       Fieri autem poterit donacio sub condicione sine modo vt ecce 'Do tibi talem
terram si ita factum sit' vel 'non factum' et sic conferatur condicio in futurum,
20   licet presencia et preterita non sint in pendenti sicut futura, quia statim condicio
infirmat obligacionem vel omnino non differt.   Tunc autem est condicio   [187]
possibilis aut inpossibilis.   Si autem possibilis et potestatiua vt si dicam, 'Do tibi
talem rem si dederis michi decem', valet donacio et suspenditur donec consistat
condicio vt si rem interim pecieris excipere potero quod tu x. michi non dederis.
25   Si vero inpossibilis vt si dicam, 'Do tibi istam rem si celum digito tetigeris,' non
valebit donacio et pro non adiecta habebitur condicio.   Item non valet donacio
ab inicio set est in pendenti in alterius potestatem collata condicione vt si dicam,
'Do tibi hanc rem si Ticius voluerit' qui cum assensum non prebuerit non valebit
donacio.   Item si condicio casualis fuerit vt si dicam, 'Do tibi talem rem si nauis
30   venerit ex Asya' vel 'si Ticius consul factus fuerit,' sic erit donacio in pendenti
quia huiusmodi donaciones dependent ex insidiis fortune.   Si autem condicio
fuerit mixta et disiuncta vt si in parte fuerit potestatiua et in parte casualis vt si
dicam, 'Do tibi hanc rem si decem michi dederis', sufficit vnum istorum adimpleri
set si plures condiciones adiecte sint donacioni coniunctim vt si dicatur, 'Si illud

---

5. *posterius* et *addidimus*.   8. simul] filii, J.   11. si *om.* J.   18. sine] siue, J.
19. sic] si, J.   21. autem] aut, J.   25. dicam] dico, J.   26. *prius* non, Br., *om.* J.
27. potestatem] potestate, J.; collata, Br., *om.* J.   29. casualis] causalis, J.   32. vt],
vel, J; casualis] causalis, J.   34. *prius* si *om.* J; sint] sunt, J.

are sometimes made for a subsequent cause: for example, if I said 'I give this thing to you so that you will serve me well', the gift will be valid.   If, however, a condition should be added qualifying the subsequent cause, the gift will be in suspense, as thus, 'I give this thing to you if you will serve me well'.   The gift will be quite absolute and complete provided it comes into effect under the condition and, until it be known whether the condition is realised or not, it will be in suspense.

Bracton,
f. 18
A gift may also be made to a man and his wife together and to the heirs common to both of them or begotten or to be begotten between them or [to the heirs] of one of them only, or to the heirs of the one who shall survive the other.
Bracton,
f. 18b
Again, the gift may be made by this mode, to several persons at the same time and in succession, as thus, 'I give to A., my first-born son, such-and-such an amount of land to hold to him and his heirs begotten of his body and, if he does not beget such or if he has them and they fail, then I will that the said land shall revert to B., my second-born son, to hold to him and his own heirs (as above), and if he has no such heirs, or if he has them and they fail, then I will and grant for myself and my heirs that the land aforesaid shall revert to C., my third son, to have and to hold to him and his heirs begotten of his body (and so of several sons, relatives or strangers), and if the aforesaid A. B. and C. should die without heirs begotten of their bodies, I then will that the aforesaid land shall revert to me and to my other heirs'.

Bracton,
f. 19
A gift may, moreover, be made under a condition without a mode as thus, 'I give you such-and-such land if such-and-such be done' or 'not done', and in this way the condition will be related to the future since events in the present and events in the past are not in suspense like events in the future, and for that reason the condition invalidates the obligation straightway or it does not defer it in any way.   Then, again, a condition is either possible or impossible.   If it is possible and within your power, for example, if I should say, 'I give you such-and-such a thing if you will give me ten', the gift is valid and in suspense until the condition is fulfilled, so that, if in the meantime you demand the thing, I can except that you have not given me ten.   If, however, a condition is impossible, for example, if I should say, 'I give you this thing if you will touch the sky with your finger', the gift is not valid and the condition will not be regarded as imposed.   Again, a gift is not valid immediately but is in suspense if a condition is introduced that lies in the power of another: for example, if I should say, 'I give you this property if Titius should be agreeable': and if he should not give his assent, the gift will not be effective.   Again, if the condition depends upon chance, for example, if I should say, 'I give you such-and-such a thing if a ship should come from Asia' or 'if Titius should be made consul', then the gift will be in suspense because such gifts are dependent upon the vagaries of Fortune.   If, however, a condition should be mixed [with another] and disjunctive, for example, if it should be in part within my power and should in part depend upon chance, as if I should say, 'I give you this thing if you will give me ten [or if a ship comes from Asia]', it suffices if one of these things is fulfilled; but if several conditions are added to the gift conjunctively, for example, if it is said 'If this and that be

et illud factum sit', omnibus est parendum si diuisim vt predictum est cuilibet vel
eorum alteri sufficit obtemperare.   Item condicionum alia expressa et fit sub verbis negatiuis vt si dicatur 'Si Ticius heres non sit tu heres esto' vel 'Si de corpore
tuo heredes non habueris tunc reuertatur terra sic data ad tales simul vel succes-
5 siue.'   Est eciam quedam condicio tacita que fit sub verbis affirmatiuis vt si dicatur, 'Si A. sit heres B. te inuicem substituo', id est heredem facio si vnus
eorum premoriatur quod viuus succedat mortuo. Est eciam quedam condicio
duplex vt si dicatur, 'Si heredes de corpore tuo non habueris vel si habueris et
decesserint tunc terra data ad me vel ad heredes meos reuertatur.' Et est
10 condicio simplex vt ecce 'Si habueris heredes et infra etatem decesserint tunc ad
me reuertatur terra,' vt supra.   Est eciam alia condicio duplex que partim fit
verbis negatiuis et partim affirmatiuis vt si dicam, 'Si filius meus non fuerit
furiosus vel si fuerit et infra furorem decesserit volo quod tu sis heres.'   Item fieri
poterit donacio sub modo pluribus condicionibus adiectis vt ecce 'Do tibi hanc
15 rem vt facias hoc (vel ne facias) quod si non feceris quod res reuertatur ad me' vel
sic 'Do tibi vt non facias sine voluntate mea et si feceris quod me extunc possim
in terram illam mittere et in eadem me licite tenere quiete de te et tuis heredibus.'
Et vnde si predicte condiciones siue conuenciones et instrumenta in quibus continentur in iudicio fuerint deducta non solum sufficit instrumenta, condiciones vel
20 conuenciones probare nisi probetur quod condicioni sit satisfactum vel non satisfactum quia probato instrumento adhuc subesse poterit quod condicioni non sit
satisfactum per veram probacionem vel saltem presumpcionem cui semper
standum erit donec probetur in contrarium.   Poterit eciam fieri donacio sub
modo vel condicione que ex alterius dependet voluntate vel potestate vt ecce si
25 quis alicui dederit aduocacionem alicuius ecclesie vt ibi faciat prioratum et illam   f. 73b
in vsus prioratus conuertat hoc sine voluntate loci dyocesani facere non poterit
cum effectu tenebit tamen donacio erga donatarium donec per dominum feodi
tollatur vel per regem nisi confirmetur.

Inpedit condicio quandoque descensum ad proprios heredes et facit liberum   [188]
30 tenementum et quandoque feodum et tollit heredibus assisam mortis antecessoris
vt ecce 'Concedo tibi tantam terram ad terminum x. annorum vt post terminum
ad me reuertatur set si interim decessero concedo pro me et heredibus meis quod
terra illa remaneat tibi ad vitam tuam' vel 'in feodo.'   Item quod fuit ab inicio
liberum tenementum et ad vitam per conuencionem mutari poterit in terminum
35 vt si quis alicui terram concedat ad vitam fieri poterit inter eos condicio quod si

---

1. et illud, Br., *om.* J; parendum] pendendum, J.   13. *post* fuerit *add.* et infuerit, J;
decesserit, Br., *om* J.   19. deducta] dedicta, J; vel *addidimus.*   21. quia *om.* J.
23. in *om.* J.   32. *post* set *add.* et, J.

done', all must be fulfilled; but if disjunctively, as aforesaid, it is sufficient to comply with one or other of them.   Again, one form of condition is express and is made with negative words: for example, if it were said, 'If Titius be not the heir, you be the heir' or 'If you should not have heirs of your body, then let the land so given revert to such-and-such, together or in succession'.   There is also a tacit condition which is made with words in the affirmative: for example, if it were said, 'If A. is the heir, I appoint you B. in his place', that is, I make him heir and, if one of them dies first, the survivor succeeds the

deceased.[1]   There is also a double condition: for example, if it is said, 'If you do not have heirs of your body or if you have them and they die, then the land given will revert to me and my heirs'.   And there is a [double] condition, as thus, 'If you have heirs and they die under age, then the land will revert to me' (as above).   There is also another double condition, which is made partly by words in the negative and partly by words in the affirmative: for example, if I should say, 'If my son is [mad], or if he is [not] mad and dies [under age], then I will that you shall be heir'.[2]   Again, a gift may be made under a mode with several conditions attached, as thus, 'I give you this thing so that you will do this (or will not do this), and if you should not do so the thing is to revert to me', or thus, 'I give to you so that you will not do [such-and-such] unless I wish it, and if you should do so, thereupon I may enter upon that land and lawfully remain therein quit of you and your heirs'.   Wherefore, if the aforesaid conditions or agreements, and the instruments in which they are contained, should be the subject of litigation, it is not sufficient merely to prove the instruments, conditions or agreements, without proving that the condition is satisfied (or not satisfied), because, once the instrument has been proved, it may still be that there is not exact proof or at least presumption (a presumption which will always hold good until there is proof to the contrary) that the condition has been satisfied.   A gift may also be made under a mode or condition that depends upon the will or power of another, as thus, if a man should give to someone the advowson of any church in order that he found a priory there and convert it to the use of a priory, he cannot give effect to this unless the diocesan of the place so wishes.   However, the gift will hold good so far as the donee is concerned until it is taken away by the lord of the fee or by the king unless it be confirmed.

Sometimes a condition prevents descent to the right heirs, and creates a freehold and sometimes a fee, and takes away from the heirs an assize of mort d'ancestor, as, for instance, 'I grant to you such-and-such an amount of land for a term of ten years so that after this term it shall revert to me but, should I die in the interval, I grant for me and my heirs that the land shall remain yours for the period of your life' or 'in fee'.   Again, what was to begin with freehold and for life may by an agreement be changed into a term [of years]: for example, if a man should grant land to someone for life, a condition might be agreed between

[1] Bracton and Fleta have the same defective reading; for another solution see Thorne, *op. cit.*, II. 72.   [2] For comparison of Bracton's corrupt text with the Digest, see Thorne, *op. cit.*, II. 72, n. 4.

tenens infra certum terminum obierit quod heredes tenentis vel assignati vel
executores terram sic datam teneant vsque ad finem termini.   Et ita fit liberum
tenementum de termino et e contrario per condicionem et dat excepcionem
contra veros dominos petentes et eorum heredes.   Oritur eciam excepcio creditori
5 contra debitorem verum dominum et eius heredes cum inter eos ab inicio conuenerit quod si pecunia suo die soluta non fuerit quod terra in vadium posita
extunc creditori et suis heredibus remaneat.   Item datur excepcio contra veros
heredes in assisa mortis antecessoris cum aliquis crucesignatus vel alius peregre
proficiscens sic deposuerit quod concesserit alicui extraneo terram suam ad
10 certum terminum, experimens vlterius quod nisi redierit quod vsufructuario
remaneat terra in feodo et sic vnum habent principium terminus et feoffamentum
quamuis exitum diuersum.   Set esto quod quis pecuniam suam credat ad plures
terminos reddendam quocienscumque in solucione alicuius termini defecerit res
inpignorata creditori in perpetuum remanebit quia sic voluit verus possessor et
15 quia non condicioni satisfactum secundum quod conuenit.   Liberatur tamen
debitori si die suo optulit denarios sub testimonio fidedignorum qui pecuniam
viderint numeratam quacumque hora diei cum tota dies cedat debitori et creditor
eos recipere contradixerit vel alias se transtulerit et sufficit debitori si vnica hora
diei sui peccuniam suam sibi creditam optulerit reddendam set creditorem oportet
20 quod per quamlibet horam se paratum exhibeat ad recipiendum et quod semper
sui copiam faciat.   Et peccunia diebus statutis non soluta nec oblata statim habet
creditor liberum tenementum et feodum si fuerit in possessione si autem extra
habet accionem ex conuencione.   Ex condicione eciam in donacione apposita
quandoque obligatur persona donatarii vt ecce 'Vt ex re data michi necessaria
25 inuenias,' et quandoque ipsa res tantum vt si dicatur, 'Do tibi et heredibus tuis
ita tamen vt non habeas illam et a te et tuis heredibus alienandi potestatem' vel
'nisi certe persone'.   Et quo casu cum alienata fuerit habebit primus donator accionem ex conuencione versus secundum donatorem qui tenetur ad conuencionem respondere et versus donatarium tenentem pro pena restitucionis et non
30 contra alterum eorum per se set simul agere oportebit contra vtrumque dum
tamen petens carte copiam habeat quoquo modo, et quamuis seruitus apponatur
in donacione ne fiat.   Donacio tamen libera est quia donatorio et heredibus
suis facta quamuis hoc verbum 'libere' in donacione non conprehendatur nec
tenentem disseysire licebit nisi talis clausula in donacione adiecta fuerit 'quod
35 si fecerit extunc liceat michi et heredibus meis rem datam in manum nostrum
capere et seysire et sine aliqua iniuria expellere omni tempore quandocumque   [*189*]
voluerimus.'   Non tamen poterit res cum tali remanere dum tamen primus
tenens suus eam velit rehabere tenendam vt prius et quo casu eiectus nichil

1. infra . . . tenentis, Br., *om.* J.   2. executores, Br., heredes, J.   20. *prius* quod *addidimus.*
23. ex conuencione, Br.; et conuencionem, J.   31. petens carte] potens parte, J; quoquo]
quoque, J.   36. omni] cum, J.

them that, if the tenant should die within a certain time, the heirs of the tenant or his assigns or executors shall hold the land so given until the end of a period of years. And so by a condition a freehold is created from a term, and conversely, and it thus gives an exception against the true owners who claim it and their heirs. Also an exception becomes available to a creditor against a debtor, who is the true owner and his heirs, when it has been agreed between them from the beginning that, should the money not be paid on the day it is due, the land given in gage shall thereafter remain with the creditor and his heirs. Again, an exception is given against the true heirs in an assize of mort d'ancestor if any crusader or anyone else setting out on a pilgrimage should dispose of his property in this way, that he grants his land to some stranger for a precise term, stating further that, if he should not return, the land would remain with the usufructuary in fee; and thus the term and the feoffment have one beginning although they have a different end. But suppose that someone should lend his money to be repaid at several terms, whensoever the debtor should fail to pay at any term the thing pledged will remain with the creditor in perpetuity, because the true possessor willed it so and because the condition as agreed was not satisfied. The thing will, however, be delivered to the debtor if on his appointed day (at whatever hour of the day, since the whole day is allowed to the debtor) he offered the money by the testimony of trustworthy men who saw the money in cash, and the creditor refused to receive it or transferred himself elsewhere. And it is sufficient if the debtor offers to pay the money lent to him at any one hour of his appointed day, but the creditor must show himself ready at every hour to receive the money and ever ready to make out his receipt. And if the money is not paid or offered on the days appointed, straightway the creditor has a freehold and a fee if he is in possession, but, if he is out of possession, he has an action on the agreement. Sometimes also, arising out of a condition inserted in a gift, the donee is personally liable, as thus, 'that out of what is given, you find me necessaries'; and sometimes only the thing itself is burdened, as if it should be said, 'I give to you and your heirs, provided, however, that you do not have it with the power of alienation by you and your heirs', or 'except to a particular person'. And in such a case where it is alienated, the first donor will have an action on the agreement against the second donor who is bound to answer in regard to the agreement, and against the donee holding the land to secure the penalty of restitution. And it will be necessary for him to bring an action against both parties together and not against either of them separately, provided that the demandant has somehow a copy of the charter. And though there is imposed in the gift a servitude that a gift be not made, nevertheless the gift is free because it is made to the [donee] and his heirs, although the word 'freely' (*libere*) is not included in the gift. Nor is it permissible to disseise the tenant unless the following clause be inserted in the gift, 'that if he should make such [gift], thereupon it is lawful to me and my heirs to take and seize what is given into our hand and without any wrong eject at any time whensoever we wish'. The property, however, cannot remain with the donor, provided the first tenant holding of him wishes to have it again to hold as before, in which case the one who is ejected will recover nothing

recuperabit set sibi inputet quod rem sic obligatam recepit quem ignorancia non excusabit.

CAP. X. DE ESCAETIS

Terra autem data bastardo cum aliqua muliere in maritagium et eorum
5 heredibus communibus ad donatorem reuerti debet quociens heredes huiusmodi
defecerint.　Si autem bastardo et suis heredibus tantum et heredes non habuerit
vel si habuerit et defecerint quamuis terram in vita sua alienauerit adhuc erit
eschaeta donatoris homagio non obstante.　Homagium enim talium cum vita
euanescit et exspirat et ideo in fauorem bastardorum inuenta fuit assignacio et
10 constituta.　Bastardus igitur si terram sibi et heredibus suis et assignatis
legitime adquisiuerit si heredes sibi non procreauerit assignatis tamen suis con-　f. 74
stituere poterit dum tamen hora congrua alioquin eschaeta remanebit donatoris.
Et quamuis constituatur quod terre de cetero date de capitalibus dominis inmediate teneantur, nullam tamen eschaetam in premissis sibi poterunt vendicare set
15 donatoribus et suis heredibus vel hiis qui ad warantiam sunt obligati reuertentur.
Mulieres autem vidue a dotibus suis non excludantur quamuis warantos producere non possint alios quam ipsos erga quos pecierint eo quod pura et simplex
et in feodo facta fuit huiusmodi viro suo donacio.　Set esto quod bastardus
filium vel filiam non habens nec assignatum facere potens terram alicui dederit et
20 post donum obierit et vxor eius petat dotem, tunc obstabit ei dotis peticio quia
warantum non habet.　Set quid si duobus fratribus bastardis fiat donacio
tenenda in communi.　Tunc moriente vno accrescit alteri pars morientis non
tamen iure successionis set per ius accrescendi et si vterque heredem sibi procreauerit ambo accionem habebunt.
25 Quandoque eciam fit reuersio quia ius et successio descendere non poterunt
ad heredes propter inpedimentum perpetuum sicut felonia antecessoris, de qua si
quis conuictus fuerit et talis terra data non erit eschaeta domini capitalis set donatoris vel heredum suorum qui pro heredibus habebuntur ad warantizandum
omnia que felo gessit perfecte ante feloniam dum voluit et potuit sicut donaciones
30 et dimissiones.　Secus vero de gestis post feloniam perpetratam. Dimissiones
statim post condempnacionem in manum regis capi debent et finitis terminis et
anno et die pro termino regis ad dominos reuertantur capitales.　Nichil tamen
firmariis debet deperire nec ad manus huiusmodi dominorum peruenire debent
huiusmodi eschaete priusquam firmariis de suis terminis conpetenter fuerit satis-
35 factum.　Donaciones eciam post feloniam perpetratam facte perfecte erunt et
perpetue nisi donatores huiusmodi de feloniis suis in vita sua conuincantur.　Et

6. defecerint] defecerit, J.　　9 exspirat] respirat, J.　　13. Westm. 3 *recentiori manu in*
margine.　　29. gessit] iessit, J.

but it will be laid against him that he received the property thus burdened, and ignorance will not excuse him.

CHAPTER 10.   OF ESCHEATS

Land which is given with some woman in marriage to a bastard and to their common heirs ought to revert to the donor whenever these heirs fail. If, however, [the land is given] to a bastard and his heirs only and he should have no heirs, or if he should have heirs and they fail, even though he should alienate the land in his lifetime, yet it will be the donor's escheat, homage notwithstanding. For the homage of such donees vanishes and expires with their lives, and therefore, assignment was invented and established in favour of bastards.   Therefore, if a bastard lawfully acquires land for himself and his heirs and assigns, if he should not beget heirs of himself, he can, however, appoint his assigns, provided he does so at the appropriate time, otherwise the land will remain the

donor's escheat.   And although it is enacted that lands given in future shall be held immediately of the chief lords, they can, however, claim for themselves no escheat in the aforesaid lands which revert to the donors and their heirs or to

those who are bound to warranty.   Widows, however, will not be excluded from their dower, although they can produce no warrantors other than those against whom they are demandants, because the gift to the husband, though a bastard, was absolute and simple and made in fee.   But suppose that a bastard, not having

a son or daughter nor capable of appointing an assign, should give his land to another and die after making the gift and his wife demand her dower, then a claim for dower will avail against that other because he has no warrantor. But what if a gift should be made to two bastard brothers to hold in common? Then, when one dies, the portion of the deceased accrues to the other, not, however, by right of succession but by right of accrual, and if each of them should beget an heir, both will have a right of action.

Sometimes, however, there is a reversion because the right and succession cannot descend to the heirs because of a permanent impediment, such as the felony of an ancestor.   And if anyone should be convicted of felony, land that has been given to him will not be an escheat of the chief lord's but of the donor's or the donor's heirs, who are regarded as heirs [of the felon] for the purpose of warranting all that the felon brought to a conclusion, such as gifts and demises, before the felony while he had the will and capacity.   But it is otherwise regard-

ing what is done after felony has been committed.   Demises should be seized into the king's hand immediately after condemnation, and when the terms [of the leases] have expired and a year and a day for the king's term, they will revert to the chief lords: but the fermors should not be deprived of anything, nor should escheats of this kind come into the hands of such lords before the fermors have properly completed their terms.   Gifts made after the commission of a felony will also be perfect and perpetual unless the donors are convicted of their felonies

ad hoc facit lex imperatoria post capitale crimen contractum donaciones facte
valent nisi condempnacio fuerit subsecuta.   Et sicut res sic data esse poterit eschaeta donatoris in dominico eodem modo poterit in homagio et seruicio quasi
medio inter ipsum et tenentem sui tenentis sublato loco cuius oportebit eum   *[190]*
5 succedere et homagium et seruicium recusare non poterit set velit nolit loco erit
heredis ei cui successerit nec poterit dominus feodi suum feodum weyuare cum
voluerit et sic a warantia soluatur tenentis.   Weyuare tamen poterit tenementum
quod in feodo tenuerit et in dominico si velit cum alii non cedit incomodum set
sibi soli in dampnum.   Nec weyuare poterit homagium vel seruicium tenentis
10 felonis magis quam ipsum tenementum.   Et cum quis feoffatus fuerit per certum
seruicium et ipse alium inde feoffauerit per maius seruicium et medius postea pro
felone conuincatur, statim ex rigore iuris obligatur terra domino capitali ex incre-
mento seruicii sibi faciendo prout suo erat medio feloni obligata et sibi accrescit
secundum cum primo tanquam eschaeta.   Ex equitate tamen decretum est sic
15 quod pro nulla constitucione felonis maioris seruicii vel minoris in suo feoffamento contenti nichil domino depereat eo quod res cum suo onere transit et quia
huiusmodi tenentes iniuste grauarentur si ad vtrumque seruicium fuerint obligati
cum pocius de suis mediis vel eorum successoribus tueri debuissent, tenendum
est hoc medium quod huiusmodi domini incrementa huiusmodi seruicorum
20 habeant vt suas eschaetas ita tamen quod minora seruicia huiusmodi dominis ex
antiquo debita in maiori seruicio tenentis inplicite conputentur.

CAP. XI.   DE DONACIONIBUS IN MARITAGIIS

Cum autem terre aliquando dentur ante sponsalia propter nupcias a patre
mulieris vel alio vel in ipso contractu vel post matrimonium contractum et
25 mencio habeatur in donacione de maritagio terra sic data supponit reuersionem
que si fiat ab ipso viro sue vxori ad hostium ecclesie non debet dici maritagium
set pocius certa dotis constitucio, et quamuis fiat mencio in donacione quod terra
data sit in maritagium tali viro cum tali vxore res data tamen est liberum
tenementum vxoris et non viri cum non habeat nisi custodiam cum vxore donec
30 liberum tenementum sibi accrescat per legem Anglie.   Secus si pro homagio et
seruicio viri et in maritagium facta fuerit donacio.   Si autem vxor donacionem
fecerit sine viro suo tunc statim competit viro restitucio per assisam noue

2. condempnacio] condempcio, J.   9. weyuare] vennare, J.   11. *prius* et *addidimus*.

in their lifetime. And on this an imperial law[1] rules that, unless condemnation follows, gifts made after a capital crime has been committed are valid. And just as property so given may be an escheat of the donor's in demesne, in the same way it may be an escheat in homage and service, as if the mesne should be removed between the donor and the tenant of his tenant to whose place he will be obliged to succeed; and he cannot reject [the tenant's] homage and service, but he must, willy nilly, take the place of the heir of him whom he succeeds. Nor can the lord of the fee waive his fee, though he might wish to do so, and thus be absolved from warranting the tenant. He can, however, waive the tenement that he holds in fee and demesne if he wishes, when this does not involve inconvenience to another but prejudices only himself. Nor can he waive the homage or service of the tenant of a felon any more than the tenement itself. And should someone be enfeoffed by a precise service and should he enfeoff another with the tenement by a greater service and should the mesne thereafter be convicted of felony, in strict law the land is immediately burdened with the increased service to be rendered to the chief lord, as it was burdened in regard to his mesne, the felon, and the second service accrues to him as an escheat with the original service. By equity, however, it has been laid down thus, that despite any creation by the felon of a greater or lesser service within his enfeoffment, the lord shall not be the loser because the property passes with its burden, and, since the tenants might be wrongfully burdened if they were bound to render both services—the more so since they ought to be safeguarded by their mesne lords or their successors—this middle course should be followed, that the superior lords shall have the additional services as their escheats, provided, however, that the lesser services due to these lords as of old shall be reckoned as included in the greater service of the tenant.

Bracton,
f. 23b

Bracton,
f. 24

CHAPTER 11.   OF GIFTS IN MARRIAGE

Bracton,
f. 21

When, as sometimes happens, lands are given by the woman's father or another [relative] before espousals in consideration of marriage or when the marriage takes place or subsequent to the marriage and [if] marriage portion is mentioned in the gift, the land so given presumes a reversion. But if such a gift is made by the husband to his wife at the church door it ought not to be spoken of as marriage portion but rather as a certain constitution of dower. And although mention may be made in a gift that the land is given to such-and-such a man in marriage with such-and-such a woman, the property given is, however, the freehold of the wife's and not the husband's, since he has nothing but the custody of it, with his wife, until the freehold accrues to him by the curtesy of England. It is otherwise if the gift should be made for the homage and service of the husband and in marriage. If, however, the wife should make a gift without her husband, then he may forthwith seek restitution by an assize of novel disseisin or by writ of

Bracton,
f. 22

Bracton,
f. 22b

---

[1] Digest 39. 5. 15.

disseisine vel per breue de ingressu.   Est autem quoddam maritagium liberum
ab omni seruicio solutum donatori vel eius heredibus vsque ad tercium heredem
vel vsque ad quartum gradum faciendo et debent gradus sic computari vt dona-   f. 74b
tarius primum faciat gradum heres eius secundum gradum heres heredis tercium
5 et heres secundi heredis quartum, qui quidem tenebitur ad seruicium vt ad homagium prius autem minime ne donator vel eius heredes per homagii accepcionem a
reuersione repellantur.   Set in quarto gradu pro eo quod tunc vehementer
presumitur quod terra non est pro defectu heredum donatarii reuersura quia
eciam si propinquos heredes non habeat vel cum habeat et defecerint ad dona-
10 torem vel eius heredes qui homagium ceperint non erit terra reuersura dum tamen
aliquis remotus de consanguinitate appareat qui ius in hereditatem poterit vendicare, alioquin euanescit homagium et reuertetur.   Et cum de sanguine homagium
factum fuerit extunc obligatur homo ad seruicium quia seruicium semper sequitur   [191]
homagium et districcio semper sequitur fidelitatem.   Et quamuis in huiusmodi
15 donacionibus non contineantur homagium, seruicium vel warantizacio expresse
nichilominus tamen tenebitur vel eius heres ad warantiam quocienscumque
fuerit vocatus eo quod femina per donatorem sic maritata vel eius pueri et
heredes si ipsa decesserit pro carta debent reputari dum tamen expresse non
excipiatur vel inhibeatur.   Et quamuis inde prestentur auxilia racionabilia que
20 personas respiciunt et non tenementum vel alie contribuantur prestaciones
communiter ad regem pertinentes nichilominus tamen liberum est.   Et est similiter maritagium seruicio obligatum et oneratum vt si quis sic dederit quod sibi et
heredibus suis aliquod seruicium reseruauerit, et quo casu faciendum est seruicium set non homagium ante tercium heredem et extunc seruicium cum homagio
25 de herede in heredem.   Poterit autem terra dari tam viro per se et suis heredibus
quam vxori per se et suis heredibus ante matrimonium et post quam vtrique
eorum et eorum heredibus communibus et vnde si a patre vel a matre vel alio
antecessore vxori facta fuerit donacio et eidem vxori per mortem sui antecessoris
cedat alia hereditas inter ipsam et alias sorores vel earum heredes participanda,
30 terra viro suo data non veniet in diuisionem nec contribuere tenetur nisi fuerit
donacio mulieri ante matrimonium tali de causa de se maritanda.   Si autem
mulieri et heredibus suis simpliciter fiat donacio ad se maritandam quamuis
heredes de corpore suo non producat succedent ei tamen heredes remoti.   Si
autem certi exprimantur heredes et tales non habuerit vel si habuerit et defec-
35 erint statim reuertetur terra ad donatorem.   Si autem viro et vxori et heredibus
suis communibus fiat donacio et filiam procreauerit quamuis ab alio viro filium
conceperit femina tamen masculo preferetur quod non esset si vxori tantum et
heredibus suis facta fuisset donacio.   Si autem viro et vxori fiat donacio
tenenda sibi et heredibus suis legitime inter eos procreatis pro homagio et
40 seruicio et in liberum maritagium, tunc omisso maritagio preferendum est

26. *prius* quam *addidimus.*   27. *prius* et] vel, J.   34. certi] ceteri, J.

entry.   There is moreover a form of marriage portion free from all service to be rendered to the donor or his heirs up to the third or even fourth degree.   And the degrees ought to be computed in this way: the donee makes the first degree, his heir the second degree, the heir of the heir the third, and the heir of the second heir the fourth, who will be required to render service.   As regards homage, however, it is not rendered previously lest the donor or his heirs, by accepting homage, should be deprived of the reversion.   But in the fourth degree [homage is accepted], because there is then a strong presumption that the land will not revert by failure of heirs of the donee, since, even if he has no near heirs or if he had them and they failed, the land will not revert to the donor or his heirs who have accepted homage, so long as anyone remote in kinship appears who can claim a right to the inheritance: otherwise the homage is extinguished and [the land given] reverts.   And when on account of kinship homage has been rendered, thereupon a man is bound to do service, because service always follows homage and distraint always follows fealty.   And although in such gifts there is no express mention of homage, service or warranty, nevertheless the [donor] or his heir will be bound to offer warranty as often as he is vouched, because the woman so endowed in marriage by the donor or, if she dies, her children and heirs ought to be esteemed as good as a charter, provided warranty is not expressly excepted or prohibited [in the gift].   And although reasonable aids are furnished therefrom, which are in respect of persons and not of the tenement, or other payments are contributed which pertain generally to the king, nevertheless the marriage portion is free.   And similarly there is a marriage portion bound and burdened with service: as for example, if the donor should so give it that he reserves some service to him and his heirs, in which case service must be done, but not homage before the third heir [inherits], and thenceforward service with homage will be done by one heir after another.   Land, moreover, can be given before marriage and afterwards not only to the husband alone and his heirs but also to the wife alone and her heirs and to both of them and their common heirs and therefore, if a gift should be made to the wife by father or mother or other ancestor, and by the death of her ancestor there should come to the wife another inheritance partible between her and her other sisters or their heirs, land given to her husband will not fall to be divided nor require to be laid under contribution, unless the gift were to the woman before marriage for such a purpose as getting her married.   If, however, the gift for the purpose of getting her married were made simply to the woman and her heirs, although she should not produce heirs of her body, nevertheless her remote heirs will succeed her.   If, however, particular heirs are specified and she has none such, or if she had them and they fail, the land will immediately revert to the donor.   But if the gift was made to the husband and wife and their common heirs and they should beget a daughter, even though the woman should conceive a son by another husband, nevertheless the female [heir] will be preferred to the male: which would not be the case if the gift were made to the wife only and her heirs.   If, however, the gift were made to the husband and wife to hold to themselves and their heirs, lawfully begotten, between them, for homage and service and in frank marriage, then 'marriage'

homagium pro homagii excellencia et dignitate.   Si autem donacio fiat alicui vt
aliquam ducat in vxorem pure vel adiecta condicione vel modo si donatarius ad
alia vota conuolauerit conpetit donatori repeticio et vnde si donator postquam
talis aliam duxerit ipsum statim eiciat eiectus per assisam noue disseisine non
5 recuperabit, secus vero si talem duxerit vt conuenit inter quos forte postea
celebretur diuorcium verumtamen conpetit inde repeticio si certi heredes in
donacione comprehensi non producantur vel defecerint.

CAP. XII. DE REUERSIONIBUS

Reuertitur autem quandoque donacio ad donatorem pro defectu heredum
10 per modum tacitum vel expressum vt si facta fuerit in maritagium vel bastardo
et quandoque non solum pro defectu heredum vel assignatorum tantum set
eciam pro defectu heredum assignatorum de quibus non fit mencio in donacione
quod res data ad ipsos descendat et quandoque cum nullus heres omnino appareat post mortem feoffati qualitercumque.   Set si mortuus heredem reliquerit   [*192*]
15 de quo plena habeatur noticia, tunc non erit donator loco heredis nec factum sui
tenentis defuncti et dotem warantizabit, secus vero si de herede dubitetur vtrum
heres fuerit vel non.   Item reuertitur terra ad donatorem quandoque per restitucionem et quandoque cum tenens suum weyuauerit tenementum et quibus
casibus euanescit homagium proinde factum.   Item reuertitur terra ad dona-
20 torem sicut ad heredem proximum feoffati vt si pater feoffauerit filium suum   f. 75
medium vel frater antenatus fratrem postnatum pro homagio et seruicio suo sibi
et heredibus de corpore suo exeuntibus et talis feoffatus obierit seysitus sine herede
de se terra data ad feoffatorem fratrem reuertitur vno modo sicut eschaeta sua
pro defectu heredum corporis sui, alio modo sicut heredi.   Set quoniam homa-
25 gium non extinguitur cum sint alii heredes remoti ac sicut primogenitus esse
non poterit dominus et heres cum homagium expellat dominicum in hoc casu et
retineat seruicium terra data cum tali fratre non remanebit.   Si quis eciam
alium feoffauerit pro homagio ac ille secundum et secundus tercium et vltra et
vltimo feoffatus primum feoffauerit feoffatorem tale feoffamentum stare non
30 poterit quia nullus esse potest simul et semel dominus et tenens.   Inpediuntur
autem reuersiones quandoque per homagium et seruicium receptum.   Prodest tamen quandoque seruicium ei assignare cuius interest donum reuocare et
homagium retinere.   Item donaciones a seruis vel sokemannis quas in villenagio
vel villano sokagio tenuerint irritari debent et dominis restitui et recenter sine

5. vt] non, J.   15. non *addidimus*; nec] in, J.   16. dubitetur] habeatur, J.
25. sicut primogenitus] primogenitus sicut, J.   31. *post* reversiones *add.* et, J.

must be disregarded and preference given to 'homage' on account of the superiority and dignity of homage. If, however, a gift is made to someone, absolutely or with a condition added or a mode, in order that he may make a certain woman his wife, and the donee should transfer his vows elsewhere, the donor has a right to reclaim it: therefore if, after the donee has married the other woman, the donor should forthwith eject him, the donee so ejected will not recover by any assize of novel disseisin. It will be otherwise, however, if the donee should marry the woman as agreed and it should befall that a divorce was afterwards decreed between them. Nevertheless, to reclaim the gift is permissible to the donor if the particular heirs, included in the gift, are not produced or if they fail.

Bracton,
f. 23

CHAPTER 12.   OF REVERSIONS

Bracton,
f. 23

Sometimes, indeed, a gift reverts to the donor on account of the failure of heirs by a mode, tacit or express: for example, if the gift were made as a marriage portion or to a bastard; and sometimes not merely for failure of heirs or assigns only, but also for failure of heirs of assigns, of whom no mention is made in the gift, [namely] that the thing given descend to them; and sometimes when no heir at all appears after the death of the feoffee, in whatsoever way [he was enfeoffed]. But if the deceased leaves an heir of whom there is full knowledge, then the donor will not occupy the place of the heir nor will he warrant what the deceased, his tenant, did and the dower; but it is otherwise if there is doubt concerning the heir, whether he should be the heir or not. Again, the land reverts to the donor sometimes by restitution and sometimes when the tenant waives his tenement, and in these cases the homage rendered therefor is extinguished. Again, the land reverts to the donor as the next heir of his feoffee: for example, if a father enfeoffs his middle son, or an elder brother enfeoffs a younger brother, for his homage and service to him and to his heirs, the issue of his body, and this feoffee dies seised without an heir of his own, the land given reverts to the feoffor, to the [older] brother, in one way as his escheat for failure of heirs of his [younger brother's] body and in another way as his heir. But since homage is not extinguished when there are other heirs, [however] remote, and since the older brother cannot be both lord and heir (since homage will in this case cast away demesne and retain service), the land given will not remain with such a brother. Also, if a man enfeoffs another for his homage, and the feoffee enfeoffs a second, and the second feoffee a third and so forth, and he who is last enfeoffed enfeoffs the first feoffor, such a feoffment cannot stand, because no one can be at one and the same time both lord and tenant. Sometimes, however, reversions are impeded by the acceptance of homage and service. So sometimes it is worth while to assign the service to him whose advantage lies in the revocation of the gift and to retain the homage. Again, gifts by villeins or sokemen of what they hold in villeinage or in villein socage ought to be annulled and restored to

Bracton,
f. 24

Bracton,
f. 26b

breui poterunt donatarii eici et inpune expelli, secus post pacificam seysinam habitam.

Fieri eciam poterunt donaciones ad terminum vite recipientis vel ad vitam donatoris vel ad terminum annorum vel donec quid fiat vel non fiat vel donec
5 fuerit prouisum donatario et tunc refert vtrum mencio fiat de donatore et heredibus vel de donatore tantum et vtrum prouideri debeat donatario tantum vel sibi et heredibus suis et quibus casibus si heredes non comprehendantur nec prouisum sit donatario in vita donatoris remanebit res data in feodo cum ipso donatario et si in vita donatoris facta fuerit prouisio ad donatorem reuertetur et si heredes
10 donatoris tantum in donacione comprehendantur et non donatarii et donatario non fuerit prouisum dum vixit cum heredibus donatarii remanebit res data in perpetuum quamuis heredibus donatarii competens satisfaccio offeratur. Set si heredes donatarii tantum in donacione contineantur tunc reuertetur terra data quamcicius per donatorem sibi prouideatur. Et contra qui quidem si non
15 prouiderit non sufficit si heredes ad satisfaccionem prouisionis se reddant beniuolos et paratos cum modus donacionis se habeat in contrarium. Si autem fiat donacio alicui ad vitam suam donatarius tamen nichil adquirit nisi liberum tenementum tantum feodum vero tamen remanet cum donatore et cum obierit statim reuertetur terra ad donatorem. Et si alicui fiat donacio ad vitam
20 donatoris quamuis heredes donatarii in donacione contineantur non tamen sibi adquirit liberum tenementum nec feodum set quamdam possessionem ad certum terminum a qua si fuerit eiectus per assisam noue disseisine non recuperabit licet per aliud remedium et tenebunt heredes vsque ad finem termini. Si autem [*193*] non fiat mencio de heredibus donatarii non statim tamen reuertetur terra ad
25 donatorem post obitum donatarii nisi decesserit intestatus, set si de residuo termini sui testato in testamento suo ordinauerit valida erit disposicio velut de catallis cum nulli cedat de exheredacione. Si autem sic fiat donacio, 'Do tali tantum terre pro me et heredibus meis,' statim fit donatario liberum tenementum tantum qui cum decesserit ad me reuertetur, ac si dixissem 'Do tali ad
30 vitam ipsius.' Ex termino vero annorum quamuis longissimo numquam fit donatario liberum tenementum, cum terminus vite incertus et ideo liberum facit tenementum et licet nichil cercius morte nichil tamen incercius hora mortis.

Potest quis alicui terram concedere ad terminum annorum et interim eidem vel alteri dare eandem in feodo et si alium vtraque tamen possessio durabit quia
35 sese conpaciuntur terminus et feoffamentum licet diuersa sint ibi iura nam ad feoffatum pertinet liberum tenementum et feodum cum proprietate. Firmarius vero nichil iuris vendicare poterit preter vsumfructum. Item dimitti poterit terra pro voluntate dimissoris tenenda de termino in terminum et anno

5. donatario] donatorio, J.   8. donatario] donatorio, J.   10. et non donatarii, Br., *om.* J.   11. prouisum] visum, J.   15. prouisionis] promissionis, J.   17. tamen] cum, J. 31. donatario] donatorio, J.   36. feoffatum] feoffamentum, J.

their lords, and if the gifts are recent the donees can be ejected without writ and expelled with impunity; but it is otherwise if peaceful seisin has been had.

Gifts may also be made for the life of the recipient, or for the life of the donor, or for a term of years, or until something be done or not be done, or until provision is made for the donee, and it is then a question whether mention is made of the donor and his heirs or of the donor only, and whether provision should be made for the donee alone or for the donee and his heirs.   And in such cases, if the heirs are not included and if provision is not made for the donee in the lifetime of the donor, the property given will remain with the donee in fee; but if provision is made in the lifetime of the donor, it will revert to the donor.   And if the heirs of the donor only are included in the gift and not the heirs of the donee and provision was not made for the donee while he lived, the property given will remain with the heirs of the donee in perpetuity, even though adequate satisfaction may be offered to the donee's heirs.   But if the heirs of the donee only are included in the gift, then the land given will revert as soon as provision has been made for them by the donor; but if, on the other hand, he has not indeed made provision, it is not enough for his heirs to show themselves willing and ready to make satisfactory provision, since the mode of the gift will be to the contrary.   If, however, the gift should be made to someone for his, the donee's, life, he acquires nothing save only the freehold, while the fee remains with the donor, and when [the donee] dies the land reverts immediately to the donor. And if a gift should be made to someone for the life of the donor, although the heirs of the donee should be included in the gift, [the donee] does not, however, acquire a freehold or a fee, but a form of possession for a fixed term, from which, if he should be ejected, he will not recover by an assize of novel disseisin, although [he will] by another remedy, and his heirs will hold until the end of the term.

Bracton,
f. 27

But if no mention is made of the heirs of the donee, the land will not, however, revert immediately to the donor after the death of the donee, unless he dies intestate; but if he should dispose of the residue of the term in his will, the disposition will be valid as in the case of chattels, since it makes for the disherison of no one.   If, however, the gift should be made thus, 'I give to so-and-so such-and-such an amount of land for myself and my heirs', at once it becomes the freehold of the donee only, and when he dies it will revert to me, as if I had said 'I give to such-and-such for his life'.   Out of a term of years, although very long, there is never created a freehold for the donee, but since a term for life is uncertain this therefore does create a freehold, for although nothing is more certain than death, yet nothing is more uncertain than the hour of death.

A man may grant land to someone for a term of years and within the term give the same land to him or another in fee, and, if he enfeoffs another, both possessions will continue, because the term and the feoffment are mutually compatible although different rights are there, for to the feoffee belongs the freehold and fee with property rights, while the fermor can claim no right except the usufruct.   Further, land can be demised at the will of the grantor to be held from term to term and from year to year, and at the end of the term the land in

in annum et finito termino in omni dimissione reuertetur terra donatori vel proprietario nisi inde feodum perquisierit.

CAP. XIII. DE DONACIONIBUS SERUIS FACTIS

Si autem a domino sub cuius potestate seruus fuerit seruo fiat donacio in
5 qua precesserit libertas cum manumissione et interueniat homagium valet   f. 75b
donacio et perfecta erit, et quamuis homagium, libertas manumissio ve in carta
non exprimantur sufficit ad libertatem tantum hec clausula 'habendum et
tenendum sibi et heredibus suis' eo quod donator per huiusmodi verba innuitur
manifeste quod in donacione voluit ipsum esse liberum quamuis hoc verbum
10 'libere' non exprimatur non obstante incerto seruicio ac vilissimo vt mercheto
sanguinis vel aliis talliagiis voluntariis contributis dum tamen huiusmodi
prestaciones fiant racione tenementi et non racione persone in donacione conprehense et reseruate.   Non enim vnum et idem est set longe aliud tenere libere
et tenere per liberum seruicium.   Libere enim tenet cuicumque alius heres quam
15 dominus succedere poterit.   Liberum enim seruicium nichil villano confert libertatis.   Tenementum enim quod conceditur villano tenendum per liberum
seruicium non facit ipsum liberum nec seruicium villanum libere feoffato
aliquid confert seruitutis nec aliquid sue detrahit persone.   Nam si tenens per
liberum seruicium tantum dum non ad vitam nec in feodo eiectus fuerit per as-
20 sisam non recuperabit.   Si autem tenuerit 'sibi et heredibus suis' per consuetudines villanas recuperaret sicut quilibet liber homo etsi a domino suo fuerit
eiectus.   Nam iura dominum contra voluntatem suam iuuare non debent et
quamuis senciat dampnum sibi non tamen iniuriatur et ex quo cum seruo suo
contraxit excepcioni villenagii tacite renunciauit nec ipsum ignorancia excusabit
25 si dicat quod nesciuit de statu suo tempore contractus quia presumitur quod
sciuit aut scire debuit cuius fuit condicionis ille cum quo contraxit.

Si autem seruo et suis heredibus fiat donacio   domino valet donacio
et qua si eiectus fuerit per aliquem dum tamen non per dominum suum sub cuius   [194]
fuerit potestate constitutus et prouisum fuerit ab ipso domino eiectus solus per
30 assisam recuperabit et per consequens conpetit suis heredibus contra quoscumque
deforciantes assisa mortis antecessoris preterquam contra verum dominum contra quem nullam habebunt replicacionem.   Si autem seruus nomine domini sui
stipulatus fuerit et perquisitum fecerit et non sibi ipsi et heredibus suis et de
perquisito per aliquem non dominum eiciatur tunc conpetit domino remedium
35 per assisam noue disseisine et non seruo, quia quodcumque per seruum iuste adquiritur domino adquiritur sicut per seruum procuratorem.   Et si seruus sibi et

4. a, *om.* J.   10. vt] vel, J.   12–13. conprehense et reseruate] conprehenso et
reseruato, J.   16. Nota J. *in margine.*   19. *post* liberum *add.* tenementum, J.   27. *post*
donacio *lacuna est in* J.   28. et qua si eiectus *iterauit* J.   35. quodcumque] quicumque, J.

every demise reverts to the donor or proprietor unless [the termor] has acquired the fee thereof.

CHAPTER 13.   OF GIFTS MADE TO VILLEINS

Bracton,
f. 24
If a gift should be made to a villein by a lord in whose power the villein is and the gift be preceded by freedom with manumission, and if it happens to be accompanied by homage, the gift is valid and will be perfect.   And although homage, Bracton,
f. 24b freedom or manumission are not expressed in a charter, this clause by itself suffices to confer freedom: 'to have and to hold to him and his heirs', because the donor by such words manifestly implies that in making the gift he wished the donee to be free, even though the word 'freely' (*libere*) is not expressly used and notwithstanding that the service may be uncertain and most servile, such as the merchet of his offspring or other tallages contributed at his lord's will, provided such renders, included and reserved in the gift, are made in respect of the tenement and not in respect of the person.   Not, however, that it is one and the same thing, but widely different, to hold freely and to hold by free service.   He, indeed, holds freely, whoever he may be, to whom there can succeed as heir someone other than the lord; but free service does not confer on a villein a particle of freedom.   For a tenement which is granted to a villein to hold by free service does not make him free, nor does villein service impose a particle of servitude upon a free feoffee or detract in any way from his personal status.   For if one who holds by free service only (provided the tenure is not for life or in fee) should be ejected, he will not recover by an assize.   If, however, he should hold 'to him and his heirs' by villein customary services, he would recover like any freeman, even if he were ejected by his lord.   For the rights of a lord should not assist him to undo what he has willed; and although he feels himself a loser, yet no wrong is done to him.   And because he has entered into a contract with his villein, he has tacitly renounced an exception of villeinage, nor will ignorance excuse him if he should say that he did not know about the status of the villein at the time of the contract, for the presumption is that he knew, or ought to have known, the status of him with whom he made a contract.

Bracton,
f. 25
If a gift should be made to a villein and his heirs, his lord [permitting], it is valid.   And if the villein be ejected from it by someone, provided that it was not by his lord in whose power he lies and that it is [permitted] by that lord, the ejected by himself will recover by an assize, and consequently an assize of mort d'ancestor is available to his heirs against any deforciants whomsoever except against the true lord, against whom the heirs will have no replication [to an exception of villeinage].   If, however, the villein has contracted and made an acquisition in the name of his lord and not for himself and his heirs, and he is ejected from the acquisition by anyone who is not his lord, then a remedy is available to the lord by an assize of novel disseisin and not to the villein, because whatsoever is lawfully acquired by a villein is acquired by the lord, as if the

heredibus suis perquisierit dominus statim possessionem apprehendat perquisiti
et seruicia in donacione contenta faciat donatori, non obstante minori etate
heredis, quod cum sic seisierit et cartam feoffamenti penes se receperit restituere
poterit seruo vel alii liberare vel in dominico inpune retinere qui se statim
5 seisinam non apprehendat poterit tamen quandocumque voluerit tam tempore
heredum quam primi donatarii dum tamen fugitiui non fuerint et clamantes in
libertatem. Si autem donatarius obierit de huiusmodi perquisito seisitus in
feodo et eius heredes fuerint inde deforciati tunc competit eis remedium per
assisam mortis antecessoris versus omnes contra quos conpeteret assisa noue
10 disseisine in persona antecessoris. Et si plurium sit seruus communis fiat par-
ticipacio eius perquisiti cum prior seysina secundam excludat. Si autem seruus
vendiderit feodum quod sibi et heredibus suis perquisiuerit antequam dominus
seysinam inde ceperit valet donacio et dominus sibi ipsi inputet quod tantum
expectauit. Si autem seruo fiat donacio priuilegiato manumisso vel fugitiuo
15 dominus nichil sibi inde vendicare poterit priusquam libertatem corpus
clamantis tanquam seruum suum disracionauerit. Quod si fieri posset, quare
deducerentur sequela tenementum et catalla in iudicium si de statu ageretur per
breue de natiuis cum in breue contineatur quod vicecomes habere faciat tali talem
natiuum et fugituum suum cum sequela sua et catallis suis. Et si ante corporis
20 disracionem sine iudicio terram sibi vsurparet et catalla vsurpanti seruum suum
per breue petenti obstabit excepcio spoliacionis ita quod nunquam audietur ante
tenementi et catallorum plenam restitucionem. Et cum corpus recuperauerit ea
que corpus sequentur recuperabit vt sequelam suam et catalla et tenementum sua
eo quod presumitur quod de catallis suis que domini sui fuisse debuerunt fuerunt
25 perquisita. Et sicut non poterit quis seruum suum fugitiuum disseysire quin per
assisam antequam corpus habeat sub sua potestate per iudicium, ita nec poterunt
liberi sub potestate dominorum constituti vt serui quamdiu in tali statu per-
manserint assisam portare versus dominos suos de perquisitis suis et recuperare   f. 76
antequam docuerint se esse liberos.
30   De re autem aliena poterunt fieri donaciones que quidem licet non valeant cum
effectu quantum ad ipsos quorum res ipse fuerint valent tamen quantum ad
donatores et donatarios et alios ius non habentes. Et quamuis valeant quoad
ipsos qui ius habuerint in tempore non valebunt tamen si per veros dominos
statim eiciantur et si per negligenciam vel pacienciam dominorum et quorum ius
35 fuerit tempus pacificum habuerint donatarii per quod liberum tenementum   [195]
habeant res cum date eis remanere non poterunt et per auxilium curie rite
fuerint reuocate. Poterit quidem res esse aliena omnino quantum ad ius et pro-

10. sit] sic, J.   11. cum prior] prior cum, J.   16–17. Quod si fieri posset, quare deducerentur, Br., om. J.   17. si] se, J.   30. fieri addidimus.   34. eiciantur] eiciciantur, J.

villein were his agent.　　And if the villein should acquire to himself and his heirs, the lord can immediately take possession of the acquisition and render to the donor the services contained in the gift, notwithstanding the minority of the heir [of the villein], and when he has thus put himself in seisin and received the charter of feoffment into his possession, he may with impunity restore the acquisition to the villein or hand it over to another or retain it in demesne; and should he not immediately take seisin, he may nevertheless do so whenever he may wish, whether during the time of the heirs or of the first donee, provided they are not fugitives who claim their freedom.　　If, however, the donee should die seised of such an acquisition in fee and his heirs are deforced thereof, then a remedy is available to them by an assize of mort d'ancestor against all those against whom an assize of novel disseisin would have been available in the person of their ancestor.　　And if the villein should belong in common to several lords, let a partition be made of his acquisition, since a prior seisin may exclude a second. If, however, the villein should sell the fee which he has acquired to himself and his heirs before his lord takes seisin thereof, the gift is valid and the lord is himself to blame because he waited so long.　　If, however, the gift is made to a villein who is privileged or is manumitted or a fugitive, the lord can claim nothing for himself therein before he has deraigned as his villein the body of him who claims freedom.　　But if he can do this, why should the villein's brood, tenement and chattels be involved in judicial proceedings if an action to determine his status may be brought by a writ of neifty, since by the terms of the writ the sheriff is to let the demandant have so-and-so his villein and fugitive with his brood and his chattels?　　And if, before the lord has deraigned the body [of the villein], he should usurp to himself, without judgement, the land and chattels, when he who thus usurps claims his villein by writ the exception of disseisin will bar him so that he will never be heard until there has been full restitution of tenement and chattels.　　But when the lord has recovered the body [of the villein], he will recover those things which follow the body, namely his brood and his chattels and tenement, because it is presumed that they were acquired from the villein's chattels which should have been his lord's.　　And just as no one can disseise his fugitive villein, on pain of an assize, before he has his body within his power by judgement of the court, neither can free men who are established like villeins in the power of lords, so long as they remain in such status, bring an assize against their lords and recover their acquisitions before they have shown that they are free men.

Gifts may be made of property belonging to another and, although they are not valid and effective as regards those who own the property, they are, however, valid as between donors and donees and as regards others who have no right [in the property].　　But although the gifts may be valid as regards those who have a temporary right, they will not, however, be valid if the donees are ejected immediately by the true owners; and if by the negligence or sufferance of the owners with a rightful claim the donees should have a period of peaceful seisin whereby they obtain a freehold, the property, although given to them, cannot remain with them and by the aid of the court the gift will be duly revoked.　　Property may,

Bracton, f. 25b

Bracton, f. 26

Bracton, f. 30b

Bracton, f. 31

prietatem feodum et liberum tenementum vsumfructum et vsum nudum in quam
si aliquis se intruserit cum rem vacantem inuenerit et in tali seysina donacionem
inde fecerit valida erit donacio quantum ad donantem et accipientem et omnes
qui ius non habuerint donec per ius habentem fuerit reuocata.   Et eodem modo
5   feoffamento facto per ipsum qui non habeat iure nisi feodum talliatum vel terminum vite vel custodiam vel terminum voluntarium in quibus casibus quoad
verum dominum nunquam erit res data liberum tenementum nisi ex longa et
pacifica seysina et vnde si incontinenti post tale feoffamentum posset verus
dominus vel ille ad quem spectat reuersio se ponere in seysinam omnes a pos-
10 sessione tenere posset exclusos vel per assisam noue disseisine recuperaret.
Verumtamen si tales feoffati post tempus pacificum et seysine post continuacio-
nem liberum tenementum habuerint quod sine iudicio eici non possint si a
vero domino fuerint inplacitati vocare poterunt feoffatores suos ad warantum
et valenciam consequi nisi doceant quod per intrusiones proprias seysinam
15 fuerint adepti et non extra seysinam feoffatorum feoffati.   Si autem proprietarius
donacionem fecerit secundo viro alicuius vxoris cuius ipse warantus fuerit de
terra quam ipsi vir et vxor simul teneant nomine dotis vxoris de dono primi viri
sui non valebit donacio quia donatario vacuam seysinam facere non potest cum
vir et vxor vnum corpus et eadem sint caro et quia seruicium vxoris viro suo
20 non poterit attornari.   Queritur si post mortem vxoris sue eiectus fuerit vir ex
tali donacione seysinam non recuperabit quia secundi viri per legem Anglie liberum tenementum non poterunt vendicare et quamuis secundus vir et vxor dotem
quam tenuerint resignare vellent in manus proprietarii ea mente vt virum
inde feoffaret non valeret donacio eo quod sic fieret fraus constitucionis.
25 Verumtamen si talis donacio facta fuerit viro qui homagium fecerit suo
feoffatori ac ipse post mortem vxoris sue se tenuerit in possessione obstabit
donatori petenti vel eius heredi excepcio donacionis.   Si autem eiciatur vir per
accionem optinebit.   Et eodem modo valebit donacio facta vxori per se vel
viro et vxori simul et heredibus suis communibus vel remotis set hoc magis est ex
30 consuetudinis anglicane permissione quam ex iuris ordine.

CAP. XIV.   DE DISTINCTIONE CARTARUM

Cartarum alia regia et alia priuata et regiarum alia priuata alia communis et
alia vniuersitatis.   Priuatarum alia de puro feoffamento et simplici alia de

1. *prius* et *addidimus*.   10. recuperaret] recuperarent, J.   14. *post* doceant *add.*
consequi, J.   15. feoffatorum] feoffamentorum, J; proprietarius] proprietatis, J.   17. vxoris]
vxor, J.   18. vacuam] veram, J.   23. vt] nec. J.   29. communibus et remotis, J,
separatis vel communibus, Br.

indeed, belong altogether to another as regards right and ownership, fee and freehold, usufruct and bare user; and if anyone should intrude therein when he finds the property vacant and, being seised in such fashion, he should make a gift thereof, the gift will be valid as between the grantor and the recipient and as regards all who have no right in the land, until the gift be revoked by him who has right. And in the same way, if a feoffment is made by one who has legally only a fee tail or a life interest or wardship or a term at will, in these cases as against the true owner the property given will never be a freehold, except in consequence of long and peaceful seisin; and therefore if, after such a feoffment, the true owner or the reversioner is able without delay to put himself in seisin, he may keep all others excluded from possession. Or he may recover by an assize of novel disseisin. Nevertheless, if such feoffees, after a period of peaceful occupation and after continuous seisin, should have a freehold from which they cannot be ejected without a judgement of the court and if they should be impleaded by the true owner, they can vouch their feoffors to warranty and sue for the value unless [the feoffors] can show that it was by their own intrusions that the feoffees have obtained seisin and that they were not enfeoffed [by livery] from the seisin

of the feoffors. If, however, an owner should make a gift to the second husband of some woman, of [whose dower] he is the warrantor, of land which the husband and wife hold together as the wife's dower by the gift of her first husband, the gift will not be valid because he cannot give vacant seisin to the donee, since husband and wife are one body and one flesh and because the service of a wife cannot be attorned to her husband. It is a question whether or not, if a husband

should be ejected from such a gift after the death of his wife, he will recover seisin, because second husbands cannot claim a freehold by the curtesy of England and, although the second husband and the wife might wish to resign the dower which they held into the hands of the owner with the intention that he should enfeoff the husband thereof, the gift would not be valid because in this way the constitution of dower would be fraudulently evaded. If, nevertheless, such a gift should be made to a husband and he should do homage to his feoffor and after his wife's death he should retain possession, an exception of gift will bar the donor or his heir claiming [the land], and if the husband is ejected he will recover by an action at law. And in the same way a gift [of land held in dower] will be valid if made to a wife by herself or to a husband and wife together and their heirs in common or distant heirs, but this is permissible rather by English custom than by a rule of law.

CHAPTER 14. OF DIFFERENCES BETWEEN CHARTERS

Some charters are royal and others private, and some royal charters are private, others are common and others are universal. Some private charters are of

feoffamento condicionali siue conuencionali, et alia de recognicione pura vel
condicionali, alia de quietaclamancia et alia de confirmacione. Carta vero de
feoffamento simplici est in qua nulla continetur adieccio condicionalis. De
recognicione autem vt si tenens rem quam ab eo petitur recognouerit ius esse
5 petentis vel si petens rem quam tenens tenet recognouerit esse ius tenentis vel si
illam remiserit et quietamclamauerit. Carta autem de quietaclamancia est vt
si petens pure remiserit et quietamclamauerit terram tenenti quam idem petens   [196]
peciit vt ius suum. Carta autem de confirmacione est illa que alterius factum
consolidat et confirmat et nichil noui attribuit quandoque tamen confirmat et
10 addit. Carte autem de pura donacione et simplici penes donatarium et eius
heredes debent remanere.

    Communes vero dupplicari debent ita quod quilibet habeat suam partem vel
si vna sit tantum tunc in equa manu communis amici vtriusque ponatur saluo
custodienda cuilibet parcium cum necesse fuerit exhibenda transcriptis tamen
15 partibus inde liberatis. Quam quidem cartam eorum alteri prout conuenit bona
fide liberatam maliciose retentam conpetit alteri cuius interest petere quam si
habere negauerit tunc aut cartam producat aut ei denegetur accio si petens fuerit
vel si ab eo petatur remaneat indefensus. Communis enim esse poterit vt si terra
detur ad terminum annorum et ad firmam, et eciam si quis alicui donacionem
20 fecerit de aliqua re retenta inde sibi aliqua parte et si tenens se dicat totum tenere
cum donator partem petat ostendere debet tenens cartam ad suam excepcionem
probandam quod si non fecerit amittet sicut indefensus quia excepcionem suam
non probat. Qui si per certa indicia docuerit et curiam instruxerit quod ad   f. 76b
cartam venire non poterit, tunc de necessitate ad patriam erit recurrendum et
25 eodem modo si casum allegauerit et eum probauerit.

    Priuatarum autem tres sunt species vna cum pro possessore loquatur alia
cum contra ipsum et tercia cirographata que tam fit pro ipso quam contra ipsum
et quo casu si quis parcium a conuencione recesserit in scripturis cirographatis
succurritur alteri parti per accionem ex conuencione. Omnium autem scriptu-
30 rarum priuatarum quibus quis vti voluerit in iudicio pro se facere copiam
tenetur aduersario suo licet contra se. Petens tamen petere non debet quod
tenentis instrumenta exhibeantur ad suam intencionem probandam vel fundan-
dam cum non teneatur aduersarium suum contra se armare nec eciam poterit
tenens petere quod ei exhibeantur instrumenta petentis prout de communibus
35 dictum est.

    De cartis vero regiis et factis regum non debent nec possunt iusticiarii regis
nec priuate persone disputare nec eciam, si in illis oriatur dubitacio, possunt eam
interpretari. In dubiis et obscuris vt si aliqua diccio vel racio duos contineat
intellectus solius regis expectanda est interpretacio et voluntas cum eius sit inter-

15. partibus] paribus, J.   20. retenta, Br., tenenda, J.   21. cartam, Br., terram, J.
27. quam] cum, J.   37. eam] eciam, J.

absolute and simple feoffment, others of conditional feoffment or feoffment subject to covenant, and others of absolute or conditional acknowledgement, others
of quitclaim and others of confirmation. A charter of simple feoffment is one
in which no conditional clause is included. A charter of acknowledgement is
one where a tenant acknowledges that property claimed from him is the right of
the demandant, or where the demandant acknowledges that the property which
the tenant holds is the right of the tenant or where he remits and quitclaims it.
A charter of quitclaim is one where the demandant absolutely remits and
quitclaims to the tenant the land which the demandant claimed as his right. A
charter of confirmation is one which ratifies and confirms the deed of another and
introduces nothing new, although sometimes it confirms and adds. A charter of
absolute and simple gift ought to remain with the donee and his heirs.

Common charters ought to be duplicated so that each party may have his
counterpart or, if there is but a single exemplar, then it should be placed in the
safe and disinterested custody of a common friend of both, to be shown when
necessary to any one of the parties, transcripts thereof being delivered to the
parties. When a charter, delivered by agreement to one of the parties in good
faith, is wrongfully retained, it is open to the other interested party to demand it;
and if one party should deny having it, then the other party will either produce
the charter or be denied his action if he should be the demandant or, if he is the
defendant, he will be without defence. A charter can, moreover, be common as,
for example, if land is given for a term of years and at farm, and also if a man
makes a gift to someone of some property but retains some part of it for himself
and, if the tenant says he holds the whole when the donor demands a part of it,
the tenant must show the charter to prove his exception and, if he does not do so,
he will lose the action as one without defence because he does not prove his exception. And if he can show and inform the court by precise information that
he cannot get access to the charter, then recourse must needs be had to a jury, and
similarly if he should allege accidental loss and prove it.

Of private charters there are three kinds, one where the charter speaks for the
possessor, the second where it speaks against him, and the third in the form of
a chirograph, which is made both for him and against him; and in this case, if
one of the parties should recede from the agreement written in the chirograph,
there is a remedy for the other party by an action based on the agreement. Of
all private writings which any one wishes to use on his own behalf in litigation, he
is bound to make a copy for his adversary, although it tells against himself. A
demandant should not, however, require the tenant's deeds to be shown in order
to prove or found his case upon them, since the tenant is not bound to arm his
adversary against himself, nor can the tenant require the demandant's deeds to
be shown to him, as we have said [must be done] in the case of common charters.

Neither the king's justices nor private persons should or can question royal
charters and the acts of kings, not even if a doubtful point should arise therein
can they interpret it. Where there are doubts and obscurities, for example, if
any phrase or definition admits of two meanings, the interpretation and pleasure
of the king alone must be awaited, since it is for him who composed to do the in-

Bracton,
f. 34

pretari cuius est condere.   Et eciam si omnino sit falsa vel suspecta propter
rasuram vel sigillum apponatur adulterium, per cautelam.

Fiant autem donaciones per hec verba:

Sciant presentes et futuri quod ego talis dedi et concessi et hac presenti
5 carta mea confirmaui tali pro homagio suo et seruicio tantam terram cum pertinenciis in N.

Et vnde per hoc quod dicit 'ego talis' vult donator quod certa persona que
dat in donacione conprehendatur.   Et vnde per hoc quod dicit 'dedi' vult quod
res data fiat accipientis.   Et per hoc quod dicit 'concessi' perpendi poterit ex hoc
10 quod donacioni consensum prebuit, nec multum differt a concessu.   Et per hoc
quod dicit 'et presenti carta mea confirmaui' innuit quod vult quod voluntas sua
per quam res transferatur ad donatarium et que firma esse debet presenti carta   [197]
sub sigilli sui munimine confirmetur.   Confirmare enim est id quod prius infir-
mum fuit simul firmare.   Et per hoc quod dicit 'tali' vult quod certa persona ex-
15 primatur cui fit donacio.   Et per hoc quod dicit 'pro homagio et seruicio suo'
vel 'pro seruicio' tantum vult quod certa causa pro qua fit donacio exprimatur.
Et per hoc quod dicit 'tantum terram cum pertinenciis' vult quod certa res
deducta sit in donacionem et certe pertinencie que tunc pertinuerint cum res
venit in donacionem.   Et per hoc quod dicit 'in tali villa' vult quod certus locus
20 conprehendatur in quo res est sita que datur.

Continentur eciam hec verba:

Habendam et tenendam tali et heredibus suis generaliter vel certis heredibus
cum coartacione libere et quiete vel in liberum maritagium vel cum condicione
adiecta vel donec et eciam tali et heredibus suis et assignatis et tali et heredibus
25 suis et assignatis assignatorum suorum.

Per hoc enim verbum 'libere' vult donator quod rem datam ad modum
liberi hominis teneat vt sui heredes in hereditate paterna succedant, quod non
est in seruo, nec vult quod rei date talis seruitus inponatur vt aliquis vtatur
in re data aliquo iure ad quam seruitus non pertineat neque vsus.   Et per hoc
30 quod dicit 'quiete' vult quod quietem habeat et pacem quod re data vti posset
pacifice et comode absque aliquo inpedimento.

Augentur enim quandoque donaciones per hec verba 'cui dare vel assignare
voluerit' adiecta clausa warantie et quo casu cum donatarius illam dederit vel
assignauerit heredes donatoris tenentur donum pocius warantizare quam
35 reuocare.   Et qualitercumque et vbicumque donacionem fecerit quis constitutum est quod nichil domino feodi depereat per translacionem set quod donatarius
rem donatam de domino capitali capiat inmediate cui donator nichilominus tene-

---

10. consensu, J, concessu, Br.   28. vt] quod, J.   29. re data, Br., etatem, J.
36. depereat] dependeat, J.

terpreting.   And it is prudent also [to follow this course] if a charter is altogether false or is suspect on the ground of erasure or because a forged seal has been affixed to it.

Bracton
f. 34b

Gifts are made by these words:

'Know all men present and to come that I, so-and-so, have given and granted and by this my present charter have confirmed to so-and-so for his homage and service such-and-such an amount of land with appurtenances in N.'

And in that he says thus, 'I, so-and-so', the donor intends that the particular person who is the giver shall be included in the gift.   And in that he says thus, 'I have given', he intends that the property given shall become the recipient's. And in that he says thus, 'I have granted', it may be inferred from this that he has given his consent to the gift, nor does consent (*consensum*) greatly differ from concede (*concessum*).   And in that he says thus, 'I have by this, my present charter, confirmed', he implies that he wishes that his intention of transferring the property to the donee, which must be firm, shall be confirmed by his present charter authenticated by his seal.   For to confirm is to strengthen at once what

Bracton,
f. 35

was previously weak.   And in that he says thus, 'to so-and-so', he intends a definite person shall be named to whom the gift is made.   And in that he says 'for his homage and service' or 'for his service' only, he intends that the particular cause for which the gift is made shall be specified.   And in that he says thus, 'such-and-such an amount of land with appurtances', he intends that a definite property shall be comprised in the gift as well as definite appurtenances which pertained to it at the time when the property became the subject of the gift.   And in that he says thus, 'in such-and-such a township', he intends a definite place to be understood in which the property that is given is situated.

These words are also included:

'To have and to hold to so-and-so and his heirs' in general, or to certain heirs with a limitation, 'freely and quietly' or 'in free marriage' or with a condition attached or 'until' and also 'to so-and-so and his heirs and assigns' or 'to so-and-so and his heirs and the assigns of his assigns'.

By this word 'freely', the donor intends that the donee shall hold the property given in the manner of a free man so that his heirs shall succeed to the paternal inheritance, which is not the case with a villein, and that he does not intend that such-and-such a servitude shall be imposed upon the property given so that any-one may exercise any right in the property given, to which neither servitude nor user pertains.   And in that he says 'quietly', he intends that the donee shall have peace and quiet so that he may use the property given peacefully and with ease without any hindrance.

Bracton,
f. 37b

Sometimes, moreover, gifts are broadened by these words, 'to whom he may wish to give or assign', with a clause of warranty attached, in which case, if the donee should give or assign the property, the heirs of the donor are bound to

St. Quia
Emptores

warrant the grant rather than revoke it.   And in whatsoever way or wheresoever a man shall make a gift, it is enacted that by the transfer nothing shall be lost to the lord of the fee but the donee shall hold the property granted from the chief lord di-

Bracton,
f. 37b

rectly, but nevertheless the donor will be bound to warrant it to the donee.   So

bitur eam warantizare.   Ampliare autem poterunt de cetero donatores minuere
autem minime.   Si autem huiusmodi assignati quibus huiusmodi donaciones
facte fuerint vlterius alios inde feoffauerint idem assignati et eorum heredes res
datas warantizare tenebuntur quibus deficientibus primi donatores et heredes
5 sui loco assignatorum et heredum suorum esse incipient quo ad warantiam, quod
quidem non esset nisi fieret mencio in prima carta de assignatis, et sic valebit pro-
lacio et ostensio aliene carte in manum extranei.   Et nota quod hoc verbum
'legare' superuacuum est preterquam in tenementis burgensium que legari
possunt vt de catallis.   Legatum enim morte tantum confirmatur donacio inter   f. 77
10 viuos sola tradicione.

    Continetur eciam 'reddendo inde annuatim tantum ad tales terminos' vel
'faciendo inde talia seruicia' vel 'tales consuetudines' que omnia esse debent
certa et in carta expressa eo quod satis acquietat qui specialiter non onerat.   Et
dicitur 'faciendo inde domino feodi' quod sibi fuerit faciendum, per quod innuit
15 quod vult quod donacionem per assensum domini feodi ingrediatur et non ipso
inuito et quod domino suo nichil depereat per translacionem.   Item dicitur 'pro
omni seruicio, consuetudine, seculari demanda et exaccione', et per istam
generalitatem videtur quod omnia alia seruicia expresse remittit.   Retineri
autem poterunt seruicia multipliciter nam retinere sibi poterit feoffator seruicium   [198]
20 cotidianum ebdomodale annuum et septennium 'reddendo semper in fine septem
annorum die sancti Michaelis vnum granum frumenti' et huiusmodi.   Retineri
eciam solent huiusmodi seruicia 'per seruicium equitandi mecum vel vxore mea'
qui rodknyghtes vocabantur vel 'per seruicium tenendi curias meas' vel 'pascendi
leporarios meos' vel alios canes vel 'mutandi aues' vel 'inueniendi arcus et sagit-
25 tas' vel 'portandi mecum', de quibus omnibus non certus numerus conpre-
henditur et que omnia dici poterunt seruicia intrinseca quia in cartis et aliis
instrumentis sunt exprimenda et ad que terre huiusmodi ex antiquo sunt obli-
gate quamuis heredes feoffatorum et huiusmodi veteribus cartis non contineantur
dum tamen a tempore regis Ricardi inde extiterint seisiti.   Innocencia enim
30 donatorum diuturnitatem seysine non aufert.   Et cum huiusmodi minuta
seruicia ad patrie tuicionem et pacis non fiunt, ideo ex talibus feoffamentis
nullam custodiam vel maritagia nec homagium poterit donator iuste vendicare.
Si autem quis feoffatus fuerit et vnum hominem equitem vel peditem vel plures
regi inueniat ad eundum pro eo in excercitum ad patrie defensionem et hostium
35 depressionem cum aliquo genere armorum, ex talibus seriantiis, que dicuntur
magne, conpetit donatori custodia et maritagium cum homagio et releuio in
suo casu hoc non obstante quod tenens aliam terram de rege ipso tenuerit in
capite.   Sunt eciam quedam seruicia intrinseca que fiunt sub disiunccione et sufficit alteram partem disiunctim facere.

40   Et sunt quedam seruicia forinseca que dici poterunt regalia que ad scutum
prestantur et inde scutagium habemus et racione scuti pro feodo militari reputa-

---

14. dicitur *addidimus*.   16. Item dicitur, Br., *om.* J; *posterius* et *om.* J.   20. ebdo-
modale] ebdomodalem, J.   25. vel portandi, Br., vel portandi mecum, J.   30. cum,
Br., quod, J.   39. disiunctim] disiuncti, J.   40. forinseca] forinceca, J.

donors will be able henceforth to enlarge but not to diminish [their gifts].   If, moreover, such assigns to whom such gifts are made should further enfeoff others therewith, those assigns and their heirs will be bound to warrant the property given, and if they fail, the first donors and their heirs will begin to take the place of the assigns and their heirs as regards warranty (though this would not be so unless there was mention of assigns in the first charter), and thus the production and exhibiting of the charter of another in the hand of a third party will be valid.

Bracton, f. 49

Be it noted that the word 'bequeath' is meaningless, except in regard to the tenements of burgesses which may be bequeathed like chattels, and a bequest is confirmed only by death, while a gift *inter vivos* is confirmed only by livery.

Bracton, f. 35

A charter also includes the words 'rendering therefor annually so much at such-and-such terms' or 'doing therefor such-and-such services' or 'such-and-such customs', all of which ought to be definite and specified in the charter, because he who does not specifically burden as good as acquits.   And it is said

Bracton, f. 35b

'doing therefore to the lord of the fee' what should be done him, by which the donor implies that he intends the donee to enter upon the gift with the assent of the lord of the fee and not against his will and that nothing shall be lost to his

Bracton, f. 35

lord by the transfer.   Again, it is said 'for every service, custom, secular demand and exaction', and by this generality it seems that the donor expressly remits all other services.   A multiplicity of services may, however, be retained; for the feoffor may retain for himself daily, weekly, annual and septennial service, 'always rendering at Michaelmas at the end of seven years one grain of wheat' and

Bracton, f. 35b

the like.   Such services as these it is also usual to retain: 'by the service of riding with me or my wife' (performed by those who are called rodknights) or 'by the service of holding my courts' or 'of feeding my greyhounds' or other dogs, or 'of mewing falcons' or 'of providing bows and arrows' or 'of carrying with me'. No precise number will embrace all these services, and all may be called intrinsec services because they ought to be expressed in charters and other instruments and, although the heirs of feoffors and the like are not mentioned in old charters, such lands from old time are burdened with the services, provided that the donees have been seised thereof from the time of King Richard, for the ingenuousness of the donors does not remove the antiquity of the seisin.   And because these petty services are not done to defend the realm and to keep the peace, therefore from such feoffments the donor cannot lawfully claim any wardship or marriage or homage.   If, however, a man should be enfeoffed and should provide a mounted-man or a foot-soldier or several of them for the king's service to go on his behalf in the army in defence of the realm and to overcome the enemy with arms of some kind, then by reason of such serjeanties, which are called 'grand', the donor is, in this particular case, entitled to wardship and marriage with homage and relief, notwithstanding that the tenant holds other land from the king in chief.   There are also certain intrinsec services which are performed in the alternative, and it suffices if either part is done separately.

Bracton, f. 36

And there are certain forinsec services which can be called royal services and which are rendered to the shield (*scutum*), and thence we have 'scutage' (*scutagium*); and by reason of the shield scutage is appropriate to a knight's fee.   All

tur. Omnis enim terra ad huiusmodi seruicium obligata feodum dici debet
militare pro quo quidem seruicio tenentur donatarii ad homagium suis donatoribus faciendum et ipsi donatores huiusmodi homagia capere tenentur quod si
refutauerint superiori domino inpune ea facere poterunt et per consequens sua
5 seruicia et medii nichilominus ad warantiam tenebuntur cum in casu fuerint
vocati. Exprimuntur enim quandoque sic 'faciendo inde michi et heredibus
meis ad scutagium cum euenerit quantum pertinet ad feodum vnius militis vel
duorum in eadem villa vel de eodem feodo militis prestantur, et ad plus plus et ad
minus minus. Per huiusmodi autem feoffamenta de sokagio fieri poterit feodum
10 militare non tamen e conuerso quamuis fieri solet. Inhibetur eciam ne donatores
de cetero a mediis seruicia sua recipiant set a tenentibus.

Sunt eciam quedam consuetudines que seruicia non dicuntur nec concomi-
tancia seruiciorum sicut racionabilia auxilia ad filium primogenitum militem
faciendum vel ad filiam primogenitam maritandam que quidem auxilia fiunt de
15 gracia et non de iure pro necessitate et indigencia domini capitalis, et non sunt
predialia set personalia secundum quod perpendi poterit in breui ad hoc
prouiso. Et ne huiusmodi auxilia cicius vel grauius quam iustum sit leuentur
prouisum est quod de feodo vnius militis integro viginti solidi tantum tribuantur
et leuentur de xx. libratis terre quam quis tenuerit in sokagio xx. solidi, et de   [*199*]
20 maiori plus et de minori minus secundum terre quantitatem, nec pro filio leuetur
priusquam quindecim fuerit annorum nec pro filia ante etatem septem annorum.
Et si pater qui pecuniam receperit obierit filia innupta executores patris respondeant filie de pecunia percepta et si bona patris non sufficiant respondeat heres
patris.
25 Sunt eciam alie prestaciones vt auxilia vicecomitis et fines communes pro
amerciamentis communibus, hydagia, cornagia, caruagia, secte hundredi et
comitatus, et alia plura de necessitate et consensu communi introducta de quibus
nullus tenetur tenentem suum acquietare eo quod personalia sunt nisi per cartas   f. 77*b*
suas ad hoc specialiter fuerint obligati.
30 Ex donacionibus autem seruicia militaria vel magne seriantie non con-
tinentibus oritur nobis quoddam nomen generale quod est sokagium.

Item continetur 'et ego et heredes mei warantizabimus tali et heredibus suis',
vel 'heredibus et assignatis' vel 'heredibus et assignatis et heredibus assignatorum'
vel 'assignatis assignatorum et eorum heredibus', et acquietabimus et defendemus
35 totam terram illam cum pertinenciis' et innuit quod obligat se et heredes suos,
propinquos remotos presentes et futuros, ad warantiam et ei succedentes in
infinitum tam principalis quam eius pertinenciarum. Sub hoc autem verbo 'pertinenciis' conprehenduntur tam corporalia vt si pertineant hameletti vel
communa pasture quam incorporalia vt libertates et iura aduocaciones ecclesi-
40 arum in proprio et seruitus in alieno. Et per largissimam warantizacionem

8. de *addidimus*; *posterius* plus *addidimus*.   9. *posterius* minus *addidimus*.   17. pro-
uiso] prouisum, J; ne] vt, J.   22. innupta *scripsimus*; inconsulta, J.   25. *post* auxilia
add. in comitatum, J., *quae duo verba punctis delevit.*   26. caruagia] cariagia, J.   26. *post*
secte *add.* et, J.   38. corporalia] corporea, J.   39. incorporalia] corporea, J.

land, indeed, which is subject to such service should be called a knight's fee, and for this service the donees are bound to do homage to their donors and these donors are bound to accept such homage. And if they should refuse it, the donees may with impunity render their homage, and consequently their services, to the superior lord, and nevertheless the mesne lords will be bound to warranty, should they happen to be vouched. Sometimes, indeed, charters are expressed thus: 'doing therefor to me and my heirs in regard to scutage, when it arises, as much as pertains to one knight's fee (or two) in the said vill' or 'is rendered [in money] from the said knight's fee', and more for more and less for less. More-over, by such feoffments a knight's fee can be created from socage but not con-

St. Quia
Emptores

versely, although it is wont to be done. It is also forbidden to donors to receive henceforth their services from mesne lords but [direct] from the tenants.

Bracton,
f. 36b

There are also some customary payments which are not called services nor the concomitants of services, such as reasonable aids to make the eldest son a knight or to marry the eldest daughter, and these aids are made of grace and not of right on account of the need and poverty of the chief lord, and they are not predial but personal, as may be inferred from the writ appointed for this purpose.

St. West-
minster,
I. c. 36

And lest such aids should be levied more frequently or more heavily than is law-ful, it has been enacted that from a complete knight's fee twenty shillings only shall be assessed and levied, from twenty pounds' worth of land which a man holds in socage twenty shillings, and more from more and less from less according to the amount of the land, nor is an aid to be levied for a son before he shall be fifteen years old nor for a daughter before the age of seven years. And if a father who has received money should die with his daughter unmarried, the father's executors will answer to the daughter for the money received, and if the father's goods should not suffice the father's heir shall answer.

Bracton,
f. 36b
Bracton,
f. 37

There are also other payments, such as sheriff's aids and common fines for common amercements, hidages, cornages, carucages, suits to the hundred and county courts, and many others introduced of necessity and by common consent, for which no one is bound to acquit his tenant because they are personal payments, unless by his charters he is specifically bound to do it.

To gifts which do not include military services or grand serjeanties, we find applicable one general name, which is socage.

A charter also includes the words, 'and I and my heirs will warrant to so-and-so and his heirs (or 'to the heirs and assigns' or 'to the heirs and assigns and heirs of the assigns' or 'to the assigns of the assigns and their heirs') and will

Bracton,
f. 37b

acquit and defend all the said land with its appurtenances'. And the donor implies that he binds himself and his heirs, near and remote, present and future, succeeding him *ad infinitum*, to warranty not only of the principal tenement but also of its appurtenances. Under this term 'appurtenances' there are included both those that are corporeal, for example, if there are appurtenant hamlets or common of pasture, and those that are incorporeal, such as franchises and rights, the advowsons of churches on one's own land and servitudes in the land of others. And by the broadest form of warranty the donor and his heirs are bound to warrant directly all included in the warranty, if the property given

tenentur donator et eius heredes omnibus in warantia conprehensis inmediate
warantizare si res data ad tot manus deuenerit alioquin oportet quod quilibet de
gradu in gradum ascendendo vocet ad warantum suum feoffatorem et suscipiat
in se obligacionem ad defendendum suum tenentem in possessione rei date et
5 assignatos suos et eorum heredes et alios si forte tenementum datum ab aliquo
petatur in dominico et ad acquietandum tenentem si quis plus pecierit seruicii
vel obligacionis quam in carta contineatur et eciam ad defendendum ipsum si
quis rei date seruitutem velit inponere contra formam feoffamenti. Per hoc
enim quod dicit 'contra omnes gentes' excludit se ipsum et heredes suos cum
10 petere non poterunt in dominico quod erga alios tenentur warantizare. Nec
eciam petere poterit quis quod defendere obligatur: non autem locum haberet
breue de warantia carte si feoffator petere posset versus suum feoffatum.

Et quoniam huiusmodi scripture non est fides adhibenda nisi signum interueniat quod talis donacio et scriptura a consciencia et voluntate donatoris prouen-
15 erit, ideo in testimonium et rei geste probacionem apponat donator signum,
adiciendo clausulam istam vel consimilem, 'In cuius rei testimonium huic
scripto sigillum meum apposui'. Ad quod quidem debent testes conuocari sub
quorum presencia omnia cum solempnitate procedant vt veritatem dicere possint
cum inde fuerint requisiti, quorum nomina in eadem carta debent inbreuiari, nec
20 noceret si omnes sigilla sua apponerent in testimonium premissorum vel si carta   [200]
in rotulo cancellarie regis vel alterius loci recordum portantis transcriberetur vel
saltem in aliquo libro parochie loci vel in curia domini feodi vel in comitatu vel
hundredo fuerit recitata et concessa. Et si testes nominati in confeccione carte
presentes non fuerint sufficit tamen si postmodum coram absentibus recitetur et
25 concedatur nec multum refert vtrum donator sigillum proprium habuerit vel
alienum acomodatum, cum semel a donatore coram testibus ad hoc vocatis
recognita fuerit et concessa. Et caueat sibi donatarius ne donacio pereat pro
defectu probacionis: contingit enim frequenter quod donatores huiusmodi
donaciones nituntur irritare.

30   CAP. XV. DE TRADICIONIBUS ET VSUCAPIONIBUS

Quia vero non sufficit alicui iuris concessio nisi donatarius donacionis possessionem consequatur ideo de possessione videndum est. Possessio autem cor-
poralis rei detencio corpore simul et animo cum iuris adminiculo concurrente.
Incorporalia vero possideri non poterunt nec vsucapi nec sine corpore tradi quia
35 per se tradicionem non paciuntur. Quasi possideri tamen poterunt per paci-

1. tenentur] tenetur,   3. suscipiat] suscipit, J.   9. cum] quod, J.   10. dominico]
dominica, J.   22. parochie] parrochie, J.   23. fuerit recitata et concessa, Br., *om.* J;
confeccione carte, B., confessione, J.   24. postmodum Br., *om.* J.   35. *post* tamen
add. non J.

should pass into however many hands.   Otherwise it behoves everyone to vouch to warranty his own feoffor, ascending rung by rung, and himself to undertake an obligation to defend his own tenant in possession of the property given and his assigns and their heirs and others, should it happen that the tenement given is claimed by someone in demesne, and to acquit his tenant, should anyone demand greater service or obligation than is contained in the charter, and also to defend him, should anyone wish to impose a servitude upon the property given against the terms of the feoffment.   And in that the donor says thus, 'against all people', he excludes himself and his heirs since they cannot claim in demesne what they are bound to warrant against others.   For no one is able to claim what he is bound to defend, nor would the writ of warranty of charter be of any use if the feoffor could claim against his feoffee.

Bracton,
f. 38

And because no trust can be put in such a writing unless a sign is present to indicate that the gift and the writing proceeded from the knowledge and intention of the donor, therefore in testimony and proof of his act the donor will affix a sign by adding this clause or something similar: 'In witness whereof I have affixed my seal to this writing'.   And to this witnesses ought to be summoned, in whose presence all things should proceed with due solemnity so that they may declare the truth, should they be required so to do, and their names should be noted in the said charter.   Nor will it do any harm if all of them should append their seals in witness of the aforegoing matters, or if the charter should be transcribed in a roll of the king's chancery or other place which can bear record, or at least in some book of the parish of the place [concerned], or read and approved in the court of the lord of the fee or in the county court or hundred court.   And if the witnesses named were not present at the making of the charter, nevertheless it suffices if it is afterwards read and approved before those who were absent.   Nor does it greatly matter whether the donor has his own seal or a seal borrowed from someone else when once [a gift] is acknowledged and approved by the donor before witnesses summoned for the purpose.   And let the donee beware lest the gift fail for lack of proof, for it frequently happens that donors strive to invalidate such gifts.

CHAPTER 15.   OF LIVERY AND USUCAPION

Bracton,
f. 38b

Because the grant of a right does not suffice for anyone unless the donee obtains with it possession of the gift, therefore possession must be discussed.   Possession, then, is the retention of corporeal property, at once physically and mentally, with the accompanying support of right.   Incorporeal things cannot be possessed or acquired by prescription nor can they be transferred apart from something corporeal, because they do not admit of livery by themselves.   They can, however, be quasi-possessed by sufferance and by user.   There are two ways

enciam et per vsum. Possessionum alia ciuilis que animo tantum retinetur et
alia naturalis que solo corpore que aliquando est iusta aliquando vero minime.
Et est tercius modus possidendi animo simul et corpore et aliter rite non poterit
fieri perquisitum et quod tamen rite adquiratur extunc nisi vtroque poterit
5 amitti. Retineri tamen poterit corpore tantum vt post mortem alicuius donec
corpus ad sepulturam efferatur.

Item possessionum alia vera, alia ymaginaria, alia nuda, alia vestita, alia
adquisita, alia adquiranda, alia bona, alia in pendenti, alia propria, alia aliena,
et alienarum quedam propinqua, quedam remota, alia vetus, alia recens et noua,
10 alia nichil iuris habens set aliquid possessionis, alia que aliquid habet possessionis
et parum iuris, alia que plurimum habet possessionis et aliquid iuris vbi vertitur
causa proprietatis, alia que multum habet possessionis et multum iuris, alia breuis,
alia tenera, alia longo tempore firmata, alia pacifica, alia contenciosa, alia continua et longa, alia interrupta et breuis, alia iusta ciuiliter et naturaliter quo ad
15 quasdam personas et quantum ad alias vtroque modo iniusta, alia precaria et alia
pro precio concessa vt si quis sine scripto concesserit alicui habitacionem vel
vsumfructum in re sua tenendi ad voluntatem suam hec quidem possessio precaria est et nuda eo quod tempestiue et intempestiue pro voluntate domini
poterit reuocari velut de seruis in villenagio qui si per dominum eici non poterunt
20 per assisam noue disseisine eicientur. Si autem certum precium in possessione
pro precio concessa constituatur tunc refert vtrum tenendi pro voluntate dimis-   f. 78
soris vel in perpetuum quod si in perpetuum tunc eici non poterit tenens pro
voluntate concedentis et si ad tempus voluntarium de die in diem poterit vtique
per semetipsum vel per assisam.

25 Tradicio vero est de re corporali aliena vel propria de persona et manu
propria vel aliena sicut procuratoris in manum alterius gratuita translacio.   [201]
Item nichil aliud est tradicio in vno sensu nisi in possessionem inductio.
Tradicionem enim facere potest omnis qui donacionem facere potest siue sit
dominus siue non dominus, que cum a vero domino fiat statim incipit donatarius
30 habere liberum tenementum propter coniunctionem iuris et seysine et mutuum
vtriusque consensum et non refert vtrum ipse dominus personaliter tradat an alius
per ipsum per litteras suas patentes ad hoc procurator constitutus cuius potestas
publice debet legi et ostendi et dupplicari et vna penes procuratorem et alia cum
donatario remaneat pro waranto.

35 Refert enim de tradicione et vsu vtrum de terra fieri debet fundo, manerio vel
domo quia si de domo tunc ea a domino et familia et catallis suis vacuata sufficit
si per haspam vel anulum hostii exterioris a vero domino donatario fiat seysina
coram testibus fidedignis. Si autem nullum sit edificium tunc per fustum vel
baculum quia sufficit pro tradicione corporali sola domini voluntas ad alium

4. tamen] cum, J.   5. amitti] admitti, J.   21. tenendi, J.   38. *post* testibus *add.*
tam, J; fustum, Br., assisam, J.

of possessing: one civil where the retention is mental only; and the other natural where the retention is physical only, and this is sometimes rightful and sometimes quite wrongful.　And there is a third way of possessing: mentally and physically combined; and acquisition cannot otherwise be made rightfully; and so what is rightfully acquired cannot thenceforth be lost except both mentally and physically, although it can be retained physically only, as, for example, by a man after death until the body is borne away for burial.

Bracton, f. 39
Bracton, f. 41b

Possession may be of several kinds: real and imaginary; bare and clothed; acquired and to be acquired; good and in suspense; of one's own and of another's; and of others' things some are near and some remote: possession is sometimes ancient and sometimes recent and new; sometimes with no particle of right but something of possession; sometimes with something of possession and little right; sometimes with a great deal of possession and something of right, where the action becomes proprietary; sometimes with much possession and much right; short or tenuous; strengthened by length of time; peaceful or disputed; continuous and long; interrupted and brief; rightful civilly and naturally as regards some persons and wrongful in both respects as regards others; sometimes precarious and sometimes granted for a price.　For example, if a man should grant to another, without a written deed, a house to live in or a usufruct in his property to be held at his will, this kind of possession is precarious and bare because it can be revoked, in season or out of season, at the will of the lord, as in the case of villeins in villeinage who, if they cannot be ejected by their lord, may be ejected by an assize of novel disseisin.　If, however, where possession is granted for a price, a precise price is agreed, then it is a question whether the tenure is at the will of the grantor or in perpetuity, for if in perpetuity then the tenant cannot be ejected at the will of the grantor, but if temporarily from day to day at will, the tenant can certainly be ejected either by the grantor himself or by an assize.

Bracton f. 39

Bracton, f. 39b

Livery is the free transfer of corporeal property, belonging to another or to oneself, from one's own person and hand or that of another (for example that of an agent) into the hand of someone else.　In one sense livery is nothing else than putting into possession.　Everyone indeed may make livery who is able to make a gift, whether he is owner or non-owner, and when livery is made by the true owner, the donee straightway begins to have a freehold because of the conjunction of right and seisin and the mutual consent of both parties.　And it does not matter whether the owner himself personally delivers or another appointed by him by his letters patent to be his agent for the purpose; but the agent's authority ought to be publicly read and exhibited and duplicated, one copy being retained by the agent, and the other remaining with the donee as his warrant.

Bracton, f. 40

It is, however, a matter of importance in livery and user whether it is to be made of land, an estate, a manor or a house; because if it is of a house, then it suffices, when it has been vacated by the owner with his family and chattels, if seisin is given by the true owner to the donee by the hasp or ring of the outer door before trustworthy witnesses.　If, however, there is no building, then [seisin is given] by staff or rod, because all that is required for corporeal livery is the owner's

translata mutata possessione cum solempnitate vt probacio non deficiat et
donatario sola pedis posicio cum possidendi affectu voluntate donatoris concurrente quamuis statim explecia non ceperit.   Vsus enim et explecia non multum
operantur ad donacionem valent tamen multociens ad possessionis declaracion-
5 em.   Nec perfecte erunt donaciones antequam de vsufructu capiatur seysina.
Nec eciam multum operantur ad seysinam cissio vel fractura arborum vel
ramorum vel segetum nondum maturarum cum pocius cedant in dampnum quam
commoditatem.   Nec eciam est necesse in seysina facienda omnes glebas
circuire nec vbique nec vndique pedem apponere set sufficit pro tradicione quo
10 ad seysinam ad liberum tenementum longa seysina et pacifica et longus vsus
quamuis de re alieni iuris vt si quis ingressum habuerit in rem vacuam et a nullo
possessam sicut in hereditatem nondum aditam.   Longa enim possessio ius parit.
Nec valebit propria intrusio in re concessa nisi a donatore fiat tradicio eo quod
voluntas donatoris inter concessionem et tradicionem mutari poterit et animo
15 retinere quod corpore concesserat et quo casu si talis intrusor teneat se in
possessione eici poterit inpune vel donator per assisam noue disseisine seysinam
suam recuperabit.   Et quamuis talis seysina infirma sit per ratihabicionem tamen
domini veri ex post facto vel per pacienciam eius conualescere poterit.   Et
eodem modo si quis alicui rem suam dimiserit ad terminum annorum et eam pos-
20 tea donauerit in feodo eidem vel saltem ad terminum vite firmario sufficit
carta donatoris publice intellecta cum voluntate et paciencia.   Fieri autem poterit
tradicio ab vno vel a pluribus vni vel pluribus dum tamen donator aliquam inde
habuerit possessionem quamuis qualem vt vsumfructum vnius anni set a non
habente nulla fieri poterit seysina.

25   Nemo enim dare potest quod non habet, et si a duobus non dominis fiat
donacio et tradicio de eadem re vni vel duobus vtraque a vero domino poterit
reuocari et quantum ad donatarios prefertur ille qui prius fuit in seysina et idem
dici poterit de duobus quibus dominus vel non dominus donacionem fecerit et
vnde versus

30   Rem domino vel non domino vendente duobus   [202]
     In iure est pocior tradicione prior.

     Donator autem nunquam desinit possidere antequam donatarius possidere
incipit vt desinente vno corpore et animo incipiat alius animo et corpore.
Poterunt enim quidam naturaliter possidere vere et iuste et eciam naturaliter
35 iniuste et non vere.   Est enim naturalis possessio iusta et iniusta, iusta vt si
facta tradicione extiterit donatarius in possessione vacua et per se, naturalis et
iniusta vt si cum donator donatarium in possessionem induxerit et sic corpore et
animo recesserit vxore tamen vel pueris vel alia familia vel catallis donatoris in

---

6. Nota, J. *in margine*.   27. donatarios, Br. *in nonnullis MSS.*, donatores, J; prefertur]
prefertus, J.   29. versus, J. *in margine*.   31. tradicione, Br., vendicione, J.   33. alius]
illius, J.

intention to transfer to another (possession being transferred with solemnity so that proof shall not be lacking) and the simple placing by the donee of his foot [on the land], with desire to possess concurring with the donor's intention, even though the donee should not immediately take the issues. User indeed and issues play no great part in a gift, although frequently they are of value as an indication of possession. Nor will gifts be complete before seisin is taken of a usufruct. Neither will the cutting down or breaking of trees or branches or [the gathering of] crops, not yet ripe, play a great part in seisin, since these acts result rather in loss than in profit. Nor also is it necessary in taking seisin to go round all the fields or to set foot anywhere or everywhere, but there suffices for livery, so far as seisin of a freehold is concerned, long and peaceful seisin and long user, even though the property is rightfully another's, as, for example, if a man should enter upon a vacant property possessed by none, such as an inheritance not yet taken up. Long possession, indeed, gives birth to right. Nor will entry by the donee himself into the property granted validate [the gift] unless livery is made by the donor, because between grant and livery the intention of the donor may be changed and he may mentally retain what physically he has granted; and in this case, if such an intruder maintains himself in possession, he can be ejected with impunity or the donor will recover his seisin by an assize of novel disseisin. And although such seisin is weak, nevertheless by the ratification of the true owner after the fact, or by his sufferance, it may be fortified. And in the same way, if a man demises his property to someone for a term of years and afterwards gives it to him in fee or at least for life, the donor's charter, made publicly known, together with his intention and sufferance, is sufficient for the fermor. Livery may, moreover, be made by one or by several to one or to several, provided that the donor has some kind of possession of the property, even such, for example, as the usufruct for one year; but no seisin can be given by one who has no kind of possession.

No one, indeed, can give what he does not have, and if gift and livery of the same property be made by two who are not the owners to one or two [donees], both [gift and livery] may be revoked by the true owner, and as regards the donees he is to be preferred who was first in seisin; and the same may be said of two donees to whom the owner or non-owner makes a gift, whence the verses:

> When property is sold by an owner or non-owner to two
> He is stronger in law to whom livery is first made.

The donor, however, never ceases to possess until the donee begins to possess, so that when one ceases his physical and mental possession the other will begin his possession mentally and physically. Men may, however, have natural possession truly and rightfully, and also natural possession wrongfully and falsely. For natural possession is both rightful and wrongful: it is rightful if, for example, livery is made and the donee stands in vacant and exclusive possession; it is natural and wrongful if, for example, when the donor inducts the donee into possession and so withdraws physically and mentally, yet his wife or children or other members of his household or the donor's chattels are left in

Bracton,
f. 42
Bracton,
f. 40

Bracton,
f. 42b

Bracton,
f. 40

Bracton,
f. 40b

Bracton,
f. 41

Bracton
f. 41b

Bracton
f. 42

possessione relictis per talem vsum nichil adquirit sibi donatarius donec per verum
dominum fuerit vacuata et iterum tradita quia non refert vtrum ipse donator cum
donatario in possessione remanserit vel eius familia vel catalla vtendo vt prius.
Per huiusmodi vero vsum manifeste apparet quod quamuis corpore recesserit
5 animo tamen non intendit recedere et vnde versus

    Monstrat per vultum
    Quod sit sub corde sepultum.

    Quod multo euidencius per factum poterit demonstrare. Per vsum enim
videri poterit quid lateat in animo donatoris secus erit cum donator familie sue
10 iniunxerit quod ex tunc sit donatario intendens vt domino cum fidelitatis sacramento vel sine et quo casu valida erit donacio. Si autem donator hoc familie
non preceperit set reuersus negocium per familiam suam gestum ratum habuerit
tunc ymaginaria est tradicio et falsa. Si autem reuersus accionem negociorum
per familiam gestorum non approbauerit adhuc valida erit donacio et tradicio
15 firmata. Et ad huiusmodi suspiciones tollendas oportet de necessitate quod f. 78b
vacua sit possessio in omni tradicione tenementi. Ad quod duo principaliter
exiguntur ad hoc vt donatario conpetat accio contra donatorem, scilicet quod res
detur cum solempnitate et quod sequatur inmissio vel introduccio rei pacifica in
vacuam possessionem ita quod donator vel eius procurator, vxor, liberi, familia,
20 colonus, inquilinus, hospes, seruiens, seruus vel amicus vel aliqua catalla nomine
donatoris in re data non remaneant aliter enim semper videbitur quod donator
nunquam desiit possidere. Et cum in possessione vacua fiat tradicio et
donator corpore simul at animo recesserit et donatarium induxerit quamuis donatarius donatorem admittat vt in re data moram suam faciat dum tamen non agat
25 vt dominus set tanquam procurator vel senescallus vel vt seruiens vel vt
ministrator vbi dominus fuerit prius maior et preceptor non erit talis admissio
donatario preiudicialis. Quia tamen non semper consistit veritas in iuratoribus
expedit vt non admittatur. Et si talis donator donatarium eiciat vel inpediat conpetit sibi remedium per assisam noue disseisine et cum per assisam seysinam
30 suam recuperauerit per hoc firma erit in perpetuum et vlterius non erit ymaginaria vel simulata et per hoc potest statim donatarius sine suspicione donatori
suo concedere quod terram sic recuperatam teneat ad vitam. Et si donator
reuersus feoffatum eiecerit si donatarius ipsum statim eicere non possit per
assisam noue disseisine recuperabit excepcione tenere seysine non obstante. [203]
35 Prodest enim possidere quociens ex voluntate eius ad quem res pertinet possidendi ceptum est et sufficit semel voluisse omnibus concurrentibus que faciunt
validam donacionem et si postquam ceptum est possidendi voluntas eius ad
quem res pertinet accesserit licet nulla ab inicio interuenerit sufficit tamen ex
post facto et prodesse debet possessori. Et sicut fit perquisitum in persona

    5. versus, J. *in margine.*   29. *posterius* assisam *scripsimus,* ar', J.   35. quociens,
Br., tradiciones, J.   39. et, Br., quod, J.

possession, for by such user the donee acquires nothing for himself until [the property] is vacated by the true owner and again delivered [to him], because it does not matter whether the donor himself remains in possession with the donee or whether he does so by the user of his household or chattels, as above.   Indeed, by such user it manifestly appears that, although he has departed physically, yet mentally the donor does not intend to depart, whence the verses:

> He shows by his face
> What lies buried in his heart.

And this can be much more plainly shown by an act.   By user, indeed, it can be shown what lies hidden in the donor's mind.   It will be different where the donor enjoins his household to be henceforth submissive to the donee as their lord, with or without an oath of fealty, and in such a case the gift will be valid.   If, however, the donor does not order his household to act thus, but returns and ratifies what his household has done, then the livery is illusory and false.   If, however, when he returns, he does not approve the conduct of affairs by his household, the gift will still be valid and the livery affirmed.   And to remove suspicions of this kind, needs must that there shall be vacant possession when any tenement is transferred.   For this two things are principally required in order that an action may be available to the donee against the donor, namely, that the property shall be given with solemnity and that there shall follow entry or peaceful induction into vacant possession of the property so that there shall not remain in the property given either the owner or his agent, his wife, children, household, labourer, lodger, guest, servant, villein or friend or any chattels in right of the donor.   For otherwise it will always seem as though the donor has never relinquished possession.   But when livery is made with vacant possession and the donor has departed physically and mentally alike and has inducted the donee, even though the donee should admit the donor to stay on in the property given, provided he does not bear himself as owner but act as agent or steward or as servant or as manager where formerly, as the owner, he was at the head and in command, to admit him in this way will not prejudice the donee. And since the truth does not always reside in jurors, it is expedient not to admit the donor.   And if such a donor should eject or obstruct a donee, a remedy is available to the donee by an assize of novel disseisin; and when he has recovered his seisin by the assize it will, in this way, be affirmed in perpetuity, and thenceforth it will not be illusory or fictitious, and in consequence the donee may at once, without arousing suspicion, grant the land so recovered to the donor to be held for life.   And if the donor returns and ejects the feoffee and the donee is not able straightway to eject the donor, the donee will recover by an assize of novel disseisin despite an exception of tenuous seisin.   For it is an advantage to possess whenever possession has begun by the will of him to whom the property belongs, and it suffices if he has once willed it, all the other things necessary for a valid gift being present together; and if, after possession has begun, the agreement of him to whom the property belongs should be added, even though it was not present from the beginning, though it is *ex post facto*, it suffices and puts

Bracton,
f. 42*b*

Bracton,
f. 51

propria ita fit per procuratorem alicuius eciam ipso hoc ignorante set si dominus
procuratoris rem gestam non approbauerit et aliquis a latere procuratorem eiecerit quero cui conpetit assisa cum donator dederit quod suum erat et procurator
nichil nomine proprio stipulatus fuerit set alieno qui se intromittere non curat
5 et reuera donatori conpetit assisa quia donatarius possidere nondum incepit.
De minori vero non sic qui versus curatorem accionem negociorum gestorum
habebit. Si autem donator ante tradicionem moriatur vel donatarius reuocari
poterit donacio quia possessionem vacuam non fuit adeptus. Sine tradicione
autem poterit quis incipere possidere per longam et pacificam seysinam et vsum
10 continuum licet alius possidere non desinat eo quod tradicionibus et vsucapionibus rerum dominia et possessiones adquiruntur. Quamuis autum tenera sit
quandoque seysina et quandoque firma, nunquam tamen erit tenera vbi ius proprietas et seysina concurrunt vt si ius alicui descenderit iure hereditario qui in
seysinam vacuam animo et corpore sine contencione se posuerit statim in ipsa
15 coniunccione liberum tenementum habebit. Si autem facta fuerit donacio de
re aliena vel contra conuencionem vel condicionem vel intrusionem vel disseysinam nunquam erit ibi possessio firma et valida set tenera erit quousque substanciam vel seysinam ceperit ex longo tempore et pacifico quod sufficere possit pro
titulo et maxime contra verum dominum vel contra conuencionem vel condicio-
20 nem. Contra donatorem vero et alios qui ius non habent firma erit et valida.

    Adquiruntur autem nobis possessiones per nosmetipsos et per liberos et seruos
quos sub potestate nostra habemus dum tamen factum eorum honestum fuerit
et illud approbauerimus et ea que ex maleficiis seruus apprehenderit ad domini
possessionem ideo non pertinent quia nec peculii causam apprehendunt.
25 Necnon et per illos qui extra nostram sunt potestatem cum eorum corpora dis-
racionauerimus nisi alieni facti fuerint serui. Minoribus eciam adquiruntur
possessiones et naturaliter fatuis et furiosis per tutores inde aliter vero minime
eo quod intellectum recipiendi non habent nec retinendi. Curatores autem
sanum intellectum oportet habere quia si minorem fatuum a natiuitate vel
30 furiosum miseris vt possideas nequaquam videris per eos possessionem appre-   f. 79
hendisse. Si autem plures fuerint seruientes per vnum poterit hereditas retineri
sicut totus redditus retinetur per vnius tenentis solucionem cum plures ad
redditum contribuere teneantur et a simili si cui data fuerit pastura ad centum
pecora per vnum inmissum pasturam ad centum retinebit. Si amicus autem
35 venditoris cui mandauit vt donatarium in possessionem induceret mortuo dona-   [204]
tore priusquam id sciret heredibus non prohibentibus donatarium in posses-

the possessor in an advantageous position. And just as an acquisition is
made by one's own self, so it is made by one's agent, even though the principal
is ignorant of it. But if the agent's principal should not approve of what has
been done and a third party should eject the agent, then it is a question to whom
an assize is available, since the donor gave what was his own and the agent had
not stipulated for anything in his own name but in that of another who may not
care to get himself involved; in truth, the assize is available to the donor,
because the donee has not yet begun to possess. It is not thus in the case of a
minor, who will have against a guardian an action upon the conduct of his
affairs. If, however, the donor or donee should die before livery, the gift can
be revoked because the donee had not obtained vacant possession. Without
livery, moreover, a man may begin to possess by long and peaceful seisin and
continuous user although the other does not cease to possess because by livery
and usucapion the ownership and possession of property are acquired. Again,
although seisin may sometimes be tenuous and sometimes firm, yet it will never
be tenuous where right, ownership, and seisin concur; for example, if a right
descends to someone hereditarily and he puts himself into vacant seisin, mentally
and physically, without dispute, straightway by that conjunction he will have a
freehold. If, however, a gift should be made of property belonging to another
or [acquired] contrary to an agreement or condition or by intrusion or disseisin,
possession in that instance will never be firm and valid, but it will be tenuous
until it attains substance or seisin after a long and undisturbed period of time,
which may suffice for title, especially against the true owner or against an agreement or condition; but against a donor or against others who have no right,
possession will be firm and valid.

　　　Possessions are acquired by us for ourselves, and by free men and by
villeins whom we have under our authority, provided that what they have done
is honest and we have approved of it. Those things, therefore, of which a
villein may obtain possession by his wrongdoings, do not fall into the lord's
possession since such things do not acquire the character of [the villein's] private
property. [Possessions are acquired for us] also by those who are outside our
authority as soon as we have established a right to their bodies (if they have not
become the villeins of others). Possessions are also acquired by minors and by
born fools and the insane through guardians for that purpose, but otherwise
most certainly not, because they have not the sense to receive or to keep. It is
necessary, however, for guardians to be of sound mind because, if you were to
send a minor, a born fool or a madman to take possession for you, never would
you see possession acquired by them. If, moreover, there should be several
bondsmen, an inheritance can be retained by one of them, just as the whole of a
rent is retained by the payment of one tenant, although several are bound to
contribute to the rent; and in like manner, if pasture should be given to someone for a hundred beasts, by turning in one he will retain pasture for the hundred.
And if a friend of a vendor should be charged to induct the donee into possession,
and the donor should die, and before he had knowledge of the death the friend
should induct the donee into possession and the heirs should not have forbidden

sionem induxerit recte tradita erit possessio set si id fecerit cum donatorem
sciret mortuum vel quod heredes id facere nollent non erit rite facta tradicio.

    Aduocaciones autem ecclesiarum sine corporibus alienari non possunt
quamuis ipse ecclesie conferri possunt tutoribus et personis nec cum corpore
5 possunt alienari nisi alienatores in seysina presentandi extiterint vel nisi in villa
in qua sita est ecclesia aliquem habeant fundum ad quem huiusmodi aduocaciones
pertinuerint. Et quamuis sic transferatur donatarius tamen aduocacionis
seysinam non gaudebit donec vacauerit vt tunc presentare possit.   Et vnde nulli
donatario valebit donacio antequam rei date seysinam fuerit adeptus quia
10 donator possidere non desinit donec eius donatarius possidere incipiat quamuis
assignatum sibi facere possit per modum donacionis sibi collate quia si tenens ab
aliquo super aduocacione inplacitatus suum vocaret feoffatorem ad warantum
excipere posset quod warantizare non tenetur eo quod nullam vnquam inde
habuit seysinam nec dare potuit quod non habuit quamuis de manerio ad quod
15 pertinuit aduocacio plene fuerit seysitus.   Et si manerium ad quod pertinuerit
aduocacio ecclesie ad diuersas manus per particulas cum pertinenciis per
vendicionem deuoluatur et donator aliquid sibi retinuerit quamuis minimam partem fundi semper remanebit aduocacio cum parte retenta nisi specialis mencio
in aliquo dono fiat de aduocacione.
20   In omni vero casu vbi confirmacio fieri debet vel recognicio oportet con-
firmantem et recognoscentem in possessione proprietatis esse vel iuris de qua
fieri debent et eodem modo ille cui fit quia si neuter locum non habebunt.

CAP. XVI.   DE HOMAGIIS

    Secundum autem diuersa genera tenementorum sunt quidam heredes qui ad
25 homagium tenentur faciendum et ad sacramentum fidelitatis et quidam ad
sacramentum fidelitatis tantum. Tenementorum autem aliud tenetur per seruicium militare vel per magnam seriantiam de quibus homagium facere oportebit
et aliud quod per paruam seriantiam vel tanquam in sokagio libero tenentur de
quibus eadem habetur consuetudo in pluribus vterque namque suum seruicium
30 scit certum neutrius enim heres in custodia domini remanebit. A soco autem
deriuatur socagium et a socco dicuntur sokemanni racione tenementorum

him to do so, possession will be rightly transferred; but if the friend should do so, knowing the donor to be dead or that the heirs did not wish it to be done, livery will not have been rightly made.

Bracton,
f. 53b

The advowsons of churches cannot be alienated without corporeal property (although the churches themselves may be entrusted to guardians and parsons), nor can they be alienated with corporeal property unless those who alienate are in seisin of the right of presentation or unless in the township in which the church is situated they have some landed estate to which such advowsons are

Bracton,
f. 54

appurtenant. And although an advowson may be transferred in this way, the donee nevertheless will not enjoy the seisin of the advowson until the church is void so that he may then present. And a gift thereof will not avail any donee until he has obtained seisin of the property given, because the donor does not cease to possess until the donee of the property begins to possess, even though

Bracton,
f. 54

by the mode of the gift made to him he may appoint for himself an assign, because if the tenant were impleaded by someone in respect of the advowson and he should vouch his feoffor to warranty, the feoffor can except that he is not bound to warrant because the tenant has never had any seisin thereof, nor could he give what he did not have, even though he was fully seised of the manor to

Bracton,
f. 55

which the advowson was appurtenant. And if the manor, to which the advowson of the church was appurtenant, should devolve to several hands through its sale in parcels with appurtenances, and the donor should retain something for himself, albeit a very small part of the estate, the advowson will always remain with the part he retained unless special mention be made of the advowson in one of the grants.

Bracton,
f. 59b

In every case where there is to be made a confirmation or acknowledgement, it is necessary that he who confirms and acknowledges should be in possession of the property or the right which is to be confirmed and acknowledged, and in like manner should he be [in possession] to whom [the confirmation or acknowledgement] is made, because, if neither is in possession, [confirmation or acknowledgement] will not hold good.

CHAPTER 16. OF HOMAGES

Bracton.
f. 77b

Depending upon the different natures of tenements, there are some heirs who are bound to do homage and take an oath of fealty and some who are bound to take an oath of fealty only. And some tenements are held by military service or by grand serjeanty, for which homage must be done, and others are held by petty serjeanty or as it were in free socage, which are in many ways subject to the same custom, for in each case the tenant knows his service for certain and the heir of neither will abide in the wardship of his lord. Socage is derived from sock,[1] and sokemen are so called from sock by reason of their

---

[1] I.e. a plough.

suorum eo quod ad culturam tantum deputati sunt quorum heredum custodia
et maritagia ad propinquiores parentes iure sanguinis pertinebit. Villani
autem sokemanni nullo priuilegio libero gaudebunt tum racione personarum
tum racione tenementorum. De tenementis autem in maritagium datis ante
5 tercium heredem donatarii capi homagium non debet racione reuersionis rei
date forte ad donatorem quod si prius captum fuerit tenet vtique. Recusatur
eciam homagium quandoque propter ius accrescendi vt si hereditas prius [205]
descendat heredibus fratribus vel sororibus nullus eorum homagium faciat ante-
natis quia si aliquis coheredum sine herede de corpore suo decedat pars dece-
10 dentis accrescet superstitibus et si homagium interuenerit ad heredes inferiores
descendet. Cum autem plures fuerint heredes omnes filie primogenite acapi-
tabunt et sacramenta facient fidelitatis et totum seruicium. Primogenita autem
domino capitali faciet homagium de toto feodo et de toto seruicio domino
respondebit ne cogatur seruicium suum recipere per particulas. Dominus
15 tamen custodiam postnatarum et maritagium habebit, primogenita vero f. 79b
nequaquam vt oues a luporum morsibus eruantur propter spem et successionis
euentum que euenire posset si ipsas infra etatem mori contingat ex aliqua
machinacione. Verumptamen si de rege tenuerint in capite omnes regi homagium facere tenebuntur.
20   Homagium autem est iuris vinculum quo quis tenetur et astringitur ad
warantizandum acquietandum et defendendum tenentem suum in seysina sua
versus omnes per certum seruicium in donacione conprehensum et vice versa quo
tenens obligatur et restringitur ad fidem domino suo obseruandam et seruicium
debitum faciendum. Contrahitur enim de mutua vtriusque voluntate et dis-
25 soluitur per contrariam vtriusque voluntatem si vterque voluerit; non sufficit
vnius voluntas. Est itaque tanta et talis connexio inter dominum et tenentem
suum per homagii vinculum quod dominus tantum debet tenenti quantum tenens
domino preter solam reuerenciam.
Capere vero debet homagium dominus feodi siue sit masculus siue femina
30 siue maior siue minor. Minor tamen maior factus valebit excepcio decep-
cionis. Maior autem ignorare non debet cuius condicionis sit ille cuius
homagium ceperit. Viri eciam superuenientes nichil nisi custodiam vxorum
habentes ante prolis suscitacionem homagium capere non tenentur. Facere
autem potest homagium liber homo masculus vel femina clericus et laycus maior
35 et minor. Electi tamen in episcopos post consecracionem homagium non
facient set sacramentum tantum fidelitatis. Abbates eciam priores conuentus
vel ecclesiastice persone qui nichil tenent nisi nomine ecclesiarum suarum
homagium facere non tenentur eo quod nomine tenent alieno et ideo nullus alii
iure succedet hereditario. In feoffamentis enim talium manifeste apparet quod
40 primo et principaliter fit donacio Deo et ecclesie de tali loco et secundario religi-

8–9. antenatis] antenatus, J.   25. contrariam, Br., mutuam, J.   33. tenentur] tenetur, J.

Bracton.
f. 78

tenements, because they are employed solely in agriculture, and the wardship and marriage of their heirs belongs to their nearest relatives by right of blood. Villein sokemen, however, will enjoy no free privilege either in right of their persons or in right of their tenements. For tenements given as a marriage-portion, however, homage should not be taken before the third heir of the donee by reason of the reversion of the property given which may perchance fall to the donor; but if homage should be taken sooner, it is assuredly binding. Sometimes also homage is refused because of the right of accrual: for example, if an inheritance should first descend to heirs, brothers or sisters, none of them would do homage to the elder-born because, if any one of the co-heirs should die without an heir of his body, the portion of the deceased will accrue to the survivors; but if homage should be rendered, the portion will descend to the heirs further down. But if there should be several heiresses, all will acknowledge their feudal subjection to the eldest daughter and will take oaths of fealty and render all the service [to her]. The eldest, however, will do homage for the whole fee to the chief lord and answer to him for the whole service lest he should be compelled to receive his service in fractions. The lord, however, will have the wardship and marriage of the younger sisters, but never will the eldest sister have them, so that the sheep may be plucked from the mouths of wolves, because there might arise a hope and prospect of succession if those under age chanced by some machination to die. However, if the sisters should hold from the king in chief, they will all be bound to do homage to him.

Bracton
f. 78b

Homage is a legal bond whereby a man is bound and constrained to warrant, acquit and defend his tenant in his seisin against all men in consideration of a definite service included in a gift and whereby, conversely, the tenant is obliged and constrained to keep faith with his lord and to render the service due. Homage, indeed, is contracted by the mutual wish of both parties and is dissolved by the wish of both to the contrary, if both so will: the wish of one does not suffice. There is, therefore, a link so great and of such a quality between the lord and his tenant through the bond of homage that the lord owes the tenant as much as the tenant owes the lord, reverence alone excepted.

The lord of a fee must take homage, whether he be a man or a woman, of age or a minor, though when a minor attains his majority, there is available to him an exception of deception. A man, however, of full age ought not to be ignorant of the condition of the one whose homage he takes. Also where husbands are concerned who have nothing except the custody of their wives, until children are begotten they are not bound to take homage. A free man can do homage, a male or female, clerk or lay man, one of full age or a minor. But those who are elected as bishops will not do homage after their consecration but take an oath of fealty only. Abbots also and priors of a convent or ecclesiastical persons, who hold nothing except in the name of their churches, are not

Bracton,
f. 79
Bracton,
f. 78b

bound to do homage, because they hold in the name of another and therefore none succeeds to another by hereditary right. For in the feoffments of such persons it manifestly appears that the gift is made first and foremost to God and the church of such-and-such a place and secondly to the religious or rectors

osis vel rectoribus ibidem Deo seruientibus et quamuis mutacio fiat capitum et
personarum per presentacionem, collacionem vel eleccionem idem tamen corpus
manet tanquam de grege nec ideo poterit fieri narracio descensus de abbate in ab-
batem sicut de herede in heredem.   Faciunt tamen tales frequenter homagium
5 per ignoranciam cum de iure non debent et tales ideo ad releuium infra tri-
cesimum annum prestandum tenentur ne capitales domini debitis seruiciis de-
fraudentur sicut in Normannia de consuetudine obseruatur.   Si autem minor
homagium faciat sacramentum tamen fidelitatis ante etatem facere non debet. [206]
Quilibet autem donatarius qui homagium facere tenetur in seysina sibi collata
10 ante seysinam et post illud facere potest quod si ante et si seysina rei non
sequatur effectum non habebit vel si nec in vita donatoris nisi donacio ratificata
fuerit per confirmacionem ab herede quod cum semel factum fuerit semper tenet
donec mors que omnia soluit eorum alterum preueniat.   Tenet tamen ex parte
superstitis quod si cadat in persona morientis tamen tenet obligacio in persona
15 heredis cum post homagium releuatur tenementum et in persona domini
renouatur homagium quod tenuit ab inicio.   Et vnde si plura fiunt homagia ab
pluribus successiue plura erunt ibi homagia racione plurium heredum et per hoc
plura releuia.   Non tamen erit nisi vnum homagium quamuis vnus dominus
plura receperit homagia vel quamuis pluries innouetur et vice versa cum tenens
20 superstes fuerit et homagium fecerit et dominus capitalis decesserit cadit homagium ex parte illa.   Durat tamen homagii obligacio in persona heredis et in
persona eius heredis releuabitur homagium ita quod de nouo erit capiendum ab
herede et de nouo faciendum a tenente.   Et sic fieri poterit de pluribus capitalibus dominis decedentibus et eorum heredibus et quo casu plura erunt homagia
25 ex parte dominorum et non nisi vnum ex parte tenentis qui semper superstes est.
Set plures homagii innouaciones propter pluralitatem dominorum et heredum
eorum et ideo non dabitur nisi vnicum releuium a tenente.   De vno eciam et
eodem tenemento simul et semel non possunt fieri plura homagia pluribus dominis capitalibus siue tenementum illud ab vno teneri debeat vel a pluribus in
30 communi quia si a pluribus in communi et vnus sit heres primogenitus ex pluribus homagium capiet ab vno.   Si autem plures tenere debeant in communi de
vno vel pluribus primogenitus faciet homagium pro omnibus.   Si autem vnus
vel plures qui tenent in communi de vno tantum tenuerint et alicui cui non
tenentur per ignoranciam vel districcionem iniustam homagium fecerint talibus
35 est subueniendum.   Si autem per maliciam et fraudem hoc fecerint ad exheredacionem domini sui eo ipso amittere debent tenementum vnde prouenit et   f. 80
obligacio homagii propter fraudem penitus extinguetur.   Et eodem modo cum

2. presentacionem *scripsimus*; priuacionem, J.   5. debent] deberent, J.   15. et *om.* J.
16. *posterius* ab *om.* J.   30. heres, J. *et* B, tenens *in nonnullis textis.*

serving God there; and although a change be made in the heads [of religious
houses] or in parsons by presentation, collation or election, nevertheless it remains the same body (like a flock of sheep); and therefore [in pleading] a count
of descent from abbot to abbot cannot be made, as it is made from heir to heir.

Frequently, however, these ecclesiastics render homage out of ignorance,
although they do not rightly owe it, and they are therefore bound to pay relief
every thirtieth year, as is a custom observed in Normandy, lest the chief lords
should be defrauded of the services due.   If a minor does homage, he should
nevertheless not take an oath of fealty before he attains his majority.   Any
donee, moreover, who is bound to do homage when seisin is conferred upon
him may render it either before or after seisin, but if he does it before seisin and
if seisin of the property does not follow, homage will be of no effect: as also if
seisin does not follow in the lifetime of the donor unless the gift has been ratified
by confirmation of the heir.   And when homage has once been done it is binding
for ever until death, which dissolves all things, shall overtake one or other of the
parties.   It is, however, binding on the part of the survivor because, if it ceases
in the person of the dying man, the obligation is nevertheless binding in the
person of the heir when the tenement is raised again after homage, and in the
person of the lord homage is renewed which was binding from the beginning.
Wherefore, if several homages are done by several [heirs] successively, there will
be several homages in that case by reason of the several heirs, and in consequence
there will be several reliefs.   It will, however, be but one [and the same] homage,
although one lord receives several homages or although homage is renewed
several times.   And, conversely, if the tenant should be the survivor and do
homage and the chief lord should die, homage lapses on his side; but the
obligation of homage endures in the person of the heir, and in the person of the
lord's heir the homage is resurrected so that it will be taken anew by the heir and
rendered anew by the tenant.   And so it can be done with regard to several
chief lords who die and their heirs, in which case there will be several homages
from the stand-point of the lords and only one from that of the tenant who
survives throughout; but [though] there would be several renewals of homage on
account of the many lords and their heirs, no more than a single relief will
be given by the tenant on that account.   Further, for one and the same tenement
several homages cannot be rendered to several chief lords at one and the same
time, whether that tenement should be held of one lord or of several in
common, for where it is held of several in common and there is one [tenant],
the eldest of the several lords shall take homage from that one.   If, however,
several should hold in common of one or several lords, the eldest tenant
shall do homage for all.   But if one or several who hold in common should
hold of one lord only and through ignorance or unlawful distraint they should
do homage to someone to whom they are not bound, they must be aided.   But

if they were to do this through malice and fraud to the disherison of their lord,
they ought on this account to lose the tenement for which homage is due, and
the obligation of homage will be wholly extinguished on account of the fraud.
And in like manner if they should once do homage to the true lord and fraudu-

semel homagium fecerint vero domino et per fraudem recesserint ab eo. Si autem ab inicio homagium fecerint non domino quod postea recuperauerit verus dominus racione alicuius finis vel attornacionis et tenens noluerit ei homagium facere cui de iure tenetur set se tenuerit ad homagium ad quod non tenetur nisi

5 de voluntate cum verus dominus postea recuperauerit homagium et seruicium de iure non liberabitur tenens ab eo cui adhesit de voluntate. Item poterit quis de pluribus tenementis plura facere homagia vni domino vel diuersis simul vel successiue et poterunt plures domini plura capere homagia racione plurium tenementorum dum tamen vnus ex pluribus dominis precipuus sit et legius vt

10 feoffator primus quia talis semper maritagium habebit heredum propter primum feoffamentum nisi tenens aliquid tenuerit de rege in capite. Et si inimicicie inter   [207] dominos suos capitales oriantur in propria persona stabit cum eo cui fecit ligeanciam et per attornatum cum aliis vel saluo eis seruicio in quo eis tenetur de tenemento.

15 De terris autem et redditibus que per seruicium tenentur militare tenetur quilibet facere homagium et semper sequetur custodia heredum et maritagium non tamen tantum propter homagium set propter seruicium regale quia ad omne homagium non sequitur custodia et maritagium. De socagio communi non debent fieri homagia et si fiant custodias tamen vel maritagia non habebunt nec

20 eciam de magnis seriantiis nisi regem tantum respiciant et patrie defensionem quod secus erit si non regem ipsum vel patrie defensionem set tantum priuatam personam respiciant. Campiones autem et seruientes quandoque homagium faciunt hoc tamen racione nudi dominii reputatur.

Ille autem qui homagium facere debet optentu reuerencie domino suo

25 debite dominum suum vbicumque inuentus fuerit adire tenetur dum tamen comode possit adire et iunctis manibus et erectis offerre debet suum homagium in signum subieccionis et reuerencie non tamen in loco secreto set publico coram pluribus qui domino vel tenenti super rebus gestis testimonium cum necesse fuerit valeant perhibere. Quod si dominus recipere voluerit tunc in signum

30 warantie acquietacionis et defensionis manus tenentis infra manus suas tenere debet dum tenens proferat hec verba:

Deuenio homo vester de feodis et tenementis que de vobis teneo et tenere debeo et fidem vobis portabo contra omnes salua fide mea versus regem et heredes suos et alios dominos meos.

35 Regi autem sic:

Deuenio homo vester de feodis et tenementis que de vobis teneo et tenere debeo et fidem vobis portabo de vita et membris corpore et catallis et omni terreno honore contra omnes qui viuere poterunt et mori.

Et facto homagio statim faciat tenens fidelitatem suam sub hiis verbis tactis

40 sacrosanctis:

Hoc auditis domine N. quod fidem vobis portabo contra omnes salua fide vt

12. *post* in *add.* vna, J.   15. et *om.* J.   16. *prius* et *om.* J.   18. communi *scripsimus*, camere, J.   21. non *addidimus*; ipsum, Br., tantum, J.   23. dominii] domini, J. 32. *prius* et *om.* J.

lently withdraw from him.   If, however, from the start they do homage to one who is not the lord and afterwards the true lord recovers by reason of some fine or attornment, and a tenant refuses to do homage to him to whom he is bound by right, but abides by the homage to which he is not bound save by his own will: when the true lord later recovers homage and service as of right, the tenant will not be freed from him to whom he adhered of his own will.   Again, a man may do several homages for several tenements to one or several lords (at one time or successively), and several lords can take several homages [from one] by reason of several tenements, provided that one of the several lords is his principal and liege lord as the first feoffor, because as such he will always have the marriage of heirs on account of the first feoffment unless the tenant should hold something of the king in chief.   And if enmities should arise between his chief lords, a tenant will stand in his own person with him to whom he did liege homage and by attorney with the others or saving to them the service in which he is bound for the tenement he holds of them.

Moreover, for lands and rents which are held by military service everyone is bound to do homage, and there will always follow wardship and marriage of the heirs, not, however, on account of the homage only, but on account of the service due to the king, because wardship and marriage do not follow upon every homage.   For common socage homages ought not to be rendered and, if they are rendered, nevertheless the lords will not have wardship or marriage; nor even for grand serjeanties except only when they concern the king and the defence of the country: it will be otherwise if they do not concern the king or the defence of the country but merely a private person.   Champions, moreover, and serjeants sometimes do homage, but this is considered to be merely on account of lordship.

Bracton,
f. 80
He, moreover, who ought to do homage is bound, on the ground of the reverence due to his lord, to go to him wherever he may be found, provided that he can conveniently do so, and, with hands joined and uplifted, he ought to offer his homage in sign of subjection and reverence, nor should this be in a secret place but publicly before several men who, should it be necessary, will be capable of bearing witness for the lord or the tenant on what has happened. And if the lord is willing to receive the homage, then, as a sign of warranty, acquittance and defence, he should hold the tenant's hands between his own hands while the tenant utters these words:

'I become your man for the fees and tenements which I hold and ought to hold of you, and I will bear you fealty against all men, saving my fealty towards the king and his heirs and my other lords'.

To the king, however, [he says] thus:

'I become your man for the fees and tenements which I hold and ought to hold of you, and I will bear you fealty in life and limb, body and chattels, and all earthly honour against all mortal men'.

And when homage is rendered, straightway the tenant should do his fealty in these words, while he touches sacred relics:

'This hear you, lord N., that I will bear you fealty against all men, saving my

supra et quod fideliter et sine diminucione contradiccione dilacione iniusta vel
inpedimento terminis statutis seruicium debitum secundum posse meum vobis
faciam.   Sic me Deus adiuuet et hec sancta.
Et regi sic:
5   Hoc auditis circumstantes quod fidem regi portabo de vita et membris et
terreno honore et arma contra ipsum non portabo.   Sic me Deus etc.
       Examinacio autem homagium precedere debet si ille qui se heredem facit sit
filius naturalis eius cuius heredem se facit et heres rectus et propinquus et propinquior quantum ad ius possessionis et proprietatis item quale et quantum
10   tenementi de eo teneat et de quo homagio facto obligatur item quid in dominico
et quid in seruicio item per quod seruicium item qualiter descendit ei hereditas
quod heres esse debeat ne in capcione homagii contingat dominum per negligenciam decipi vel errorem.
       Effectus autem homagii est quod si quis homagium alteri fecerit domino vel
15   non domino a tali domino vel homagio suo sine iudicio recedere non potest
quamdiu tenuerit tenementum per quod obligatur ad homagium in dominico vel   [208]
in seruicio.   Nec eciam poterit tenens aliquid facere propter obligacionem
homagii quod domino suo vertatur ad exheredacionem vel aliam atrocem
iniuriam nec e conuerso dominus tenenti quod si fecerint dissoluitur homagium
20   et omnis homagii connexio et obligacio et vnde merito in iudicio considerabitur
si in persona domini quod dominium amittat et si in persona tenentis quod amittat tenementum.   Aliquando eciam tenet homagium et homagii connexio in
persona tenentis et extinguitur in persona domini propter ipsius defectum vel   f. 80b
delictum set releuatur et viuificat in persona alterius domini superioris.   Propter
25   defectum vt si dominus omnino sine herede decesserit vel alteri homagium et
seruicium eius attornauerit in casibus licitis et concessis vel alio modo de voluntate tenentis et quo casu extinguitur homagium quoad ipsum dominum semper
tamen durat in persona tenentis quia in persona alterius reuiuiscit.   Propter
delictum vt si dominus feloniam fecerit vel aliquid ad exheredacionem sui
30   tenentis propter quod ipse dominus iusto iudicio debeat exheredari et quo casu
quod superior dominus capitalis prius per medium optinuit modo inmediate
capiet medio omnino sublato et extunc incipit obligacio homagii inter tenentem
et capitalem dominum superiorem.   Et tenebitur talis dominus homagium
capere velit nolit nec weyuare poterit feodum suum neque homagium et serui-
35   cium recusare vt sic a federe warantie absoluatur pro inconuenienti quod sequeretur contra voluntatem tenentis sui quominus teneatur ad warantiam et escambium nec eciam tenens quominus faciat domino suo seruicium debitum quamdiu
tenuerit tenementum propter quod obligatur ad seruicium.   Nunquam enim
faceret aliquis warantyam suo tenenti de magna quantitate terre pro minimo

       31. prius] primus, J.   35-36. quod sequeretur *scripsimus*; prosequeretur, J.

fealty (as above), and that faithfully and without diminution, contradiction, wrongful delay or impediment I will perform due service to you at the stated terms to the best of my ability. So help me God and these sacred relics.'

To the king [he says] thus:

'This hear you, who stand by, that I will bear the king fealty in life and limb and earthly honour, and against him I will not bear arms. So help me God etc.'

Bracton,
f. 80b

And, lest in taking homage the lord should happen by negligence or error to be deceived, an examination ought to precede homage thus: whether he who claims to be heir is a natural son of him whose heir he claims to be, and is right and near heir and nearer [than others] in the matter of right of possession and ownership; further, what kind of tenement and how much he holds of the lord and, when homage is rendered, for what he will be bound; what in demesne and what in service; and by what service; again, in what manner the inheritance descends to him so as to constitute him the heir.

The effect of homage is that, if a man does homage to another, be he [true] lord or non-lord, from that lord or his homage he may not depart without a judgement of the court so long as he holds the tenement in demesne or in service for which he is bound to render homage. Moreover, by reason of the obligation of homage, a tenant cannot do anything that would result in his lord's

Bracton,
f. 81b

disherison or do him any other grave harm, nor, conversely, can the lord [behave thus] to the tenant; and if they should do so, the homage is dissolved and

Bracton,
f. 80b

every tie and obligation of homage, and therefore it will be justly awarded in judgement, if the lord [has offended], that he lose his lordship, and if the tenant, that he lose his tenement. Sometimes, moreover, homage and the tie of homage hold in the person of the tenant and are extinguished in the person of the lord by reason of the failure of heirs or felony; but [the homage] is raised again and revived in the person of another, the superior lord. On account of failure of heirs, as, for example, if the lord should die entirely without an heir or should attorn the tenant's homage and service to another in cases where it is lawful and permitted or otherwise with the agreement of the tenant; and in this case homage is extinguished as regards the lord, though it continues in the person of the tenant because it comes to life again in the person of another [lord]. On account of felony, as, for example, if the lord should commit a felony or do anything to the disherison of his tenant on account of which the lord should by rightful judgement be disinherited; and in this case what the superior lord previously had obtained through a mesne he will now receive immediately, the mesne being entirely removed, and thereupon an obligation of homage begins

Bracton,
f. 81b

between the tenant and the superior lord. And such a lord will be bound to take the homage willy nilly, nor can he waive his fee or refuse homage and service against the wish of his tenant in order to be absolved from the bond of warranty, because of the mischief that would follow if he should not be bound to warranty and exchange. Nor can the tenant [refuse] so that he does not render to his lord the service due as long as he holds the tenement on account of which he

Bracton,
f. 80b

is bound to render the service. Never, indeed, would anyone make warranty to his tenant of a great quantity of land for a very small service if, of his own

seruicio si pro voluntate sua posset feodum suum weyuare et homagium et
seruicium sui tenentis recusare. Tenere eciam poterit homagium in persona
domini et dissolui in persona tenentis et conualescere in persona alterius vt si
tenens cum domino suo fecerit homagium se ex toto dimiserit de hereditate sua
5 et alium feoffauerit tenendi de domino capitali et quo casu tenens ab homagio
absoluitur et extinguitur homagium velit nolit dominus et incipit in persona
feoffati qui obligatur propter tenementum quod tenet de feodo domini. Extingui eciam poterit homagium et eius obligacio dissolui ex vtraque parte propter
defectum vel delictum tenentis vt tenementum ad manus domini descendat
10 quoquo modo per eschaetam vel si tenens cum homagium domino fecerit
maliciose in locum recordi deaduocauerit tenere de eo propter exheredacionem
ipsius domini et quo casu licet homagium et obligacio teneat ex parte domini si
voluerit non tamen tenet ex parte tenentis cum per abnegacionem domini sui
homagium suum et vinculum fidelitatis infringit et quo casu domino conpetit
15 quod petat tenementum tenentis sui quod de eo tenere debuit in dominico quia
deaduocatus est per tenentem in cuius persona defuit obligacio per tale breue:

Precipe tali quod reddat tali tantum terre cum pertinenciis vel tot feoda
que predictus talis de eo tenuit et inde homagium ei fecit et seruicium et que [209]
debent esse escaeta sua eo quod predictus talis tenens contra homagium suum et
20 fidelitatis sacramentum quod ei inde fecerat ipsum maliciose et ad exheredacionem suam deaduocauit et nisi fecerit.

Et vnde cum sic probatum fuerit per inquisicionem et iuratam non erit necesse
vlterius querere de aliquo iuris descensu. Si autem petere velit per breue de
recto incongrue tamen petet per aliquem descensum cum tenens in possessione
25 extiterit per descensum ab antecessoribus suis. Set qualitercumque agatur non
erit locus magne assise neque duello set capietur iurata et inquisicio ad similitudinem magne assise sub hiis verbis:
vtrum videlicet ille qui tenet maius ius tenendi tenementum illud habeat vel
feodum in dominico an ille qui petit et cui idem tenens aut aliquis eius ante-
30 cessorum inde homagium et seruicium fecit et quem postmodum contra homagium et fidelitatem suam maliciose deaduocauit.

Quod si probatum fuerit petens recuperabit in dominico quod tenens in
dominico tenuit. Si autem seruicium pecierit id recuperabit et de cetero non erit
medius inter tenentem et dominum et sic extinguitur homagium in persona medii
35 et reuiuiscit in persona inferioris tenentis.

Vbi autem eadem est racio ibi idem ius erit. Si tenens domino suo atrocem
iniuriam facit vel si steterit in bello cum inimicis domini sui consilio vel auxilio
contra dominum suum excepto principe vel capitali domino suo cui ligeanciam
fecit vel si manus violentas in dominum suum felonice iniecerit vel aliquid fecerit

3. *posterius* et *om.* J; in persona alterius, Br., *om.* J.   26–27. neque . . . assise, Br.,
om. J.   38. cui] cum, J.

volition, he could waive his fee and refuse the homage and service of his tenant.

Bracton,
f. 81

Again, homage may hold in the person of the lord and be dissolved in the person of the tenant and revive in the person of another tenant, as, for example, where a tenant does homage to his lord and he divests himself entirely of his inheritance and enfeoffs someone else to hold of the chief lord, for in this case the tenant is released from homage and homage is extinguished, whether the lord likes it or not, and it begins in the person of the feoffee, who is bound [to homage] by reason of the tenement which he holds of the lord's fee. Homage may also be extinguished and its bond be dissolved on each side on account of the failure of heirs or felony of the tenant, so that the tenement will fall into the lord's hands somehow by escheat; or where the tenant, when he has done homage to his lord, wrongfully disavows holding of him in a place of record, by reason of the disherison of the lord; and in this case, although the homage and the obligation will be binding on the part of the lord, if he wishes, it will not, however, be binding on the part of the tenant, since by denying his lord he breaks his homage and the bond of fealty; and in this case it is competent for the lord, because he is disavowed by the tenant in whose person the obligation has ceased, to demand in demesne his tenant's tenement which he ought to have held of him by this writ:

Bracton,
f. 81b

'Command so-and-so to render to so-and-so such-and-such an amount of land with appurtenances (or so many fees) which the aforesaid so-and-so held of him and for which he did him homage and service and which ought to be his escheat because the aforesaid so-and-so, the tenant, against his homage and the oath of fealty which he made to him therefor, has disavowed him wrongfully and to his disherison. And if he should not do so [etc.].'

Bracton,
f. 81

And thereupon, when this has been proved by inquisition and jury, there will be no necessity to enquire further into any descent of right. Moreover, if the lord wishes to claim [the tenement] by writ of right, it will nevertheless be incongruous to claim it by any descent since the tenant has been in possession by descent from his ancestors. But in whatsoever form he brings his action there will be no place for a grand assize [or battle, but a jury and inquisition similar to a grand assize will be taken], employing these words:

Bracton,
f. 81b

'whether he who holds has a greater right to hold the tenement (or fee) in demesne than he who demands it, to whom the said tenant (or someone of his ancestors) did homage and service therefor and whom subsequently, against his homage and fealty, he wrongfully disavowed.'

And if this is proved, the demandant will recover in demesne what the tenant held in demesne. If, however, he has claimed service he will recover that service. And henceforward there will not be a mesne between the tenant and the lord, and so homage is extinguished in the person of the mesne and revives in the person of the tenant further down.

Where there is the same reason, there the same right will be. If a tenant does grave harm to his lord or if in war he takes sides with his lord's enemies, by counsel or aid, against his lord (excepting the prince or his chief lord to whom he has done liege homage) or if he lays violent hands feloniously upon his lord

ad eius exheredacionem et quo casu iustum erit iudicium quod tenens ex-
heredetur propter obligacionem homagii quam confringit. Et plura hiis
similia tenentem exheredant.

    Poterit eciam tenens domino suo reddere homagium suum simul cum
5 tenemento propter capitales inimicicias vt liberius appellum suum versus eum
sequatur et sic dissoluitur homagium.   Homagium autem contra voluntatem   f. 81
hominis attornari non poterit eo quod sic posset dominus suum hominem capitali inimico subiugare per quod teneretur sacramentum facere fidelitatis ei qui
ipsum dampnare niteretur.   Et differt leuis inimicicia a capitali.   Leuis enim in-
10 imicicia non inpedit quin dominus homagium et seruicium sui tenentis attornare
possit inuito ipso tenente per finem factum in curia regis et quo casu summon-
endus est ille cuius homagium et seruicium conceditur vt ibi cognoscat
seruicium et homagium vel dedicat, que si cognoscat extunc attornabitur
donatario et nisi recedere velit a domino suo quantum ad homagium: quantum
15 tamen ad seruicium considerabitur quod donatario sacramentum faciat fidelitatis quod si nolit extunc liceat tali donatario distringere tenementa ad hoc obligata donec fidelitatem sibi fecerit, quantum tamen ad homagium a priori
domino suo inuitus non recedet set cum talis decesserit tunc statim euanescit
homagium in personis heredum defuncti qui alienauit et conualescit in persona
20 illius cui attornabatur.   Et eodem modo si quis terram dederit in maritagium
cum filia sua cum homagio et seruicio alicuius liberi hominis, item si pro
redempcione corporis sui, in quibus casibus attornabitur velit nolit nisi causas
pretenderit racionabiles quare non debeat attornari.   Et cum considerabitur
quod donatarius distringat donec fidelitatem gratis fecerit et districtus aueria   [210]
25 sua replegiari faciat et dicat quod iniuste ipsum distrinxit eo quod non est
dominus eius nec vnquam ei fecit homagium set alio tali a quo nondum recessit
et quod nichil clamat tenere de distringente non tamen propterea cesset districcio
set continuetur quia seruicium concedere sine districcione nichil aliud est quam
concedere haustum aque in fonte set non accessum ad fontem et in hoc casu
30 stare possunt simul deaduocacio et districcio ante homagium.   Causa vero
quare non poterit est vt si velit homagium attornare tali qui nichil habet in bonis
vnde possit warantizare vel escambium facere si necesse fuerit pro inconuenienti
nam si hoc esset licitum sic posset quilibet dominus ad warantiam centum
libratarum terre obligatus pro vno denariato seruicii per annum exonerare se
35 cum vellet ne suo tenenti ad warantiam teneretur vel escambium occasione
paruitatis seruicii, quod esset iniquum.

    Cum domino offeratur homagium a tenente ac ille capcionem iniuste deferat
vel recuset in fraudem forte ne ei teneretur ad warantiam tunc omne seruicium et
releuium licitum est tenenti retinere quia non erit dominus eius antequam ipsum
40 tanquam tenentem suum admiserit qui si seruicium per iudicium curie regis de-

or does anything to his disherison, in this case it will be rightfully adjudged that the tenant shall be disinherited because of the bond of homage he has broken. And there are many similar things that disinherit a tenant.

A tenant may also return his homage to his lord, together with the tenement, on account of deadly enmities so that he may prosecute his appeal against him the more freely, and in this way homage is dissolved.   Homage, however, cannot be attorned against the will of the man because in this way the lord could sub-jugate his man to his deadly enemy, and thereby the man would be bound to take an oath of fealty to him who sought to do him harm.   And a slight enmity differs from deadly enmity.   For, although the tenant is unwilling, slight enmity does not prevent a lord from attorning the homage and service of his tenant by a fine levied in the king's court, and in this case he whose homage and service are granted must be summoned so that he may there acknowledge or refuse service and homage.   If he acknowledges them, he will thereupon be attorned to the donee so far as homage is concerned and [provided] he wishes to depart from his lord.   But as regards service it will be adjudged that he shall take an oath of fealty to the donee, and if he will not, thereupon it will be lawful for such donee to distrain the tenements subject to the service until [the tenant] does fealty to him.   As regards homage, however, [the tenant] will not depart, against his will, from his former lord but, when that lord dies, then immediately the homage is extinguished in the persons of the heirs of the deceased who alienated but it revives in the person of him to whom he was attorned.   And in like manner, if a man should give land in marriage with his daughter, together with the homage and service of some free man, or if [he should give it] for the ransoming of his body : in these cases the tenant will be attorned, willy nilly, unless he can show reasonable cause why he ought not to be attorned.   And when it is adjudged that the donee may distrain until the tenant freely does fealty and the distrainee causes his beasts to be replevied and says that the donee distrained him unlaw-fully because the donee is not his lord and never did he do homage to him but to another from whom he has not yet departed, and that he does not claim to hold anything from the distrainor, the distress will not cease on that account but will continue, because to grant service without distress is nothing else than to grant the right of drawing water from a spring but not access to the spring.   And in this case disavowal and distress before homage can stand at the same time. There is indeed a case where, on account of the mischief [that would result], this could not be : for example, if [the lord] wishes to attorn homage to someone who has no property whereby he can warrant or make an exchange if need be.   For if this were allowed, then any lord, who was bound to warrant a hundred pounds' worth of land, could discharge himself when he pleased for one penny-worth of service a year from liability to warrant his tenant or provide an exchange because of the insignificance of the service.   And this would be unjust.

When homage is offered by a tenant to a lord and he unlawfully delays or perchance fraudulently refuses to take it lest he should be bound to warrant for him, then it is lawful for the tenant to keep back all service and relief because he will not be his lord until he has admitted him as his tenant.   And if the lord

Bracton,
f. 82

Bracton,
f. 82b

Bracton,
f. 82

Bracton,
f. 82b

beat recuperare considerabitur quod non faciat ei seruicium antequam eius
receperit homagium qui si tunc homagium ceperit arreragia omnium seruiciorum
non recuperabit. Poterit eciam tenens si voluerit oblato homagio coram
pluribus testibus fidedignis et precise recusato attornare se superiori domino
5 capitali et si ipse homagium recusauerit tunc alteri superiori et sic de domino in
dominum donec peruenerit ad regem qui nemini curiam claudit non magis quam
ecclesia. Et cum superior dominus homagium eius ceperit, ille qui homagium
recusauit vlterius seruicium nec homagium petere poterit et nichilominus
tenebitur ad warantiam acquietanciam et defensionem hoc tamen probato quod
10 homagium iniuste recusauit et illum sequetur seruicium cui factum est homagium.

    Verumtamen si tenens velit omni modo inmediato domino suo acapitare et
non alii tunc consulitur ei per breue quod dominus homagium capiat et nisi
fecerit quod veniat coram iusticiariis ostensurus quare non fecerit. Et cum
15 summonitus in curia venerit pretendat querens suas raciones quare summonitus
debet suum homagium capere. Dicere enim poterit quod pater eius tenuit de
tali et homagium ei fecit vel de tali alio antecessore summoniti et per tale
seruicium ita quod ille tali racione tenere debeat de eo et ipse homagium suum
capere tenetur. Ad quod respondere poterit summonitus defendendo verba
20 curialia homagium oblatum et seruicium et dicere precise quod ille querens nullam
terram de eo tenet nec tenere debet et hoc profert defendere per campionem vel
poterit se ponere in magnam assisam per hec verba: 'vtrum ille de quo queritur   f. 81b
maius ius habeat tenendi terram illam in dominico an idem qui queritur tenendi
de eo'. Poterit enim esse quod querens vel antecessores querentis homagium
25 fecerunt antecessoribus eius de quo queritur nunquam tamen seysinam in vita
antecessorum fuerunt consecuti vel quod ipse homagium tale cepit et talis propria auctoritate et sine waranto et contra voluntatem donatoris se posuit in   [211]
seysinam et sic poterit petere terram in dominico.

    Si autem tenens per districcionem homagium fecerit alicui non domino et
30 verus dominus postea petat homagium eiusdem tenentis non poterit tenens ab
eo cui fecit homagium recedere sine iudicio et quo casu consulitur vero domino
per breue de consuetudinibus et seruiciis ad quod oportebit tenentem respondere
quod libenter faceret ei homagium et seruicia recta si a tali cui per districcionem
fecit homagium possit inpune recedere vel dicere quod nichil tenet nec tenere
35 clamat de petente set de alio tali cui fecit homagium. Et quibus casibus
rex venire faciet talem qui homagium cepit vt inter eos procedat veritatis discussio vt homagium per iudicium remaneat cum quo remanere debet et tunc
puniendi sunt per misericordiam regis tam ille qui homagium iniuste cepit vel
peciit quam tenens. Et si petens recuperauerit dampna consequentur ne

    2. omnium, Br., enim, J.   10. iniuste] iuste, J.   26. tale] talis, J.   39. consequentur]
consequetur, J.

should recover the service by judgement of the king's court, it will be adjudged
that the tenant shall not do him service until he receives his homage, and if then
he takes the homage, he will not recover the arrears of all the services. Having
offered homage before several trustworthy witnesses and homage having been
categorically refused, the tenant may also, if he wishes, attorn himself to the
superior chief lord; and if he too should refuse his homage, then to the next
superior lord, and so from lord to lord until he comes to the king, who shuts his
court to no one, any more than does the church. And when the superior lord
takes the tenant's homage, he who refused the homage can no longer claim either
homage or service, yet nevertheless he will be bound to warrant, acquit and
defend [the tenant], provided that it is proved that he unlawfully refused the
homage; and the service is attached to him to whom the homage has been done.

Bracton
f. 83b

Yet if the tenant wishes in every way to acknowledge his subjection to his
immediate lord and to none other, then he has a remedy by a writ [commanding]
the lord to accept his homage and, if he does not do so, to come before the justices
to show why he has not done so. And when the defendant comes into court, the
plaintiff may put forward his arguments why the defendant should accept his
homage. For he can say that his father held of so-and-so and did him homage,
or of some other ancestor of the defendant, and by such-and-such service, so
that for such reason he ought to hold of him and he is bound to accept his homage. To which the defendant can answer by denying the words of court and the
offer of homage and service and say categorically that the plaintiff holds and
ought to hold no land of him and offer to deny this by a champion, or he may put
himself on the grand assize, employing these words, 'whether he of whom complaint is made has greater right to hold that land in demesne than the plaintiff
has to hold it of him'. It may indeed be that the plaintiff or ancestors of the
plaintiff did homage to the ancestors of him against whom the complaint is made
but had never secured seisin in the lifetime of those ancestors. Or that [the
donor] accepted such homage but that [the donee], of his own authority and
without warrant and against the will of the donor, put himself in seisin, and so
the defendant may claim the land in demesne.

Bracton,
f. 82b

Bracton,
f. 83

If, however, a tenant should do homage to someone who is not the lord because he is distrained and the true lord should afterwards claim the homage of
the said tenant, the tenant cannot without a judgement of the court withdraw
from him to whom he has done homage, and in this case a remedy is available
to the true lord by a writ of customs and services. To this the tenant must either
answer that he would willingly render homage and right services to the true lord
if he could withdraw with impunity from him to whom, by reason of distraint,
he has done homage, or else say that he holds nothing and does not claim to hold
anything of the demandant but of the other man instead to whom he has done
homage. In these cases the king will cause him to appear who has accepted
homage in order that a discussion of the truth may proceed between them and
that homage may remain by judgement of the court with him with whom it
should remain. And then both he who received or demanded homage wrongfully as well as the tenant will be punished by amercement of the king. And if

maleficia inpunita remaneant et sic euanescit homagium non domino factum et
ad pristinum statum reuertetur. Et cum tenens verum dominum suum deaduocauerit in iudicio et ei nullo modo velit adherere tunc primo vertetur placitum
inter ipsos tantum. Et si dominus agat per breue de consuetudinibus et
5 seruiciis tunc refert vtrum super ipso iure agat vel super seysina homagii et
seruicii hoc est vtrum contineatur in breui: 'quod faciat ei consuetudines et recta
seruicia que ei facere debet et solet' vel tantum 'que facere solet'. Si autem super
ipso iure siue dominus petat quod tenens faciat siue tenens petat quod dominus
capiat per breue de homagio capiendo in vtroque casu per interrogaciones et
10 responsiones perueniri poterit ad duellum vel ad magnam assisam secus erit si
dominus terram petat in dominico pro deaduocacione. Si autem euitare voluerit duellum et magnam assisam tunc omisso hoc verbo 'debet' et petat consuetudines et recta seruicia que ei facere solet tantum et sic loquetur breue
tantum de seysina et non de ipso recto per omissionem alterius verbi. Et cum
15 seysinam suam verificauerit considerabitur quod extunc recuperanti attornetur
et licitum erit tali distringere pro arreragiis et seruiciis donec conpetenter
fuerit inde sibi satisfactum quamuis ipsum deaduocauerit pro domino suo pro
homagio alteri facto quod sine morte vel iudicio extingui non potest in persona
captoris. Verumtamen succurritur domino deaduocato per assisam noue dis-
20 seisine cum per deaduocacionem incipiat esse non tenens eo quod breue de consuetudinibus et seruiciis nichil prodest omnino deaduocato. Si autem petens
seruicia per manum tenentis fuerit seysitus et de tali recenti seysina pecierit aut
tenens confitebitur aut nichil respondet aut omnino negabit. Si autem con-
fiteatur planum est iudicium si nichil respondeat indefensus remanebit et si
25 precise negauerit per patriam debet veritas declarari.

CAP. XVII. DE RELEUIIS

Capitis igitur homagiis et fidelitatibus ab illis qui plene fuerint etatis statim
oportet quod tenementum quod fuit in manus antecessorum et hereditas que
iacens fuerit per eorum decessum releuetur in manus heredis et propter talem
30 releuacionem facienda erit ab herede quedam prestacio que dicitur releuium. [212]
Racionabile autem releuium est secundum constitucionem magne carte de
libertatibus vt de comitatu integro centum libre sterlingorum, per heredes vero

24. planum, Br., plenum, J.

the demandant should recover, damages will follow [the judgement], lest wrong-doings should remain unpunished. And so homage done to him who is not the lord will be extinguished and there will be a reversion to the former position. And if a tenant should disavow his true lord in judicial proceedings and wishes in no wise to cleave to him, then in the first place an action will proceed between these two only. And if the lord proceeds by writ of customs and services, then it is a matter of importance whether he bases his action on the right itself or upon seisin of the homage and service, that is whether the writ will read 'that [the tenant] shall render him the customs and right services which he ought and is wont to do him' or only 'which he is wont to do'. If the action is based upon the right itself, whether the lord claims that the tenant shall do [homage] or the tenant claims that the lord shall accept [homage] by a writ for the taking of homage, in each case by means of questions and answers the matter may

Bracton,
f. 83*b*

eventuate in battle or the grand assize. It will be otherwise if the lord, on account of the disavowal, demands the land in demesne. If, however, he wishes to avoid battle and the grand assize, then he omits the word 'ought' (*debet*) and only claims the customs and right services which he is 'wont' (*solet*) to do him, and so by the omission of the other word the writ speaks only of seisin and not of the right itself. And when he has established his seisin, it will be adjudged that straightway attornment shall be made to him who recovers it, and it will be law-ful for him to distrain for arrears and services until full satisfaction has been made to him therefor, although the tenant disavowed him as his lord in order to do homage to another; and this homage cannot be extinguished in the person of

Bracton
.84

the receiver except by death or judgement of the court. If by reason of the disavowal the tenant begins to be no longer tenant, nevertheless the disavowed lord is aided by an assize of novel disseisin, because a writ of customs and services is no use to one who is entirely disavowed. If, however, the demandant has been seised of the services by the hand of the tenant and should base his claim on this recent seisin, either the tenant will admit the claim or answer nothing or deny the claim entirely. If, however, he admits the claim, judgement is clear; if he answers nothing, he will stand without defence; and if he should deny the claim categorically, the truth should be declared by a jury.

CHAPTER 17.　OF RELIEFS

Bracton,
f. 84

Moreover, when homages and fealties have been taken from those who are of full age, the tenement which was in the hands of their ancestors and the inheritance which lies vacant through their decease must needs be raised again at once into the hands of the heir, and because of this raising again (*rele-vatio*) a certain payment must be made by the heir, which is called relief (*rele-vium*). A reasonable relief, according to the enactment of the Great Charter of

Magna Carta
c. 2

Liberties, is for a whole earldom a hundred pounds sterling; by the heirs of barons

baronum de baronia integra dari debent centum marce, de herede militis de
feodo militari integro centum solidi sunt petendi, et qui minus tenuerit minus det
secundum porcionem tenementi sui.   Et omnes illi hereditates suas releuare
tenentur qui alicui succedunt hereditarie et in quorum personis releuantur
5 hereditates que iacentes fuerint per mortem antecessorum nisi minores fuerint
heredes propter quorum minorem etatem in custodiis fuerint dominorum
quamuis per modicum tempus.   Et releuium dare non debent nisi semel quamuis   f. 82
plures decesserint domini successiue quia vnicum erit releuium quantum ad tenentem quamdiu idem tenens vixerit.   Nec ante homagium captum debet dari
10 releuium nec ante hereditatem suam plenarie sibi restitutam cum cartis ad ipsam
spectantibus si quas habuerit.   Et sicut non tenetur quis duo facere homagia
duobus dominis ambo viuentibus de vno tenemento sic nec duo releuia.   De
pluribus tamen heredibus successiue succedentibus plura capi poterunt homagia.
Nullus autem qui tenementum adquisierit aliquo genere adquisicionis, nullus
15 eciam cui dominus mutatur, nullus eciam qui ad vitam tenuerit tantum quoquo
modo, nullus eciam qui aliquam duxerit in vxorem que aliquamdiu in
custodia domini sui extiterit, nullus eciam a quo dominus receperit racione
custodie ad valenciam vnius denarii, nullus eciam qui semel releuauerit terram
suam isti autem a releuio sint absoluti.   Nulli autem dandum est releuium dum
20 fuerit infra etatem et in custodia domini sui nec antequam sue hereditatis habeat
possessionem.   De sokagio autem fiat secundum quod de feodo militari in iuris
ordine non tamen in releuii quantitate eo quod dominus feodi homagium petere
non poterit eo quod tales per seruicia regalia non feoffantur.   Nec aliquid
petere poterunt nomine releuii nisi solummodo tantum quantum reddit ei per
25 vnum annum in redditu assiso nec propterea sit tenens quietus de redditu suo
sibi prestando in terminis in donacione conprehensis et sic habebit dominus in
vno anno pro releuio et pro redditu redditum vnius anni dupplicatum.   Omnes
tamen hoc petere non poterunt antequam heres sibi facere valeat fidelitatis
sacramentum.   De tenementis autem que ad feodi firmam tenentur reddendo
30 inde minus per annum quam valorem quarte partis obseruetur idem processus
set si amplius dederint ab omni releuio sint quieti.

CAP. XVIII.   DE HERIETTIS

Est autem quedam alia prestacio que dicitur heriettum vbi tenens liber vel
seruus in morte sua dominum suum respicit de meliori auerio suo vel de secundo
35 meliori que quidem prestacio magis fit de gracia quam de iure et nullam habet
comparacionem ad releuium eo quod heredem non contingit quia factum est
antecessoris.

8. successiue] successione, J.

a hundred marks should be given for a whole barony; from the heir of a knight a hundred shillings should be demanded for a whole knight's fee; and he who holds less should give less according to the size of his tenement.   And all those are bound to give a relief for their inheritances who succeed anyone hereditarily, and in their persons the inheritances are relieved which fall vacant through the death of their ancestors, unless the heirs should be minors who, on account of their minority, are in the wardship of lords, although it may be for only a little while.   And heirs should not give relief except once only, even though several lords die successively, because, so far as the tenant is concerned, there will be a single relief so long as he shall live.   Nor should relief be given before homage is taken nor before his inheritance is fully restored [to the heir] with the charters relating to it, if he has any.   And just as no one is required to do two homages for one and the same tenement to two lords who are both alive, so no one is required to give two reliefs.   From several heirs, however, who succeed each other in turn, several homages may be taken.   Anyone, however, who shall acquire a tenement by any form of acquisition, anyone also whose lord is changed, anyone also who holds only for life in any way, anyone also who marries a woman who for some time has been in her lord's wardship, anyone also from whom the lord receives so much as a penny by reason of his wardship, anyone also who has once given a relief for his land: all these shall be absolved from a relief.   To no one, moreover, must a relief be given while he is under age and in the wardship of his lord or before he has possession of his inheritance.   In regard to socage, the legal position accords with that for a knight's fee, but not as regards the amount of the relief, because the lord of the fee cannot demand homage since socagers are not enfeoffed by services to the king.   Nor can lords demand anything by way of relief save only as much as the tenant renders to the lord for one year in fixed rent, nor shall the tenant on this account be quit from paying him his rent at the terms included in the grant.   And so the lord will have in one year, for relief and for rent, double the rent for one year.   Every lord, however, is not able to demand this before the heir is in a position to take an oath of fealty to him.   For tenements, which are held at fee farm rendering therefor less than the fourth part of the yearly value, the same course should be followed; but if [the tenants] give more than this, they will be quit of all relief.

CHAPTER 18. OF HERIOTS

There is, moreover, a certain other payment which is called a heriot, whereby a tenant, free or bond, on his death remembers his lord with his best beast or his second best; but indeed, this payment is made rather by way of grace than of right, and it bears no comparison with a relief because, since it is the deed of the ancestor, it does not concern the heir.

Bracton,
f. 84b

Bracton,
f. 85

Bracton,
f. 85b

Bracton,
f. 86

Bracton,
f. 86

LIBER QUARTUS

CAP. I. DE RERUM ACCIONIBUS

Quia a iusticia tanquam a fonte emanant iura nostra ideo de iusticia et de f. 82
iure primo dicamus.   Est autem iusticia constans et perpetua voluntas ius suum
vnicuique tribuens vel hoc saltem affectans.   Ius enim a iusticia deriuatur et cum
5 multiplex sit est tamen ius possessionis et ius proprietatis.   Ius vero possessionis per se descendere potest vt cum ius proprietatis descendat ad antenatum
tanquam propinquiorem ac postnatus se ponat in seysinam et moriatur seysitus
transmittit ad suos heredes quoddam ius proprietatis cum iure possessionis quod
sequi debuit primam proprietatem et sic de herede in heredem, set primi heredes
10 maius ius habent.   Semper tamen prefertur possessio secundis heredibus donec
primi ius suum euicerint.   Et cum accio super proprietate summum sit remedium
et vltimum de accionibus possessoris intentemus.

Agentibus enim in iure possessorio plura ordinantur breuia remediorum.
Quatuor autem sunt breuia assisarum sicut assisa noue disseysine cum suis mem-
15 bris que sunt breuia de intrusione, quare eiecit, de redisseysinis et huiusmodi,
preterea assisa vltime presentacionis cum suis membris que sunt breuia quare
inpedit et quare incombrauit, item assisa mortis antecessoris cum suis membris
que sunt de consanguinitate, de auo, nuper obiit et quod permittat et eciam assisa
de vtrum cum conuiccionibus.   Est autem assisa in iure possessorio quedam
20 recognicio xij. hominum iuratorum per quam iusticiarii cerciorantur de articulis
in breui contentis tam in absencia tenentis quam eius presencia quibus infligitur
pena conuiccionis si in modum assise periurium committant.

Fit autem disseysina multis modis et non refert an domino fiat ipso presente f. 82*b*
vel procuratori vel familie sue ipso absente et non solum disseysitur quis cum a
25 seysina sua violenter iniuste et sine iudicio de tenemento suo qualitercumque
eiectus fuerit verum eciam cum ad nundinas vel peregre profectus fuerit vel alias
se diuerterit nemine in possessione relicto alius possessionem ingreditur et ipsum
reuersum non admittit vel cum ingredi voluerit per se vel assumptis viribus

BOOK IV

CHAPTER 1. OF REAL ACTIONS

Bracton,
f. 2b

Because our rights arise from justice as from a spring, therefore we will first speak of justice and of right.   Justice then is a constant and perpetual intention to award to everyone his right or at least to strive to do this.   For right (*jus*) is

Bracton,
f. 3

derived from justice (*justitia*) and, since it is manifold, there is a right of possession and a right of ownership.   The right of possession may, indeed, descend by itself, as, for example, where the right of ownership descends to the first-born as the nearest heir and a younger [brother] puts himself in seisin and dies seised, he transmits to his heirs, along with the right of possession, a certain right of ownership which ought to have attended the first ownership, and so from heir to heir, but the heirs of the first-born have the greater right.   Yet possession by the heirs of the second-born is always given preference until the heirs of the first-born have established their right.   And since an action upon ownership is the highest and final remedy, we will turn to possessory actions.

For those who sue for the right of possession there are ordained several remedial writs.   There are thus four writs of assizes: namely, the assize of novel disseisin with its members, which are the writs of intrusion, *quare ejecit*, redisseisin and the like; next the assize of darrein presentment with its members, which are the writs of *quare impedit* and *quare incumbravit*; then the assize of mort d'ancestor with its members, which are cosinage, aeil, *nuper obiit* and *quod permittat*, and, further, the assize *utrum*.   And there are corresponding attaints. An assize in possessory right is a certain recognition by twelve sworn men by which the justices are certified upon the particulars contained in the writ, whether in the absence of the tenant or in his presence, and upon these jurors there is inflicted the penalty of attaint if they commit perjury when sitting as an assize jury.

Bracton,
f. 161b

Disseisin is done in many ways, and it does not matter whether it is done to the owner when he is present or to an agent or to his household when he is absent. And not only is a man disseised when he is in any way ejected forcibly, wrongfully and without judgement from his seisin of his tenement, but also when he sets off to a fair or on a pilgrimage or travels elsewhere, leaving no one in possession, and someone else enters into possession and does not admit him when he returns or, when he wishes to enter, repels him forcibly, either by him-

violenter repellat vel eciam si ipsum vel eius procuratorem vel familiam in
possessione existentem vti omnino non permittat vel saltem iniuste inpediat
quominus comode vti possit.   Item fit disseysina cum quis prepotens vti voluerit
in alterius tenemento contra ipsius domini voluntatem vel contendendo tene-
5   mentum esse suum cum sit alienum vel pecora inmittendo vel alio quocumque   [214]
modo seruitutem libero fundo inponendo cum auferat libertatem quominus possessor libere teneat.   Item eciam fit disseysina cum quis non nisi nudam habens
possessionem alteri feodum fecerit vel liberum tenementum, et si custos hoc fecerit vel firmarius et statim per verum dominum vel eius nomine eiciatur dona-
10   tarius neuter recuperabit.   Et fiunt quandoque disseysine per iusticiarios et
quamuis cum iudicio iniuste tamen quia sine waranto per breue originale de
quo rex fuerit testis ac eciam per escaetores et vicecomites et alios ministros regis
quibus inhibitum est ne per colorem officiorum suorum sine waranto aut
speciali precepto aut certa auctoritate officio suo appendente aliquem de libero
15   tenemento suo eicere vel aliquo modo disseysire presumant et si fecerint prouisum est quod in eleccione disseysitorum sit quod sibi perquirant per assisam
noue disseysine vel per peticiones regi factas debitum apponatur remedium et
in vtraque via de iniuria conuincantur dampna reddentur dupplicata et in
misericordia regis remanebunt.   Fit eciam disseysina cum quis vltra mandatum
20   regis admissum vel ostensum quod liberet vel quod ne diucius teneat tenementum iniuste detinuerit vel reddere noluerit.   Fiunt eciam disseysine in
districcionibus vt si quis distringat pro seruicio cum nullum ei debeatur vel cum
ei solutum fuerit vel cum modum districcionis excedat.   Item disseysitur quis
cum a distringendo iniuste inpediatur vt si tenens feodum domini sui muro fossato
25   haya vel huiusmodi sic incluserit quominus dominus liberum aditum habere possit ad distringendum in feodo suo vel cum tenens debitam vetuerit districcionem
vel iniuste replegiauerit vel cum waynagium alicuius liberi per crebras et indebitas inpediatur districciones.   Fit eciam disseysina cum quis optinuerit possessionem a qua fuerit ipso presente vel in casu absente abiudicatus vel cum quis
30   alienum ingrediatur tenementum per iudicium quod non ligat vel cum quis
firmarius vel custos liberum tenementum clamauerit habere cum non habeat in
exheredacionem proprietarii.   Fit eciam disseysina firmario in casu vt cum
tenentes in dotem vel aliter ad terminum vite alicui dimiserint statum quem
habuerint et ipsi inde fuerint eiecti viuentibus dimissoribus.   Item fit eis dis-
35   seysina cum a tenemento expelluntur qui tenuerint per feodum talliatum vel per
legem Anglie vel donec prouideantur vel per iudicium curie regis donec tanta
pecunia inde fuerit leuata.

Hec quidem assisa non solum locum habet in rebus corporalibus sicut in
tenementis pratis boscis pasturis vastis piscariis turbariis gurgitibus estoueriis
40   nucibus glandis et aliis fructubus colligendis deliberacionibus et aliis que in sey-

3. comode] comodo, J.   18. dupplicata] dupplicatur, J.   19. *post* disseysina *add* q, J.
28. *post* quis *add* alienum ingrediatur tenementum per iudicium quod non ligat, J., *quae
verba punctis delevit.*   35. tenemento] tenente, J; tenuerint] tenuerit, J.

self alone or taking his men with him; or again, when he or his agent or his household is in possession [of the tenement], someone does not permit them to use it at
all or at least wrongfully hinders them from being able to use it with ease.
Disseisin is also done when someone more powerful wishes to have user in
another's tenement against the wish of its owner, or makes a claim that the
tenement is his when it belongs to another, or turns in cattle, or imposes a servitude in any way whatever on a free estate, since he takes away its freedom so
that the possessor holds less freely.   Again, disseisin is also done when someone
who has nothing but bare possession creates a fee or a freehold for someone else;
and if a guardian or fermor should do this and the donee is straightway ejected
by the true owner or in his name, neither of them will recover.   And disseisins
are sometimes done by justices (and although with a judgement of the court,

St. West-
minster,
I. c. 24

nevertheless done unlawfully because there is no warrant by an original writ
witnessed by the king), and also by escheators and sheriffs and other royal
ministers who are forbidden to eject any one from his freehold or to presume in
any way to disseise him by colour of their office unless they have a warrant or
special instructions or definite authority belonging to their office.   And if they
should do so, it is provided that it shall be in the election of the disseisees either
to look after their interests by an assize of novel disseisin or to make petitions to
the king for appropriate redress to be provided.   And those convicted of wrongdoing in either of these ways shall pay double damages and remain subject to
amercement by the king.   A disseisin is also done when someone, who has
received or been shown the king's mandate that 'he hand over' or 'no longer
retain' a tenement, in defiance unlawfully detains or refuses to surrender it.

Bracton,
f. 162

Disseisins are also done through distraints: for example, if anyone distrains for
service when none is due to him or when it has been rendered to him or when he

Bracton,
f, 221b

goes beyond the mode of distraint.   Again, a man is disseised when he is unlawfully hindered from distraining: for example, if a tenant encloses his lord's fee
with a wall, dyke, hedge or the like so that the lord cannot have free access to
distrain in his fee, or where the tenant should forbid just distraint or unlawfully
replevies it, or where by frequent and unjust distraints any free man is hindered
from cultivating his land.   Disseisin is also done if a man should keep possession
from which he has been ousted by judgement of the court in his presence or
perchance absence; or if he should enter another's tenement by a judgement that
is not binding; or if some fermor or guardian should claim to have a freehold
which he does not have, in disherison of its owner.   Disseisin is also done to a
fermor on occasion where, for example, tenants in dower or otherwise for life
demise to another the estate they have and the fermors are ejected therefrom in
the lifetime of the lessors.   Again, a disseisin is committed when those are
ousted from a tenement who hold by fee tail or by the curtesy of England or until
other provision is made for them or by judgement of the king's court until
a certain sum of money has been levied therefrom.

   This assize not only holds good in respect of corporeal things such as
tenements, meadows, woods, pastures, wastes, fisheries, turbaries, sluices, estovers, gathering nuts, acorns and other produce, liveries [of food] and other things

sina alicuius sunt aliquo iusto titulo in feodo vel ad terminum vite possessoris vel
dimittentis in casu, verum eciam in rebus incorporalibus sicut in seruitutibus et
iuribus et pertinenciis pertinenciarum que pertinent ad tenementa, et ad hoc facit
hoc statutum:

5   Quia non est aliquod breue in cancellaria per quod querentes habent tam
festinum remedium sicut per breue noue disseysine, rex voluntatem habens   [*215*]
quod conquerentibus iniuriatis celeris fiat iusticia et quod dilaciones in placitis   f. 83
amputentur et abbreuientur prouidit et ordinauit quod assisa noue disseysine
locum habeat in pluribus casibus quam prius habuit et concessit quod de
10 estoueriis bosci et proficuo capiendo in bosco de nucibus et glande et aliis
fructubus colligendis ac eciam de corrodio et liberacione bladi aut aliorum
victualium aut necessariorum in certo loco annuatim recipiendorum necnon de
tolneto tronagio pontagio passagio et hiis similibus in certis locis capiendis ac
eciam in custodiis parcorum boscorum forestarum chaciarum warennarum por-
15 tarum et aliis balliuis et officiis in feodo de cetero iaceat assisa noue disseysine.
Et in omnibus supradictis modo consueto fiat breue de libero tenemento. Et
sicut breue prius iacuit et locum habuit in communa pasture ita de cetero locum
habeat in communa turbarie, piscarie et aliis communis hiis similibus quas quis
habet pertinentes ad liberum tenementum suum vel eciam sine tenemento per
20 speciale factum ad minus ad terminum vite. In casu eciam quando quis tenet
tenementum ad terminum annorum vel in custodia et illud alienat in feodo et
per illam alienacionem transfert liberum tenementum in feoffatum fiat remedium
per breue noue disseysine et habeantur pro disseysitoribus tam ille qui feoffat
quam feoffatus ita quod viuente altero eorum locum habeat predictum breue et
25 si per mortem personarum cesset remedium per predictum breue fiat remedium
per breue de ingressu. Item de domo muro mercato ad nocumentum leuato et
huiusmodi habeant querentes remedia per eandem assisam. Et si alienacio fiat
de vno ad alium tunc ambo nominentur sicut tenens et disseysitor.

Fit eciam disseysina de fossato muro vel stagno iniuste leuato vel prostrato
30 vel exaltato sepe leuata vel prostrata via obstructa vel artata et de cursu aque
diuerso vel ad nocumentum artato.

Sunt tamen quedam ad nocumentum leuata de quibus non dabitur assisa set
ad vicecomitem in comitatibus pertinent placitanda veluti de virgulto porta ouili
molendino ventricio gurgite furno bercaria vaccaria wayeria augmentacione
35 curie et curtilagii. Item fit disseysina cum quis depascerit alterius separale vel
cum quis piscatus fuerit in alterius piscaria et in consimilibus. Nam si quis
terram possideat prope ripam ex vtraque parte aque per totum licebit piscari sicut
in libero tenemento suo quod si sine inpedimento alicuius facere non possit succurritur ei per assisam, et si ex vna parte tantum tunc vsque ad filum in medio
40 aque erit piscaria suum liberum tenementum et quicquid inde pro dote fuerit
assignatum liberum tenementum erit mulieris.

6. habens *in statuto*, habet, J.   7. celeris] sceleris, J.   13. in *addidimus*.   15. *post* officiis
add. d, J.   18. *ante* hiis *add.* et, J; quis *om.* J.   22. feoffatum] feoffamentum, J.
25. *prius* per *in statuto*; post, J.   28. vno ad alium, *in statuto*, manu ad manum, J; dis-
seysitor] disseytor, J.   38. si sine] seysine, J.

which are in someone's seisin by any rightful title, in fee or for the life of the possessor or, on occasion, of the lessor, but also in respect of incorporeal things, such as servitudes and rights and appurtenances of appurtenances which pertain to tenements.   And this statute provides accordingly:

St. West-
minster,
II. c. 25
Because there is in the chancery no writ whereby plaintiffs have so speedy a remedy as they have by a writ of novel disseisin, the king, wishing that speedy justice should be done to complainants who have been wronged and that delays in hearing pleas should be cut and shortened, has provided and ordained that the assize of novel disseisin shall hold good in more cases than it did before, and he has granted that an assize of novel disseisin shall in future lie in respect of estovers of wood and the profit taken in a wood by gathering nuts and acorns and other produce as well as in respect of a corrody and a livery of corn or other victuals or necessaries to be received annually at a specified place, and also in respect of toll, tronage, pontage, passage and such like to be taken in specified places, and also in respect of the custody of parks, woods, forests, chaces, warrens, gates, and other bailiwicks and offices in fee.   And in all the abovesaid cases a writ of free-hold (*de libero tenemento*) shall be made in the accustomed manner.   And just as a writ formerly lay and held good in respect of common of pasture, so henceforward it shall hold good in respect of common of turbary, fishery and other suchlike rights of common which anyone has appurtenant to his freehold or else, even without a freehold, by special deed for at least the term of his life.   Also in the case where anyone holds a tenement for a term of years or in wardship and alienates it in fee and by this alienation conveys a freehold to the feoffee, a remedy shall be provided by a writ of novel disseisin, and both the feoffor and the feoffee are to be regarded as disseisors so that during the lifetime of either of them the aforesaid writ shall hold good, and if upon the death of these persons redress by the aforesaid writ ceases, redress is to be made by a writ
St. West-
minster,
II. c. 24
of entry.   Again, with respect to a house, a wall, a market set up so as to cause nuisance, and the like plaintiffs shall have redress by the same assize.   And if an alienation is made from one to another, then both parties shall be named as tenant and disseisor.

Bracton,
f. 221 *b*
Disseisin is also done by unlawfully setting up or knocking down or raising a dyke, wall or pool or erecting or cutting down a hedge or obstructing or narrowing a path or diverting a watercourse or causing a nuisance by narrowing it.

St. West-
minster,
II. 46
There are, however, some things done that cause a nuisance for which an assize will not be given, for cognizance belongs to the sheriff and they are to be pleaded in the county court, such as arise from an orchard, gate, sheepfold, windmill, sluice, bakehouse, sheepcote, cowhouse, horsepond, encroachment of court and curtilage.   Further, disseisin is done if anyone should depasture the severalty
Bracton,
f. 208*b*
of another or fish in another's fishery and the like.   For if a man should possess land adjoining the bank on both sides of a river, he will be allowed to fish the whole of the stretch as his freehold, and if he is not able to do so without hindrance from someone else, he is helped by an assize.   And if he possesses land on one side only, then the fishery will be his freehold up to a line in mid-stream. And whatsoever shall be assigned therein for dower will be the woman's freehold.

CAP. II. DE REMEDIO SPOLIACIONIS

Si vero aliquo predictorum modorum facta fuerit disseysina primum et principale competit remedium quod ille qui ita disseysitus est per se si possit vel sumptis viribus vel resumptis dum tamen sine aliquo interuallo flagrante dissey-
5 sina et maleficio reiciat spoliantem.   Incontinenti autem vim vi repellere licitum est vel quamcito sciri possit vim esse illatam priusquam ille cui illata fuerit ad [216] actum contrarium diuertat.   Vel si cum fuerit in possessione alius cum eo vti voluerit ipse nichilominus vtatur nisi omnino iniuste vtentem tenere possit ab vtendo exclusum vt per vsum suum iuste suam retineat seysinam et quo casu
10 tenens iniuste in alieno nichil sibi per vsum iniustum adquirit quem si nullo modo expellere possit ad superioris auxilium erit recurrendum et illa via electa et facta inpetracione ad reieccionem redire non poterit nec seysinam suam propria auctoritate resumere in preiudicium superioris ad quem deuoluta est cognicio. Si autem verus possessor absens fuerit ex quacumque causa, tunc locorum dis-
15 tanciam distinguere oportebit secundum quod fuerit prope vel longe quo tempore videlicet scire potuit disseysinam esse factam vt sic allocatis ei racionabilibus dilacionibus primo die cum venerit statim suum reiciat disseysitorem qui si primo die reicere non possit in crastino vel die tercio vel vlterius dum tamen sine fic- ticia hoc facere poterit vires sibi resumendo arma colligendo auxiliumque f. 83b
20 amicorum conuocando quod satis erit incontinenti cum non currat tempus nisi a tempore sciencie ex quo post scienciam comode venire possit quod si per longum tempus hoc expectauerit videbitur per hoc iniuriam dissimulasse et per hoc illam penitus aboleri.   Si autem extra regnum fuerit in peregrinacione sim- plici sicut apud sanctum Iacobum vel in Vasconia in seruicio regis tunc xl.
25 dierum dilacionem habebit duorumque fluminum et vnius ebbe quia de vltra mare et similiter spacium xv. dierum postquam venerit in regnum et eciam quatuor dierum vt vires sibi resumat si necesse fuerit, et si extra regnum fuerit in simplici peregrinacione in terra sancta tunc dabitur dilacio vnius anni xv. dierum et qua- tuor dierum.   Si autem in generali passagio ad terram Ierosolymitanam inpune
30 poterit quemquam seysitum eicere quandocumque redierit dum tamen negligencia sua vel dissimulacio ipsum non inpediat.   Et si aliquis infra tempus illud a disseysitore feoffatus fuerit si verus dominus reuersus eum incontinenti eiciat eiectus non recuperabit quia tempus tale quamuis longum preiudiciale non erit absenti.   Taliter igitur prouideant sibi qui disseysitores reicere velint quod statim
35 flagrante maleficio expellantur ita quod iniuriam disseysine per pacienciam

5. vi] si, J.   6. esse] esset, J.   10. adquirit, Br., *om.* J.   17. statim] statum, J.
18. reicere, Br., *om.* J; vlterius] alterius, J.   26. spacium, Br., *om.* J.   35. maleficio] malificio, J.

CHAPTER 2.   OF THE REMEDY FOR DISPOSSESSION

Bracton,
f. 162b

If disseisin is done in any of the aforesaid ways, the first and principal remedy available to him who is thus disseised, is for him, by himself if he is able or by employing more and more assistance, to eject his dispossessor in turn, provided no interval of time has elapsed and the disseisin and wrongdoing are fresh.   For

Bracton,
f. 163

it is lawful to repel force by force immediately or as soon as it can be known that force has been employed and before he, against whom force is employed, takes any inconsistent action.   Or again, if one man is in possession and another wishes to have user with him, if the former cannot keep the altogether unlawful user excluded from user, he nevertheless should himself so use that by his lawful user he may retain his seisin, in which case he who unlawfully occupies another's property acquires nothing for himself by his unlawful user.   And if he can in no way expel [the intruder], he must have recourse to the aid of a superior and, having chosen this course and having sued out a writ, he will not be able to go back to ejection or of his own authority regain his seisin to the prejudice of the superior upon whom cognisance of the matter has devolved.   If, however, the true possessor should be absent for some reason or other, then it will be necessary to make a distinction according to the distances of places, whether he was near at hand or far away, that is to say, at what time he could have learned that disseisin had been done, and thus, after reasonable delays have been allowed him, he may on the first day of his arrival straightway eject his disseisor.   And if he is not able to eject him on the first day, then on the next day or the third day or later, provided that, without subterfuge, he can do so by gathering his forces, collecting arms and summoning the help of his friends, and that will be quick enough since time will run only from the time when he knew about the disseisin and after that from the time at which he can conveniently arrive.   But if he waits for a long time, he will seem thereby to have been indifferent to the wrong and in consequence entirely to extinguish it.   If, however, he is outside the realm on a simple pilgrimage to Saint James [of Compostella], for example, or in the king's service in Gascony, then he will have a delay of forty days and two flood-tides and one ebb-tide because he is overseas, and likewise a period of fifteen days after his arrival in the kingdom, and also four days to gather his

Bracton,
f. 163b

forces if it should be necessary.   And if he is out of the kingdom on a simple pilgrimage to the Holy Land, then a delay of a year, fifteen days and four days will be granted.   But if he [takes part] in a general passage to the land of Jerusalem, whenever he returns he may with impunity eject whoever is seised, provided that his own negligence or indifference does not bar him.   And if anyone is enfeoffed by the disseisor within that time and the true owner on his return ejects him without delay, the ejected will have no recovery because, however long such time may be, it will not prejudice the absent man.   Those, therefore, who intend to eject disseisors should make such provision for expelling them immediately while the wrongdoing is fresh so that they do not allow the

dissimulacionem negligenciam inpotenciam desperacionem vel negligentem
inpetracionem non tepescant per quod vtramque possessionem naturalem videlicet et ciuilem amittant et disseysitor vtramque habere incipiat ita quod sine
iudicio licite eici non possit.   Et si verus possessor contra spoliatorem assisam
5 contempnat et possessionem suam viribus et non iudicio sibi vsurpare presumat
conpetit spoliatori assisa propter vsurpacionem quia sine iudicio quamuis iuste
fuerit spoliatus quia per negligenciam veri domini incepit vtramque habere possessionem nec habere poterit recursum ad assisam quia frustra legis auxilium
inuocat qui in legem committit.

10   Ad ipsos autem pertinet querela qui nomine proprio tenuerunt et non alieno
in feodo vel saltem ad vitam propriam vel in vadium sed non ad terminum
quoquo modo per feoffamentum vel per constitucionem mercatorum vel
iudicium curie regis pro delicto recognito vel dampnis adiudicatis vel huiusmodi.
Et quamuis iniuste possidentes contra veros dominos nullam habeant accionem
15 si eiciantur habebunt tamen querelam accionem et assisam contra tales qui ius   [217]
non habent propter comodum possidendi quia si tales qui ius non habent extra
seysinam peterent numquam versus possidentes recuperarent set remaneret suo
loco possessio quia secundus spoliator nullum ius habuit eiciendi.   Eiecto eciam
conpetit assisa versus omnes a quocumque fuerit feoffatus domino vel non
20 domino qui pro se titulum habuerit et tempus seysine pacificum.   Et eciam
conpetit ei qui sine iudicio disseysitus fuerit de aliquo tenemento de quo in
seysina fuerit quoquo modo quamuis nullum titulum habuerit set tempus tantum
quod sufficere poterit pro titulo.   Conpetit enim cuicumque libero et statu libero
existenti quod dicitur de hiis qui in nayuitate sunt procreati verumtamen qui a
25 magno tempore extra astrum suum villanum ad loca remociora se transtulerint
et liberum tenementum perquisierint: si eiciantur conpetit eis remedium per
assisam noue disseysine contra dominos suos sicut contra quascumque extraneas
personas quia quousque huiusmodi domini tales fugitiuos suos repugnantes in
seruitutem per iudicium redigerint ad perquisitum eorum seysiendum manum
30 apponere non possunt.   Villanis autem in veteribus astris suis commorantibus
non conpetit huiusmodi remedium contra veros dominos quamuis contra alias
quascumque personas tam de villenagio quam de perquisito quia quamuis
villanus quo ad dominum suum vnum vel plures pro villano et natiuo habeatur
contra tamen alios pro libero debet reputari in conquerendo sicut sokemannus
35 de antiquo dominico corone regis licet contra dominum vel alium sokemannum
vicinum suum de eodem sokagio placitare non possit nisi per breue de recto
clausum secundum consuetudinem manerii, versus quemcumque tamen extraneum ipsum eicientem a sokagio suo vel perquisito conpetit ei remedium per   f. 84
assisam noue disseysine.   Item conpetit liberis a magno tempore in seruitutem

2-3. naturalem . . . ciuilem, Br., *om.* J.   3. quod *om.* J.   11. sed non ad, Br., ante, J.

wrong of disseisin to grow cold by their sufferance, indifference, negligence, weakness, apathy or failure to apply for aid, and thus lose possession of both kinds, natural, that is, and civil, while the disseisor begins to acquire both and thus cannot lawfully be ejected without a judgement of the court. And if the true possessor spurns an assize against the dispossessor and presumes to usurp his possession by force and not by judgement of the court, an assize is available to the [first] dispossessor on account of the usurpation, because he was dispossessed (however rightly) without judgement, since through the negligence of the true owner he had begun to have possession of both kinds, nor can the true possessor have recourse to an assize because he who sins against the law will invoke the aid of the law in vain.

Bracton
f. 165
The plaint lies for those who hold in fee, in their own name and not in another's, or for at least the term of their own life or in gage (but not for a term of years) in whatever way, by enfeoffment or by statute merchant or by judgement of the king's court for a confessed delict or damages awarded or the like. And although unlawful possessors have no right of action against the true owners, if they are ejected they will have a plaint, a right of action and an assize by reason of the advantages of possession against such as have no right because, if those who have no right sue when they are out of seisin, they will never recover against those in possession, but possession will remain where it lies,
Bracton,
f. 165b
since the second dispossessor had no right to eject. An assize is available also against all men to one who is ejected, by whomsoever he may have been enfeoffed, whether owner or non-owner, if he has a title in his favour and a peaceful period of seisin. And an assize is also available to him who has been disseised, without judgement of the court, of any tenement of which he was in seisin in any way, even though he has no title but only a period of time which can
Bracton
f. 166
suffice for a title. An assize is available, too, to any man who is free and living in a free condition, as is said of those who are born in villeinage and nevertheless have removed themselves for a long while to far distant places away from their villein hearth and have acquired a freehold. If they are ejected, a remedy is available to them by an assize of novel disseisin against their lords, just as it is against any third party whatsoever, because until such lords have by judgement of the court brought these rebellious fugitives of theirs back to servitude they cannot lay hands on what they have acquired and take seisin of it. To villeins, however, who dwell by their ancestral hearths such a remedy is not available against their true lords, although it is available against any other persons whomsoever with regard both to a villein holding and to an acquisition, because, although a villein is held to be a villein and a neif with respect to his lord (whether one or several), yet against others, he ought, when he has a plaint, to be regarded as a free man, just as a sokeman of the ancient demesne of the Crown, although he cannot plead against his lord or any neighbouring sokeman of his regarding his socage tenement except by writ of right close according to the custom of the manor, yet has a remedy available to him against any third party, who ejects him from his socage tenement or acquisition, by an assize of novel disseisin. Again, a remedy is available to free men who for a long time have been reduced

redactis quorum patres et alii antecessores sui a tempore quo currit breue de
recto in statu extiterint seruili si in astris suis fuerint commorantes conpetit eis
remedium ad liberum tenementum rehabendum per breue ne vexes et si ab huiusmodi tenemento omnino fuerint eiecti conpetit eis remedium per assisam noue
5 disseysine. Conpetit eciam viro quandoque contra vxorem suam in casu quo
vxor pro fuga liberum tenementum viri alienat vel proprium vel cum teneat se
seysitam inuito viro postquam semel virum reliquerit et pro adulterio recesserit.
Conpetit eciam ei remedium per assisam licet personaliter vel per procuratorem
eiectus non fuerit verum eciam cum nemine in seysina relicto quamuis recessit
10 non admittatur vel repellatur cum redire voluerit.   Item eciam ei conpetit assisa
qui per iudicem et iudicium iniustum sicut sine breui originali de tenemento
fuerit eiectus.   Si autem seruus ingrediatur ad liberam vxorem habentem liberum
tenementum vt dotem vel hereditatem si eiciantur recuperabunt per assisam non
obstante seruitute viri secus si econuerso.   Et de libero tenemento bene conpetit
15 assisa viro versus omnes si eiciatur non obstante vxore sua villana vel eius
villenagio.   Item iacet assisa inter dominum et non dominum cum non dominus
iniuste distrinxerit tenentem domini.   Et si tenens gratis soluerit non domino
tunc habebit assisam contra vtrumque.   Preterea conpetit ei cuius pater obiit in   [218]
statu libero si post mortem patris a seysina perquisiti patris fuerit eiectus et
20 contra dominum suum si sub eius potestate non fuerit constitutus.   Item eciam
ei qui feoffatus fuerit donec ei prouideatur si ante terminum fuerit eiectus et
omnibus qui in consimilibus casibus fuerint feoffati eiecti.   Si autem duobus
facta fuerit donacio et vterque se posuerit in seysinam sine waranto si recenter
eiciantur non recuperabunt et idem dicatur de eorum altero.   Si autem non
25 eiciantur per donatorem set inter ipsos tenentes habeatur contencio tunc ille debet
preferri cuius seysinam donator ratam habuerit vt sic si duo contendant de
aliqua hereditate quorum nullus ius habuerit vt si ambo fuerint bastardi ei conpetit assisa qui prius fuerit in seysina et possessione donec maius ius habens per
iudicium recuperauerit vel sic si duo se gerant pro herede et de eorum iure
30 dubitetur melior erit condicio possidentis.   Cum autem donacio fiat ob causam
si donatarius ad alia vota conuoluerit et non satisfaciat condicioni si eiciatur per
donatorem per assisam non recuperabit licet ab inicio perfecta sit donacio cum
causa non sequatur.
    Et sicut vnus disseysiri poterit de re propria sic plures possunt de re communi
35 sicut res que communis est inter virum suum et ipsam vxorem et de quo neutri

2. statu] statum, J.   10. eciam] et, J.   20. eciam] et, J.   24. eorum *scripsimus*,
eodem, J.   26. sic] hic, J.   31. conuoluerit] conualuerit, J.   35. sicut . . . est, Br.,
om. J.

to servitude, whose fathers and other ancestors of theirs have been of servile condition from the period from which the writ of right runs:[1] if they are dwelling by their hearths, a remedy is available to them to have the freehold back by the writ *ne vexes*; and if they have been utterly ejected from such freehold, a remedy is available to them by an assize of novel disseisin. Sometimes an assize is available to a husband against his wife in a case where the wife deserts her husband and sells his freehold or her own or where against her husband's will she retains the seisin after she has left him once for all and has departed to live in adultery.

Bracton, f. 165b A remedy by an assize is also available to a man, even though he has not been ejected in person or through an agent, and even though he departed leaving no one in seisin, if he is not admitted but repelled when he wishes to return. Again, an assize is also available to him who has been ejected from his holding by a

Bracton, f. 168b judge and unjust judgement, for example, without an original writ. If, moreover, a villein should come by a free-born wife having a freehold as dower or as inheritance and they are ejected, they will recover by an assize, notwithstanding the husband's servile condition, though in the converse case it is otherwise. And an assize will certainly be available to the husband against all men in respect of a freehold if he is ejected, notwithstanding that his wife is a villein or [has] villeinage. Further an assize lies between the lord and one who is not the lord if the latter unlawfully distrains the lord's tenant, and if the tenant freely makes payment to one who is not his lord, the lord will have an assize against them both. Further-

Bracton, f. 165b more, an assize is available to him whose father was of free condition when he died, if after his father's death he is ejected from the seisin of what his father had acquired, and even against his lord if he is not living under his authority.

Bracton, f. 166 Again, an assize is available to him who has been enfeoffed until other provision is made for him if he should be ejected before his term [is completed], and to all those ejected who have been enfeoffed in similar circumstances. If, however, a gift should be made to two donees and both put themselves in seisin without a warrant and they are ejected soon after, they will not recover, and the same may be said of each of them. If, however, they are not ejected by the donor but a dispute arises between the donees themselves, then he ought to be preferred whose seisin is ratified by the donor, as for instance, if two contest some inheritance to which neither has a rightful claim—for example, if both should be bastards—an assize is available to him who was first in seisin and possession until the one who has a greater right recovers by judgement of the court; or again, if two set themselves up as heir and it is doubtful whose claim is rightful, he who is in possesssion will be in the better position. If, however, a gift is made for a certain cause and the donee changes his mind and does not fulfil the condition, then, even though the gift was complete to begin with, if he is ejected by the donor, he will not recover by an assize because [fulfilment of] the cause does not follow [the gift].

Bracton, f. 166b And just as one may be disseised of one's own property, so several may be disseised of common property, such as property which is common to a husband

---

[1] That is, 1 Richard I.

sine alio conpetit querela.   Conpetit tamen viro contra vxorem suam in casu.
Poterit enim tenementum esse commune inter duos vel plures sicut bunde et mete
et racionabiles diuise que ponuntur in terminis et finibus agrorum ad distinguendum predia et dominia vicinorum quorum quilibet dominus est proprietatis
5 non tamen in solidum set in communi et talibus conpetit assisa coniunctim vel
diuisim quia quicumque diuisas arauerit lapidem vel arborem finalem amouerit
et asportauerit facit disseysinam quia huiusmodi diuise solo cedunt.   Poterit
eciam res esse communis inter plures sicut inter coheredes et participes in tenementis communibus non partitis et eciam inter vicinos in aliquo tenemento
10 quod aliquando fuit litigiosum et de communi voluntate relinquitur ad aliquem
vsum communem et si quis ex talibus participibus alium suum participem disseysiuerit eiectus assisam habebit versus participes suos ad tenendum in communi:
si autem duos quilibet suam habebit assisam.   Et idem erit de pluribus in causa
possessionis adquirende ante particionem hereditatis cum semel fuerit adquisita
15 et sunt ibi diuersa iura licet de re incerta.   De seysina vero propria si eiectus f. 84b
fuerit particeps vnus vel plures a participe vel a participibus vel ab extraneis personis, quilibet per se assisam habebit sine participe quia plures sunt ibi disseysine
et vice versa si vnus vel plures coheredes disseysinam fecerint coheredibus vni vel
pluribus siue extraneis vni vel pluribus quilibet de facto suo per se respondebit
20 quia pena tenebit suos auctores.   Ante adicionem vero hereditatis coniunctum
est ius et seysina antecessoris et ideo coniunctim ab omnibus petere debent per
assisam mortis antecessoris qui coniuncti sunt tanquam vnus heres, set cum adita
fuerit vel adiri inceperit adhuc manet vnum ius coniunctum et seysina diuersa sed
communis tamen quousque fuerit partita.   Et ideo nullus sine alio respondebit
25 cuicumque seysinam petenti vel ius alicuius antecessoris sui nec in causa proprietatis neque possessionis per assisam mortis antecessoris cum omnia sint eis
communia proprietas et possessio et post diuisionem hereditatis communis erunt [219]
plures seysine et plura iura separata.   Set tamen non debet quis sine alio respondere in causa proprietatis nisi velit quod si faceret nullum regressum haberet erga
30 suos participes si forte amitteret.   Et quod dictum est de participibus dici poterit de vicinis.
     Conpetit eciam assisa contra liberum hominem et seruum, masculum et femi-
nam, clericum et laycum, maiorem et minorem, furiosum et stultum et contra
omnes spoliatores et tenentes et non solum contra eos qui spoliant et tenent set
35 eciam contra illos quorum nomine spoliacio fit vel perquisitum dum tamen ad hec
fuerint aduocati vel saltem quod non deaduocati precise vel quod iniuriam non
emendauerint cum de hoc eis constiterit quia non refert an quis propriis manibus
eiciat an per alium.

     6. amouerit] ammouerit, J.   8. et *om.* J.   13. assisam, Br.; seysinam, J.
19. extraneis] extraneus, J.   20. coniunctum] conuictum, J.   21. antecessoris] ancessoris, J.
22. qui] quia, J.   23. et] vt, J; sed *om.* J.   35. illos] illorum, J.

and his wife, and for which an action is available to neither without the other, although in a certain case[1] an assize is available to a husband against his wife. There may also be a holding common to two or more, such as bounds and metes and rightful balks which are placed at the limits and ends of fields to distinguish the estates and lordships of neighbours, and everyone is the owner thereof, not, however, as a whole but in common; and to such owners an assize is available jointly or severally, because whosoever ploughs up these balks or moves and takes away a boundary stone or tree does disseisin, since balks and the like belong to the soil. Property may also be common to several, as between co-heirs and parceners in common holdings that have not been partitioned, and, again, as with any holding that was at some time in dispute between neighbours and by common agreement is let remain in some common user, and if any of these parceners disseises any fellow-parcener, he who is ejected will have an assize against his fellow-parceners to hold in common with them, and if two are ejected each will have his assize. And the same will be true of several persons in an action for obtaining possession before partition of the inheritance, when it has once been acquired; and there are different rights there, although in respect of an uncertain thing. If one or more parceners are ejected from their own seisin by a parcener or parceners or by third parties, each will have an assize by himself, without a parcener, because there are several disseisins there; and, conversely, if one or more co-heirs do disseisin to one or more co-heirs or to one or more third parties, each will answer by himself for his own deed, because the penalty will attach to its authors. But before an inheritance is taken up, the right and the seisin of the ancestor are conjoined and should therefore be claimed jointly by an assize of *mort d'ancestor* by all who are joined together as one heir. But when the inheritance is, or has begun to be, taken up, there still remains a single joint right, and seisin in severalty but yet common until the inheritance is partitioned. And therefore none will answer without the other to anyone who claims the seisin or right of any ancestor of theirs, whether in a proprietary action or in a possessory action by an assize of *mort d'ancestor*, for all things are common to them, property and possession; but after the common inheritance has been divided, there will be several seisins and several separate rights. Nevertheless, none ought to answer without the other in a proprietary action unless he wishes, for if he did so he would have no recourse against his parceners, should he happen to lose. And what is said about parceners may be said about neighbours [who hold jointly].

An assize is also available against free man and villein, man and woman, clerk and layman, one of full age and a minor, madman and fool, and against all who dispossess and retain, and not only against those who dispossess and retain but also against those in whose name the dispossessing or acquiring is done, provided that they avowed these acts or at least did not categorically disavow them or that they did not amend the wrong when it became known to them; for it does not matter whether one ejects by one's own hands or through another.

Bracton, f. 167

Bracton, f. 167b

Bracton, f. 170b

---

[1] Adultery, see above, p. 51.

Contra dominum vero regem non habebitur remedium per assisam quamuis in eleccione spoliati sit vel prouidere sibi per supplicacionem versus ipsum regem vel quod omnino procedat assisa versus spoliatores hoc excepto quod ipse rex in assisa non conprehendatur.   Et si spoliator dicat quod sine rege respondere
5 non poterit cuius nomine fecit id quod fecit non propter hoc differatur assisa set capiatur et si spoliator euidentem racionem et manifestam habeat differatur inde iudicium donec cum rege fuerit inde tractatum, sin autem seisynam recuperet cum dampnis dupplicatis tam versus escaetorem, vicecomitem et alios ministros regis quam versus quascumque priuatas personas.
10 Heredes autem in hereditatem antecessorum succedentes a pena disseysine sint quieti teneantur tamen ad penam restitucionis per breue de ingressu dum tamen lis in suis antecessoribus extit contestata non obstante eorum minori etate pro re viciosa quam sunt ingressi.   Et eodem modo de successoribus in rem litigiosam succedentibus dum tamen predecessor spoliator in breui nominetur
15 nomine dignitatis et non nomine proprio tantum quia licet diuersum nomen eadem tamen dignitas manet.   Contingit autem quandoque quod spoliator rem transfert ad alium et cum disseysitus assisam arramiare voluerit spoliator timens assisam suum spoliat feoffatum super quem ipse spoliatus statim perquirit assisam et tunc sunt due assise in vnicam concurrentes personam et vtrique
20 conquerenti conpetit assisa.   Refert tamen cui primo conpetit et reuera in omni casu spoliacionis vbi plures assise arramiuntur versus vnum de vno tenemento de vltima disseysina prius erit cognoscendum.   Et nota quod tenens dum non fuerit principalis disseysitor set a disseysitore feoffatus quamuis tanquam disseysitor nominetur pro eo quod alius ab eo restituere non potest vocare poterit
25 ad warantum suum feoffatorem sine alio breui si presens sit in capcione assise et si absens fuerit tunc obseruetur idem processus velut in assisa mortis ante-   f. 85 cessoris.

CAP. III.   QUIBUS NON COMPETIT ASSISA

Nulli autem conpetit querela nec remedium per assisam noue disseysine qui
30 in possessione fuerit nomine alieno quia quamuis talis in possessione fuerit non possidet tamen quia ipse possidet cuius nomine possidetur.   Item non competit eis assisa qui statim a vero domino post disseysinam flagrante disseysina sunt [220] eiecti.   Item nec intrusori nisi longum tempus habuerit et pacificum et sufficere possit pro titulo.   Item nec villano vel villane sub potestate domini existenti de
35 villenagio contra dominum suum nec contra alios quoscumque nec racione per-

26. obseruetur] obser, J.   32. a vero, Br., annexo, J.

Bracton,
f. 171b

Against the king in truth there will be no remedy by an assize, although he who is dispossessed has the choice either of looking after his interests by way of petition vis-à-vis the king himself or of proceeding by an assize solely against the dispossessors, with this reservation that the king himself is not included in the assize.   And if a dispossessor should say that he is unable to answer without the king, in whose name he did what he did, the assize will not be put off on this account, but it will be taken, and if the dispossessor should have a plain and obvious reason [for what he did], judgement in the matter will be deferred until there has been consultation with the king thereon: otherwise the disseisee will recover seisin with double damages, not only against an escheator, sheriff or other ministers of the king but also against any private persons.

Bracton,
f. 172

Heirs who succeed to the inheritance of their ancestors are quit of a penalty for disseisin, nevertheless, provided that issue was joined in an action against their ancestors, they are liable to the penalty of restitution by a writ of entry, notwithstanding that they are under age, because of their defective title to the property into which they have entered.   And likewise as regards those who succeed to property disputed in court, provided that the predecessor-dispossessor is named in the writ by the title of his office and not merely by his own name, because, although a name may differ, yet the title of an office remains unaltered.   It

Bracton,
f. 172b
Bracton,
f. 177

sometimes happens that a dispossessor transfers the property to another and, when the disseissee proposes to arraign an assize, the dispossessor in fear of the assize dispossesses his feoffee, who, being dispossessed, at once brings an assize against him, and then there are two assizes running together against one and the same person, and an assize is available to both complainants.   It is then a question to whom it is first available; and, truly, in every case of dispossession where several assizes are arraigned against one defendant regarding one tene-

Bracton,
f. 177b

ment, cognisance shall first be taken of the last disseisin.   And be it noted that the tenant, while he is not the principal disseisor but his feoffee, although he is named as disseisor because none other than he can make restitution, is able to vouch his feoffor to warranty without another writ if he is present when the assize is taken and, if he should be absent, then the same procedure will be observed as in an assize of *mort d'ancestor*.

CHAPTER 3.   WHO ARE NOT ABLE TO BRING AN ASSIZE

Bracton,
f. 167b

Neither a plaint nor a remedy by an assize of novel disseisin is available to one who is in possession in the name of another because, although he may be in possession, nevertheless he does not possess: for he possesses in whose name it is

Bracton
f. 168

possessed.   Again, an assize is not available to those who after disseisin are immediately ejected by the true owner while the disseisin is fresh, nor to an intruder unless he has had a long and peaceful period [of occupation] which may suffice for a title; nor to a villein or neif, living under the authority of a lord, with respect to the villeinage, neither against their lord nor against any other

sonarum nec racione tenementi nec eciam de perquisito contra dominum quamuis
contra alios quousque dominus sub cuius fuerint potestate huiusmodi tenementum in manum suam ceperit. Item nec de terris perquirendis in manum mortuam
si a domino capitali infra annum vel a superiori infra alium dimidium annum
5 eiciantur. Item nec ei qui se cognouerit ad villanum disseysitoris nisi excepcionem habeat sibi adiutricem. Item nec ei a cuius tenemento spoliata fuerint
edificia aliena per ignoranciam vel mala fide constructa et per edificatorem aspor-
tata nisi prohibicio precesserit ne amouerentur vel denunciacio ne fierent. Item
nec ei qui a tenemento suo eicitur qui tenuerit per legem Anglie racione liber-
10 orum qui conuicti sunt ad bastardos vel quod heredes non possunt esse quoquo
modo. Item nec donatario cum quo donator semper extitit in seysina si a vero
herede eiciatur recenter post mortem donatoris secus vero ab extraneo cuius non
interfuerit et quo casu recuperabit propter comodum possessionis verus tamen
heres post tempus per assisam mortis antecessoris recuperabit. Item nec viro
15 per se sine vxore de iure vxoris disseysito nec e conuerso. Item nec ei qui
secundum conuencionem suam fuerat eiectus. Item nec ei qui inpeditur
racione vasti per ipsum facti donec transgressionem emendauerit. Item nec
domino contra tenentem suum de seruicio detento cum districcio sufficiat et non
sit vetita vel per breue replegiata et quo casu locum habet districcio. Item nec
20 ei qui semel se retraxerit coram iusticiario ab assisa et a breui. Item nec ei qui
semel de bona voluntate sua dederit tenementum. Item si quis tenens cum
presens non sit velit rem petenti restituere hoc possit per scriptum fieri sine
solempnitate tradicionis quod non est in donacione. Item nec mulieri
clamanti dotem de qua probatum est quod nunquam fuit ei cuius nomine
25 dotatur legitimo matrimonio copulata si a vero herede eiciatur. Item nec viro
tenenti hereditatem vxoris a qua prolem non suscitauit si a vero herede fuerit
spoliatus. Item nec secundo viro clamanti tenere per legem Anglie quamuis
heredes habuerit ab vxore. Item nec ei qui rem spoliatori dissimulando remiserit vel omnino quietam clamauerit vel iniuriam condonauerit vel confirmauerit.
30 Item nec ei qui tenentem de eodem tenemento per breue de alciori natura in-
placitauerit lite pendente. De cimiteriis et huiusmodi dedicatis tenementis in
sacris ac eciam de muris theatris stadiis viis et stratis publicis et aliis ad vsum
publicum deputatis non iacent assise set querele de transgressione quia nulla sin-
gularis persona in huiusmodi rebus aliquod singulare ius sibi poterit vendicare
35 et ideo non disseysiri.

2. quousque] quoscumque, J.; fuerint] fuerit, J.   8. amouerentur] amoueretur, J.
21-22. *Post* semel *add.* bona, J; nonnulla verba desinunt: *scripsimus* de bona voluntate . . . hoc
possit.   32. theatris] teatris, J.; vsum] suum, J.

persons, neither on account of their persons nor on account of their holding, nor
even in respect of an acquisition [is the assize available] against their lord,
although it is against others, until the lord, under whose authority they are, has
taken the said tenement into his hands.   Nor in respect of lands taken into
mortmain, if the tenants are ejected by the chief lord within a year or by a superior
lord within another half year.   Nor to him who acknowledges himself to be the
villein of the disseisor, unless he has an exception to help him.   Nor to him from
whose tenement there are removed buildings belonging to another, which had
been erected in ignorance or bad faith and taken away by the builder, unless
there had previously been a prohibition that they were not to be removed or a

Bracton,
f. 170

warning that they were not to be erected.   Nor to him who is ejected from a
tenement that he holds by the curtesy of England by reason of children [of the

Bracton
f. 168

marriage], who are adjudged to be bastards or incapable in any way of being
heirs.   Nor to a donee with whom the donor always remained in seisin if,
immediately after the death of the donor, he should be ejected by the true heir,
though it would be otherwise if he were ejected by a third party who had no
interest in the property, for in this case he will recover because possession gives

Bracton,
f. 168b

him an advantage, though the true heir will recover eventually by an assize of
mort d'ancestor.   Nor to a husband by himself without his wife who is disseised

Bracton,
f. 169

[of property held] in right of the wife, nor conversely.   Nor to him who had been
ejected in accordance with his own agreement.   Nor to him who is barred on
account of the waste he has committed, until he has made the trespass good.
Nor to a lord against his tenant for a service withheld, where distraint is sufficient
remedy and it has not been prevented or replevied by writ: in this case

Bracton,
f. 169b

distraint is appropriate.   Nor to him who has once withdrawn from the assize
and writ before a justice.   Nor to him who has once of his own good will given
a tenement.   Again, if a tenant wishes to restore property to a claimant when he
himself is not present, this can be done by a deed, without the ceremony of
livery: which is not the position in the case of a gift.   Nor to a woman who
claims dower, of whom it was proved that she was never joined in lawful
matrimony to him in whose name she is endowed, if she is ejected by the true
heir.   Nor to a husband who holds the inheritance of a wife, with whom he has
not begotten children, if he is dispossessed by the true heir.   Nor to a second
husband who claims to hold by the curtesy of England, even though he should

Bracton,
f. 170

have heirs by his wife.   Nor to him who through indifference concedes the
property to the dispossessor or quitclaims it absolutely or condones the wrong or
confirms it.   Nor to him who impleads the tenant of the said tenement by a
writ of a higher nature while the suit is pending.   For cemeteries and the like

Bracton,
f. 170b

tenements dedicated to sacred uses, and also for walls, theatres, race-courses,
public roads and streets and other things set apart for public use, assizes do not
lie but plaints of trespass, because no private person can claim for himself any
private right in these things and cannot therefore be disseised.

CAP. IV. DE VI SIMPLICI ET ARMATA

Duo autem maxime paci sunt contraria vis et iniuria.   Est autem vis maioris
rei inpetus cui resisti non potest.   Est autem vis quociens quis quod sibi debere
putat non per iudicium reposcit.   Virium autem alia simplex alia armata alia   [221]
5 expulsiua omnino sine armis alia expulsiua cum armis alia clandestina et de nocte
alia publica et de die alia iusta alia iniusta alia per violenciam alia sine violencia
sicut in rem vacuam alia perturbatiua alia inquietiua alia ablatiua alia conpul-   f. 85d
siua que quandoque metum inducit alia iniuriosa et illicita alia iusta et licita.
Siue fuerit simplex siue violenta inermis vel armata, est enim vis armata non
10 solum si quis venerit cum telis verum eciam omnes illos dicimus armatos qui
habent quod nocere potest.   Telorum autem appellacione omnia in quibus
singuli homines nocere possunt accipiuntur, set si quis venerit sine armis et in ipsa
certacione ligna sumpserit fustes vel lapides talis dicitur vis armata.   Et si quis
venerit cum armis tamen cum non vsus fuerit ad deiciendum et deicerit vis armata
15 dicitur esse facta.   Sufficit enim terror armorum vt videatur armis deiecisse.   Si
autem cum dominus a peregrinacione vel a nundinis reuersus fuerit et qui
possessionem inuaserit ei prohibuerit ne ingrediatur talis armis est eiectus et talis
vis dicitur esse repulsiua.   Item cum procurator generalis armatus venerit siue
dominus hoc mandauerit siue ratum habuerit et eiecerit ipse dominus videtur
20 armis deiecisse.   Hoc idem dicendum erit in familia cum ipsa venerit armata et
quo casu non videor esse armatus set ipsa familia nisi hoc iussi vel ratum
habui.   Et secundum precedencia qualitas facti penam habet grauiorem vel
minus grauem et quibus casibus tales fiunt constituciones.

Quicumque autem de disseysina cum robberia de aliquibus mobilibus vel
25 catallis vel absque robberia dum tamen vi et armis conuinci contigerit per
recognicionem iuratorum assise primo adiudicetur querenti seysina cum dampnis
tam tenementi quam catallorum ablatorum eo insuper pene carcerali manci-
petur et inde redimatur pro transgressione siue presens fuerit vel absens.   Et eodem modo fiat de disseysitore vno vel pluribus conuicto de disseysina facta vi et
30 armis eciam sine robberia.

Et si disseysitor non habeat vnde dampna reddere possit respondeant illi ad
quorum manus tenementum medio tempore deuenerit ita quod quilibet tenens
pro suo tempore oneretur.

Siue fuerit vis armata vel inermis quelibet talis non erit iniuriosa quia
35 armorum quedam sunt tuicionis et quod quis ob tutelam sui corporis fecerit vel
sui iuris iuste fecisse videtur.   Sunt eciam arma pacis et iusticie et arma pertur-
bacionis pacis et iniurie et sunt arma vsurpacionis rei aliene et talis vis dici poterit

5. armis] aliis, J; clandestina] clamtestina, J.   10. dicimus] dominis, J.   13. certacione, J.; concertacione, Br.   16. peregrinacione] peregrinacone, J.   35. quod] quo, J.

CHAPTER 4. OF SIMPLE AND ARMED FORCE

Bracton,
f. 162
Two things are especially against the peace, force and tort. Force is the assault of a greater body which cannot be resisted, and there is force whenever anyone demands what he thinks is his, otherwise than by judgement of the court. Force may be of several kinds: simple or armed; expulsive *in toto* without arms, or expulsive with arms; clandestine and by night, or open and by day; lawful or unlawful; with violence or without violence, as in vacant property; causing an uproar or unease; ablative[1] or compulsive, which sometimes leads to fear; wrongful and illicit or lawful and licit. For whether it be simple or violent, unarmed or armed, there is armed force not merely if someone comes with weapons, for we also call those armed who have anything which may do hurt.

Bracton,
f. 162b
Under the description of arms everything is included by which individuals may do hurt: even if one comes without arms and in the struggle itself lays hold of sticks or cudgels or stones, that is said to be armed force. And if a man comes with arms, even though he does not use them in order to eject, but he does eject, armed force is said to be used; for the terror of arms suffices to give the appearance of ejecting by arms. If the owner is returning from a pilgrimage or from a fair and he who has invaded his possession prohibits him from entering, the owner is ejected with arms, and such force is said to be repulsive. And if a general agent comes armed, whether his lord ordered or ratified it, and ejects, the lord himself is regarded as having ejected with arms.   And the same will be said of [members of the] household, if they should come armed; though in this case I am not deemed to be armed but the household, unless I have ordered or ratified it.   The nature of the deed carries a heavier or lighter penalty according to the antecedent circumstances, and for such cases the following enactments are made:

St. West-
minster,
I. c. 37
Whosoever shall fall to be convicted, by the recognition of the jurors of an assize, of disseisin with the robbery of any movables or chattels (or without robbery, so long as it is with force and arms), in the first place seisin shall be adjudged to the plaintiff, with damages both for the tenement and for the chattels taken, and thereupon the defendant shall be committed to prison, from which he may ransom himself for the trespass, whether he has been present [at the disseisin] or absent.   And the same course shall be followed in the case of one or more disseisors convicted of disseisin, done with force and arms, even without robbery.

St. Glou-
cester,
c. 1
And if the disseisor has not the wherewithal to enable him to pay the damages, they shall answer into whose hands the tenement has passed in the meantime so that each tenant shall be charged in respect of his own period.

Bracton,
f. 162b
Whether force be armed or unarmed, it will not in every instance be wrongful, because some arms are for protection, and what one has done for the protection of his body or his right is deemed to have been done lawfully.   There are also arms of peace and justice and arms for the disturbance of the peace and wrong.

---

[1] Defined later, p. 56.

ablatiua vnde ei qui iuste possidet licitum erit cum armis repellere vt per arma
tuicionis et pacis que sunt iusticie repellat iniuriam et vim iniustam et arma
iniurie set tamen cum tali discrecionis moderamine quod iniuriam non committat.
Non enim poterit quis sub tali pretextu hominem interficere vulnerare vel male
5 tractare si alio modo tueri possit suam possessionem et igitur qui viribus vult vti
erit viribus viriliter resistendus. Venit eciam quis vt iuste possidentem cum
viribus eiciat set cum possidens ei resistat quod opere adimplere non possit quod
in animo habuit et voluntate in assisam non incidit nec debet obesse conatus vbi
iniuria nullum habuit effectum.

10   CAP. V. DE BREUI NOUE DISSEYSINE   [222]

Audita a superiore ad quem pertinet vim et iniuriam propulsare et ad quem
recurritur de necessitate querela statim transmittet breue suum vicecomiti loci in
quo continebitur tam nomen querentis quam eius de quo queritur siue fuerit vnus
vel plures. Facta itaque inpetracione statim tradatur breue vicecomiti ne per
15 negligenciam et minus diligentem prosecucionem efficiatur seysina pacifica que
ab inicio fuit litigiosa per diligentem inpetracionem. Officium vicecomitis in
hac parte est in principio plegios recipere de prosequendo nisi querens in
cancellaria regis plegios inuenerit vel aliam securitatem fecerit de prosequendo
vt per fidei interposicionem pro paupertate querentis secundum quod in breui
20 continebitur, et tales plegios recipiat qui sibi sint distringibiles et sufficientes ad
misericordiam regis soluendam si querens forte se retraxerit vel non fuerit prosecutus, alioquin ipse idem pro plegio habeatur. Duo autem plegii sufficiunt de
prosequendo quamuis plures fuerint in breui querentis nominati sicut vir et vxor
et plures querentes in communi. Ad vicecomitem vero pertinet quod tene-
25 mentum de quo fit querimonia reseisiri faciat de catallis que in ipso fuerint inuenta hodie tamen aliter obseruatur quia querens omnia dampna post capcionem   f. 86
assise per sacramentum iuratorum declaranda recuperabit, item quod ipsum
tenementum cum catallis esse faciat in pace hoc est quod non permittat quod res
ad alium sine iudicio transferatur vel quod disseysitus seysinam sine iudicio sibi
30 vsurpet donec iusticiarii venerint, quod sic debet interpretari quod si spoliator
rem spoliatam a recessu querentis a domicilio suo versus curiam regis alienauerit
dum tamen querens diligentem fecerit prosecucionem in inpetrando donatarius
tenebitur ad restitucionem quamuis in breui non fuerit conprehensus nec a

3. cum tali] talis cum, J; discrecionis] discrescionis, J.   11. Audita] Audito, J.
19. interposicionem] interpretacionem, J.   25. reseisiri] reisiri, J.   27. declaranda]
declarandam, J.   28. cum] in, J.

And there are arms for usurping the property of others; and force of this kind may be called ablative, and it will be lawful for him who rightfully possesses to repel it with arms so that by the arms of protection and peace, which are those of justice, he may repel wrong and unrightful force and the arms of wrong, but yet be so governed by discretion that he commits no wrong.　Nor indeed may anyone under such a pretext kill a man or wound or illtreat him if he can protect his possession in any other way.　And therefore he who intends to use force must be manfully resisted by force.　Furthermore, if there comes someone in order that he may with force eject him who rightfully possesses but, when the possessor resists him, is unable to fulfil the task he had in mind and intention to perform, he does not fall within the assize: an attempt ought not to be prejudicial where the wrong has had no practical result.

CHAPTER 5.　OF THE WRIT OF NOVEL DISSEISIN

Bracton,
f. 179

When the superior, whose function it is to repulse force and wrong and to whom recourse is had of necessity, has heard the plaint, straightway he will send his writ to the sheriff of the district: in this writ there will be contained both the name of the plaintiff and that of those against whom the plaint is made, whether they be one or many.　And when the writ has thus been sued out, it should be delivered immediately to the sheriff lest the seisin, which at the beginning through the prompt suing out of the writ was contentious, should turn into peaceful seisin through negligence and lukewarm prosecution of the suit.　The duty of

Bracton,
f. 179b

the sheriff in this matter, to begin with, is to receive pledges of prosecution, unless the plaintiff finds pledges in the king's chancery or gives some other security to prosecute, such as by pledging his faith on account of his poverty, as will be set out in the writ.　And the sheriff will receive such pledges as are distrainable to him and have the wherewithal to pay an amercement to the king if the plaintiff should chance to withdraw from the suit or not prosecute it; otherwise the sheriff himself will be regarded as the pledge.　Two pledges suffice for prosecuting, even though several [plaintiffs] are named in the writ, such as a husband and wife, or several persons complaining in common.　It is the function of the sheriff to see that the tenement, regarding which complaint is made, is repossessed of the chattels that have been found in it; though today the practice is different, for after the assize is taken the plaintiff will recover all [in] damages, which will be made known by the oath of the jurors.　It is also his function to see that the tenement with its chattels is in peace, that is, until the coming of the justices he will not permit the property to be transferred to anyone else without judgement of the court or permit the disseisee without judgement to usurp the seisin for himself.　This should be interpreted thus: that if the dispossessor should alienate the property he has taken after the plaintiff has departed from his home to the king's court, provided the plaintiff is diligently occupied in suing out his writ, the donee will be bound to make restitution even though he is not

donatore escambium consequatur nisi sibi in seysina sua per breue de warantia
carte caucius prospexerit.   Et interim faciat xij. liberos et legales homines de
visneto illo videre illud tenementum.   Per hoc preceptum pertinet ad vicecomitem quod conuenire faciat plures liberos et legales homines de visneto illo
5 et in presencia parcium si velint interesse inde eligere xij. qui neutri parti sint
affines essoniabiles vel suspecti nec qui sint languidi vel de stipite villani vel in alia
prouincia commorantes vel infra etatem vel nimis senes quos statim mittat tenementum illud videre, et non solum ab vno fiat visus vel tantum a duobus set eciam
ab omnibus si fieri possit vel a vij. ad minus quia assisa per pauciores visores
10 procedere non potest et qui debent poni in assisis et qui non denotatur per istas
constituciones:

Quia hundredarii, balliui et seruientes regis populum sibi subditum grauare
consueuerunt ponendo in assisis et iuratis homines languidos et decrepitos et
perpetua vel temporali languore detentos ac homines tempore summonicionis in
15 patria non morantes necnon et summonendo superfluam hominum multitudi-
nem ita quod quosdam dimitterent in pace prece vel precio et a quibusdam
denarios et alia munera extorquerent per quod assise et iurate frequenter per
pauperes et insufficientes capiebantur diuitibus et discretis pro suo dando
domi commorantibus statutum est quod de cetero non summoneantur in vna
20 assisa plures quam viginti quatuor.   Senes eciam lxx. annorum et vltra perpetuo   [*223*]
languidi vel eciam tempore summonicionis infirmi vel in patria non morantes in
minoribus assisis non ponantur nec iuratis vel assisis quamuis in eodem comitatu
capi debeant aliqui qui minus tenuerint quam xx. solidatas terre per annum, et si
extra comitatum tunc non ponantur aliqui qui minus habuerint quam xl. soli-
25 datas exceptis dumtaxat testibus in cartis et scriptis.   In magnis autem assisis
milites terram habentes in comitatu licet moram non facientes in eodem pro
defectu militum eiusdem comitatus ponere licebit.   Si quis autem balliuus conuincatur quod contra hoc statutum euenerit restituet dampna grauatis et in
misericordia regis remanebit.   Et habeant iusticiarii ad assisas capiendas
30 assignati cum in comitatu venerint potestatem audiendi querimonias singulorum
conquerencium in premissis et iusticiam exhibendi in forma predicta.

Et quia spoliatores pocius viribus quam iudicio vtuntur quod est manifeste
contra pacem ideo causare non poterunt quod per quindenam non fuerint pre-
muniti secundum racionem racionabilis summonicionis ideo essonia non habe-
35 bunt nec longas inducias nec iudiciorum solempnitates set pro voluntate vicecomitis attachiari poterunt quia siue quindenam habuerint siue non venire
poterunt per balliuos et per amicos suos qui personaliter adesse non possunt et
quorum responsiones admittentur ad instruccionem iuratorum et eciam ad
declinandum assisam.   Cognoscere autem non poterunt disseysinam remittere
40 neque pacisci.

Et cum iuratores visum fecerint statim inbreuientur nomina, et summoniantur

5. sint] sunt, J.   6. affines] affinies, J.   10. denotatur per *scripsimus*, decipiant, J.
13. decrepitos et] despitos, J.   15. non] ante, J.   16. dimitterent] dimitteret, J.
28. statutum, J. *in margine*.   39. declinandum, Br., declinandam, J; autem] cum, J.

included in the writ, nor may he sue for an exchange of property from the donor unless, while he is in seisin, he has taken the precaution to safeguard himself by a writ of warranty of charter.   And the sheriff should meanwhile arrange for twelve free and law-worthy men of the neighbourhood to view the said tenement. According to this instruction, it is his duty to require many free and law-worthy men of the neighbourhood to assemble and, in the presence of the parties if they wish to be present, to arrange for twelve to be chosen therefrom who are akin to neither party nor essionable nor under suspicion and who are not sick or of villein stock or dwelling in another county or under age or too old, and these he will send forthwith to view the said tenement.   And the view is not to be made by one alone or by two only but, indeed, by all, if this can be done, or by seven at least, because an assize cannot proceed with fewer viewers.   And who should be and should not be put on assizes is indicated by these enactments:

St. West-
minster,
II. c. 38
Because hundredors, bailiffs and serjeants of the king, to harass the people within their jurisdiction, have been wont to put on assizes and juries sick and decrepit men, confined to bed with chronic or temporary illness, and men who, at the time of summons, were not dwelling in the district, and also to summon an excessive number of men so that they might let some of them go in peace at their prayer or for a price and from some of them might extort money and other gifts, with the result that assizes and juries have been frequently taken by poor and incapable men, while wealthy and responsible men remained at home by reason of their gifts, it is enacted that henceforth no more than twenty-four are to be summoned for one assize and that old men of seventy years and over, those chronically ill, and also those who at the time of summons are sick or not dwelling in the district, shall not be put on petty assizes, nor should any be put on juries or assizes, though these be taken in their own county, who hold less than twenty shillings' worth of land a year and, if taken outside the county, then none should be put on them who hold less than forty shillings' worth, except only witnesses to charters and deeds.   On grand assizes, however, it will be permissible to put knights who have land in the county although they do not dwell therein, if there is a lack of knights of that county.   And if any bailiff is convicted of offending against this statute, he shall pay damages to those who are injured and be amerciable to the king.   And the justices assigned to hold assizes, when they come into the county, shall have authority to hear the plaints of all complainants regarding the above matters and to administer justice in the aforesaid form.

Bracton,
f. 182
And because dispossessors use force rather than a judgement of the court and this is manifestly against the peace, therefore they cannot grumble that they have not been given a fortnight's warning as a reasonable summons requires, nor for that reason will they have essoins or long postponements or the formalities of judicial proceedings; but they can be attached at the discretion of the sheriff, because, whether they have a fortnight's summons or not, those who cannot be present in person can appear by their bailiffs and friends, and their answers will be admitted for the information of the jurors as well as for abating the assize, but they cannot acknowledge the disseisin or repudiate it or compromise it.

And when the jurors have made the view, their names are to be noted; and

per bonos summonitores hoc est per duos liberos homines et ideo bonos quia
terras tenentes quod sint coram talibus iusticiariis ad certo diem et locum
secundum mandatum iusticiariorum vicecomiti directum parati inde facere
recognicionem.   Set tunc refert vtrum in comitatu vel extra comitatum ad quod
5   nos instruit magna carta de libertatibus que dicit quod communia placita non
sequantur curiam regis set teneantur in banco apud Westmonasterium.   Recog-   f. 86*b*
niciones autem assisarum noue disseysine et mortis antecessoris non capiantur
nisi in suis comitatibus.   Iurate tamen alibi capi poterunt sine iuris offensa non
autem assise noue disseysine et mortis antecessoris.   Ad idem in constitucioni-
10   bus secundis Westmonasterii assignentur duo iusticiarii ad minus in singulis comitatibus qui sibi associent duos vel vnum de discrecioribus militibus de comitatu
in quo declinabunt coram quibus capiantur assise noue disseysine et mortis antecessoris et iurate conuiccionum et certificacionum ad minus ter per annum
videlicet semel inter quindenam Natiuitatis sancti Iohannis Baptiste et primum
15   diem Augusti et iterum inter festum Exaltacionis sancte Crucis et octabas sancti
Michaelis et tercio inter festa Epiphanie et Purificacionis et in quolibet comitatu
ad quamlibet capcionem assisarum antequam recedant statuant diem de redditu
suo quod ita omnes de comitatu scire valeant de eorum aduentu et de termino in
terminum adiornent assisas super vocacionibus warantorum per resummoniciones
20   et per defectus recognitorum si ad alium diem earum capcio differatur.   Et si de
aliqua causa viderint vtile esse quod assise mortis antecessoris per essonium vel
per vocaciones warantorum ponantur in respectum tunc liceat iusticiariis partes
adiornare in banco vt difficultates si que fuerint terminentur ibidem et tunc   [224]
mittant iusticiariis de banco recordum cum breui originali.   Et cum loquela
25   perueniatur ad capcionem assise remittatur loquela cum breui originali per
iusticiarios de banco ad priores iusticiarios assignatos coram quibus capiatur
assisa.   Et iusticiarii de banco de cetero dent in huiusmodi assisis iiij^{or} dies ad
minus per annum.

    Apponatur eciam terminus in breui noue disseysine quia assisa noue dissey-
30   sine infra certum tempus limitatur et vltra non extenditur.   Tempus enim est
modus tollende obligacionis et accionis quia tempus currit contra desides et sui
iuris contemptores et ita poterit quis amittere accionem et seysinam suam per
negligenciam suam et inde habebit tenens contra querentem excepcionem.   Et
vnde fit talis constitucio quod in breui de recto non narretur de longiori seysina
35   quam de tempore regis Ricardi, in breuibus noue disseysine et nuper obiit non nisi
post primam transfretacionem domini Henrici regis patris regis Edwardi in
Vasconiam, in breuibus mortis antecessoris, consanguinei, aui, de ingressu et de
natiuo habendo nisi a tempore coronacionis regis Henrici patris regis Edwardi.

    Et sicut tempus est modus tollende obligacionis et accionis ita est modus

    2. sint] sicut, J.   11. duos vel vnum *in statuto, om.* J.   13. minus, J., plus *in statuto.*
18. ita *in statuto, om.* J; *ulterius* de *addidimus.*   20. alium] vnum, J.   22. *post* warantorum, J. *add.* quod assise.   30. est *om.* J.   31. tollende] tollendo, J.

they are to be summoned by good summoners (that is, by two free men and, because they hold land, therefore they are good) to be before such-and-such justices at a stated day and place according to the instructions addressed to the sheriff by the justices, prepared to make their recognition thereon. But then it is a question whether [the land] is within or outside the county. On this point the Great Charter of Liberties instructs us, for it says that common pleas are not to follow the king's court but to be held in the Bench at Westminster; but recognitions of assizes of novel disseisin and *mort d'ancestor* are to be taken only in the counties to which they belong. Yet juries can be taken elsewhere without offending the law, but not assizes of novel disseisin and *mort d'ancestor*. For this purpose the second Statute of Westminster assigns two justices at least in every county, who are to associate with themselves two or one of the more discreet knights of the county they are visiting, before whom are to be taken assizes of novel disseisin and *mort d'ancestor* and juries of attaint and certifications three times a year at least, namely, once between the Quinzaine of the Nativity of Saint John the Baptist[1] and the first day of August, and secondly between the Feast of the Exaltation of the Holy Cross[2] and the Octave of Michaelmas,[3] and thirdly between the Feasts of the Epiphany[4] and the Purification.[5] And in every county at every taking of assizes, before their departure they shall appoint a day for their return so that everyone of the county can learn of their coming, and they shall adjourn assizes from term to term, if the taking of them may be deferred to another day on vouchers to warranty for resummons and for lack of recognitors. And if for any reason they think it expedient that assizes of *mort d'ancestor* shall be respited by essoins or vouchers to warranty, then the justices are permitted to adjourn the parties to the Bench so that, if there are any difficulties, they may be determined there, and then they shall send the record with the original writ to the justices of the Bench. And when the action arrives at the taking of the assize, it will be remitted with the original writ by the justices of the Bench to the former justices assigned, before whom the assize is to be taken. And the justices of the Bench will henceforth give to these assizes four days in the year at least.

A term is also to be put in a writ of novel disseisin, because an assize of novel disseisin is limited to a certain period and does not extend beyond. For time is a means of getting rid of an obligation and an action because time runs against the slothful and those who are scornful of their right; and thus a man may lose his right of action and his seisin by his negligence, and on that account the tenant will have an exception against the plaintiff. And in this regard is a statute made as follows, that in the writ of right no longer seisin shall be counted than from the time of King Richard; in writs of novel disseisin and *nuper obiit* only after the first passage of King Henry, father of King Edward, to Gascony; in writs of *mort d'ancestor*, cosinage, aiel, entry and neifty only from the time of the coronation of King Henry, father of King Edward.

And just as time is a means of getting rid of an obligation and an action, so

Bracton
f. 179*b*

Magna Carta,
cc. 11, 12

St. Westminster,
II. c. 30

Bracton,
f. 212*b*

St. Westminster,
I. c. 39

Bracton,
f. 212*b*

---

[1] 8 July.　　[2] 14 September.　　[3] 6 October.　　[4] 6 January.　　[5] 2 February.

inducende obligacionis et accionis et ex tempore adquirunt sibi plures acciones
vt si quis intruserit se in tenemento vel alium iniuste disseysiuerit si statim non
reiciatur post tempus habebit accionem si fuerit eiectus.   Si quis eciam ingressum
fecerit in communam pasture per vsurpacionem ante tempus quo currit assisa
5   mortis antecessoris non poterit inde eici quin recuperet.   Preterea si quis aren-
tauerit in curia sua finem pro pulcre placitando a tempore quo rex Henricus pater
regis Edwardi transfretauit in Britanniam non poterit de huiusmodi redditu
disseysiri.   Mulieres eciam rapte vltra xl. dies nullatenus audiantur.   Idem eciam
parcorum et viuariorum vltra annum in prosecucione contra malefactores eo-
10   rundem ab accione repellantur, et eodem modo ipsi qui wreckum prosequantur
vel weyuium vel qui finem velint clamare.   Et idem tempus limitatur in sectis
petendis.

CAP. VI.   DE MODO VIDENDI IN TENEMENTIS

Missis itaque visoribus necesse est quod discrete fiat visus quod certa res in
15   iudicium possit deduci iuratores verum et certum facere possint sacramentum
et iusticiarii proferre iudicium.   Videre autem debent iuratores vtrum terra sit
vel redditus et vtrum res sacra vel priuata et quale sit tenementum vtrum priuatum vel commune et quid et quantum querens posuerit in visu suo vtrum plus
vel minus, quia si querens superfluum in visu suo posuerit in misericordia pro
20   superdemanda remanebit, sicut et in assisa mortis antecessoris, et vtrum totum
in vno comitatu vel in diuersis in qua villa et in quo loco et in qua parte loci inter
quos fines et quos terminos tenementum contineatur.   Si autem de redditu de   f. 87
estoueriis bosci de corrodiis vel liberacionibus bladi aut aliorum victualium aut
necessariorum tolneto tronagio pontagio passagio et hiis similibus vel de cus-
25   todiis parcorum boscorum forestarum chaciarum warennarum portarum et huiusmodi officiis vel de communa pasture turbarie piscarie et aliis communis similibus   [225]
fieri debeat visus tunc fiat de tenemento vnde proveniunt vel saltem de hiis ad
que dicuntur pertinere adeo de abbaciis et prioratibus sicut de aliis locis priuatis.
Item cum spoliatus visum faciat iuratoribus videre debent an proprium sit vel
30   commune et si commune sit inter coheredes vel vicinos tunc fiat visus de toto
tenemento in communi a quocumque facta fuerit disseysina.   Videre eciam
debent an sit commune sicut diuise communes sunt que diuidunt et distingunt
dominia et fines agrorum siue sit arbor, fossatum, lapis vel murus.   Regis via

4. fecerit *addidimus*.   7. regis] rex, J.   10. prosequantur] prosequitur, J.   17. sit]
fit, J.   19. pro] per, J.   22. de *om*. J.   24. similibus] similia, J.   25. warennarum]
warannarum, J.   30. visus] vnus, J.   32. commune] certe, J.   33. via *om*. J.

it is a means of giving rise to an obligation and an action, and many actions are produced through the efflux of time: for example, if a man intrudes himself into a tenement or unlawfully disseises another, and he is not ejected forthwith, after a time he will have a right of action if he is ejected.   Again, if a man should have entered into common of pasture by usurpation before the period from which the assize of *mort d'ancestor* runs, he cannot be ejected therefrom without his recovering.   Further, if a man should have arrented in his court a fine for beaupleader from the time when King Henry, father of King Edward, crossed into Brittany, he cannot be disseised of this rent.   Women also who are ravished will in no wise be heard after forty days.   Again, [those who complain of offences in] parks and stews who prosecute after a year's delay will be refused an action against trespassers therein, and likewise those who sue for wreck or waif or who wish to challenge a fine [after a year's delay].   And the same period of limitation[1] applies to demanding suits of court.

St. Marlborough,
c. 11
St. Westminster,
I. c. 13
Ibid.,
c. 20
Ibid.,
c. 4
Modus
levandi fines
St. Marlborough
c. 9

CHAPTER 6.   HOW THE VIEW OF A TENEMENT IS MADE

Bracton,
f. 179*b*

So when the viewers are sent, it is necessary that the view should be made with care so that something certain can be brought to adjudication and the jurors can make a true and precise oath and the justices can deliver judgement.   The jurors ought to see whether the property is land or rent, and whether it is sacred or private, and what kind of tenement it is, whether it is privately held or held in common, and what and how much the plaintiff includes in his view, whether it is too much or too little; because if the plaintiff should include too much in his view, he will be amerciable for an excessive demand (as is also the case in an assize of *mort d'ancestor*).   And [the jurors ought to see] whether the whole of the tenement is in one county or in several, in which township and in which place and in which part of that place, and between which limits and which bounds it is contained.   If, moreover, a view is to be made of rent, of estovers of wood, of corrodies or liveries of corn or other victuals or necessaries, of toll, tronage, pontage, passage or such like, or of the keeping of parks, woods, forests, chaces, warrens, gates and such like offices, or of common of pasture, turbary, fishery and other similar rights of common, then let it be made of the tenement from which these things issue or, at least, of those tenements to which they are said to be appurtenant, both in the case of abbeys and priories and in the case of other places in private hands.   Further, when the dispossessed presents the view to the jurors, they ought to see whether the tenement is his own in severalty or is held in common; and, if it is held in common between coheirs or neighbours, then a view should be made of the whole tenement held in common, whosoever made the disseisin.   The jurors ought also to see whether it is common, as are the common bounds which divide and distinguish lordships and limits of fields, whether the bound is a tree, a dyke, a stone or a wall.   The king's highway, although it

Bracton,
f. 180

Bracton,
f. 180*b*

1 Henry III's passage to Brittany.

quamuis communis sit non tamen inter vicinos communis est et quicumque inde
aliquid occupauerit excedendo fines et terminos terre sue dicitur fecisse purpres-
turam super regem et transgressionem et idem dici poterit de via militari que
ducit ad mare et ad portus et ad mercata.   Set de diuisis prediorum de consensu
5 vicinorum factis secus est quod huiusmodi diuise communes sunt et dicuntur
diuise eo quod agros diuidunt et tenementa.   Aqua vero currens non dicitur
diuisa nisi quamdiu rectum cursum tenuerit et cum alueum mutauerit desinit
esse diuisa inter vicinos.

Item sicut oportet facere visum de tenemento de quo redditus prouenerit ita
10 videre oportet tenementum propter quod prestatur redditus, vt si quis certum redditum constituerit alicui et heredibus suis de camera sua vt aquam ducere possit
per fundum suum et quo casu videre oportebit si talis aquam duxerit vel non
duxerit.   Item si quis redditum constituerit eodem modo vt habeat in
alieno fundo ius pascendi vel eundi vel quid tale faciendi siue alius aquam
15 duxerit vel diuerterit vel quid tale fecerit vel non semper tamen debetur redditus
et pro redditu seruitus vnde si aliquis ipsorum contrahencium recedere voluerit
a contractu tamen alius nisi voluerit non recedet et vnde si ille qui seruitutem concesserit redditum recipere noluerit nichilominus tamen debetur seruitus vt ius
eundi aquamue ducendi vel pascendi vel huiusmodi.   Si autem seruitus con-
20 cedatur et redditus denegetur vel detineatur nec sit locus vel tenementum vbi
districcio fieri possit, locus erit assise noue disseysine quasi de libero tenemento,
et si non sit tenementum de quo redditus prouenerit et de quo visus fieri possit
sufficit tamen si fiat visus de tenemento propter quod debetur redditus.   Item
videre debent si fiat aliquid in fundo alicuius iniuste quod vicino noceat vt si
25 fossatum vel murus vel huiusmodi leuetur vel prosternatur vel aliud quid fiat tale
ad nocumentum iniustum vel iniuriosum nec sufficit videre tantum tenementum
quod nocet set eciam illud cui nocitum est.   Item si ius eundi vel pascendi vel
quid tale debeatur non sufficit videre tenementum in quo ius illud constituitur
verum eciam illud ad quod ius pertinet vnde oportet videre tenementum vbi
30 pastura est et tenementum ad quod pertinet pastura.   Si autem cum querens
locum designat visoribus nescit tamen designare in qua parte loci sufficit si in
aliquo loco detur ei seysina per sacramentum iuratorum.   Si autem de certa
parte loci constiterit set nesciat querens terminos et fines distinguere eo quod
termini et lapides finales amoti sunt forte tunc ei assignetur tantum quantum
35 iuratores crediderint ipsum esse disseysitum quia etsi iusticiarii semper certum
non possunt reddere iudicium eo quod de incerta re agitur apud illos tamen hoc
facere debent quantum eis fuerit possibile.

1. et Br., set, J.   4. *post* mercata *add.* dici poterit, J.   9. prouenerit] prouenit, J.
11. et *om.* J.   13. *post* constituerit *add.* quamuis, J.   15. tamen] cum, J.   17. tamen]
cum, J; nisi] non, J; si *om.* J.   18. noluerit] voluerit, J; seruitus] seruiciis, J.   20. nec] vel, J.
22. prouenerit] prouenit, J.   29. vnde *om.* J.   29. *post* oportet *add.* enim, J.
30. cum querens] conquerens, J.

is common, is not, however, common between neighbours, and whosoever seizes anything thereof beyond the limits and bounds of his own land is said to commit a purpresture and trespass against the king; and the same may be said of a military highway that leads to the sea and to ports and markets.   But it is otherwise where the bounds of estates are concerned, which are made with the consent of neighbours, because these bounds are common and they are called *divisae* because they 'divide' fields and holdings.   Running water, however, is not called a bound, except for so long as it holds its proper course; and when it changes its bed, it ceases to be a boundary between neighbours.

Bracton
f. 181

Again, just as it is necessary to make a view of the tenement out of which a rent issues, so it is necessary to view the tenement in respect of which the rent is paid: for example, if a man has arranged for a certain rent to be paid out of his chamber to someone and his heirs so that he may lead water through his estate, in such a case it will be necessary to see if he does so or does not.   Again, if a man should likewise establish a rent in order that he may have in someone else's land a right of pasture or a right of way or a right to do this or that, whether he leads water or diverts its course, or does this or that or does not do it, the rent will always be due, and for the rent the servitude: wherefore, if any one of the contracting parties wishes to resile from the contract, the other party shall not resile unless he wishes to do so; and, therefore, if he who has granted the servitude refuses to accept the rent, nevertheless the servitude remains, such as a right of way or of leading water or of grazing or the like.   If, however, the servitude is granted and the rent denied or withheld, and there is no place or tenement upon which distraint may be made, an assize of novel disseisin will lie as if for a freehold, and if there is no tenement out of which the rent issues and of which a view can be made, nevertheless it suffices if a view is made of the tenement in respect of which the rent is due.   Again, the jurors ought to see whether anything is unlawfully done in anyone's land which is a nuisance to a neighbour: for example, if a dyke or a wall or the like is erected or knocked down, or anything else is done unlawfully or harmfully to his nuisance: nor does it suffice to view merely the tenement that is the cause of the nuisance but also that to which the nuisance is done.   Again, if a right of way or of grazing or a right to do this or that is owing, it does not suffice to view the tenement in which that right is based but also the tenement to which the right is appurtenant; wherefore it is necessary to view the tenement where the grazing is and the tenement to

Bracton,
f. 181*b*

which the grazing is appurtenant.   If, however, when the plaintiff indicates the place to the viewers, and yet finds it impossible to indicate the precise part, it suffices if seisin is given to him in any [part of the] place by the oath of the jurors. If, however, there is certainty regarding the particular part of the place, but the plaintiff does not know how to decide its metes and bounds because the metes and boundary-stones have perchance been removed, then there shall be assigned to him as much as the jurors believe him to have been disseised of, since, although the justices are not always able to deliver a precise judgement because an uncertain thing is in action before them, yet they ought to do this as far as it is possible for them to do so.

Item continetur in breui 'Pone per vadium et saluos plegios talem vel [226]
balliuum suum si ipse inuentus non fuerit' vnde videndum erit quid pertineat ad
dominum et quid ad balliuum.   Balliuus enim non potest quicquid dominus
poterit.   Non enim poterit balliuus cognoscere disseysinam quominus procedat
5 assisa ad veritatem declarandam nec eciam transigere nec pacisci nec iocum f. 87b
partitum facere nec aliud quo magis dominus suus seysinam amittat in toto vel
in parte nisi hoc sit per iudicium et assisam.   Dicere tamen poterit sicut ipse dominus quare assisa remanere debet in perpetuum vel ad tempus.   Dicere enim
poterit contra iuratores et causas suspicionis pretendere sicut ipse dominus, et
10 eciam contra ipsum iusticiarium si forte iurisdiccionem non habuerit et contra
querentem et contra breue et generaliter omnes habebit excepciones quas
haberet ipse dominus principalis.   Attornatus vero hec omnia facere poterit.
Est tamen differencia magna inter attornatum et responsalem.

Item habere debet vicecomes nomina plegiorum quia si querens coram iusti-
15 ciariis retraxerit sic ipse et plegii sui in misericordia remanebunt et ei facienda
est securitas quem comoda sequi debent quia si securitas defecerit difficilis erit
prosecucio misericordie satisfaccionis propter libertates.   Item habere debet
breue coram iusticiariis nam sine breui cognoscendi non habebunt potestatem.

CAP. VII.   DE INTENCIONE QUERENTIS

20   In aduentu vero iusticiariorum partibus vocatis et non conparentibus, omnes
plegii querentis et tenentis vel eius balliui erunt in misericordia.   Petens tamen
semel poterit essoniari secundum tenorem huius constitucionis:

In breuibus autem assisarum et attinctarum et iuratarum vtrum non habeat
petens nisi vnicum essonium tenens autem nullum nec tenenti nec petenti post
25 apparenciam nullum essonium allocetur set faciant attornatos si velint alioquin
capiantur assise vel iurate per eorum defaltam.

Querens tamen eandem habeat accionem quam prius set per aliud breue consimile.   Si autem querens venerit et alius non, attachiatus et plegii sui in misericordia remanebunt et in odium defalte capiatur assisa.   Si autem venerit querens
30 et ille de quo queritur statim capiatur assisa.   Si vero querens simpliciter se
retraxerit in quocumque fuerit placito numquam per consimile breue recuperabit.
Si incepta fuerit assisa vel placitum quodcumque inceptum et error forte fuerit
in breuis inpetracione ita quod cadere oportebit tanquam viciosum siue querens
dicat quod sequi noluerit breue illud vel se simpliciter retrahat vel licenciam retra-

1. saluos] certos, J.   5. pacisci] pacissi, J.   8. iocum partitum, Br.; locum petitum, J.
7. Dicere tamen poterit, Br.; om. J.   8. assisa remanere] assisam vendicare, J; contra
assisam quare remaneat, Br.   15. ei] eius, J.   28. alius] attachiatur, J.   30. capiatur]
capiatus, J.   33. inpetracione] perpetracione, J.   34. noluerit] voluerit, J.

Bracton,
f. 212b

Also included in the writ are the words: 'Put under gage and safe pledges so-and-so, or his bailiff if he himself should not be found'; whence it must be seen what pertains to the lord and what to the bailiff.   For the bailiff cannot do whatever the lord can.   For the bailiff cannot acknowledge a disseisin to prevent the assize from proceeding to declare the truth, nor can he make an agreement or compromise or put in jeopardy or do anything else whereby his lord is the more likely to lose his seisin, wholly or in part, except it be by judgement and assize. He can, however, say, as the lord himself might, why the assize should be stayed for ever or for a time, and, like the lord himself, he can challenge the jurors and put forward reasons for suspicion, and likewise challenge the justice himself (if perchance he has no jurisdiction) and the plaintiff and the writ and, in general, he will have all the exceptions that his principal, the lord himself, might have.   An attorney, indeed, can do all these things [that the principal can], but there is a great difference between an attorney and a respondent [bailiff].

Bracton,
f. 213

The sheriff should have the names of the pledges because, if the plaintiff should withdraw before the justices, then both he and his pledges will be amerciable, and security must be given to him to whom the payments ought to accrue because, if security is lacking, the pursuit of satisfaction for the amercement will be difficult on account of franchises.   Further, he should have the writ before the justices, for without the writ they will have no authority to hear the action.

CHAPTER 7.   OF THE PLAINTIFF'S STATEMENT OF CLAIM

Bracton,
f. 182

At the coming of the justices, if the parties are called and do not appear, all the pledges of the plaintiff and the tenant or the tenant's bailiff will be amerciable. The demandant can, however, be essoined once, according to the terms of this enactment:

St. West-
minster,
I. cc. 42, 43
St. West-
minster,
II. c. 28

In writs of assizes and attaints and juries of *utrum* the demandant shall have one essoin only, but the tenant none, and no essoin shall be allowed to either the tenant or the demandant after appearance in court but, if they wish, they may appoint attorneys, and otherwise the assizes or juries shall be taken in their default.

Bracton,
f. 182

The plaintiff will, however, have the same action as formerly, but by another and similar writ.   If, however, the plaintiff appears and the other does not, the defendant who was attached and his pledges will be amerciable and, in reprobation of the default, the assize will be taken.   If, however, both the plaintiff comes and he of whom complaint is made, the assize will be taken forthwith. But if the plaintiff simply withdraws from whatever action it may be, he will never recover by a similar writ.   If an assize or any other action should be begun and there should perchance be an error in the suing out of the writ so that it must be quashed as defective, whether the plaintiff says that he does not wish to prosecute that writ, or simply withdraws, or prays leave to withdraw, or withdraws

Bracton,
f. 182b

hendi petat vel alio quocumque modo ad melius tantum breue poterit recuperare.
Quia ad accionem non respondetur nec contra accionem excipitur set tantum
contra vicium et breuis errorem et accio in se integra manet et non incepta et ideo
nulli preiudicabitur retraccio nisi ei qui a breui se retraxerit et accione.   Set
5   qualitercumque se retraxerit inpune non recedet quia ipse et plegii sui de
prosequendo in misericordia regis remanebunt nisi eis per iusticiarios gratis
licencia recedendi concedatur.   Si autem breue conpetens sit nec excipi poterit
contra personam si res et accio in iudicium deducantur et non sit error in
quantitate rei petite et tunc petat licenciam recedendi simpliciter recedat ab
10   vtroque et numquam per aliud breue consimile recuperabit.   Si autem sic   [227]
dicam 'Retraho me versus talem,' quia nichil tenet forte, nichilominus recu-
perabo ad aliud breue versus alium qui tenet quamuis versus non tenentem me
retraxerim ab vtroque, nec obstat michi illa subtraxio si non tenens de nouo inceperit possidere et super eum iterum inpetrauero, quia iam incepit accio de
15   nouo conpetere que tunc non conpeciit et non in tali casu.   Semper est videndum
vtrum me retraxero de breui tantum pro vicio vel de breui et assisa, tacite vel expresse, et si eadem sit persona vel eadem res vel diuersa et vtrum accio primo non
conpeciit quia tenens non tenuit et postea conpetere incepit.   Si autem tenens
dicat quod nichil habet nec aliquid clamat in tenemento de quo queritur ab omni
20   accione tam rei quam huiusmodi pertinenciarum excluditur in perpetuum nisi
ex nouo contractu sibi aliquo genere adquisicionis generetur.

Partibus autem in iudicio conparentibus et audito breui patente per quod iu-
dices cognicionem habeant et iurisdiccionem ad officium eorum pertinet
querentem de iure suo diligentissime examinare vt scire possint si accionem
25   habeat vel querelam et vtrum recognicio procedere debeat in modum iurate vel
assise.   Interrogare vel eciam debent reum si ad ipsum pertineat excepcio et
qualis qui si presens disseysinam cognouerit mittendus est gaole eo autem si
iniuriam cognouerit que est contra pacem.   Docere autem oportet petentem et   f. 88
plenius ostendere quod sua intersit queri quia non sufficit dicere quod aliquis dis-
30   seysiuit me de libero tenemento meo sic vnde proponendo intencionem meam
nisi illam fundauero aliqua racione probabiliter vel presumptiue vt si dicam quod
talis disseysiuit me de tali libero tenemento, oportebit me docere qualiter fuit michi
liberum tenementum vel denegabitur michi accio ita videlicet quod quia michi
descenderit ex causa successionis escaete reuersionis dotis vel ex aliqua alia iusta
35   causa adquirendi et vnde fui in seysina per tantum tempus donec ipse de quo
queritur me iniuste disseysiuit vel saltem quod tenementum illud qualemcumque

3. et accio Br., *om.* J.   7. licencia, *om.* J.   16. vel de breui, Br., *om.* J.
18. postea, Br., petens, J.   28. iniuriam, Br., disseysinam, J.

in some other way, he will be able to recover by merely obtaining a better writ. Because no answer is made to the action and no exception against the action, but only against the defect and error in the writ, the right of action remains unimpaired and no action is begun, and therefore a withdrawal is prejudicial to none except to him who withdraws from the writ and the action. But howsoever the plaintiff may withdraw, he will not depart with impunity, because he and his pledges of prosecution will remain amerciable to the king unless licence to withdraw is freely granted to them by the justices. If, however, the writ is in order and no exception is possible against the person [of the plaintiff], and if the property and action are brought to trial, and there is no error in the amount of property claimed, and the plaintiff then seeks leave to withdraw, he shall simply withdraw from both writ and action and he will never recover by another similar writ. If, however, I should say thus, 'I withdraw myself against so-and-so', because perchance he holds nothing, nevertheless I will recover on another writ against another who does hold, even though I have withdrawn from both [writ and action] as against the non-tenant. Nor does this withdrawal estop me if the non-tenant should begin afresh to get possession and I again sue out a writ against him, because a right of action has now begun to be freshly available to me which was not then available, and not in regard to the same case. It is always to be considered whether I withdraw from the writ only on account of its defect or from both writ and assize, tacitly or expressly, and whether the person and the property are the same or different, and whether at first the action was not admissible because the tenant did not hold, and subsequently began to be admissible. If, however, the tenant should say that he has nothing and claims nothing in the tenement regarding which the plaint is made, he is excluded for ever from any action regarding either the property or its appurtenances, unless an action should arise for him out of a new contract through some kind of acquisition.

Bracton,
f. 183b

When the parties appear at the trial and the writ patent has been heard under which the judges have cognisance and jurisdiction, it is their duty to examine the plaintiff very closely concerning his claim so that they may know whether he has an action or plaint and whether the recognition should proceed by way of jury or assize. They ought also to examine the defendant to see whether an exception is available to him and what kind it is; and if he is present and acknowledges the disseisin, he must be sent to gaol if indeed he has acknowledged a wrong which is a breach of the peace. The plaintiff must also set forth and show in detail what grounds he has to complain, because it is not sufficient to say that someone has disseised me of my freehold, thus setting out my statement of claim, unless I base it on some probable or presumptive reason: for example, if I say that so-and-so has disseised me of such-and-such a freehold, I shall be obliged to set forth in what way the freehold belonged to me (or an action will be denied me), for instance, that it was because it descended to me by cause of succession, escheat, reversion, dower or some other lawful cause of acquisition, and that I was in seisin thereof for such-and-such a period of time, until he, of whom I complain, unlawfully disseised me; or, at least, that I have held the said tenement

Bracton
f. 183
Bracton,
f. 183b

ingressum habuero per tantum tempus pacifice tenui quod sine iudicio non
debui disseysiri quia cum quis agere velit quod possessionem alicuius adipiscatur
docere debet de iure suo per quod probet illam rem ad se pertinere alioquin sub-
cumbet accio quamuis res illa non pertineat ad disseysitorem vel dicere potero in
5 casu quod qualitercumque tempus siue per longum siue per modicum ad illum
non pertinuit me disseysire cum nullum ius haberet vel iuris scintillam eiciendi
nec aliquam accionem in causa proprietatis haberet si eiceretur. Et sicut
necesse est quod petens doceat in causa proprietatis quo iure petat cum non
sufficiat simpliciter dicere quod ius habeat in re nisi doceat de iure, ita nec sufficit
10 proponere querelam nisi querens doceat ius querele et quo iure ad ipsum pertineat
et quo titulo an per titulum successionis hereditarie vel feoffamenti et perquisiti
vel escaete vel per alium. Si autem per successionem tunc sufficiet ad liberum
tenementum habendum sola pedis posicio dum tamen sit verus heres et vacuam
inuenerit possesssionem et non solum de mesuagio verum eciam de toto quod
15 tenementum admittitur quod secus esset de herede non vero sicut de bastardo in
vtroque membro vel de herede remoto quibus non conpetit assisa si a vero herede   [228]
ab eius hereditate eiciantur quamuis per dimidium annum fuerint in possessione.
Huiusmodi enim possessio pocius dicitur intrusio quam seysina. Vel si heres
remotus ingrediatur statim post mortem antecessoris et ambo diu simul manserint
20 et vnus postea alium eiciat pro vero herede semper iudicabitur. De titulo autem
liberi tenementi per feoffamentum et perquisitum multa sunt consideranda quia
cum quis alium feoffauerit statim transfertur liberum tenementum infeoffatum
dum tamen feoffamentum illud nulli cedat in dampnum vel preiudicium et
eciam si donator in donacione nichil sibi retinuerit nisi nudum dominium et
25 seruicium alioquin non statim transfertur. Nam si tenentes ad terminum vite
tantum custodes intrusores vel tenentes per feodum talliatum feoffamenta fecerint
de facto, et de iure non possint, non statim fit donatariis liberum tenementum
nisi per tempus pacificum subueniatur. Et si tales eiecti fuerint et ipsi assisam
portauerint consideranda sunt remota absencia illius cuius interest, tempus
30 noticiam portans eius resistendi et multa alia. Et similiter de villano alienante villenagium et balliuo tenementum in custodia sua existens alienante in quibus casibus non adquiritur donatariis liberum tenementum nisi ex longa et pacifica
seysina. In titulo autem per escaetam que quandoque adquiritur capitali domino
per feloniam tenentis vel cum tenens obierit sine herede et huiusmodi in quibus
35 casibus et hiis similibus sicut in reuersione post feodum talliatum in iure eciam
quod alicui conpetit per formam donacionis de facili adquiritur liberum tenementum perquisitoribus. In istis tamen duobus casibus diuersa exigitur veri-
ficacio et intencio. Adquiritur eciam titulus per quietamclamanciam per finem

2. adipiscatur] adipiscat, J.   4. quamuis, Br., quod, J.   8. petat, *om.* J.
23. preiudicium] per iudicium, J.

peacefully for such-and-such a length of time, whatever kind of entry I may
have had, that without a judgement of the court I ought not to be disseised:
because, when a man wishes to bring an action to obtain someone's possession,
he should explain his rights whereby he proves the said property to belong to
him, otherwise his action will fail, even though the property may not belong to
the disseisor. Or I could say, where appropriate, that whatever the period
of my possession, whether long or short, it was not for him to disseise me since
he had no right or glimmer of right to eject me, nor would he have any right of
action in a proprietary suit if he were ejected. And just as it is necessary that
a demandant in a proprietary action should set forth by what right he makes his
claim, since it is not sufficient to say simply that he has a right to the property
unless he specifies his right, so it is not sufficient merely to put forward a plaint
unless the plaintiff can set forth the grounds of his plaint and by what right [the
property] belongs to him and by what title, whether by title of hereditary succession or feoffment and acquisition or escheat or by any other title. If by succession, then, in order to have a freehold, it will be sufficient if merely a foot be
placed thereon (provided it be the true heir [who does this] and he finds possession
to be vacant) and not only for the messuage but for the whole of what is admitted
to belong to the tenement. But it would be otherwise if one were not the true heir,
such as a bastard on either side or a remote heir, to neither of whom an assize is
available if they are ejected by the true heir from his inheritance, even though they
should be in possession for half a year. For this kind of possession is called intrusion rather than seisin. Or if a remote heir should enter immediately after
the death of the ancestor and both [he and the true heir] should for a long time
remain [in possession] together, and if subsequently one should eject the other,
judgement will always be given for the true heir. Where the title to the freehold
is by feoffment and acquisition, there are many things to be considered because,
if one enfeoffs another, he forthwith transfers the freehold so enfeoffed, provided
that the said feoffment does not result in damage or prejudice to anyone, and
provided also that the donor, in making his gift, does not retain anything for
himself except bare lordship and service, for otherwise the freehold is not forthwith transferred. For if tenants for life only, guardians, intruders or tenants in
fee tail, make feoffments *de facto* when they cannot *de jure*, a freehold is not forthwith created for the donees, unless a period of peaceful possession comes to their
aid. And if such donees should be ejected and they themselves bring an assize,
consideration must be given to the absence afar of an interested party, the time
necessary for bringing notice of his opposition, and much else. And, similarly,
if a villein alienates his villein tenement or a bailiff alienates a tenement in his
keeping, in these cases the donees do not acquire a freehold, except through long
and peaceful seisin. Where the title is by escheat, which sometimes accrues to
the chief lord through the felony of a tenant, or where a tenant dies without heir
or the like, in these and similar cases, as in reversion after a fee tail, even where
the right belongs to someone by the terms of a gift, a freehold is easily obtained
by the acquirers. In these two cases, however, a different statement of claim and
proof are required. A title is also acquired by a quitclaim, by an indented fine,

Bracton,
f. 184

cirographatum et per iudicium curie regis et per pacienciam disseysiti et mulieri
per dotem et homini per legem Anglie et multis aliis modis et vnde si disseysitus
in intencione sua probanda nullum titulum sue possessionis velit exprimere
videtur quod accione merito debet expelli.   Et vt igitur certa res in iudicium de-
5 ducatur et certi reddantur iusticiarii et in aliqua certitudine instruantur iuratores
oportebit iusticiarios interrogaciones facere ad cautelam de quo tenemento
querens fuerit disseysitus et qualiter sit eius liberum tenementum et de qualitate
vtrum de terra vel de redditu et si de terra vtrum propria fuerit vel communis
publica vel res sacra vel vtrum sit hereditas descendens reuertens vel perquisitum
10 vel escaeta et vtrum in feodum vel ad vitam propriam vel alienam vel ad terminum
annorum vel donec fuerit prouisum ita quod ad minus presumi possit quod suum
possit esse liberum tenementum et quamuis fuerit alienum dum tamen seysinam
habuit quod sufficiens fuerit ita quod inpune sine iudicio non potuit inde
spoliari et quo casu necesse est de tempore seysine querendum.   Si autem de
15 redditu tunc inquirere oportebit si de illo redditu qui domino capitali debetur vel   f. 88*b*
de redditu annuo de aliquo tenemento percipiendo vel de redditu camere vel de
redditu concesso pro aliquo tenemento et pro aliquo iure tenendo vel libertate in
fundo alieno.   Oportet eciam inquirere si de corrodio vel aliis in constitucione
necnon et de quantitate tenementi vt sciri possit vtrum querens plus posuerit in
20 visu suo quam recuperare debeat per assisam et ne querens plus vsurpet in
seysina quam recuperauerit per assisam.   Inquirendum est eciam vtrum omnino   [*229*]
eiectus fuerit vel repulsus vel inpeditus quominus vti possit seysina sua.

     Et quamuis querens docere nesciat quare liberum tenementum habeat oportet
tamen tenentem docere quod non habet et quod iuste se posuit in seysina sicut per
25 iudicium iustum vel alio modo.   Si autem proferat cartam donacionis querentis
non sufficit nisi sola voluntas donatoris probari possit in donacione.   Si autem
negauerit se possidere dicens quod nichil inde teneat nec tenere clamat non propterea remaneat quominus assisa capiatur per quam si conuincatur quod tenens
sit et quod iniuste possideat querens tunc inpune ipsum eicere poterit.

30   Presentibus siquidem partibus vel saltem querente et recognitoribus omnibus
quamuis disseysitor presens non fuerit per se nec per balliuum suum nec per
alium qui per se verba facere possit procedat assisa et recognicio per defaltam
quia nulli parcendum est nec differenda erit assisa pro aliquo et in quo casu non
minus examinetur querens nec minus instruantur iuratores.

     5. *prius* et *om.* J.   12. et *om.* J.   23. querens] tenens, J.   24. tenentem] verum, J.
29. tunc] tamen, J.   32. procedat] procedit, J; et *om.* J.   33. pro] pre, J.

and by judgement of the king's court, and by the sufferance of the disseised and, for a woman, by dower, and, for a man, by the curtesy of England, and in many other ways.   And therefore, if the disseised will not state what his title to possession is when proving his statement of claim, he will seem to merit the dismissal of his action.

In order, therefore, that a specific thing should be brought to trial and that the justices should be precisely informed and the jurors instructed in a matter of certainty, the justices must, as a precaution, make enquiries as to the holding of which the plaintiff was disseised and how it came to be his freehold and what kind it is, whether land or rent, and, if land, whether it is severalty or common, public or consecrated property, or whether it is an inheritance by descent or reversion or an acquisition or escheat and whether in fee or for the life of the plaintiff or of another or for a term of years or until provision is made, so that it can, at least, be presumed that the property could be the plaintiff's freehold and, even though it should be another's, nevertheless he had a seisin which was sufficient to secure that he could not with impunity be dispossessed thereof without a judgement of the court; and in this case it is necessary to make enquiry regarding the length of time of the seisin.   If, however, it is a matter of rent, then enquiry must be made whether it is a rent due to the chief lord or an annual rent issuing from some tenement or a rent issuing from a chamber or a rent granted for some tenement or for holding some right or franchise in another's land.   Enquiry must also be made if it is in respect of a corrody or other things contained in an agreement and, again, about the extent of the holding so that it may be known whether the plaintiff put more in his view than he ought to recover by the assize and to prevent him usurping in seisin more than he should recover by the assize. Enquiry must also be made whether the plaintiff has been utterly ejected or repelled or obstructed so that he is unable to use his seisin.

And although the plaintiff may be unable to explain why he should have the freehold, nevertheless it behoves the tenant to show that the plaintiff does not have it and that he lawfully put himself in seisin, as by a lawful judgement of the court or in some other way.   If, however, he produces the plaintiff's deed of gift, this is not sufficient, unless it can be proved that the gift was made by the free will of the donor.   But if the tenant denies that he is in possession [of the property], saying that he neither holds nor claims to hold anything therein, there will be no stay on this account so that the assize is not taken; but if it is adjudged by the assize that the defendant is the tenant and that he is not in lawful possession, the plaintiff may then eject him with impunity.

When, therefore, the parties are present or at least the plaintiff, and all the recognitors, even though the disseisor is not present in person or by his bailiff or by anyone else who can speak formally on his behalf, the assize and recognition will proceed by default, because none is to be spared nor must the assize be postponed on anyone's behalf.   And in this case the plaintiff will be none the less examined and the jurors none the less instructed.

CAP. VIII. DE EXCEPCIONIBUS CONTRA IURATORES

Sunt autem quidam disseysitores qui cum in iudicio venerint aliquid nolunt vel forte nesciunt dicere quare assisa debeat remanere set statim negando quod disseysinam non fecerint se simpliciter ponunt in assisam et sic procedit assisa in
5 modum assise si omnes iuratores presentes sint contra quos excipi non poterit et si presentes non fuerint differatur assisa ad alium diem. Partibus vero in iudicio comparentibus et iuratoribus excipi enim poterit contra iuratores multipliciter. Eisdem enim modis amoueri poterunt a sacramento quibus eciam testes amouentur a testimonio. Repellitur autem sacramento infamis qui alias conuictus
10 fuerit de periurio quia iam legem liberam amisit nec vlterius dignus est legis libertate gaudere quia publice in legem commisit. Item repellitur propter inimiciciam magnam dum tamen presentem secus vero propter leuem que si aliquando fuit modo tamen non est. Item propter amiciciam presentem sicut propter odium. Item pro eo quod iurator repulsus aliquid iuris clamat in re petita de qua
15 debet iurare. Item repellitur ille qui in patria non moram fecit, excommunicatus, senex habens lxx. annos et amplius, seruus absque sacramento iuratorum simplici testimonio coniuratorum absque sacramento dum tamen a pluribus dictum fuerit et testatum quod fuerit in statu seruitutis et in possessione domini sui constitutus vt seruus. Item propter nimiam familiaritatem, consanguinitatem
20 et affinitatem presentem quia fere paribus passibus incedunt nisi eadem familiaritate, consanguinitate et affinitate vel consimili alteri parti sit coniunctus. Et idem dici poterit de amicicia et inimicicia. Item repellitur si fuerit cum eo pro quo iurare debet commensalis continue vel de eius familia et similiter si ita sit sub eius potestate quod ei possit inperari vel noceri vel iniuste distringi pro con-
25 suetudinibus vel seruiciis. Item repellitur iurator si fuerit in eadem causa sicut vna parcium vel si fuerit aduocatus alterius partis vel consiliarius.

CAP. IX. DE VEREDICTO IURATORUM [230]

Cum autem partes in iuratores consenserint statim procedat assisa qui per hec verba iurabunt: 'Hoc auditis iusticiarii quod veritatem dicam de assisa ista et de

2. nolunt] volunt, J.   8. eciam] et, J.   15. patria] patriam, J.   24. inperari] inpetrari, J.   24. noceri vel iniuste distringi] nocere vel iuste distringere, J.   25. in om. J.   26. post partis add. domini J. sed om. Br.

CHAPTER 8. OF EXCEPTIONS AGAINST JURORS

Bracton,
f. 184b

There are some disseisors who, when they appear in court, will not say anything or perchance cannot say why the assize should be stayed, but at once deny that they committed disseisin and simply put themselves on the assize.   And so, if all the jurors are present against whom there can be no exception, the assize proceeds in the manner of an assize; but if all the jurors are not present, the assize

Bracton,
f. 185

is adjourned to another day.   When the parties and the jurors, however, appear in court, the possible exceptions against the jurors are manifold.   They may be prevented from taking the oath in the same ways whereby witnesses also are prevented from testifying.   There will be excluded from taking the oath a man of ill-fame who has been convicted on another occasion of perjury, because he has already lost his free law-worthiness and is no longer worthy to enjoy the freedom of the law, because he has openly offended against the law.   Again, a man is excluded on account of great enmity, provided it still exists; but it is otherwise on account of a slight enmity, which, if it once existed, does not now, however, exist; again, on account of present affection as well as on account of hatred; again, because the juror who is challenged claims some right in the property demanded, regarding which he has to swear an oath.   He too is excluded who does not dwell in the district; or who is an excommunicate, or an old man of seventy years or more; or a villein (without the jurors being sworn but on the simple testimony of his fellow jurors without oath, provided it is said and testified by several that he is in servile condition and stands in the possession of his lord as a villein).   Again, on account of too much friendship, kinship and present affinity because they walk in almost even step, unless they are linked to the other party by the same friendship, kinship, affinity or the like.   And the same may be said of both affection and enmity.   Again, he is excluded if he should be a constant mess-mate of a party on whose behalf he is required to swear or a member of his household and, similarly, if he should be to such an extent under a party's authority that he can give him orders or harm him or unlawfully distrain him for customs or services.   Again, a juror is excluded if he should be involved in the same case as one of the parties or if he should be the advocate or counsellor of either party.

CHAPTER 9. OF THE VERDICT OF THE JURORS

Bracton,
f. 185

When the parties have agreed to the jurors, the assize forthwith proceeds and the jurors shall swear in these terms: 'Hear this, O Justices, that I will speak the

tenemento de quo visum feci per preceptum regis', vel sic 'de tenemento vnde
talis redditus prouenit' vel 'de pastura et tenemento' vel 'de communa vnde
visum feci.'　Vel si assisa aramietur de aliquo quod fiat ad nocumentum in fundo
vnius quod noceat fundo alterius tunc dicatur de eo quod nocet et postea de
5　tenemento cui nocitum est sic, 'de muro et tenemento vel huiusmodi vnde visum
feci'.　Et ita generaliter de omnibus racione quorum capiuntur assise prinici-
paliter et tunc dicant, 'et pro nichilo omittam quin veritatem dicam sic Deus me
adiuuet et hec sancta.'　Postea iurent alii sic: 'Tale sacramentum quale iste
primus iurauit tenebo erga me sic me etc.'　Et si plures assise capi debeant sub
10　vno sacramento tunc sic, 'de assisis et tenementis de quibus visum feci' vel sic,
'de assisis et tenementis istis et similiter de tenemento vnde talis redditus
prouenit' vel sic, 'de talibus tenementis et communa pasture' vel 'huiusmodi
tenementis de quibus visum feci' vel sic, 'de assisa ista et corrodio et tenemento
vnde visum feci' et sic de omnibus aliis assisis noue disseysine, mortis antecessoris
15　et vltime presentacionis et aliis.

Facto autem sacramento tunc legat prenotarius virtutem breuis ad instruc-　f. 89
cionem iuratorum hoc quidem modo: 'Vos dicetis per sacramentum quod
fecistis si talis N. iniuste et sine iudicio disseysiuit talem N. de libero tenemento
suo in tali villa post triennium vel non.'　Iusticiarii eciam ad instruccionem
20　iuratorum recitabunt querelam petentis et ipsis iniungent dicere prout tucius
fuerit faciendum.　Et tunc recedant iuratores et inde adinuicem interloquantur
ad quos si aliquis non iuratus accedat vel colloquium cum eis habeat sine licencia
iusticiariorum committendus est gaole dum tamen per maliciam hoc fecerit
excogitatam et iuratores in misericordia nisi racionabilem pretenderint ex-
25　cusacionem nec ipsi eciam signo vel verbo alicui manifestent quod fuerint in
veredicto suo prolaturi.　Si autem iuratores sibi inuicem fuerint contrarii quia
in vnam non poterunt consentire sentenciam in eleccione iusticiariorum erit vel
de consilio curie assisam afforciare per alios dum tamen summonitos iuxta
numerum maioris partis dissencientis vel eosdem iuratores conpellere ad con-
30　cordiam quod vicecomes videlicet ipsos sine cibo et potu custodiri faciat donec
vnanimes fuerint et concordes.

Cum autem post sacramentum suum pro vna parte vel alia veredictum suum
dixerint secundum eorum dicta proferatur iudicium nisi quid dixerint obscurum
propter quod iusticiarii inducantur ad examinandum alioquin adiudicabitur
35　seysina querenti vel ipse tenens quietus recedat cum seysina sua.　Contingit
tamen quandoque quod eorum alter vel ambo in misericordia remanent, et si
plures fuerint disseysitores nominati quidam cadunt in penam disseysine et quidam quieti recedunt.　Si autem querens prosecutus est quamuis ipse in miseri-

4. *posterius* de] quod, J.　　　5. vel *om*. J.　　　16. breuis ad instruccionem, Br., *om*. J.
33. *ante* secundum *add*. et, J; obscurum] obstructum, J.　　　38. est *om*. J.

truth concerning this assize and the tenement of which I have made view by the king's command' or thus, 'concerning the tenement from which such-and-such a rent issues'; or 'concerning the pasture and tenement'; or 'concerning the common of which I have made view'.　Or if the assize is arraigned regarding some nuisance done in the land of one man which is a nuisance to the land of another, then that which creates the nuisance is first spoken of and afterwards the tenement which is subject to the nuisance, thus, 'concerning the wall and tenement (or the like) of which I have made view', and thus generally with regard to everything by reason of which assizes are mainly taken.　And then they say, 'and for nothing will I fail to speak the truth, so help me God and these holy relics.'　Afterwards the others swear thus: 'The oath, as this our foreman swore it, I will keep for my part, so help me God etc.'　And if several assizes are to be taken under one oath, then thus: 'concerning the assizes and tenements of which I have made view'; or thus; 'concerning these assizes and tenements and likewise concerning the tenement from which such-and-such a rent issues'; or thus, 'concerning such-and-such tenements and common of pasture' or 'concerning such tenements of which I have made view'; or thus, 'concerning this assize and the corrody and tenement of which I have made view'; and likewise as regards all other assizes of novel disseisin, *mort d'ancestor*, darrein presentment and others.

Bracton,
f. 185b

When the oath has been taken, the chief clerk will then read the substance of the writ for the information of the jurors in this fashion: 'You shall say by the oath you have taken whether this M. unlawfully and without a judgement disseised that N. of his freehold in such-and-such a township three years ago or not'. The justices will also, for the information of the jurors, recite the plaint of the demandant and will enjoin them to speak as carefully as can be.　And then the jurors will retire and discuss the matter among themselves.　And if anyone who is not sworn should approach them or have speech with them without leave of the justices, he shall be committed to gaol, provided he did this of malice aforethought, and the jurors will be amerciable if they cannot put forward a reasonable excuse.　Nor may they indicate to anyone by sign or word what they will declare in their verdict.　If, however, the jurors are at odds among themselves because they cannot agree on a unanimous verdict, it will be at the discretion of the justices either by counsel of the court to afforce the assize by others, provided those summoned number the same as those who disagreed with the majority of the jury, or to compel the said jurors to come to an agreement, that is to say, the sheriff is to arrange for them to be kept without food and drink until they shall be of one mind and in agreement.

When, however, after taking their oath, they declare their verdict for one party or the other, judgement will be pronounced according to their words, unless what they have said is obscure, whereupon the justices will be led to examine them: otherwise seisin will be adjudged to the plaintiff, or the tenant will depart quit with his seisin.　It sometimes happens, however, that one or both parties are amerciable: and if several disseisors are named, some of them incur the penalty of disseisin and some depart quit.　But if the plaintiff has prosecuted his suit, although he himself may be amerciable, nevertheless his pledges of pro-

cordia remaneat plegii tamen eius de prosequendo non erunt conuicti licet
iudicium habuerit sibi contrarium. Possunt autem recognitores veredictum
suum breuibus et paucis verbis pronunciare dicendo quod sic numquam fuit
seysitus quod de libero tenemento suo potuit inde disseysiri vel precise quod dis-
5 seysitus sit vel huiusmodi. Verumtamen si difficultas oriatur vel obscuritas [231]
tunc necesse habent facti veritatem declarare vel narracionem expressam et quo
casu si iuratores ignorauerint si manifesta fuerit disseysina vel non conpelli non
debent vlterius set petere debent instruccionem iusticiariorum quibus si
difficile sit iudicium pronunciare tunc ponatur iudicium vsque ad bancum vt ibi
10 de consilio curie prouideatur qualiter in hac parte fuerit iudicandum. Si autem
plana omnia sunt cum bene iurauerint stabitur eorum veredicto si vero male
locus erit conuiccioni et si dubie vel obscure vbi vnica diccio vel oracio dupli-
cem habere poterit intellectum vel si partes minus bene fuerint examinate locus
erit certificacioni. Videndum est igitur vtrum certum dixerint vel incertum
15 clarum vel obscurum vel vtrum dubitauerint in veredicto suo vel omnino ignorauerint vel si aliquid dixerint contra personam querentis quare assisam portare
non possit vel contra personam tenentis quare contra assisam excipere non possit
vel contra breue quod stare non possit propter errorem. Si autem iuratores
factum omnino ignorauerint et nichil de veritate sciuerint tunc dicere oportebit
20 de credulitate et consciencia et quo casu non committunt periurium quia contra
conscienciam non vadunt. Si autem falsum dixerint contra personas conuincendi sunt quia capienda erit assisa in modum assise secus vero si in modum
iurate vt si causa status conuencio vel condicio vel huiusmodi a parte parti
opponeretur et vtraque pars de hoc se poneret in iuratam cum aliam forte non
25 haberent probacionem. Si autem iuratores dicant quod breue inepte fuit concep-
tum quia erratum forte in comitatibus nominibus villarum personarum vel digni-
tatum vel in cognominibus vel huiusmodi, non erit de hoc multum curandum
quia hoc ab inicio non fuit a tenente excipiendo obiectum quia ex quo semel in
assisa se posuit errorem dissimulans breue tanquam validum approbauit, et
30 quamuis recognitores in hac parte errauerint periurium tamen non committunt
cum falsitati non consenciant et qui errat non consentit. Et quia ad iudicem
pertinet iustum proferre iudicium et reddere diligenter oportebit eum deliberare
et examinare si dicta iuratorum in se contineant veritatem ne eorum sequens
errorem fatuum vel falsum ferat iudicium.
35   Post hoc insuper inquirant iusticiarii diligenter que dampna facta sint in
domibus boscis gardinis et locis aliis et quod vastum fecerint disseysitores quod
exilium et quam destruccionem et quid medio tempore perceptum fuerit in fruc-
tibus redditibus et aliis terrarum commoditatibus et quale comodum spoliatus f. 89b

---

1. non *om.* J.   8. quibus] qui, J.   9. difficile] dificile, J.   12. oracio, Br., racio J.
13. minus] nimis J.   14. certificacioni] cerciorum, J.   16. portare] parcare, J.
23. vel condicio, Br., *om.* J; *post* huiusmodi *add.* conuencio, J.   27. de *om.* J.
33. ne] nec J.

secution will not be condemned even though he has judgement given against him.
The recognitors, moreover, may declare their verdict in few and short words,
saying that the plaintiff was never so seised of the freehold that he could be disseised thereof, or saying categorically that he is disseised, or the like.   If, indeed,
difficulty or obscurity should arise, then it is necessary for them to declare the
truth about the facts or say what actually happened; and if it happens that the
jurors do not know whether the disseisin is palpable or not, they should not be
compelled to say anything more but rather they must seek the guidance of the
justices, and if judgement is difficult for them to pronounce, it should then be remitted to the Bench so that there, by counsel of the court, it may be provided
how judgement should be given in this matter.   If, however, everything is plain
with the jury duly sworn, their verdict will stand; but if their verdict is bad there
will be occasion for an attaint, and if their verdict is doubtful or obscure where
a single word or sentence may have a double meaning, or if the parties have not
been properly examined, there will be occasion for a certification.   It must be
seen, therefore, whether the jurors' verdict is certain or uncertain, clear or obscure,
or whether they have expressed therein a doubt or whether they have been quite
ignorant [of the facts] or whether they have said anything against the person of
the plaintiff why he cannot bring an assize or against the person of the tenant
why he cannot except against the assize or against the writ which cannot stand
on account of error.   If, however, the jurors are quite ignorant and know
nothing of the truth of the matter, then it behoves them to speak according to
their belief and conscience, and in this case they do not commit perjury because
they do not go against their conscience.   If, however, they speak falsely against
the persons, they must be attainted because the assize will be taken in the manner
of an assize, but it will be otherwise if the assize be taken in the manner of a jury,
for example, if cause, status, agreement or condition or the like should be brought
forward by one party against the other and both parties put themselves thereon
on a jury when they happen to have no other proof.   If, however, the jury say
that the writ was wrongly drawn, perhaps because there was a mistake in the
counties, names of townships, persons or dignities, or in surnames or the like,
not much notice will be taken of this if objection was not taken to it at the
beginning by the tenant when excepting; for when once he has put himself on the
assize and has disregarded the error, he has approved the writ as valid, and although the recognitors should fall into error in this respect, yet they do not commit perjury since they do not consent to the falsity, and he who errs does not
consent.   And because it is the duty of the judge to set forth and deliver a rightful judgement, it will behove him diligently to consider and examine the state-
ments of the jurors to see whether the truth is contained in them lest, following
their error, he should pass a foolish or false judgement.

After this the justices should further diligently enquire what damage has been
done to buildings, woods, gardens and other places and what waste the disseisors
have made, what exile [of villeins] and what destruction, and what in the meantime
has been received in crops, rents and other profits of the lands, and what profit
the dispossessed would have had if he had not been ejected from the tenement,

Bracton,
f. 186

Bracton,
f. 186b

Bracton,
f 187

habuisset si a tenemento non fuisset eiectus et de omnibus rebus et catallis
ablatis certificentur. Ex virtute autem breuis habetur quod cum ipso fundo
restitui debent catalla tempore spoliacionis inuenta vtpote sunt arma vtensilia
oues et boues et huiusmodi et que restitui debent sine re ipsa et de quibus dup-
5 plicem actor habeat accionem criminalem et ciuilem et que si non restituantur
semper tamen durabit iurisdiccio iusticiarii dum recordum habeat donec sibi
fuerint restituta et non solum que propria fuerint ipsius disseysiti verum eciam
omnia illa que sibi comodata fuerint inpignorata vel deposita vel quorum vsum
vel vsumfructum habuerit et donec de bestiis medio tempore mortuis plena fiat   [232]
10 restitucio quia licet disseysitor amiserit et dampna sencierit hoc tamen non erit
inputandum disseysito. Tenebitur eciam disseysitor ad casus fortuitos vt si edes
incendio consumpte fuerint earum precium restitui debet per assisam et non
solum restituende sunt res quas illuc habuit disseysitus cum disseyseretur verum
eciam siue in eo loco a quo deiectus est siue in omni possessione quia ad omnem
15 partem possessionis refertur qua quis caruit cum disseyseretur.

CAP. X. DE EXCEPCIONIBUS

Et caueant sibi de cetero qui nominati disseysitores qui falsas excepciones
proponunt per quas capcio assise differatur, dicendo quod assisa alias transiuit
inter easdem partes de eodem tenemento vel dicendo in menciendo quod breue de
20 alciori natura pendet inter easdem partes de eodem tenemento et super hiis et
consimilibus vocet rotulos vel recordum ad warantum vt per illam vocacionem
asportare posset vesturam et leuare redditus et alia proficua ad magnum detri-
mentum querentis quia namque licet prius aliam penam non habuit ille qui
huiusmodi falsas excepciones mendaciter proposuit nisi tantum quod post men-
25 dacium suum conuictum processum fuit ad capcionem assise, prouisum est quod
si quis disseysitor nominatus personaliter proponat huiusmodi excepciones si
defecerit de waranto quod vocauit habeatur pro disseysitore absque recognicione
assise et restituat dampna prius inquisita vel post inquirenda in duplo et nichilominus pro falsitate sua puniatur per prisonam vnius anni. Et si illa excepcio
30 proponatur per balliuum non propter hoc differatur capcio assise neque iudicium
super restitucione seysine et dampnorum ita tamen quod si dominus illius
balliui qui absens fuerit veniat postea coram iusticiariis qui assisam illam
ceperint et offerat verificare per recordum vel per rotulos quod assisa alias
transiuit de eodem tenemento inter easdem partes vel quod querens alias retraxit

8. fuerint] fuerunt, J.   10. non *om.* J.   14. quia ad omnem, Br., que aliquam, J.
15. disseysiretur] disseyseretur, J.   17. Et *in statuto*; Aut J; disseysitores] seysitores, J.
21. vt] vel, J.   23. penam] partem, J.   28. post inquirenda *in statuto*; post quirenda, J.
31. tenementi *in statuto*, seysine, J.   32. fuerit] fuit, J.

and they should be informed of all the property and chattels removed.　Moreover, by virtue of the writ it follows that there should be restored with the land itself the chattels found there during the period of dispossession, such as arms, utensils, sheep and oxen and the like, and these ought to be restored irrespective of the property itself, and in respect of them the plaintiff has a two-fold right of action, criminal and civil, and if these are not restored, nevertheless the jurisdiction of the justice will always remain while he has record until they are restored to the plaintiff (and not only those things which were the property of the disseisee but also all those things which were lent to him, pledged or deposited with him, or of which he had the use or usufruct) and until full restitution is made for beasts that have died in the meantime, because although the disseisor may incur losses and suffer damage, nevertheless this shall not be charged against the disseisee. The disseisor will also be held responsible for casualties: for example, if buildings should be destroyed by fire, their value ought to be restored [to the disseisee] by

Bracton,
f. 187b

the assize, and not only should those things be restored which the disseisee had there when he was disseised but also [any others], whether in that place from which he was ejected or in every possession of his because what anyone lost when he was disseised involves every part of what he possessed.

CHAPTER 10.　OF EXCEPTIONS

Stat. Westm.
II. c. 25

And let those beware henceforth who are named as disseisors and who put forward false exceptions whereby the taking of the assize may be deferred, saying that at another time an assize passed between the same parties concerning the same tenement or telling a lie that a writ of a higher nature is pending between the same parties concerning the same tenement, and upon these and like matters they vouch rolls or record to warranty so that through this vouching they may carry away the crops and levy the rents and other profits to the great damage of the plaintiff; for whereas hitherto he who lied in putting forward such false exceptions incurred no other penalty than that, after his falsehood was proved, the taking of the assize was proceeded with, it is provided that, if anyone who is named as a disseisor should personally put forward such exceptions and fail to produce the warranty he has vouched, he shall be held to be a disseisor without need for a finding of the assize and he shall restore double the damages previously or subsequently made the subject of inquiry, and furthermore he shall be punished for his falsity by a year's imprisonment.　And if the exception be put forward by a bailiff, the taking of the assize shall not be deferred on this account nor judgement on the restitution of the seisin and damages; provided nevertheless that, if the said bailiff's lord who was absent shall afterwards come before the justices who took the assize and offer to prove by record or by rolls that an assize passed at another time between the same parties concerning the same tenement, or that

se de consimili breui vel quod placitum pendet per breui de alciori natura, fiat
ei breue ad faciendum venire super hoc recordum, et cum illud habuerit et
iusticiarii viderint quod recordum ante iudicium ei valuisset ita quod querens ab
agendo illa vice saltem repelleretur statim faciant iusticiarii scire parti que
5 recuperauerit quod sit coram eis ad certum diem ad quem rehabeat defendens
seysinam suam et dampna sua si qua prius soluit per primum iudicium simul
cum dampnis que habuit post primum iudicium redditum et illa restituantur ei
in duplo vt predictum est.   Et nichilominus puniatur ille qui primo recuperauit
per prisonam secundum discrecionem iusticiariorum.   Et eodem modo si
10 defendens contra quem transiuit assisa ipso absente ostendat cartas vel quietas-
clamancias super quarum confeccione non fuerint iuratores examinati nec
examinari poterunt pro eo quod tunc non fiebat mencio in placitando et probabiliter ignorare potererunt confecciones huiusmodi scriptorum iusticiarii visis
scriptis illis faciant scire parti que recuperauerit quod sit coram eis ad certum
15 diem et similiter venire faciant coram eis iuratores eiusdem assise.   Et si per
veredictum iuratorum vel forte per irrotulamentum scripta illa verificauerit
puniatur ille qui assisam inpetrauit contra factum suum per penam supradictam. [233]
    Quedam autem sunt que restitucionem inpediunt ad tempus et quedam in
perpetuum: prius debent terminari, quia excepcionem pariunt cum primo
20 fuerint proposita, et terminantur in modum iurate et non in modum assise, et
ideo non recipiunt conuiccionem propter consensum parcium cum de hoc se gratis vel de necessitate ne sint indefensi posuerunt se in iuratam.   Qualia sunt questio status, causa successionis, causa donacionis, pactum siue condicio vel conuencio, incertitudo, voluntas et dissimulacio, transaccio vel quietaclamacio vel
25 remissio, confirmacio siue consensus, propria vsurpacio rei proprie, difficultas iudicii, iustum iudicium, finis et cyrographam, intrusio in rem alienam vel disseysina
si incontinenti reiciatur, negligencia que per cursum temporis excludit accionem
et assisam.   Sunt autem excepciones in assisa noue disseysine que conpetunt f. 90
contra breue et assisam differunt set non perimunt et sunt quedam contra per-
30 sonam querentis que assisam omnino perimunt.   Est enim peremptoria breuis
et dilatoria iudicii et quedam peremptoria quantum ad personam vnius et
dilatoria iudicii et non peremptoria quantum ad personam alterius, vt si querens
accionem non habeat licet alius et conpetat accio alteri et non sibi et sicut conpetit contra personam ita et contra assisam et si breue non valeat ab inicio non
35 erit vlterius procedendum quod si valeat tunc recurrendum est ad personam et

3. querens *in statuto*, tenens J.   5. quem rehabeat *in statuto,* quam rem habeat, J.
12. examinari] examinare, J.   14. illis *in statuto*, vel, J.   15. venire] ne iur', J.
19. prius] peius, J.   19. pariunt] perimunt, J; primo, Br., post J.   22. de *om.* J.
23. *prius* causa] cum, J.   31. quedam peremptoria Br., quod perpatoria, J.

the plaintiff at another time withdrew from [an action on] a similar writ, or that
an action is pending by a writ of a higher nature, a writ shall be made out to him
for the production of the record on this matter.   And when he has it, and the
justices see that the record would have availed him before judgement was made,
with the result that the plaintiff on that occasion would at least have been barred
from his action, the justices shall forthwith cause the party who had recovered
to be warned that he is to be before them at a certain day, at which the defendant
shall have his seisin again and his damages, if he has already paid any under the
first judgement, together with the damages he has sustained since the first judgement was delivered, and these shall be restored to him twofold, as aforesaid.
And furthermore he who first recovered shall be punished by imprisonment at
the discretion of the justices.   And, in the same way, if the defendant, against
whom an assize passed in his absence, shall show charters or quitclaims, upon
the making of which the jurors were not examined nor could be examined because no mention was then made of them in pleading and they might in all prob-
ability not know that such writings had been made, the justices, when they have
looked at the said writings, shall cause the party who has recovered to be warned
that he is to be before them at a certain day, and they shall likewise cause the
jurors of that assize to come before them.   And if the defendant shall prove
those writings by the verdict of the jurors or perchance by an enrolment, he who
sued out the assize contrary to his own deed shall be punished by the penalty
aforesaid.

Bracton,
f. 213

There are certain things which prevent restitution for a time and certain things
which prevent restitution for ever.   These ought first to be determined, because
they give rise to an exception as soon as they are put forward.   And they should
be determined in the manner of a jury and not in the manner of an assize, and
therefore the jurors are not liable to attaint since of their own accord, whether
voluntarily or of necessity lest they should be without defence, the parties put
themselves in this matter on a jury.   Such things are a question of status; a cause
of succession; a cause of gift; an agreement or a condition or a covenant; uncertainty, willingness or indifference, compromise or quitclaim or remission; confirmation or consent; one's own usurpation of one's own property; difficulty of
judgement; rightfulness of judgement; fine and chirograph; intrusion in another's
property or disseisin if it is immediately repelled; negligence which by lapse of

Bracton,
f. 187b

time precludes a right of action and an assize.   There are, however, exceptions
in an assize of novel disseisin which are available against the writ and defer the
assize but are not fatal to it, and there are certain exceptions against the person
of the plaintiff which are altogether fatal to the assize.   For there is an exception
which is peremptory as regards the writ and dilatory as regards the judgement
and some are peremptory as regards the person of one man and dilatory as regards the judgement but are not peremptory as regards the person of another:
for example, if the plaintiff should not have a right of action although another
has and an action is available to the other and not to him.   And just as an exception is available against a person, so it is available against an assize, and if
from the beginning the writ is not valid there will be no further proceedings but,

videndum si conpetit ei querela vel non.   Postea vero ad assisam si tenens iniuste
et sine iudicio disseysiuerit ipsum querentem de libero tenemento suo sicut dicit
in tali villa post terminum.   In primis excipere poterit tenens super iurisdiccione
iusticiariorum vt supra, et concessa iurisdiccione excipere poterit contra breue
5   vt si non sit conpetens accioni vel si in se sit viciosum vt si rasura fuerit in loco
suspecto vbi nomina scripta fuerint et non iura, si appensum fuerit sigillum
adulterinum, vel si non habeat verbis cancellarie ordinatam disposicionem nec
verborum ordinem nec stilum calami.   Suspicio vero esse poterit de breui cum
non concordet manibus notariorum et eciam in rasura nominum locorum tene-
10   mentorum et date et aliorum que sunt iudicii principalia.   In aliis autem que
iuris sunt non est multum curandum de rasura.   Iura enim et consuetudines et
ea que omnibus sunt communia vbique scribi possunt nisi huiusmodi sus-
picionem inducant calami diuersitas vel attramenti.   Si autem in loco suspecto
inueniatur rasura vel correccio tunc distinguendum erit an facta fuerit cor-
15   reccio vel incrementum quando breue sigillatum fuit vel post sicut per clericum
vicecomitis vel iusticiarii quod si ante sustinendum est si autem post et inde
quis conuincatur vltimo puniendus est iudicio tanquam falsarius.   Item videndum erit si tempore date aliquam habuit occasionem inpetrandi vel nullam.
Item si querens de consimili breui et eciam assisa omnino retraxerit.   Item si
20   prius inceperit agere de seysina aliena quam de propria aut per breue de alciori
natura lite pendente ordine accionum non obseruato.   Item si inpetratum
fuerit contra ius commune quod plures querentes in vno breui contineantur vbi
diuerse sunt disseysine et res partite et non in communi.

     Error autem perimit breue set non iudicium neque assisam.   Error vero mul-
25   tipliciter in persona querentis esse poterit vt si errauerit in inpetrando contra
personam eius qui nomine possidet alieno et non proprio vt firmarius, custos   [234]
vel canonicus.   Perimitur autem breue propter errorem nominis vt si Matheus
ponatur pro Andrea et eciam cognominis vt si ponatur Matheus filius Willelmi
vbi dici debuit filius Petri et idem erit si erratum fuerit nomine ville vel in littera
30   vel silliba vel in nomine dignitatis vel cum filius eodem nomine vocetur sicut eius
pater quamuis idem nomen habeant et cognomen non tamen recuperabit quia
erratum est in persona et in accione quia filio nulla facta est iniuria set patri.

     Error autem quandoque versatur circa personam siue circa corpus quan-
doque circa officium siue dignitatem quandoque circa ipsam rem et quandoque

2. querentem] tenentem, J.   4. supra Br.; *littera* J *in* J.   6. non iura, Br.; non iurat, J.
11. sunt *om.* J.   11. constituciones, J; consuetudines, Br. in nonnullis textis.
15. fuit *addidimus.*   20. aut] vt, J.   21. lite pendente] li pen, J.   27. Perimitur]
Permittitur, J.

Bracton,
f. 188

if it is valid, then attention must be turned to the person to see whether or not a plaint is available to him, and afterward to the assize to see if the tenant has unlawfully and without judgement disseised the plaintiff of his freehold, as he says, in such-and-such a township after the period [of limitation]. To begin with, the tenant can except against the jurisdiction of the justices, as above,[1] and if their jurisdiction is conceded he can except against the writ: for example, if it is not appropriate to the action, or if it is defective in itself, as, for instance, if there were an erasure in a suspicious place where names should be written (but not matters of law) or if a false seal should be appended, or if its words do not follow the practice of the chancery either in their order or the style of writing. The writ can be regarded as suspicious when it does not agree with the handwriting of the clerks and also when there is erasure in names, places and tenements as well as in the date and other things which are of prime concern in judgement. In other matters, however, which relate to the law, erasure is not of much account. Laws indeed and customs and matters that are common to all may be written any time unless a difference of pen or of ink induces any suspicion. If, however, an erasure or a correction should be found in a suspicious place, then it will be necessary to distinguish whether the correction or addition was made when the writ was sealed or afterwards, as, for example, by a sheriff's or justice's clerk, for if it was done before sealing it must be sustained, but if it was done afterwards and someone is convicted thereof he must be punished with the supreme penalty as a forger. Again, it must be seen whether at the date of the writ the plaintiff had or had not any ground for suing it out; and again, whether the plaintiff had withdrawn completely from a similar writ as well as from the assize; again, whether he had previously begun an action in respect of a seisin other than his own, or by a writ of a higher nature, on which an action is pending, thus not observing the proper order of actions; again, if the writ were sued out against the common law so that several plaintiffs are included in one writ where there are different disseisins and the property is divided and not held in common.

Bracton,
f. 188b

Error destroys a writ but not a judgement or an assize. Error can indeed be manifold in regard to the person of the plaintiff: as, for example, if he errs in suing out a writ against him personally who is in possession in another's name and not his own, such as a fermor, guardian or canon. A writ is also destroyed on account of a mistake in the Christian name: as, for example, if Matthew is put for Andrew; and also in the surname, as, for example, if Matthew fitz William is put where it ought to be fitz Peter, and the result will be the same if there should be a mistake in the name of the township, or in a letter or a syllable, or in the name of an office, or where a son is summoned by the same name as his father has, for though they may have the same Christian name and surname nevertheless the plaintiff will not recover because the writ is in error as regards the person and the action, because the injury is done not to the son but to the father.

The error sometimes turns upon the person or upon the body, sometimes upon the office or dignity, sometimes upon the property itself and sometimes

[1] See p. 61.

circa causam.   Circa personam dupliciter vt ex negligencia vel inpericia inpetrantis quandoque ex dolo aduersarii.   Si quis vero binominis sit siue nomine proprio vel cognomine illud nomen tenendum erit quo in partibus vel frequencius et
communius appellatur.   Cognomina enim ideo inposita sunt vt voluntatem
5 dicentis demonstrent et vtantur vocis ministerio.   Ex impericia vero impetrantis
vt si quis nominauerit Petrum pro Paulo et idem erit in errore prenominis,
agnominis, cognominis, idem eciam erit in errore nominis appellatiui vt si
vestum posuerit pro pecunia.   Ex dolo aduersarii vt cum aduersarius dolose in
absencia inpetrantis commutat possesssionem vt sic breue suum amittat et
10 querelam dum tamen ante breuis inpetracionem facta fuerit transmutacio et ante
recessum querentis versus curiam ad inpetrandum.

Poterit eciam error esse circa officium siue dignitatem vt si quis precentorem
nominauerit pro decano.   Circa ipsam vero rem vt si quis nominauerit vineam
vbi nominare deberet ecclesiam vel lanceam vbi vestem.   Rerum vocabula in-
15 mutabilia sunt vel quasi et hominum mutabilia.   Error eciam poterit esse in qualitate rei et quantitate in precio numero pondere et mensura in genere colore et
loco.   Circa causam vt si quis inpetrando dederit intelligi quod iuste possideat
cum non possedit, et tunc videndum est si causa sit casualis et tunc non inpedit
processum vel condicionalis et tunc inpedit omnino.   Circa locum vt si dis-
20 seysitus inpetrauerit ad vicecomitem in cuius comitatu tenenementum non
fuerit vel si dicat tenementum esse in vna villa cum sit in alia vel si dicat
tenementum esse in hameletto pertinente ad villam et non in villa.   Agris enim f. 90b
sunt termini positi et edificia tollata et vicinata ex quibus fiunt hameletti ville
tamen manent et eosdem habent terminos et sua tenementa diffinita vt prius quod
25 prius dignius et a dignioro fieri debet denominacio quamuis ambo fuerint in vna
quia villa continebitur in alia et sic poterit tenementum esse in vtraque.

Plures autem sunt excepciones contra breue inferius assignate in causa proprietatis quarum quedam locum habent hic quedam vero non et sunt quedam
excepciones que hic assignate sunt contra breue in causa possessionis que locum
30 habent hic et non ibi.   Si autem breue fuerit deperditum vel deletum sequitur
quod eo ipso cessabit iurisdiccio iudicis quasi deficiente suo waranto quia si
iudicium non cessauerit et recordum coram ipso rege debeat demandari nisi
breue originale mitteretur cum recordo non esset recordum admittendum set
remittendum et vanum et pro nullo haberetur quasi deficiente waranto et [235]
35 caderet iusticiarius in assisa cum vicecomite et tenente si seysina in hoc casu
fuerit petenti adiudicata et quiscumque conuincatur de huiusmodi maliciosa sub-

3. cognomine] cognicione, J.   5. dicentis Br., dantis, J.   9. commutat] conuincat, J.
18. possedit] fecerit, J.   18. casualis] causalis, J.   19. vt] et, J.   20. inpetrauerit]
inpetrauit, J.   36. quiscumque] quicumque, J.   36. post conuincatur add. et, J.

upon the cause.　About the person in two ways: for example, from the negligence or inexperience of him who sues out the writ, and sometimes from the guile of his adversary.　If a man bears two names, whether a Christian name or a surname, that name shall be kept by which he is most frequently and most commonly called in the locality, for surnames are added so that they may indicate the wishes of the speaker and utilise the services of speech.　From the ignorance of him who sues out the writ: as, for example, if anyone names Peter instead of Paul; and it will be the same if he makes mistakes in a forename or any of the surnames; and also if he errs in naming things, for example in putting a garment instead of money. From the guile of the adversary: as, for instance, if during the absence of the one who sues out the writ his adversary deceitfully changes the possession and so the plaintiff loses his writ and his plaint, provided the change was made before the writ was sued out and before the plaintiff left for the court to sue out the writ.

　　　Error can also be made as regards an office or a dignity: for example, if one should call a precentor the dean.　Or as regards the property itself: for example, if one should speak of a vineyard where one ought to speak of a church, or of a lance instead of a garment.　The names of things are unchangeable or almost so, the names of men changeable.　Error may also lie in the quality or quantity of a thing: in price, number, weight and measure, in kind, colour and place.　It may lie as regards the cause: for example, if someone suing out a writ gives it to be understood that he lawfully possesses when he does not possess, and it must then be considered whether the cause is casual, for then it does not bar the proceedings, or conditional, for then it bars them altogether.　As regards the place: for example, if the disseisee should sue out a writ to the sheriff of a county in which the tenement did not lie, or if he should say the tenement lies in one township when it is in another, or if he should say that the tenement lies in a hamlet pertaining to a township and not in the township.　Boundaries are put to fields and buildings are brought together and grouped and out of them hamlets are formed.　Yet the townships remain and keep the same boundaries and their tenements are defined as before and what exists first is the higher in dignity and it is by the higher in dignity that the naming should be made although both may be a single entity, because one township will be included in another and thus the tenement could be in both.

　　　Several exceptions against a writ are assigned below[1] in a cause of proprietary action, some of which have a place here but others not, and there are some exceptions which are assigned here against a writ in a cause of possession which are appropriate here but not there.　If, however, a writ should be lost or destroyed, it follows that by that very fact the jurisdiction of the judge will cease as though his warrant was lacking, for if the proceedings were not brought to an end and if the record should be ordered to come before the king's bench, then unless the original writ were sent with the record, the record would not be admitted but sent back and considered as worthless and void as lacking a warrant. And the justice would be subject to the assize with the sheriff and the tenant if seisin should in these circumstances be adjudged to the plaintiff.　And whoso-

1 Book VI.

traccione carcerali custodie committetur ibidem moraturus donec regium fauorem per condempnacionem, redempcionem vel alio modo valeat adipisci.

CAP. XI. DE EXCEPCIONIBUS STATUS

Conpetit eciam excepcio tenenti contra querentem ex persona querentis vt si
5 querens excommunicatus fuerit quod si tenens hoc docuerit per litteras ordinarii patentes oportebit querentem docere de absolucione priusquam audiatur. Dicere eciam poterit quod querela ad ipsum non pertinet nec assisa quia non tenuit tenementum petitum nomine proprio set alieno sicut procurator, custos, firmarius, seruus vel familia et quo probato vel recognito cadet assisa quia talibus
10 non conpetit assisa nisi nomine proprio tenuerint per disseysinam vel intrusionem et tempus habuerint quod sine iudicio disseysiri non debuissent. Si autem tenens dicat quod querens seruus sit et tenuit tenementum petitum in villenagio cadit assisa quia alienum petit nomine proprio nisi replicando docere poterit contrarium quod libere tenuit nec sufficit ipsum probare seruum alienum nisi
15 probetur quod in villenagio tenuerit.   Contra dominum suum sufficit ipsum probare seruum suum et in potestate eius constitutum quamuis tenementum petitum in villenagio non tenuerit et hoc probare licet dupliciter vel per parentes vel per assisam et quo comperto cadit accio et assisa donec in causa proprietatis si probauerit ipsum esse liberum et quo casu non nocebit ei probacio probata cum
20 nichil operatur nisi ad declinandum assisam.   Et quia seruus est aliquando sub potestate domino constitutus et in statu seruili et in possessione seruitutis et aliquando extra potestatem in statu libero et in possessione libertatis aliquando eciam tenet libere et aliquando in villenagio et questio status cum incidat in assisam preiudicialis sit et ideo videndum est cui obiciatur et a quo.   Cui: vtrum
25 seruo qui fuerit sub potestate domini constitutus proprio vel alieno bona fide possesso vel libero sub potestate existenti in statu seruili qualitercumque siue per vim et iniustam detencionem siue per copulam maritalem vel ei qui omnino fuerit extra potestatem et tunc vel ei qui fugitiuus suus fuerit et recenter fugit de terra sua et recenter fuit insecutus vel non recenter ita quod sine breui reuocari non
30 possit in seruitutem vel ei qui nunquam fuit sub potestate sua set de natiuis suis qui fugerunt a terris antecessorum suorum vel eis qui omnino fugitiui sunt excep-

7. nec] nisi, J.   10. nisi nomine *scripsimus*; quia tali, J.   11. habuerint] habuerit, J. 19. ei] ea, J; probata] pᵃ, J.   26. siue *om.* J.   28. vel] vtrum, J.   31. qui fugerunt *addidimus.*

ever is convicted of thus maliciously abstracting a writ will be committed to the custody of a prison, there to remain until he is able to obtain the king's favour by fine, ransom or in some other way.

CHAPTER 11.   OF EXCEPTIONS ON ACCOUNT OF STATUS

Bracton,
f. 190

Bracton
f. 203

Bracton,
f. 190

Bracton
f. 190b

An exception is also available to the tenant against the plaintiff in respect of the plaintiff's person: for example, if the plaintiff should be excommunicate and, if the tenant shows this by letters patent of the Ordinary, it will be necessary, before the plaintiff is heard, for him to show that he has been absolved.   The tenant can also say that the plaintiff has neither a plaint nor an assize because he did not hold the tenement claimed in his own name but in that of another, as agent, guardian, fermor, villein or one of the household, and when this is proved or acknowledged the assize abates because an assize is not available to such persons unless they hold in their own name by disseisin or entry and have a period [of peaceful possession] so that they must not be disseised without a judgement of the court.   If, however, the tenant says that the plaintiff is a villein and held the tenement in question in villeinage, the assize abates because the villein is demanding the property of another in his own name unless in his answer he can show that on the contrary he held freely, nor is it sufficient for the tenant to prove that the plaintiff is another's villein unless he proves also that he held in villeinage.   [As regards an exception] against his lord: it suffices for the lord to prove that the plaintiff is his villein and living under his authority, although he does not hold the tenement in question in villeinage.   And it is open to the lord to prove this in two ways, either by the plaintiff's relatives or by an assize, and when the proof is established the action abates as well as the assize until in a proprietary action the plaintiff proves himself to be free, and in this case the proof of the exception will do him no harm because it serves no other purpose than to abate the assize.   And because sometimes a villein lives under his lord's authority and in a servile condition and possessed of servitude, and sometimes he lives outside the authority of the lord in free condition and possessed of liberty, and sometimes also he holds freely and sometimes in villeinage, and the question of status, when it falls into an assize, is prejudicial, therefore it must be considered against whom objections may be made and by whom.   Against whom? whether against a villein living under the authority of a lord, possessed *bona fide* by his own lord or by another; or a free man living under authority in a servile condition in any way whatsoever, whether by force or unlawful detention or by the bonds of marriage; or against a man who is altogether outside a lord's authority, and then it is either against one who is fugitive from his lord and recently fled from his land and was immediately pursued (or not immediately, in which case he cannot be recalled to servitude without a writ); or against one who was never under the lord's authority but was descended from his villeins who fled from the lands of his ancestors; or against those who are

cione tamen perpetua muniti vel priuilegio quibus semper tueri possunt quia
nunquam forte a terra opponentis fugerunt et huiusmodi vel quia manentes in
ciuitate aliqua vel villa priuilegiata vel dominico regis per vnum annum et vnum
diem sine clamio domini vel priuilegio clericali vel milicie quorum ordines pro
5 priuilegio sufficiunt donec per aliquod iudicium fuerint degradati. A quo:
vtrum a proprio domino vel alio, et in qua causa vtrum in iudicio petitorio vel
possessorio.

Si autem excepcio seruitutis apponitur seruo proprio opponentis sub cuius
fuerit potestate constitutus cum talis seruus excepcionem habere non possit
10 neque accionem contra dominum suum quia quicquid per ipsum iuste adquiritur   [236]
id domino adquiritur et cum ipse a domino suo possideatur nichil possidere potest
nec aliquid proprium habere nec oportebit producere parentes set sufficit si per
assisam tantum probetur quam si seruus recusabit denegabitur ei accio et si
iuratores male iurauerint conuincendi sunt per parentes. Verumtamen si par-
15 entes producantur qui querentem seruum sub potestate domini constitutum
probauerint terminatur per hoc tam causa status quam assisa et talis liberabitur
domino suo vt villanus suus. Idem erit si villanus sub potestate domini constitutus contendens se esse liberum perquirat breue quod dominus non exigat
ab eo alias consuetudines vel alia seruicia quam ea que de iure facere debet si
20 dominus opposuerit villenagium et parentes produxerit vtrumque placitum per   f.19
hoc terminabitur quamuis indirecte. Idem erit cum villanus a domino suo
iusticiari non possit quod ei faciat seruicia vel cum villanus breue de pace perquisierit cum sit sub potestate domini et nullum breue naiuitatis precesserit et
dominus sibi perquisierit per breue quod faciat ei consuetudines et seruicia que
25 ei facere debet de tenemento quod de eo tenet in villenagio et parentes produxerit et probauerit villenagium vtrumque terminabitur quamuis indirecte
siue liber tenuerit villenagium siue villanus et in hoc casu querens se ponat in
assisam velit nolit vel negabitur ei accio quod secus esset se esset extra domini
potestatem. Si autem seruo obiciatur alieno vel libero in statu tamen seruili
30 possesso et constituto tenebit excepcio donec ille liber in seruitute detentus se
liberum probauerit et donec seruus probetur alienus. Si autem seruo alieno
bona fide possesso a possidente obiciatur huiusmodi excepcio parentes produci
non debent set standum erit presumpcioni et tenebit excepcio propter possessionem donec possessus se probet liberum. Et eodem modo si seruo alieno bona
35 fide possesso semper stabitur excepcioni donec verus dominus eum euincat et si
ille qui possidet aliquo casu parentes illius produxerit ad probandum non valebit
quia per hoc non probabit eum esse suum seruum quamuis alienum cum

1. muniti] inimici, J.   13. recusabit] recusabitur, J.   15. seruum] suum, J.
17. sub potestate, Br., *om.* J.   20. vtrumque placitum, Br., vtrum, J.   21. villanus]
balliuus, J.   25. parentes] petens, J.   27. se] si, J.   30. se] si, J.   35. si] siue, J.

completely fugitive but protected with a permanent exception or privilege by which they can always be protected: because they perhaps have never fled from the land of their adversary and so forth, or because they have been dwelling for a year and a day in some city or privileged town or the royal demesne without being claimed by their lord or [because they are protected by] the privilege attaching to clerks or knights whose orders are sufficient to constitute privilege until they are degraded by some judgement of the court. By whom? whether by their own lord or someone else. And in what cause? whether in petitory or possessory proceedings.

Bracton,
f. 191
If, however, an exception of villeinage is put forward, alleging the plaintiff to be the villein of him who brings the exception against him and living under his authority: since such a villein can have neither exception nor action against his lord because whatever is rightfully acquired by him is acquired for his lord, and
Bracton,
f. 192b
since he who is possessed by his lord can possess nothing nor have anything of his own, it will not be necessary to produce his kinsmen but it is sufficient if the exception is proved by the assize alone and, if the villein refuses the assize, a right of action will be denied him and, if the jurors swear falsely, they must be
Bracton,
f. 192
attainted by means of the kinsmen. Nevertheless, if kinsmen are produced who prove the plaintiff to be a villein living under a lord's authority, both the cause of status as well as the assize will thereby be determined and the plaintiff will be delivered to the lord as his villein. The result will be the same if a villein, living under a lord's authority, asserts that he is free and sues out a writ that the lord shall not exact from him other customs or other services than those which he ought to do of right: if the lord alleges his villeinage and produces kinsmen [to prove it], both pleas will be determined by this, although indirectly. The result will be the same when a villein cannot be justiced by his lord to render services to him, or when the villein purchases a writ of peace when he is under the authority of a lord and there is no previous writ of neifty and the lord looks after his own interests by a writ that the villein render him the customs and services which he ought to render him from the tenement which he holds from him in villeinage and produces kinsmen and proves the villeinage: both pleas will be determined, although indirectly, whether he who holds the villein tenement is a freeman or a villein, and in this case the plaintiff will put himself on the assize willy nilly or a right of action will be denied to him; but it would be different if he were outside the lord's authority. If, however, the objection is raised against the villein of another or against a free man possessed and living even in a servile condition, the exception will hold until the said freeman detained in villeinage proves himself to be free or until the villein proves that he belongs to another. If, however, such an exception is raised against the villein of another, possessed *bona fide* by his possessor, his kinsmen should not be produced but the presumption will stand and the exception hold by reason of the possession until the man who is possessed
Bracton,
f. 192b
proves that he is free. And likewise if it is raised against another's villein possessed in good faith, such an exception will always hold until the true lord claims him and, if he who possesses should as it happens produce his kinsmen, this will not avail as proof because he will not thereby prove that he is his villein though

parentes sui serui sunt alieni. Cum autem opposita fuerit excepcio a vero
domino ei qui fuerit extra potestatem domini sui qui recenter fugerit tenebit excepcio contra eum quamdiu dominus eum repetere possit sine breui et licite
capere si in feodo inueniatur, set cum ad villanum suum recuperandum habere
5 non possit regressum nisi per breue non valebit excepcio donec fugitiuus in domini venerit potestatem quia cum dominus seruum suum possidere desierit per
inpotenciam vel necligenciam et vtramque possessionem amiserit naturalem et
ciuilem tempus nec locum habebit excepcio.   Set villano conpetit restitucio per
assisam et dominus nisi in causa proprietatis versus eum non habebit accionem
10 set cum corpus disracionauerit in causa proprietatis tunc adiudicabitur domino
cum omnibus terris bonis et catallis suis et tota sequela sua nec prius sibi
quicquam auferri poterit quin seruus recuperet tamen quia non poterit quis
recuperare nec habere pertinencias ante quam habuerit id ad quod res pertineat.   Tamen quia vana essent verba in breui contenta vbi rex preceperit tali
15 quod habere faciat tali talem natiuum et fugituum suum cum tota sequela sua et
cum catallis suis et vnde si catalla serui fugitiui sine iudicio vsurpare possit illud   [237]
verbum catallis perperam esset positum et effectum non haberet.

Quid eciam iuris clamare poterit dominus in catallis vel tenementis quasi in
accessorio cum nichil iuris clamare poterit in corpore quod est principale.   Set
20 reuera in questione status per breue de natiuis obstabit semper domino petenti
excepcio spoliacionis donec seruus restituatur ad plenum et semper prius inquirendum erit de spoliacione et inde fiat plena restitucio quam de statu.   Set
refert vtrum queratur et petat restitui de spoliacione propria vel petat sibi rem
reddi de possessione aliena sicut de seysina alicuius antecessoris serui quam ante-
25 cessor habuit die quo obiit in causa possessionis vt de feodo.

Cum igitur dicat querens quod iniuste disseysitus fuerit oportet quod tenens
ostendat quod iuste et quo iure quia forte statim reeiecit post disseysinam
querentis.   Ad quod replicari poterit quod iniuste eo quod post longeuum interuallum et vbi sibi perquirere debuit per assisam fecit se iusticiarium vel sic iuste
30 quia querens nullum ius habuit nec liberum tenementum nec feodum quia per
disseysinam vel intrusionem nec hoc valebit quia si disseysitus nullum habeat
ius tenendi ille qui eiecit nullum habuit ius eiciendi quia disseysitus iuste fuit in
possessione quantum ad ipsum eicientem qui nichil iuris habet.   Vel si dicatur
quod iuste quia seruus est et non potest assisam portare, hoc non sufficit cum
35 non sit seruus eius et ideo nichil ad eum.   Nec dicere poterit quod iuste eum
eiecit cum sit seruus alienus et sic non defenditur ex quo nichil ad eum nec

1. excepcio *om.* J.   13. pertinencias] pertinencia, J; quod] quos, J.   14. vbi] nisi, J.
19. in corpore, Br., *om.* J.   25. die] de, J.   27. iuste] iniuste, J; reeiecit, Br., *om.* J.
29. per assisam, Br., *om.* J; iusticiarium, Br., iusticiari, J.   30. ius *om.* J.   32. *post* quia
add. si, J.   34. hoc] set, J.   36. et] quia, J.   36. nec] quod, J.

Bracton,
f. 191

he is another's, since his kinsmen are the villeins of another. If however, an exception should be put forward by the true lord against him who is outside his lord's authority and has recently fled, the exception will hold against him so long as the lord can reclaim him without a writ and lawfully seize him if he is found in his fee but, when he cannot have recourse to recover his villein except by a writ, the exception is of no avail until the fugitive comes within the lord's authority because, if a lord through weakness or negligence ceases to possess his villein and loses both natural and civil possession, there will be neither time nor place for an exception. But restitution is available to the villein by an assize and the lord will not have an action against him except in a proprietary action, but when the lord has deraigned his person in a proprietary action, then he will be adjudged to his lord with all his lands, goods and chattels and all his brood. But before that he cannot take anything away from the villein without his recovering it, both because no one can recover or have appurtenances before he has that to which the things pertain, and also because the words contained in the writ would be worthless where 'the king commands so-and-so to cause so-and-so to have so-and-so, his villein and fugitive, with all his brood and with his chattels' for, if he can usurp the chattels of a fugitive villein without a judgement of the court, then that word 'chattels' would be wrongly included and would have no effect.

Bracton,
f. 191b

What right can the lord claim in chattels or tenements, in as it were accessories, when he can claim no right in the body [of the villein] which is the principal [subject of action]? But in truth in any question of status, raised by a writ of neifty, the exception of dispossession will always bar the lord who is the demandant until the villein is given restitution in full, and enquiry must always first be made about dispossession, and full restitution made, before enquiry is made about status. But it is important whether he complains and demands restitution of something taken from himself, or whether he bases a claim that the thing be delivered up to him upon the seisin of another, for example the seisin of some ancestor of the villein: in a possessory action, [the seisin] which the ancestor had as of fee on the day he died.

Bracton,
f. 190b

Bracton,
f. 196

When therefore the plaintiff says that he was unlawfully disseised, it behoves the tenant to show that it was done lawfully, and by what right, because he may have ejected immediately after a disseisin by the plaintiff. To which answer can be made that the ejection was unlawful because it occurred after a long interval of time, and where he ought to have aided himself by an assize he made himself the judge; or thus, that the ejection was lawful because the plaintiff had no right, neither freehold nor fee, because [he held] by disseisin or intrusion. Yet this will not avail because, if the disseisee has no right to hold, he who ejected had no right to eject since the disseisee was lawfully in possession so far as the ejector was concerned who has no right. Or if it is said that [the ejection] was lawful because he is a villein and cannot bring an assize, this does not suffice when he is not the disseisor's villein and therefore is nothing to him. Nor can the disseisor say that 'he lawfully ejected him' when he is another's villein, and if he does, he is without defence inasmuch as it is no concern of his, nor could he say,

dicere potuit quod res fuit empta de denariis suis sicut posset dicere verus dominus. Item sine iudicio quia si disseysitor vltimus iudicium expectaret et per
accionem petere vellet nullam in mundo inueniret que ei competere possit. Et
ideo cum nullam habere posset accionem nulla ei competere debet excepcio con-
5 tra seruum qui alienus est omnino quia sic sequeretur hoc inconueniens quod
retinere posset per excepcionem et maliciam quod nunquam adquirere posset per
accionem.

Et cum exceperit de seruitute quamuis hoc verificare petat per assisam
querens tamen contra extraneum non dominum non habet necesse replicare de
10 libertate quia si gratis inde se poneret in assisam et de statu seruili conuictus
esset non tamen propterea conuictum erit quod non ipsum iniuste non disseysiuit cum sit seruus alienus et non suus. Et si dominus serui habere non possit
assisam ex quo tenementum nondum cepit in manum suam ante disseysinam nec
ipse seruus sic sequeretur quod terra remaneret cum disseysitore et sic de malicia   f. 91*b*
15 lucrum reportaret quod esse non debet. Sequitur ergo quod excepcio seruitutis
in ore extranei locum habere non debeat cum ille qui in possessione fuerit maius
ius habeat in re possessa quam ille qui fuerit extra cui nullum ius conpetit et
ideo semper in tali casu prius terminanda erit disseysina et spolacio quam
questio status. Nullus autem in statu libero existens necesse habet ponendi
20 statum suum in assisam vel iuratam verumtamen si hoc per stulticiam fecerit non
tamen preiudicabitur statui nisi tantum ad hoc quod assisa non procedat licet
producti fuerint parentes ad excepcionem probandam. Quilibet autem in tali
casu petere debet iudicium si ponere se debeat in assisam de aliquo quod tangat
statum suum antequam fuerit de spoliatis restitutus et si tenens excepcionem   [*238*]
25 weyuiare noluerit nec querens replicacionem ex officio iudicis capienda erit assisa
vtrum disseysitus fuerit vel non. Et eodem modo de libero existente in statu
seruili et de omnibus preterquam de villano sub potestate domini constituto
tenente villenagium de eo contra quem nullum liberum tenementum poterit
vendicari.

30 Si autem seruus sub potestate domini sui perquisitum fecerit tenendum
libere et feoffator suus eum inde eiecerit antequam dominus tenementum illud
ceperit in manum suam statim conpetit accio villano per assisam noue disseysine
et non domino contra feoffatorem suum et omnes alios preterquam contra
verum dominum sub cuius potestate fuerit constitutus non obstante excepcione
35 villenagii. Et vbi sequitur assisa noue disseysine in persona antecessoris
sequitur assisa mortis antecessoris in persona heredis et versus easdem personas.
Si autem a domino suo feoffatus fuerit tenendi libere sibi et heredibus suis si
per dominum suum postea eiciatur conpetit restitucio per assisam contra
dominum suum et contra omnes quamuis aliam terram tenuerit in villenagio de

---

1. quod] quia, J.   2. si *repetitur in* J.   2-3. per accionem] paccionem, J.   24. et]
vt, J.   25. weyuiare noluerit] veyuiare voluerit, J.   39. tenuerit] tenuerint, J.

Bracton,
f. 196b

as the true lord could say, that the property was bought with his money. Likewise [he cannot say] 'without a judgement of the court' because, if the last
disseisor should await judgement and wish to proceed by action, he would find no
action in the world that could avail him. And therefore since he can have no
right of action, no exception should be available to him against a villein who
belongs completely to another, because there would thus follow an incongruity
in that he could retain by an exception and malice what he could never acquire
by an action.

Bracton,
f. 197

And should he except on the ground of villeinage, though he may ask for this
to be verified by an assize, yet the plaintiff is under no necessity to answer a third
party who is not his lord regarding his free status because, if he voluntarily put
himself on the assize on that issue and was adjudged to be of servile condition,
nevertheless it will not on that account be adjudged that [the defendant] did not
unlawfully disseise him, since he is another's villein and not his. And if the
villein's lord cannot have an assize because he has not yet taken the tenement
into his own hand before the disseisin, nor the villein himself, it would thus
follow that the land would remain with the disseisor and he would thus gain
profit from his wrongdoing, which must not be. It follows therefore that the
exception of villeinage should not lie in the mouth of a third party, since he who
is in possession has greater right to the property possessed than he who is out of
possession and to whom no right attaches, and therefore in such a case disseisin

Bracton,
f. 199

and dispossession must always be determined before the question of status.
There is, however, no need for anyone of free condition to put [the question of]
his status to an assize or jury: indeed, if he should stupidly do this, it will not
however prejudice his status save only to this extent, that the assize will not proceed even though his kinsmen have been produced to prove the exception. Yet
anyone in such a case ought to pray judgement whether he must put himself on
an assize concerning anything which touches his status before there is restored
to him what he has lost by dispossession. And if the tenant will not waive his
exception nor the plaintiff his answer the assize will be taken on the judge's
authority whether the plaintiff was disseised or not, and likewise with regard to
a freeman living in a servile condition and with all others save a villein living
under his lord's authority who holds a villein tenement of him, for against his
lord he can claim no freehold.

Bracton,
f. 192b

If, however, a villein under the authority of his lord has made an acquisition
to be held freely, and his feoffor ejects him therefrom before the lord takes the said
tenement into his hands, an action is forthwith available to the villein, and not
to the lord, by an assize of novel disseisin against his feoffor and all others (except against his true lord under whose authority he is living), notwithstanding an
exception of villeinage. And where an assize of novel disseisin lies in the
person of an ancestor, an assize of *mort d'ancestor* follows in the person of the
heir and against the same persons. If, moreover, a villein should be enfeoffed
by his lord to hold freely, to him and his heirs, and if he is afterwards ejected by
his lord, restitution is available by an assize against his lord and against all men
(even though he may hold other land of his lord in villeinage) notwithstanding

domino non obstante excepcione villenagii quia villenagium non aufert a libero
libertatem manumissionis.   Set si dominus seruo suo petenti opponat excepcionem seruus habebit replicacionem ex facto et manumissione domini, et eodem
modo si dominus cum seruo suo faciat conuencionem per quam manumittatur
5 tunc agere potest contra dominum suum et multo forcius contra non dominum.
Si autem villenagium opponatur alicui petenti contra quem non producantur
parentes ad excepcionem probandam et petens statim inde se ponat in assisam
et tenens similiter cadit assisa et vertitur in iuratam et inde verba sacramenti iuratorum talia erunt quod veritatem dicent de hiis que ab eis exigentur ex parte
10 regis et non secundum verba assise quia non est actum principaliter ad assisam
vtrum disseysitus fuerit vel non set quantum ad iuratam inquisicionem si
querens sit vel seruus vel paritatem habeat a domino priusquam cum domino
respondeatur quia si conuincatur per iuratam quod seruus sit cadit assisa nec
villanus aliquid capiet per assisam set erit in misericordia pro falso clamore.
15 Non tamen propter hoc erit seruus domino suo pro seruo liberandus quia per
iuratam nichil agitur nisi quod seruus a querela repellatur et si conuincatur per
iuratam quod libere sit condicionis pro querente iudicabitur nec latebit conuiccio quia in modum assise non transiuit non tamen in potestate domini liberandus
quia talis excepcio in breui noue disseysine opposita statum non mutat neque
20 condicionem set secus esset in placito de consuetudinibus et seruiciis quamuis
indirecte.   Et si iuratores non opposita excepcione villenagii dicant quod querens
habere non possit liberum tenementum quia seruus tenentis conuinci poterunt
de periurio dum tamen assisa in modo assise processerit et similiter si dicant quod
liber sit conuinci poterunt per parentes vel alio modo et si de statu fiat discussio
25 et iuratores veraciter nesciuerint vtrum seruus sit vel liber pro libertate erit iudicandum.   Si autem sic seruo obiciatur quod villanus sit et pater suus villanus fuit
replicare poterit seruus quod etsi pater suus villanus fuerit mater tamen sua libera
fuit et in partu soluta.   Si autem vxor liberi petatur ab aliquo quamuis natiua
obstabit petenti excepcio liberi thori cum viro suo.   Si autem causa talis adici-
30 atur quia pater suus villanus fuit non sufficit nisi dicat quod in statu seruili obiit   [239]
sub potestate domini constitutus et quamuis ad hoc agi non possit quod mortuus
ad villanum probetur quia hoc esset in principali causa status ad probandum ipsum esse talem per testes et parentes et ita mutare statum defuncti.   Poterit
tamen inquiri per iuratam vtrum ipse villanus obiit vel liber sicut inquireretur si
35 legitimus obiit vel bastardus statu propter hoc non mutato quia villenagium
oppositum in modum excepcionis statum defuncti vel viui non alterat neque

    5. potest *addimus*.   8. sacramentum iurate, J. *in margine*.   12. vel] vt, J.
15. Nota J. *in margine*.   26. et] qualiter, J.   27. *post* tamen *add*. cum, J.   28. partu]
parte, J.   28. quamuis] nunquam, J.   29. cum *om*. J.   32. in *om*. J.   35. legitimus]
legatarius, J.

the exception of villeinage, because villeinage does not take away from a free
man the freedom given by manumission.   But if the lord puts forward this exception against the villein who is the plaintiff, the villein will have an answer from
the act and manumission of the lord, and likewise, if the lord makes an agreement with his villein by which he is manumitted, then he can bring an action
against his lord and with even greater force against one who is not his lord.
If, however, [the exception of] villeinage is raised against any plaintiff, against
whom his kinsmen are not produced to prove the exception, and on this issue the
plaintiff forthwith puts himself on the assize and the tenant does likewise, the
assize abates and is turned into a jury, and the words of the juror's oath thereon
will be to the effect that they will speak the truth concerning those things which
are demanded of them on behalf of the king, and not according to the words of
the assize, because the judicial proceedings are not principally an assize to decide
whether the plaintiff was disseised or not but simply a sworn inquest to find out

Bracton,
f. 193

whether the plaintiff is a villein or is the equal of the lord before he is answered
by the lord because, if it is found by the jury that he is a villein, the assize abates
and the villein will take nothing by the assize but will be amerciable for a false
claim.   Nevertheless, the villein will not on this account be delivered to his lord
as his villein because nothing is decided by the jury except that the villein should
be denied his plaint and, if the jury finds that the plaintiff is of free condition,
judgement will be given for the plaintiff, nor will an attaint lie, because it was not
done in the manner of an assize.   He is not to be delivered into the authority of
the lord because such an exception, put forward against a writ of novel disseisin,
changes neither status nor condition, but it would be otherwise in a plea of

Bracton,
f. 193

customs and services, although indirectly.   And if, when an exception of
villeinage is not put forward, the jurors say that the plaintiff cannot have a freehold because he is the tenant's villein, they can be attainted of perjury, provided
the assize has proceeded in the manner of an assize, and similarly, if they say that
the plaintiff is a free man, they can be attainted by [the production of] kinsmen or
in some other way, and if the status of the plaintiff is made an issue and the jurors

Bracton,
f. 194b

do not in truth know whether he is a villein or a free man, judgement must
be in favour of freedom.   If, however, objection is raised against a villein
to the effect that he is a villein and his father was a villein, the villein can reply
that, although his father was a villein, yet his mother was free and was single
when he was born.   If, however, the wife of a free man is claimed by anyone,
although she is a neif the exception of a free bed with her husband will bar the
claimant.   If, however, such a plea is added to the effect that [he is a villein]
because his father was a villein, it does not suffice unless one says that he died
in servile condition while living under the authority of his lord, although
proceedings cannot take place for the purpose of proving that he died as a villein

Bracton
f. 194

because to prove him to be such by witnesses and kinsmen would constitute a
principal plea of status and so could change the status of the deceased.   It can,
however, be enquired by the jury whether he died a villein or a free man, just
as it can be enquired whether he died legitimate or bastard, but his status is not
thereby changed because, where villeinage is put forward by way of an exception,

mutat.   Et sicut villanus in iudicio petitus per breue in statu libero se defenderit
vsque ad mortem vel quamuis numquam petitus fuerit in possessione domini
tamen non fuerit constitutus vt seruus cum sine placito et breui reuocari non
poterit in seruitute, ita nec liber homo in statu serui sub potestate domini
5 existens et in possessione seruitutis constitutus sine placito peruenire poterit ad
libertatem.

Excipere autem poterit seruus et replicare in multis modis vt si dominus in   f. 92
curia regis recognouerit ipsum esse liberum et hoc docere possit item si dominus
eum aliquando produxerit in curia regis vt liberum hominem suum ad dis-
10 racionacionem vel legem aliquam faciendam vel purgacionem et hoc docere possit
per recordum curie regis vel comitatus item si dominus eum manumiserit item si
homagium eius ceperit item si ipsum feoffauerit sibi et heredibus suis item si
totum ius quod in eo habuit et in sequela et in catallis suis ei remisit et quietum-
clamauit item si contra dominum petentem ipsum vt natiuum suum quietus
15 recesserit per iudicium.   Et nota quod manumissio sine tradicione magis obesse
poterit in persona heredis si proferatur contra dominum ipsum petentem quam
prodesse quia inperfecta fuit empcio siue manumissio eo quod nunquam fuit in
vita venditoris tradicio prosecuta.   Et si quis replicando dicat quod quamuis
aliquando fuit villanus ab ipso tamen tenente fuit manumissus licet certam manu-
20 missionem proferat non recuperabit contra dominum pro cognicione quia si
dominum mutauerit per manumissionem statum tamen non mutat.   Nam si
huiusmodi manumissus prolem suscitauerit eciam ex libera hereditatem
habente si post mortem matris eiciatur non recuperabit per assisam.   Esto quod
villanus feoffatus sit a domino suo sub cuius fuerit potestate tenendi libere nulla
25 facta mencione de heredibus quamuis per feoffatorem fuerit eiectus non recuperabit per assisam quia status suus in aliquo non mutatur quia omnis homo aut
est omnino liber aut omnino seruus nec habetur medium.   Si autem simpliciter
opponatur quod querens villanus sit et querens hoc neget tunc procedet assisa
ac si nichil dictum esset quare assisa remaneret.   Et nota quod contra nullum in
30 statu libero existentem set tantum contra seruum sub potestate domini constitutum produci debent parentes nec per eos admitti debet probacio set tantum
per iuratores.   Est enim in statu libero quicumque potestatem habet standi in
iudicio sicut liber et cum de statu suo sine breui respondere non teneatur.   Et
sicut seruus esse poterit in statu liberi ita poterit liber esse in statu serui.   Seruus
35 autem fugitiuus non solum infra annum et diem capi poterit in feodo domini set
vbicumque inuentus fuerit in regno dum tamen recenter post fugam sequatur   [240]
comprehendi poterit et inpune retineri: secus vero si infra annum et diem non
sequatur vel petatur.

3. cum *addidimus*.   7. et *om*. J.   14. natiuum] vacuum, J.   15. Nota, J. *in*
margine.   23. habente] habuit, J; matris, Br., patris, J.   29. Nota J. *in margine*.
32. potestatem] personam, J, *sed corrigitur in margine*.   37. *prius* et] eciam, J.

it does not alter or change the status of a man, whether dead or alive.   And just as a villein, claimed by writ in judicial proceedings, may defend himself in a condition of freedom until his death or, although he is never claimed, nevertheless is not placed in the possession of a lord as a villein, since he cannot be recalled into servitude without an action and a writ, so neither can a free man, who lives in servile condition under a lord's authority and remains possessed of servitude, attain freedom without an action.

A villein can except and answer in many ways: for example, if the lord has acknowledged in the king's court that he is free and he can show this; or if the lord has at some time produced him in the king's court as his free man to deraign or to make some compurgation or purgation and he can show this by a record of the king's court or of the county court; or if the lord has manumitted him or if he has accepted his homage or if he has enfeoffed him, to him and his heirs; or if he has remitted to him and quitclaimed all the right he had in him and his brood and his chattels; or if, when the lord claimed him as his villein, he went quit of him by judgement of the court.   And it is to be noted that, in the person of the heir, manumission without livery can be more of a hindrance than a help if it is put forward against the lord who claims him because the purchase or the manumission was incomplete in that livery was never sued for in the lifetime of the vendor.   And if anyone in answering should say that, although he was once a villein, nevertheless he has been manumitted by the tenant himself, although he should put forward a definite manumission, he will not recover against the lord on account of this acknowledgement, because if by manumission he changes his lord, yet he does not change his status.   For if he who is thus manumitted should beget children, even with a free woman who has an inheritance, if after the death of the mother he is ejected, he will not recover by an assize.   Suppose that a villein is enfeoffed by his lord, under whose authority he is, to hold freely, and no mention is made of heirs, although he should be ejected by the feoffor he will not recover by an assize because his status is in no wise changed, since every man is either altogether free or altogether bond nor is there anything in between. If, however, it is simply objected that the plaintiff is a villein and the plaintiff denies it, then the assize will proceed as if nothing had been said why the assize should be stayed.   And it is to be noted that against no one living in a state of freedom but solely against a villein living under the authority of a lord ought kinsmen to be produced, and proof should not be admitted by them but only by the jurors.   For everyone is in a state of freedom who has the power to stand in court as a free man and who is not bound to answer as to his status without a writ.   And just as a villein can be in a condition of freedom, so can a free man be in a condition of villeinage.   A fugitive villein, however, may be seized within a year and a day not only in the lord's fee but wherever he may be found in the realm; provided he is pursued immediately after his flight, he can be arrested and detained with impunity; but it would be otherwise if he were not pursued or claimed within a year and a day.

Bracton,
f. 194b

Bracton,
f. 195

Bracton,
f. 199

Bracton,
f. 197b

CAP. XII. DE EXCEPCIONE RACIONE ADIUNCTI

Si autem mulier libera nupta sit villano existenti sub potestate domini sui et ipsa liberum habeat tenementum et dominus serui illos eiecerit non recuperabunt viuente viro set post mortem viri recuperabit mulier quasi sublato inpedimento
5 qualitercumque mortuus fuerit morte naturali vel ciuili et cum ab extraneo non domino eiecti fuerint neuter de iure vxoris sine alio petere poterit secus vero de iure viri. Si autem vxor de re propria donacionem fecerit in vita viri sui ambo assisam portare non poterunt simul nec quilibet per se vir tamen recuperabit per aliud breue. Si autem de re vxoria simul disseysiti fuerint et assisam simul
10 inpetrauerint si alter eorum moriatur ante capcionem assise cadit breue. Si autem vir premoriatur vxor per assisam non recuperabit set per breue de ingressu in qua non habet ingressum nisi per disseysinam quam fecit ei et tali viro suo. Si autem mulier fuerit disseysita et assisam perquisierit et ante capcionem assise nupta fuerit cadit breue racione adiuncti et non assisa et quo casu fiat tale
15 breue: Questi sunt nobis A. et B. vxor eius quod C. iniuste disseysiuit predictam B. Si autem vxor eiciatur viro agente longe in remotis vt in peregrinacione vel in nuncio vel huiusmodi non conpetit vxori restitucio per assisam racione adiuncti et ideo prouisum fuit breue de generali attornato. Si autem vxor virum relinquens virum suum disseysiuerit conpetit viro remedium per assisam
20 per tale breue: 'Questi sunt nobis A. et B. vxor eius quod B. de tali loco', ita quod ipsa vxor nominetur, si res de qua fit disseysina fuerit ius vxoris, simul cum viro suo in querela et iterum per idem nomen set cognomen diuersum sicut de villa in qua nata fuit vel tanquam filia patris eius et quo casu habebitur vxor pro disseysitrice.

25 ## CAP. XIII. DE EXCEPCIONE EX PERSONA TENENTIS

Conpetit eciam excepcio tenenti ex persona sua propria contra querentem vt si dicat quod quamuis disseysina ibi fuerit ipse tamen disseysinam non fecit set alius antecessor vel predecessor qui mortuus est et iniuria personalis est et se non extendit ad heredes neque ad successores quia penalis est et pena suos debet

2. existenti] existente, J.   11. recuperabit] moriatur, J, *sed corrigitur in margine.*
12. qua] quam, J.   25. Tenentis] Petentis, J.

CHAPTER 12.   OF AN EXCEPTION ARISING BY REASON OF ONE CONJOINED IN MARRIAGE

Bracton,
f. 202

If a free woman should be married to a villein living under the authority of his lord and she has a freehold and the villein's lord ejects them, they will not recover while the husband is alive but after his death the woman will recover, the impediment being as it were removed, howsoever the deceased died, whether by natural or civil death, and if they are ejected by a third party who is not their lord, neither of them can claim in right of the wife without the other.   But it is

Bracton,
f. 202b

otherwise in right of the husband.   If, however, the wife should make a gift of her own property in the lifetime of her husband, both will not be able to bring an assize together nor either of them alone: the husband will recover by another writ.   But if they should be disseised together of the wife's property and should sue out an assize together, if either of them dies before the assize is taken, the writ abates.   If, however, the husband were to predecease the wife, she will not recover by an assize but by a writ of entry 'in which he has no entry except by the disseisin he did to her and to so-and-so, her husband'.   But if a woman should be disseised and sue out an assize, and before the assize is taken she should get married, the writ abates by reason of the person joined to her, but not so the assize.   And in such a case a writ is made as follows: 'A. and B., his wife, have complained to us that C. has unlawfully disseised the aforesaid B.'

Bracton,
f. 203

If, however, the wife is ejected while the husband is busy far away in distant places, as on a pilgrimage or on a mission or the like, restitution is not available to the wife by an assize by reason of the person joined to her, and for that reason

Bracton,
f. 202b

a writ of general attorney was provided.   If, however, the wife leaves her husband and disseises him, a remedy is available to the husband by an assize by means of a writ as follows: 'A. and B., his wife, have complained to us that B. of such-and-such a place', so that the wife herself is named along with her husband in the plaint, if the property which is the subject of the disseisin is the right of the wife, and again by the same Christian name but with a different surname, such as of the township in which she was born or as the daughter of her father, and in which case a wife will be regarded as a disseisor.

CHAPTER 13.   OF AN EXCEPTION ARISING OUT OF THE PERSON OF THE TENANT

Bracton,
f. 203b

An exception is also available to the tenant against the plaintiff arising from the tenant's own person: for example, if he says that, although there was a disseisin there, he did not commit the disseisin but another, an ancestor or predecessor who is dead, and the wrong is personal and does not extend to heirs or successors because it is penal, and a penalty ought to attach only to those

tenere tantum auctores et quo conperto cadit breue. Si autem procuratores,
custodes, firmarii, serui vel familia disseysinam fecerint, quamuis dominus cuius
nomine disseysinam fecerint de disseysina non sciuerit non propter hoc remaneat assisa set capiatur in odium disseysitorum. Si assisa faciat contra eos
5 recuperabit querens et dominus cum redierit si factum eorum aduocauerit incidit f. 92b
in penam disseysine cum suis. Item conpetit excepcio contra querentem vt si
dominus capitalis petat per assisam vbi conpetit ei districcio. Si autem distringere non audeat ad auxilium regis habeat recursum et ipse precipiet vicecomiti
loci quod sit ei in auxilium nam si tenens ad tuicionem sui excipiat quod assisa
10 procedere non debeat de seruicio nisi seruicium negaret set palam confitetur
quod tenet de tali statim propter confessionem iacebit districcio et cadet assisa [241]
et sine alio breui precipietur vicecomiti ex parte regis ex officio iusticiariorum
quod sit tali domino in auxilium ad distringendum. Si autem tenens omnino
ipsum deaduocauerit tunc statim cessat districcio propter quod dominus petere
15 potest terram in dominico post biennium. Prius tamen agere poterit per breue
noue disseysine in casu cum tenens contendat contra dominum distringentem et
faciat districcionem replegiari et quibus casibus facit disseysinam domino suo et
quamuis assisa non iaceat inter dominum et tenentem suum tenens tamen districcionem replegiando vel dominum suum deaduocando se facit non tenentem.
20 Esto quod extraneus non dominus per vim conpellat alienum tenentem quod ei
soluat redditum domino debitum vel quod domino suo non soluat talis extraneus
domino facit disseysinam et non tenens quasi de libero tenemento domini. Et
illud idem erit si tenens de voluntate sua soluat extraneo et quo casu conpetit
domino districcio contra tenentem et assisa contra extraneum distringentem de
25 altero tamen istorum habeat se contentum. Si quis autem recenter rem ingressus
fuerit post disseysinam flagrante maleficio non est mirum si teneatur de disseysina cum res in se sit viciosa propter disseysinam. Scit enim aut scire debet que
et qualis sit res quam ingreditur si viciosa sit per disseysinam sicut ille qui rem
emit scire debet vtrum libera sit vel serua per inposicionem seu constitucionem
30 seruitutis vel vtrum onerata sit nec ne et vtrum sit contenciosa per diligentem inpetracionem siue sic siue sic semper tenebitur accipiens ad penam vel ad restitucionem vel ad vtramque.

3. fecerint] fecerit, J.   10. debeat] debet, J.   22. quasi, Br.; quia, J.
26. maleficio] malefacto, J.

Bracton,
f. 204

Bracton,
f. 204b

Bracton,
f. 203

Bracton,
f. 203b

Bracton,
f. 204b

Bracton,
f. 205

responsible and, when this is made known, the writ abates. If, however, agents, guardians, fermors, villeins or members of a household commit disseisin, even though the lord in whose name they committed the disseisin did not know about it, the assize will not on this account be stayed but will be taken in reprobation of the disseisors. If the assize goes against them the plaintiff will recover, and if the lord avows their deed when he returns, he will fall with them under the penalty for disseisin. Again, an exception is available against the plaintiff if, for instance, the chief lord should proceed by an assize where distraint was open to him: if, however, he does not dare to distrain, he may have recourse to the king for aid and he will command the sheriff of the district to go to his aid, for if the tenant to save himself excepts that the assize ought not to proceed as to the service because he does not deny the service but openly admits that he holds of so-and-so, forthwith on account of the admission distraint will lie and the assize abates and without any further writ the sheriff will be commanded by the justices *ex officio* on behalf of the king that he give aid to such-and-such a lord to distrain. But if the tenant disavows him altogether, the distraint will end forthwith, because of which after two years the lord can claim the land in demesne. But before then he can sue by writ of novel disseisin in a case where the tenant disputes with the lord who is distraining and causes the distress to be replevied, and in such cases he commits disseisin against his lord, and although an assize does not lie between the lord and his tenant, yet the tenant, by replevying the distress or disavowing his lord, makes himself a non-tenant. Suppose that a third party who is not the lord compels another's tenant by force to pay him a rent that is due to the lord or not to pay it to the lord, such third party and not the tenant commits a disseisin against the lord as it were of the lord's freehold. And it will be the same if the tenant of his own free will makes payment to the third party, in which case distress is available to the lord against the tenant and an assize against the third party who distrains, but he will have to content himself with one or other of those remedies. If, however, anyone enters a property immediately after a disseisin while the wrongdoing is fresh, it is no wonder if he be guilty of disseisin, since the property is in itself defective on account of the disseisin, for he knows or ought to know what and of what kind the property is into which he enters, whether it is defective by disseisin, just as the purchaser of a property ought to know whether it is free or servient by the imposition or creation of a servitude, or whether it is burdened or not, and whether it is subject to dispute by constant claims, and whether it is this or whether it is that, the acquirer will always be held liable to a penalty or to restitution or to both.

CAP. XIV.   DE EXCEPCIONIBUS IUDICIALIBUS

Continetur enim in breui 'Questus est nobis talis quod talis iniuste et sine iudicio disseysiuit talem'.   Iniuste autem et sine iudicio accipi poterunt copulatiue vel disiunctiue iniuste propter iniuriam vel iniuste quamuis non sine iudicio set non
5 a suo iudice et ideo iniuste quia iudex non habuit warantum per breue et ideo eius iudicium nullum de iure habere potuit effectum nec execucioni demandari et non solum facit curia que iudicat iniuriam et disseysinam verum eciam balliuus qui tale iudicium iniustum fuerit executus nec eciam ipse balliuus tantum cum iudice et curia set eciam ille qui tali iudicio nactus fuerit possessionem.   Et
10 si querens per assisam recuperare non poterit, poterit tamen per breue de falso iudicio, set ad hoc requiritur regium consilium et auxilium quia nullum breue originale ab inicio sine quo non admittetur recordum sine regio assensu et precepto et quo casu semper poterit tenens vocare ad warantum recordum tam curie regis quam alterius male iudicantis et cum iudicium falsum inueniatur que-
15 rens recuperabit simul cum dampnis.

Conpetit eciam excepcio tenenti racione tenementi et rei que sancta est, sicut sunt loca Deo dedicata et que ab aliquo possideri non possunt et ideo nulli de talibus tenementis conpetit assisa et in quo casu cadit assisa et non breue et vertitur assisa in iuratam ad inquirendum de transgressione si facta fuerit in re
20 sacra quia nulla ibi est disseysina vt per iuratam emendetur transgressio et vterque tam tenens quam querens in misericordia.   Item si tenementum fuerit [242] vniuersitatis vel publicum et in ciuitate vel burgo si ibi fuerit edificatum vel presumptum ad dominum regem pertinebit emendacio et quo casu pocius erit transgressio et purprestura quam disseysina.   Si autem via publica vel regia ex-
25 tra ciuitatem vel burgum eodem modo pertinebit ad regem emendacio.   Si autem locus fuerit communis alicuius vniuersitatis extra ciuitatem vel burgum qui deputatus sit ad aliquem vsum communem hic erit transgressio et nulla disseysina.

CAP. XV.   CADIT ASSISA

30 Quandoque autem cadit breue et non assisa vt si tenens excipiat contra breue ita quod tenementum non sit in villa in breui comprehensa set in alia et querens dicat contrarium per officium iudicis inquiratur prestito sacramento et siue dicant iuratores hic vel ibi non propter hoc terminabitur negocium quia

3. et *om.* J.   23. regem, Br., ciuitatis, J.   27. hic, Br., sic, J.

CHAPTER 14.   OF JUDICIAL EXCEPTIONS

Bracton,
f. 205

Included in the writ are the words, 'So-and-so has complained to us that so-and-so has disseised so-and-so unlawfully and without a judgement of the court.' 'Unlawfully' and 'without a judgement' may be construed together or separately: 'unlawfully' on account of the wrong; or 'unlawfully', though not 'without a judgement', but one not given by the appropriate judge, and so 'unlawfully' because the judge did not have a warrant by writ, and therefore his judgement could have no effect in law and could not be brought to execution.

Bracton,
f. 205b

And not only does the court which judges commit a wrong and disseisin but also the bailiff who might execute such an unlawful judgement, and not only the bailiff together with the judge and the court but also he who by such a judgement gains possession.   And if the plaintiff cannot recover by an assize, yet he can do so by a writ of false judgement, but for this the royal counsel and aid are needed, because there was no original writ at the start and without it the record will not be admitted without the king's assent and command, and in this case the tenant can always vouch to warranty the record not only of the king's court but also the court of anyone else which judges badly, and when false judgement is found the plaintiff will have recovery together with his damages.

Bracton,
f. 210b

An exception is also available to the tenant by reason of a tenement and a thing which is holy, such as the places dedicated to God which cannot be possessed by any man, and therefore an assize in respect of such tenements is available to no one, and in this case the assize abates but not the writ, and the assize is turned into a jury to enquire into the trespass whether it was committed in a holy place (because there is no disseisin there) so that the trespass can be redressed by the jury and both the tenant and the plaintiff will be amerciable. Again, if the tenement should belong to a community or be public property and be within a city or borough and if building or usurpation takes place there, amendment will belong to the lord king, and in this case it will be trespass and purpresture rather than disseisin.   And if it is a public or royal highway outside a city or borough, amendment will likewise belong to the king.   But if the place is common belonging to some community, outside a city or borough, which is assigned to some common use, it will then be trespass and not disseisin.

CHAPTER 15.   THE ABATEMENT OF AN ASSIZE

Bracton,
f. 211

Sometimes the writ abates and not the assize; for example, if the tenant excepts against the writ in this way: that the tenement is not in the township contained in the writ but in another and the plaintiff says the contrary, an *ex officio* enquiry will be made by the judge after an oath has been administered, and whether the jurors say that the tenement lies here or lies there, the business will

excepcio proponitur contra breue et non contra assisam et ideo stat assisa set
cadit breue forte nec erit locus ioco partito eciam si partes consentire vellent
quod vnus amittat si ita sit, et si non sit quod lucretur alius quia si iuratores
dicant quod tenementum non sit in villa in breui nominata cadit breue et non
5 assisa et ad consimile breue redire poterit siue petat licenciam recedendi de
breui suo et habeat siue sine licencia a breui suo se retrahat quamuis enim quis   f. 93
propter breue male impetratum sine licencia a breui se retraxerit nec propter
hoc se retrahit ab accione.   Et si dicant iuratores quod tenementum est in villa
in breui nominata siue ita sit vel non procedet assisa et per assisam terminabitur
10 negocium nec erit locus conuiccioni quia vtraque pars de hoc se posuit in
iuratam.   Si autem iuratores forte dubitauerint et nesciuerint in qua villa tenementum illud fuerit tunc inquiratur a querente si clamet in villa non nominata
qui si dicat quod non cadet assisa set non breue, statim tamen sine alio breui fiant
racionabiles diuise inter villas vel inter maneria secundum quod inter certas
15 diuisas fuerint distincta.   Et eodem modo fiat cum fuerit contencio de
finibus et terminis comitatuum vt si tenens dicat quod in vno comitatu et
querens in alio et inde se posuerint super iuratam et iuratores distinguere sciant
fines et terminos comitatuum per eorum sacramentum procedat negocium vt si
dicant quod tenementum fuerit in comitatu non nominato cadet breue et per
20 aliud breue procedet negocium modo quo predictum est et in comitatu nominato
tunc procedat assisa et per assisam terminabitur negocium.   Si autem iuratores
nullo modo distinguere sciant fines et terminos comitatuum non propter hoc cadit
breue set sine alio breui per officium iudicis cadit assisa in perambulacionem et
per perambulacionem terminabitur negocium, dum tamen partes prius coher-
25 centur ad certum et ita quod a querente sciatur si aliquid clamet in comitatu non
nominato et e conuerso a tenente si aliquid clamet in comitatu nominato.   Et
sic procedet perambulacio, habita tamen racione vtrum querens maioris fuerit
etatis vel minoris quia nullus infra etatem consentire poterit in perambulacionem
et sine eius consensu ante etatem non procedet perambulacio.   Si autem iura-
30 tores dicant quod quedam pars tenementi vnde visus factus est sit in villa vel in
comitatu nominatis et quedam pars in villa et in comitatu non nominatis pro-   [243]
cedet assisa pro ea parte tenementi que est in villa vel in comitatu nominatis et
pro alia non et uterque erit in misericordia.   Et cadit assisa quandoque in
perambulacionem propter incertitudinem de consensu parcium modo predicto
35 vt si fuerit contencio inter partes in cuius baronia vel feodo tenementum
fuerit et si iuratores nesciant designare tunc per perambulacionem terminabitur

2. ioco] loco, J   3. quod . . . alius, Br., *om.* J.   7. impetratum] perpetratum, J.
17. posuerint] posuerit, J.   24. perambulacionem] ambulacionem, J.   25-26. non
. . . comitatu, Br., *om.* J.   32. et *om.* J.   35. fuerit] fuit, J.

not be brought to an end on this account because the exception is put forward against the writ and not against the assize and therefore the assize stands but the writ perforce abates.   Nor will there be place for jeopardy, even if the parties are willing to agree that, if it is so, one will lose and, if it is not so, he will win because, if the jurors say that the tenement is not in the township named in the writ, the writ abates and not the assize.   And the plaintiff can have recourse to a similar writ whether he prays and obtains leave to withdraw from the writ or whether he withdraws from his writ without leave, for although a man withdraws without leave from a writ because it is badly conceived, he does not on this account withdraw from the action.   And if the jurors say that the tenement is in the township named in the writ, whether it is so or not, the assize will proceed and the business will be brought to an end by the assize and there will be no room for attaint because both parties have put themselves as to this matter on a jury.   If, however, the jurors should perchance be in doubt and should not know in which township the said tenement is situated, then the plaintiff is to be asked if he claims in a township that is not named, and if he says that he does not the assize abates but not the writ.   But forthwith without another writ agreed boundaries are to be made between the townships or between the manors so that they may be set apart between specified boundaries.   And let it be done likewise when there is a dispute regarding the metes and bounds of counties: for example, if the tenant says that [the tenement] is in one county and the plaintiff says it is in another and they put themselves thereon on a jury and the jurors are able to distinguish the metes and bounds of the counties, the business will proceed by their oath: for example, if they say that the tenement was in a county not named, the writ will abate and the business will proceed by another writ in the manner aforesaid, and if they say the tenement is in the county named, the assize is to proceed and the business will be brought to an end by the assize.   If, however, the jurors cannot in any wise distinguish the metes and bounds of the counties, the writ does not abate on this account, but without any other writ at the instance of the judge the assize descends to a perambulation and by the perambulation the business will be resolved, provided, however, the parties are previously compelled to make a precise statement and it is thus known from the plaintiff whether he claims anything in a county that is not named, and conversely from the tenant whether he claims anything in the county named.   And so the perambulation will proceed, account having been taken, however, whether the plaintiff is of age or a minor, because no one under age can agree to a perambulation and without his consent the perambulation will not proceed before he is of age.   If, however, the jurors say that some part of the tenement, of which a view has been made, is in the township and in the county named and some part in a township and in a county not named, the assize will proceed in respect of that part of the tenement which is in the township or in the county named but not for the other part, and each party will be amerciable.   An assize sometimes descends to a perambulation with the consent of the parties in the manner aforesaid because of an uncertainty: for example, if there is a dispute between the parties as to the barony or fee in which the tenement lay and if the jurors do not know where to place it,

Bracton, f. 211b

Bracton, f. 212

negocium. Et sicut fieri poterit perambulacio inter priuatas personas ita inter ipsum regem et aliquem querentem de eo vel de ministris eius assensu tamen regio interueniente.

Item non conpetit restitucio per assisam propter falsam inpetracionem vt si
5 quis inpetrauerit antequam facta fuerit disseysina quod perpendi poterit per datam breuis et eodem modo si causa fuit inpetrandi et postea desiit esse vt disseysitor rem disseysitam domino proprietatis restituerit illam gratis accipienti desinit esse restitucio per assisam, quod secus esset si verus dominus seysinam suam sibi viribus vsurpauerit. Item cadit assisa pro falso iudicio vt si quis per
10 iudicium alicuius curie ingressum habuerit et non per disseysinam et quo casu vocare poterit curiam ad warantum et si iudicium compertum fuerit falsum cadit assisa et agat de falso iudicio. Item cadit assisa propter incertitudinem rei nec vertitur in iuratam neque in perambulacionem sicut videri poterit inter mulierem et warantum suum de dote sua ante assignacionem dotis vt si ambo
15 eiecti fuerint de tenemento et mulier per se petat restitucionem tercie partis per assisam non recuperabit quia suam terciam partem designare non potest quia nunquam fuit specificata nec ei assignata. Et eodem modo si heres eam eicerit de toto cum ad etatem peruenerit, versus eum per assisam non recuperabit racione predicta qualecumque sit feodum, socagium vel militare. Eodem modo
20 dici poterit inter eos qui tenent in communi ante diuisionem sicut sunt coheredes et participes vel vicini si de consensu teneant in communi propter contencionem habitam ex causa transaccionis. Et vnde si quis a latere omnes eiecit vel aliquem ipsorum et vnus per se restitucionem petat de aliqua certa parte nichil capiet per assisam quia nullam certam partem per se designare potest. Si autem petat
25 totum vnus vel omnes tenendum in communi bene procedet assisa. Et idem erit si particeps a participe eiciatur et ita fiat de aliis huiusmodi que tenentur in communi. Item cadit assisa quandoque per incertitudinem persone vt si iuratores de eo nullam habeant noticiam per quam scire possint quis sit vel vtrum in possessione fuerit nomine proprio vel alieno. Item cadit assisa propter in-
30 certitudinem vt si ius alicuius terre recognitum sit duobus et vnus se posuerit in seysinam sine participe nulla facta particione et disseysitus fuerit non recuperabit per assisam. Cadit assisa cum iuratores nesciant ad quem pertineat tenementum ad tenentem vel ad querentem cum visum fecerint. Item cadit assisa cum tradiccio donacionis non fuit in vita donatoris secuta. Item si due sorores tulerint
35 assisam in communi et obiectum fuerit vni quod vir suus fuerit vtlagatus nec constat vtrum mortuus fuerit vel viuus cadit assisa.

Manerium autem poterit esse per se ex pluribus edificiis coadunatum siue f. 93b

7. domino] dominio, J.　　　　24. *post* designare *add.* non, J.　　　　27. vt] vel, J.
28. possint] possunt, J; in *om.* J.　　　　31. nulla facta particione] facta participacione, J.
34. donacionis] donacionem, J.　　　　35. fuerit] fuit, J.　　　35. *posterius* fuerit] fuit, J.
36. viuus] minus, J.　　　37. coadunatum, Br., *om.* J.

then the business will be resolved by a perambulation.   And just as a perambulation can be made as between private persons, so it can as between the king and anyone complaining of him or his ministers, provided the king's assent is obtained beforehand.

Recovery by an assize is not available if a writ has been fraudulently sued out: for example, if a man were to sue out a writ before a disseisin was committed and this can be ascertained from the date of the writ.   And likewise if there was cause for suing out a writ but afterwards the cause ceased to exist: for example, if the disseisor restores the property disseised to the owner of the property who freely accepts it, there ceases to be recovery by an assize; but it would be otherwise if the true owner should usurp his seisin to himself by force.   Again, the assize abates on account of a false judgement: for instance, if a man had entry by the judgement of some court and not by disseisin, in that case he can vouch the court to warranty, and if the judgement is found to be false, the assize abates and there may be an action of false judgement.   Again, the assize abates on account of uncertainty regarding the property nor does it turn into a jury or into a perambulation, and this may be seen as between a woman and her warrantor with regard to her dower before assignment of dower: for example, if both are ejected from the tenement and the woman on her own claims restitution of her third, she will not recover by an assize because she cannot specify her third, for it was never specified or assigned to her.   And likewise, if the heir ejects her from everything when he comes of age, she will not recover against him by an assize for the reason aforesaid, whatever be the nature of the fee, socage or military. The same may apply between those who hold in common before partition, such as co-heirs or parceners, or neighbours if by agreement they hold in common by reason of a compromise arising out of a dispute.   And therefore, if anyone on his own has ejected all or any one of them, and one independently claims restitution of some particular part, he will take nothing by an assize because he cannot specify any particular part by itself.   If, however, one or all of them claim the whole as held in common, the assize will indeed proceed.   And the same will apply if a parcener is ejected by a parcener.   And thus it will be done with regard to such other [tenements] as are held in common.   Again, the assize sometimes abates on account of uncertainty about the person: for example, if the jurors have no knowledge of him by which they can know who he is or whether he is in possession in his own name or that of another.   Again, the assize abates on account of uncertainty: for example, if the right of two men to some land is acknowledged and one should put himself in seisin without his parcener and without a partition being made and he is disseised, he will not recover by an assize.   The assize abates when the jurors do not know to whom the tenement belongs, whether to the tenant or to the plaintiff, when they have made the view.   Again, the assize abates when livery of the gift did not follow during the lifetime of the donor.   Again, if two sisters should bring an assize together and it is objected to one of them that her husband has been outlawed or it is not clear whether he is dead or alive, the assize abates.

A manor can exist on its own, put together out of several buildings or out of

Bracton,
f. 212b

Bracton,
f. 212

villis vel hamelettis adiacentibus et eciam per se et cum villis et hamelettis
adicientibus et poterit esse manerium capitale plura sub se continens maneria non　[244]
tamen capitalia quod poterit continere plures villas et plures hamelettos sub
capite vno et plures hameletti poterunt pertinere ad vnam parochiam et plures
5　parochie ad vnam villam.　Et si quelibet parochia nomen habeat separale et
quamuis in qualibet sit ecclesia et cimiterium quo inferantur mortui et vnde si
nomen parochie nominetur in breui nisi nominetur villa integra cadit breue.

CAP. XVI.　QUALITER ASSISA VERTITUR IN IURATAM

Vertitur autem assisa in iuratam multipliciter.　Ex causa successionis sic.
10　Esto quod querens sic fundat intencionem suam et dicat quod de tali tenemento
obiit antecessor eius seysitus vt de feodo et ipse sicut heres propinquior se posuit
in seysinam et fuit in seysina per tantum tempus donec talis eum iniuste eiecit.
Ad quod excipi poterit quod talis antecessor non obiit seysitus vt de feodo set ad
vitam quocumque modo vel ad terminum tenuerit vel in vadium et quod ipse
15　querens nichil habeat nisi per intrusionem et vnde statim eiectus fuit per tenentem qui est verus dominus vel iustus heres vel dominus capitalis vel quod posuit
se in seysinam licet heres esse possit super dominum capitalem qui primam
habuit seysinam suam vt dominus capitalis et ipse se intrusit super seysinam suam
antequam sciretur vtrum ipse heres esset vel non vel quis esset heres et si obiit
20　seysitus vt de feodo ille tamen querens non potuit esse heres quia non fuit filius
nec heres set bastardus vel si filius et heres propinquus alius fuit propinquior scilicet talis.　Ad quod replicari poterit a querente quod ipse heres est vel licet heres
esse non possit tamen fuit ibi per tantum tempus quod sine iudicio eici non debuit.　Et alie infinite excepciones inde elici poterunt que omnes per assisam in
25　modum iurate debent terminari que non recipiunt conuiccionem.

Multe eciam conpetere poterunt excepciones ex donacione vt si querens
dicat quod fuit in seysina illius tenementi de dono talis per tantum tempus donec
talis eum eiecit.　Set excipi poterit contra eum quod ille qui donasse debuit nunquam habuit inde aliquam seysinam quod donacionem inde facere posset vel quia
30　omnino nullam habuit vel si habuit tenementum tamen illud prius dederat tali
per cartam suam priusquam aliquam cartam fecisset predicto querenti.　Vel sic
respondere poterit quod si aliquam seysinam inde habuit nullam tamen
habuit nisi post mortem donatoris per intrusionem et de qua recenter fuit eiectus
et quo casu cadit breue et assisa vertitur in iuratam vt sciatur si seysinam habuit
35　in vita donatoris vel non et per hoc terminabitur negocium.　Si iuratores autem
dicant quod nichil sciunt de seysina, querens nichil capiet per iuratam.　Si

1. adiacentibus, Br., coadunatis, J; *posterius* et *om*. J.　　11. obiit] obiis, J.　　18. et
om. J.　　22. vel] et J.　　23. quod] et, J.　　33. mortem *om*. J.　　35. negocium, Br.,
breue, J.

adjacent townships or hamlets, and it can also exist on its own and with adjacent townships and hamlets.   And it can be a chief manor, including within itself several manors that are not chief manors and so it can comprise several townships and several hamlets within one chief manor.   And several hamlets can belong to one parish and several parishes to one township.   And if each parish has a separate name and even if in each parish there is a church and a cemetery to which the dead are brought and if the name of the parish is given in the writ, nevertheless, unless the entire township is named the writ abates.

CHAPTER 16.   HOW AN ASSIZE IS TURNED INTO A JURY

Bracton,
f. 213

An assize is turned into a jury in many ways.   Arising out of a cause for succession it happens in this way.   Suppose that the plaintiff should base his declaration thus and say that his ancestor died seised of such-and-such a tenement as of fee and he as the nearest heir put himself in seisin and was in seisin for such-and-such a length of time until so-and-so unlawfully ejected him.   To this it can be excepted that so-and-so, the ancestor, did not die seised as of fee but held for life in some way or other, or for a term of years, or in gage, and that the plaintiff has nothing [in the property] save by intrusion and that he was immediately ejected therefrom by the tenant who is the true owner or rightful heir or chief lord; or that the plaintiff, even though he may be the heir, put himself in seisin over the chief lord who had his primer seisin as chief lord and intruded upon his seisin before it was known whether he was the heir or not or who was the heir; or if the ancestor died seised as of fee, yet the plaintiff could not be the heir

Bracton,
f. 213b

because he was neither son nor heir but a bastard or, if he was a son and near heir, another was nearer, namely so-and-so.   To which answer can be made by the plaintiff that he is the heir or, even though he may not be the heir, nevertheless he was there for such a long time that he ought not to be ejected without judgement of the court.   And other exceptions without number can be formulated thereon, all of which ought to be determined by an assize in the manner of a jury, which is not subject to attaint.

Many exceptions can also be available, arising from a gift: for example, if the plaintiff says that he was in seisin of the said tenement by the gift of so-and-so for such-and-such a length of time until so-and-so ejected him.   But it can be excepted against him that he who was said to have made the gift never had any seisin therein that enabled him to make a gift thereof either because he had no seisin at all or, if he had, he had previously given the tenement to so-and-so by his charter before he had made any charter in favour of the aforesaid plaintiff. Or he can reply thus: that if the plaintiff had any seisin therein, nevertheless he had none save by intrusion after the donor's death and from it he was immediately ejected, in which case the writ abates and the assize is turned into a jury so that it may be known whether he had seisin in the lifetime of the donor or not, and by that the matter will be determined.   And if the jurors say that they know

autem dubitauerint pro possessore iudicabitur.   Si autem dicant quod de seysina
querentis bene sunt certi et quo die positus fuit in seysinam set de morte donatoris nichil sciunt quia obiit in remotis et in alio comitatu ideo in comitatu in
quo obiit per aliam iuratam inquiratur de veritate et sic coniunctis illis duabus
5 inquisicionibus terminabitur negocium.

Cadere eciam poterit in assisam pactum siue conuencio si apposita fuerit in
inicio donacionis et ita inerit donacioni et donacionem informabit.   Et eodem   [245]
modo inesse poterit modus vt si dicatur Do vt facias condicio vt si dicatur Do si
feceris vel potest condicio apponi sic quod quis teneatur ad duo coniunctim vt si
10 dicatur Do vt facias istud et illud et quo casu non sufficit vnum fieri nisi fiat
vtrumque.   Vel potest fieri condicio ad duo disiunctim sic Do si feceris hoc vel
illud et quo casu sufficit vnum fieri.   Alio autem modo poterunt inesse donacioni modus et condicio vno modo verbis affirmatiuis vt si dicatur Do vt facias
et alio modo verbis negatiuis vt si dicatur Do ne facias.   Poterit eciam esse modus
15 siue condicio verbis affirmatiuis et negatiuis coniunctim et sic erit dupliciter vt
si dicatur Do vt facias et si non feceris volo quod terra data reuertatur ad me vel
ad alios tales vel quod liceat michi et heredibus meis ponere me in terram illam
e conuerso eciam verbis negatiuis et affirmatiuis coniunctim et sic erit dupliciter
vt si dicatur Do ne facias et si feceris tunc liceat michi etc. et fieri poterit verbis
20 negatiuis vt si dicatur Do ne facias sine voluntate et consensu meo et si feceris
quod tunc ponam me, et cum hoc fecerit adhuc non sufficit hoc fieri nisi sciatur
vtrum hoc fecerit de voluntate vel contra voluntatem et siue satisfactum sit
condicioni siue non si vnus se ponere possit in seysinam et se tenere in eadem
excepcionem habebit ex conuencione.   Cum igitur querens proposita querela
25 sua illam fundauerit sic et vnde queritur quod talis iniuste disseysiuit eum de tanta terra quam habuit in dono ipsius talis et vnde idem talis cepit homagium
suum et posuit eum in seysinam per se vel per procuratorem suum vel per litteras vel huiusmodi et vnde fuit in seysina per tantum tempus donec idem talis
ipsum iniuste et sine iudicio disseysiuit et inde posuit se super assisam.   Et no-
30 tandum quod omnis intencio querentis in assisa noue disseysine fundari poterit   f. 94
secundum omnia genera adquisicionis liberi tenementi siue ex causa successionis
vel quacumque alia siue in feodo siue ad vitam vel secundum quod possessio
alicuius pacifica fuerit vel turbata vel secundum quod disseysina facta fuerit
in ipso principali scilicet in corpore vel in eius pertinenciis sicut in iuribus vt
35 si quis ius habeat eundi vel pascendi in fundo alieno vel huiusmodi.   Et talis venit

1. seysina, Br., disseyna, J.   3. et *om.* J; ideo in comitatu, Br., *om.* J.   6. apposita]
opposita, J.   7. informabit] non formabit, J.   9. Nota J. *in margine.*   12-13. donacioni]
condicioni, J.   23. si] et J.   33. *prius* fuerit] erit, J.   34. iuribus] viribus, J.   35. si
quis] sicut, J.

nothing about the seisin, the plaintiff will take nothing by the jury.   And if they are in doubt, there will be judgement for the possessor.   If, however, they say that they are quite certain as to the seisin of the plaintiff and the day when he was put in seisin but know nothing about the death of the donor because he died in distant parts and in another county, therefore the truth should be enquired into by another jury in the county in which he died, and so by a combination of these two inquests the matter will be determined.

A pact or covenant may also fall into an assize if it is introduced when the gift is first made, and thus will inhere in the gift and give it its character.   And likewise a mode can inhere, as where it is said 'I give so that you do'; or a condition: as where it is said 'I give if you will do'; or a condition can be added to the effect that a man is obliged to do two things conjointly: as where it is said 'I give so that you will do this and that', and in this case it is not enough for one to be done if both are not done.   Or a condition can be made for two things to be done alternatively thus: 'I give if you will do this or that', and in this case it suffices for one to be done.   A mode and a condition can inhere in the gift otherwise: in one way by words in the affirmative, as where it is said 'I give so that you do'; and in another way by words in the negative, as where it is said 'I give so that you do not do'.   A mode or a condition can also inhere by words in the affirmative and in the negative conjointly, and thus it will be twofold: as where it is said 'I give so that you do and, if you should not do, I wish that the land shall revert to me' (or to such-and-such others) or 'that it shall be lawful for me (and my heirs) to put myself in the said land'.   Conversely this can also be done by words in the negative and affirmative conjointly and so it will be twofold: as where it is said 'I give so that you do not do and, if you should do, it is then lawful for me etc'.   And it can be done by words in the negative: as where it is said 'I give so that you do not do without my wish and consent and, if you should do, then I will put myself [in that land]'.   And though he has done this, it still does not suffice for this to be done unless it is known whether he did it with his consent or against his will.   And whether the condition has been satisfied or not, if anyone should put himself in seisin and maintain himself therein, he will have an exception arising out of the covenant.   When, therefore, the plaintiff propounds

Bracton,
f. 214

his plaint, he should frame it thus: 'and whereof he complains that so-and-so unlawfully disseised him of such-and-such an amount of land which he had by the gift of so-and-so and for which the said so-and-so accepted his homage and put him in seisin in person' or 'by his agent' or 'by letter' or the like 'and whereof he was in seisin for such-and-such length of time until the said so-and-so disseised him unlawfully and without a judgement of the court, and as regards this he puts himself on the assize'.   And be it noted that every declaration of a plaintiff in an assize of novel disseisin can be supported according to all the kinds of acquisition of a freehold, whether by the cause of succession or any other cause, whether in fee or for life or according to whether someone's possession is peaceful or disturbed, or according to whether the disseisin is committed in the principal property itself, that is the *corpus*, or in its appurtenances such as the rights: for example, where a man has a right of way or grazing in the land of

et defendit quod ipsum iniuste non disseysiuit nec aliquam ei fecit iniuriam et
bene cognoscit donum et homagium factum et seysinam et totum quod proponitur a querente.   Set dicit quod antequam homagium suum capere voluit de tali
tenemento concessit idem querens quod si ille tenens infra certum tempus in-
5 quirere posset quod idem querens aliquid teneret de rege in capite vel si quid
faceret vel non faceret et sic secundum quamcumque conuencionem vt supra
quod bene liceret ei ingredi predictum tenementum et tenere sibi et heredibus
suis quiete in perpetuum sine contradiccione et inpedimento predicti talis
querentis et heredum suorum.   Et quia inquisiuit infra predictum terminum
10 quod tenuit de rege in capite talem terram et talem vel quia fecit contra predictum conuencionem vel quia non fecit secundum conuencionem ideo posuit
se in seysinam iuxta predictam conuencionem, et vnde dicit quod licet donacio
valida esset et perfecta ab inicio tamen effecta est inualida per conuencionem
predictam.   Ad quod querens respondere poterit aut dedicit omnino illam
15 conuencionem aut cognoscit.   Si autem cognoscat predictam conuencionem et
factum sit contra, tunc erit manifestum quod nullam fecit ei iniuriam.   Si
autem illam omnino negauerit vel defenderit cum ex tali negacione fiat res dubia   [246]
oportebit eum de necessitate quod illam probet si fuerit extra seysinam.   Alioquin indefensus remanebit quasi excepcione nulla et per hoc recuperabit
20 querens sine aliqua iurata.   Et si fuerit in seysina dabitur ei excepcio.   Probari
autem poterit conuencio per scripturam cum fuerit extra seysinam vt si scriptum
confectum fuerit inter eos super predicta conuencione sub presencia virorum
fidedignorum qui presentes erant et audientes predictam conuencionem ante
capcionem homagii vel post et qui loqui possunt de proprio visu et auditu, que
25 quidem si fuerit a querente dedicta probetur carta et conuencio per testes licet
domestici sint simul cum aliis de iurata vel per collacionem vel alio modo.   Et
si probatum fuerit instrumentum sic manifestum erit quod talis fuit conuencio.
Non tamen propter hoc probatur quod satisfactum sit conuencioni.   Oportebit
igitur vlterius procedere inuestigando per assisam in modum iurate capiendam
30 et per testes nominatos in scripto vtrum factum sit secundum conuencionem,
vtrum ita sit vel non secundum quod dicitur in conuencione.   Et eodem modo
erit procedendum probato scripto et probata conuencione ac si ab inicio essent
concessa quia etsi concessa essent adhuc videndum esset vtrum satisfactum esset
conuencioni vel non et quod ita sit procedendum videri poterit per cartam que
35 confecta est super donacione aliqua.   Et si carta fuerit dedicta non sufficit nisi
donum dedictum nam si dicat 'Defendo cartam et donum' tunc tenentem
oportet probare vtrumque.   Si autem dicat tantum 'Defendo donum' sufficit
quod donum poterit esse validum et perfectum esse sine carta, et carta bene

6. *posterius* faceret] fecerit, J.   10. Nota de conuencione J. *in margine.*   11. vel . . .
conuencionem, Br., *om.* J.   13. effecta, Br., perfecta, J.   14-15. aut . . . cognoscit, Br., *om.* J.
29. inuestigando] in vestigando, J.

another, or the like.   And the defendant comes and denies that he disseised
the plaintiff unlawfully or did him any wrong and freely acknowledges the gift
and the homage rendered and the seisin and everything that is propounded by
the plaintiff.   But he says that, before he would accept his homage for such-and-
such a tenement, the plaintiff agreed that, if the said tenant could find within a
certain period of time that the said plaintiff held anything of the king in chief, or
if he did or did not do something and thus acted according to some covenant or
other (as above), it would be quite lawful for the tenant to enter and to hold the
aforesaid tenement to himself and his heirs peacefully in perpetuity without
gainsaying and obstruction from the aforesaid plaintiff and his heirs.   And
because he found out within the aforesaid period of time that the plaintiff held
such-and-such land of the king in chief or because he acted against the aforesaid
covenant or because he did not act according to the covenant, he therefore put
himself in seisin in accordance with the aforesaid covenant, and hence he says
that, although the gift was valid and complete to begin with, nevertheless it has
been rendered invalid by the aforesaid covenant.   To this the plaintiff can reply,
either to deny the covenant altogether or to acknowledge it.   If, however, he
acknowledges the aforesaid covenant and it had been broken, then it will be quite
plain that the tenant did him no wrong.   If, however, the plaintiff categorically
denies or repudiates the covenant, since such a denial puts the issue in doubt,
the defendant must needs prove it if he is out of seisin, otherwise he will be without defence as if his exception did not exist, and the plaintiff will by this means
recover without any jury.   And if the defendant is in seisin, the exception will be
allowed him.   And the covenant can be proved by a writing if the defendant is out
of seisin: for example, where a writing has been drawn up between them upon the
aforesaid covenant, in the presence of trustworthy men who were present and
heard the aforesaid covenant read, before or after the acceptance of homage, and
who are able to say that they personally saw and heard.   And if this should be
denied by the plaintiff the charter and covenant will be proved by the witnesses,
even though they are of the defendant's household, together with others of the
jury, or by collation [of documents] or some other way.   And if the instrument
should be proved, thus it will be made plain that such-and-such was the covenant.
Nevertheless it is not thereby proved that the covenant was satisfied.   It will be
necessary therefore to proceed further with the investigation by means of an
assize taken in the manner of a jury, and by the witnesses named in the writing, to
ascertain whether the terms of the covenant have been complied with, and whether
this is so or not depends upon what is said in the covenant.   And when the
writing and the covenant have been proved, the procedure will follow the same
course as if they had been admitted from the beginning because, even if they had
been admitted, it must still be seen whether the covenant was satisfied or not.
And that the procedure should be thus can be seen from the charter which is
drawn up in regard to any gift.   If the charter should be denied, this is not
sufficient unless the gift is denied, for if the plaintiff says 'I deny the charter and
the gift', then it is necessary for the tenant to prove them both.   If, however,
he merely says 'I deny the gift', it is sufficient that the gift should be valid and

Bracton,
f. 214*b*

poterit esse vera et sine dono perfecto vacua erit et inualida. Si autem donum
validum fuerit et perfectum vtrumque iuuari poterit per aliud et sic donum
poterit esse validum licet carta sit falsa et carta poterit esse valida licet donum
inualidum vel inperfectum vt si donatarius intruserit se propria auctoritate
5 sine waranto. Non igitur sufficit cartam esse veram nisi probetur donum esse
validum et perfectum. Cum igitur probata sit scriptura et conuencio et opor-
teat de necessitate vlterius procedere aut bene sciunt conuencioni esse satisfactum vel bene sciunt quod non est satisfactum secundum hoc pro vna parte vel
pro alia erit iudicandum. Si autem nichil sciuerint de aliqua conuencione per
10 hoc recuperabit querens quasi excepcione nulla. Si autem dubitauerint vtrum
satisfactum sit conuencioni vel non licet constiterit eis de conuencione facta si
presumpciones inducant probabiles pro vna parte vel pro alia in hoc dubio
standum erit presumpcioni cum nulla sit pro aliqua parte vera probacio que vin-
cere possit presumpcionem. Poterit tamen presumpcio in posterum iuuari si
15 fecerit pro eo qui forte conuencionem cognouerit. Set forte replicando dicat
illam esse remissam si presumpcio facit pro eo iuuari poterit presumpcio per
instrumentum postea compertum ex parte illa quod contineat veritatem. Si
autem tenens nullum omnino habeat instrumentum tunc oportebit quod alio
modo probet excepcionem conuencionis et vnde aut ponit se in assisam in modum
20 iurate capiendam aut non. Si autem velit probare per domesticos et familiares
suos excepcionem non licet et si per domesticos et familiares alterius partis non
prodest. Si autem communiter per vtrosque nunquam conuenient. Oportet [247]
igitur de necessitate recurrere ad assisam assumptis aliquibus qui interfuerint
conuencioni dum tamen neutram partem contingant. Si autem instrumentum
25 non habuerit neque se ponere velit in iuratam habet tamen sectam vnam forte
vel plures siue sint familiares siue non, et ex secta habetur ad minus pre- f 94b
sumpcio donec probetur in contrarium. Probari tamen poterit contrarium per
defensionem per legem quia lex vincit sectam. Et si donator per conuencionem
non sufficiat quod se ponere possit in seysinam dabitur ei accio ex conuencione
30 cum sit extra seysinam et ad superiorem erit recurrendum. Et cum sit in
seysina dabitur ei excepcio ex conuencione.

4. intruserit se] intruse, J.   7. sciunt] sciuit, J.   8. sciunt] sciuit, J.
14. presumpcionem] probacionem, J.   16. si] et, J.   24. contingant] contingat, J.
25. non om. J; habuerit] habuit, J.   29. seysinam] seysina, J.

complete without a charter. And the charter can well be authentic but, unless the gift is complete, it will be void and invalid. If, however, the gift is valid and complete, each can be strengthened by the other. And so a gift can be valid although the charter is false, and the charter can be valid although a gift is invalid or incomplete: as, for example, if the donee of his own authority intrudes himself without warrant. It is not therefore sufficient for the charter to be authentic unless the gift is proved to be valid and complete. When therefore the writing and covenant are proved and one must needs proceed further, either the [jurors] well know that the covenant has been satisfied or they well know that it has not been satisfied and judgement will be given accordingly for one party or the other. But if they should know nothing of any covenant, the plaintiff will on that account recover as if the exception did not exist. If, however, they should be in doubt whether the covenant has been satisfied or not, even though it is plain to them that the covenant had been made, if the probabilities raise a presumption in favour of one party or the other, the presumption will stand in this doubtful situation when there is no true proof for either party which will overcome the presumption. The presumption can, however, be subsequently strengthened if it works in favour of him who has perchance acknowledged the covenant. For if he happens to say when replying that it has been lost and the presumption works in his favour, the presumption can be strengthened by an instrument, subsequently discovered relating to this matter, that contains the truth. But if the tenant has no instrument whatsoever, then it will behove him to prove the exception of a covenant in some other way, and therefore he either puts himself on an assize to be taken in the manner of a jury or he does not. If, however, he wishes to prove his exception by members of his own household and family, this is not allowable; and if by members of the household and family of the other party this profits him nothing. If, however, by both together, they will never reach agreement. Therefore one must needs have recourse to an assize and summon any who were present at the covenant, provided they are kin of neither party. But if he has no instrument and does not wish to put himself upon a jury, yet he has a single suit, or perhaps more, whether they are members of his household or not, and out of the suit a presumption at least arises until there is proof to the contrary. The contrary can, however, be proved by a denial by wager of law because the wager of law overcomes a suit. And if a covenant is not sufficient to enable the donor to put himself in seisin, a right of action on the covenant will be given to him when he is out of seisin and there will be recourse to a superior. And when he is in seisin, an exception arising out of the covenant will be given him.

CAP. XVII. QUE INPEDIUNT RESTITUCIONEM

Incertitudo autem restitucionem inpedit siue fuerit in ipsa re sicut in corpore de tenemento siue in iure pertinente ad tenementum siue in ipsa persona que queritur.   Non dico tamen si aliqua racione posset esse certitudo vel saltem
5 presumpcio immo si omnino nulla possit haberi certitudo nec eciam presumpcio. Negligencia vero et dissimulacio ad tempus que trahuntur ad consensum inpediunt restitucionem non tamen quod omnino tollatur accio set quod auferatur disseysito recens reieccio.   Et dissimulacio et negligencia que trahuntur ad consensum dant quasi liberum tenementum disseysitori ita quod sine iudicio eici non
10 potest et tollit priuilegium disseysito quia ex quo negligens est presumitur quod voluit disseysiri et per hoc presumitur eciam quod vtramque amiserit possessionem naturalem videlicet et ciuilem.   Et eodem modo voluntas si hoc voluit ab inicio vel post tempus iniuriam remiserit et tenementum quietum clamauerit. Transaccio autem inpedit restitucionem vt si partem tenementi remiserit et partem
15 receperit nomine concordie quod quidem de gracia ei concedi poterit et pro bono pacis et non de iure quia de hiis que presumpte sunt contra pacem regis nulla transaccio siue concordia set ipsum iudicium secundum quod querens se retraxerit vel ipse disseysitor cognouerit seysinam.   Confirmacio eciam vel consensus restitucionem inpedit vt si disseysitus confirmauerit disseysitori rem
20 disseysitam quia confirmacio gratuita tollit iniuriam.   Consensus vt si disseysitor donacionem fecerit et disseysitus donacioni consenserit et illam ratam habuerit siue ab inicio siue post.   Item propria vsurpacio rei proprie post disseysinam sine iudicio set post tempus vt si disseysitus fuerit quis et negligens in inpetracione fuerit vel prosecucione vel in vtraque sine iudicio rem propriam sibi vsurpare non
25 poterit, tamen illam recipere si ei gratis offeratur non tamen in omni casu.   Item difficultas iudicii inpedit restitucionem.   Item iustum iudicium secus si iniustum nisi ad tempus.   Item intrusio inpedit restitucionem dum tamen non currat tempus per negligenciam hoc est si incontinenti reiciatur.   Item excepcio finis facti.   Et alia.
30 Sunt eciam quedam excepciones que assisam non perimunt nec accionem set breue tantum licet ad tempus differatur, sicut excepciones contra iurisdiccionem, excepciones contra breue, excepciones contra personam querentis, excepciones que conpetunt ex loco et tempore et hec que conpetunt contra iura- [248] tores.   Et cum omnes iste excepciones siue sint peremptorie siue dilatorie sunt
35 quasi extra assisam vel preter, ideo non in modum assise set in modum iurate ter-

---

2. fuerit] fuit, J.   3. de] et, J.   8. ad] et, J.   11. quod] quam.   12. videlicet et ciuilem, Br., *om.* J.   13. tenementum *om.* J.   16. que presumpte] qui presumpti, J; 16–17. nulla transaccio, Br., in illas terras accio, J.   18. Confirmacio, Br., Confirmat, J. 20. disseysitam] disseytam, J.   21. habuerit] habuit, J.   24. vtraque] vtramque, J. 26–27. Item iustum iudicium secus si iniustum nisi ad tempus, J, Item res iudicate, maxime si iustum interuenerit iudicium, Br.   34-35. sunt quasi, Br., fiunt eciam, J.

CHAPTER 17.   WHAT THINGS STAND IN THE WAY OF RECOVERY

Bracton,
f. 214b

Uncertainty stands in the way of recovery whether it is in regard to the property itself, such as the *corpus* of the tenement or in regard to a right appurtenant to the tenement, or in regard to the person of the complainant.   I am not speaking, however, about where for any reason there could be certainty or at least a presumption but rather about where it is not possible by any means to

Bracton,
f. 215

attain any certainty or even presumption.   Negligence indeed and indifference for a period of time drag on into consent and stand in the way of recovery although a right of action is not altogether taken away, but what is taken away from the disseisee is immediate ejection.   And indifference and negligence which drag on into consent give a quasi-freehold to the disseisor, so that without a judgement of the court he cannot be ejected, and take away an advantage from the disseisee, because, since he is negligent, it is presumed that he wished to be disseised, and by that it is also presumed that he has lost both kinds of possession, that is natural and civil.   Intention also impedes recovery if he willed it from the beginning or after a time remits the wrong and quit-claims the tenement.   A compromise also impedes recovery: for example, if he remits one part of the tenement and accepts another part by way of agreement, which may be allowed him as a matter of grace and for the sake of peace but not as a matter of law, because in regard to those matters which are presumed to be against the king's peace there is no compromise or agreement but only judgement according as the plaintiff withdraws or the disseisor acknowledges [the plaintiff's] seisin.   A confirmation or consent also impedes recovery: for example, if the disseisee confirms the property disseised to the disseisor, for a confirmation freely made destroys a wrong.   Consent: for example, if the disseisor makes a gift and the disseisee consents to the gift and ratifies it, whether at the beginning or subsequently.   Again, one's own usurpation of one's own property after disseisin without judgement of the court but after a period of time has elapsed: for example, if a man is disseised and is negligent in suing out a writ or in prosecuting it or in doing either of these things he may not usurp his own property to himself without a judgement of the court, although he can accept it if it be freely offered to him: but not in every case.   Again, difficulty in giving judgement impedes recovery.   So also a just judgement (but otherwise if the judgement is illegal except for a time).   Again, intrusion impedes recovery, provided time does not run through negligence, that is, if the intruder is ejected without delay.   Also the exception that a fine has been made.   And there are others.

Bracton,
f. 215b

There are also certain exceptions which do not destroy the assize or the action but only the writ, although there is postponement for a time, such as exceptions against the jurisdiction; exceptions against the writ; exceptions against the person of the plaintiff; exceptions which lie from considerations of place and time and those which lie against the jurors.   And since all these exceptions, whether they are peremptory or dilatory, are as it were outside the assize or

minabuntur quasi per consensum parcium cum vnus dicat ita esse et alius dicat
contrarium quasi extra assisam et petat quilibet quod sua veritas inquiratur.
Ideo conuiccionem non recipiunt quia si qua parcium venire vellet contra dicta
iuratorum ita dicerent probacionem suam falsam cum veredictum iuratorum in
5 hoc casu non sit assisa set probacio excepcionis quia qui excipit probare debet
excepcionem replicans replicacionem sicut agens suam accionem.

Vt autem sciatur quando locum habet conuiccio et quando non videndum
erit vtrum assisa capiatur in modum assise vel in modum iurate sic vt si fundata
intencione querentis tenens se statim ponat in assisam sine aliqua excepcione et
10 respondeat simpliciter ad intencionem querentis quod non disseysiuit eum et
inde ponat se super assisam et iuratores dicat simpliciter quod disseisiuit talem
iniuste cum non disseysiuerit vel e conuerso vel si dicant quod tenens disseysiuit
querentem de libero tenemento cum tenuerit illud in villenagio vel e conuerso et
huiusmodi vel si dicant aliquid quod tangat excepcionem et non accionem neque
15 assisam non tamen simpliciter set cum adieccione sic dicendo quod querens liberum tenementum habere non potuit quia villanus est et tenuit in villenagio cum
liber sit et libere tenuerit vel e conuerso si querens postmodum docere potest
contrarium iuratores conuincendi erunt de periurio quia assisa capta est in
modum assise et non in modum iurate. Si autem proposita querela re-
20 spondeat tenens intencioni quod querens disseysiri non potuit de libero tenemento quia villanus est et tenuit in villenagio et querens dicat simpliciter quod
non, nichil replicando, cum per negacionem fiat res dubia oportet quod tenens
probet excepcionem per parentes quos statim habeat ad manum si possit vel ad
diem vel per assisam. Et quo casu siue per parentes siue per assisam pro-
25 bauerit cum inde se posuerit in assisam in modum iurate capiendam siue
iuratores dicant pro vna parte vel pro alia non sunt conuincendi quia hoc est
pocius probacio excepcionis per iuratam quam capcio assise per assisam. Nec
eciam siue verum dicant siue falsum propter hoc preiudicabitur querenti in   f. 95
causa status et sic in hoc casu semper incumbit probacio tenenti. Set esto
30 quod querens excepcioni seruitutis dicens quod liber sit adhuc incumbit probacio
tenenti quam quidem si aliquo modo probauerit probet querens contrarium si
possit per probacionem validiorem replicando. Si autem excipiens non probauerit non erit necesse quod querens probet contrarium replicando quasi excepcione nulla. Si autem non sint parentes qui ex aliqua parte producantur de
35 necessitate recurrendum erit ad assisam vt in modum iurate terminetur negocium
et hinc inde erit probacio et non assisa. Probat enim tenens excepcionem per

3. qua, J *et* Br.   7. de conuiccione, J. *in margine.*   9. se *om.* J.   10-11. eum . . .
disseisiuit, Br., *om.* J.   12. dicant] dicat, J.   13. villenagio] villenagium, J.
20. querens] tenens, J.   29. status, Br., *om.* J.

irrespective of it, therefore they will be determined not in the manner of an assize but in the manner of a jury, as if by consent of the parties since one says it is so and the other says the opposite and each asks that the truth of his assertion be enquired into. Therefore the jurors are not subject to attaint because, if either party should wish to refute the verdict of the jurors, they would say that their own proof was false, since in this case the verdict of the jurors is not an assize but the proving of an exception, because he who excepts must prove his exception and he who replies must prove his replication, just as a plaintiff must prove his action.

However, in order that it may be known when there is occasion for an attaint and when there is not, it must be seen whether the assize is taken in the manner of an assize or in the manner of a jury: for example, if after the declaration of the plaintiff has been made the tenant straightway puts himself on the assize without any exception and simply replies to the plaintiff's declaration that he did not disseise him and thereof puts himself on the assize, and the jurors say simply that he disseised so-and-so unlawfully although he had not disseised him (or conversely) or if they say that the tenant disseised the plaintiff of a freehold when he held it in villeinage (or conversely) and the like; or if they say something which touches an exception and not the action or the assize, and say it not simply but with an addition, saying, for instance, that the plaintiff could not have a freehold because he is a villein and held in villeinage though he is a free man and holds freely (or conversely), then if the plaintiff can subsequently show to the contrary, the jurors must be convicted of attaint for perjury because the assize has been taken in the manner of an assize and not in the manner of a jury. If, however, when the plaint has been propounded, the tenant should answer to the declaration that the plaintiff could not be disseised of a freehold because he is a villein and held in villeinage, and the plaintiff simply says that it is not so, with nothing more by way of reply, then because by denial the matter is put in doubt it behoves the tenant to prove the exception either by kinsmen, whom he should have immediately at hand if he can or at an appointed day, or by the assize. And in this case, whether he proves it by kinsmen or by the assize, since on this issue he puts himself on the assize to be taken in the manner of a jury, whether the jurors find for one party or the other they are not to be attainted because this is the proving of an exception by a jury rather than the taking of an assize by an assize. Nor, whether their finding be true or false, will the plaintiff be prejudiced thereby in an action on status, thus in this case the burden of proof is always on the tenant. But suppose the plaintiff to say to an exception of villeinage that he is a free man, the burden of proof is still on the tenant and, if he should in some way prove the exception, let the plaintiff, if he can, prove the contrary by giving a stronger proof in his reply. If, however, the exceptor should not prove the exception, there will be no necessity for the plaintiff in his answer to prove the contrary because the exception is as it were non-existent. If, however, there are no kinsmen who may be produced by either party, recourse must needs be had to the assize so that the matter may be determined in the manner of a jury, and hence there will be the proof [of an exception] and not an assize. For the tenant proves an

Bracton,
f. 216

iuratam in quam de necessitate consentire oportet propter defectum alterius probacionis quia si non habeat parentes de necessitate recurritur ad iuratam alioquin nulla erit excepcio quasi deficiente probacione. Et eodem modo dici poterit de replicacione querentis. Set esto quod querens parentes non habeat
5 quos producat sequitur quod cum tenens probare voluerit excepcionem per iuratam et querens hoc recusauerit querenti eo ipso denegabitur accio et assisa. Si autem tenens hoc recusauerit procedet assisa in modum assise quasi excep-   [249] cione nulla. Si autem tenens fundata intencione querentis excipiat de villenagio et probacionem habeat ad manum parentes vel iuratam, querens replicare
10 poterit de priuilegio si fuerit dominus qui petat.
    Vertitur eciam assisa in iuratam alio modo vt si querens sic fundauerit intencionem et dicat quod duxerit vxorem hereditatem habentem vel maritagium et post mortem vxoris sue fuit in seysina per tantum tempus donec talis eum iniuste disseysiuit et ita fuit in seysina per legem Anglie quia pueros genuit de
15 vxore sua. Ad quod sic tenens contra ipsum exceperit quod nullum omnino habuerit puerum vel si habuerit mortuus tamen fuit in vtero vel si natus fuerit monstrum fuit et non puer et si puer fuit et viuus nunquam tamen auditus fuit clamare. Si autem querens dicat replicando contrarium inquiratur veritas per assisam in modum iurate. Si autem iuratores dicant quod bene viderunt eum
20 seysitum et postea eiectum per tenentem set de aliquo puero nichil sciuerint quia mater obiit in pariendo extra comitatum in remotis recurrendum erit ad comitatum et ad visnetum vbi mater obiit quia eorum veredictum insufficiens est et quia ipsi ignorare possunt ea que fiunt in remotis et ibi facta inquisicione de veritate terminetur negocium. Preterea dicere poterit tenens quod si filios
25 habuit non nocet tamen eo quod postea coniucti fuerint ad bastardos quod si querens negauerit veritas per assisam in modum iurate declarabitur. Si autem dicat quod pueri bastardi sunt et hoc paratus est docere quando et vbi tunc aut dicat quod ita bastardi sunt quod nati fuerunt ante matrimonium vel quod pater eius nunquam matrem eorum desponsauit. Si primo modo et alius dicat quod
30 post vterque se posuerit in iuratam poterit negocium terminari et si secundo modo et querens replicando dicat quod sic remanebit assisa quousque in foro ecclesiastico constiterit de veritate.
    Vertitur eciam quandoque assisa in iuratam propter transgressionem vt si quis contra voluntatem domini vti velit in alieno vel contra voluntatem participum
35 vti voluerit in communi et de communi facere proprium vel excessum proprium

---

1. *post* consentire *add.* poterit, J.   2. *post* parentes *add.* et, J.   3. *post* deficiente *add.* condicione, J.   5. quod] et, J.   7. Si . . . assisa, Br., *om.* J.   15. sic] si, J.   17. *post* viuus *add.* et, J.   21. obiit] obiis, J.   23. fiunt] fuerunt, J.   24. negocium, Br., *om.* J. 27. tunc aut] tenens autem, J.

exception by a jury to which he must needs consent because of the lack of other proof because, if he has no kinsmen, recourse must necessarily be had to a jury, otherwise the exception will be void as lacking proof.   And the same may be said of the answer by the plaintiff.   But suppose that the plaintiff has no kinsmen to produce and, when the tenant wishes to prove the exception by a jury, the plaintiff refuses: it follows that for that very reason a right of action and an assize will be denied to the plaintiff.   If, however, the tenant refuses [proof by a jury], the assize will proceed in the manner of an assize as if the exception were non-existent.   But if when the plaintiff has made his declaration, the tenant should put forward an exception of villeinage and have proof ready to hand, whether kinsmen or jury, the plaintiff can reply by pleading a privilege,[1] if it should be the lord who demands [him as his villein].

An assize also turns into a jury in another way: for example, if the plaintiff has made his declaration in this way, saying that he married a wife who had an inheritance or a marriage-portion, and after his wife's death he was in seisin for such-and-such a length of time until so-and-so unlawfully disseised him, and he was thus in seisin by the curtesy of England because he begat children with his wife.   To which the tenant might thus except against him that he had no child at all or, if he did, yet the child died in the womb or, if it was born, it was a monster and not a child, and if it was a child and alive, nevertheless it was never heard to cry.   If, however, the plaintiff in his replication says the opposite, the truth is to be enquired into by the assize in the manner of a jury.   But if the jurors say that they did indeed see him seised and afterwards ejected by the tenant but that they knew nothing about any child because the mother died in childbirth afar off outside the county, then recourse will be had to the county and the neighbourhood where the mother died, because their verdict does not suffice and because they cannot know what happened afar off, and, after an inquest has been held there as to the truth, the matter will be determined.   The tenant can say further that, if the plaintiff had children, nevertheless that does him no harm because they were subsequently adjudged to be bastards and, if the plaintiff should deny this, the truth will be made known by the assize in the manner of a jury.   If, however, he says that the children are bastards, and he is ready to show this when and where [he ought], then he may say that they are bastards in that either they were born before marriage or that [their] father never espoused their mother.   If the tenant [excepts] in the first way and the other says that [they were born] after marriage and both put themselves on a jury, the matter may be [thus] determined; and if in the second way and the plaintiff in his replication says that [the father did espouse the mother], the assize will be stayed until the truth is established in an ecclesiastical court.

An assize is also sometimes turned into a jury on account of a trespass: for example, if a man against the will of the owner should wish to have the user of another's property, or against the will of parceners should wish to have the user of common property and make a severalty out of what is common or to make too

Bracton.
f. 216b

---

1 Above, p. 73.

vt si sibi appruare voluerit aliquam partem que communis est vel vtendo excessum facere et ita sibi vsurpare quod alienum est vel commune sibi et aliis, facit
disseysinam et similiter transgressionem secundum quod transgressio non est
disseysina et si eo animo forte ingrediatur fundum alienum non quod sibi
5 vsurpet tenementum vel iura non facit disseysinam set transgressionem. Set
quoniam incertum est quo animo hoc faciat ideo querens sibi perquirat per
assisam et quo casu querendum erit per iudicem quo animo hoc fecerit vtrum eo
quod maius ius habuerit in re vel non habuerit vt si forte ductus errore probabili
vel ignorancia non tamen grassa vt si omnes de patria sciuerint rem ad ipsum non
10 pertinere et ipse solus ignorauerit non excusatur. Si autem ignorancia iusta
fuerit et probabilis error et ita ingrediatur fundum alienum quem suum esse
crediderit et clam vel palam arbores succiderit vel herbam falcauerit vel aliud
genus investiture et non nomine seysine asportauerit set per errorem vel ignoranciam excusatur a disseysina quia ibi est pocius transgressio quam disseysina
15 quam quidem si cognouerit emendet et si dedixerit vertatur assisa in iuratam ad   [250]
inquirendum de transgressione et per hoc stet vel cadat. Et idem erit si teneat
in communi et hoc maxime nisi ita fecerit sepius et de consuetudine. Fre-
quencia enim mutat transgressionem in disseysinam vt si sepe transgressionem
faciat et respondeat ad assisam quod nichil clamat in tenemento vel eius perti-
20 nenciis per se vel in communi vt per hoc penam disseysine possit euadere non
audietur set sustinebit penam disseysine et redisseysine. Et idem erit si in delicto
captus fuerit vel alius quem aduocauerit qui vadium dare noluerit per iuratam   f. 95b
agrauetur pena transgressionis si hoc fuerit per iuratam declaratum. Si autem
dicat se ius habere in re cum nullum omnino habeat vel ipsam dicat esse suam
25 propriam cum sit communis, statim procedat assisa in modum assise et per assisam terminabitur negocium et quo casu si res fuerit communis locum habere
poterit iudicium de communi diuidendo. Si autem talis sibi ius vsurpauerit in
alieno prosternendo arbores vel succidendo vel lapides finales amouendo primo
ante assisam capienda sunt vadia et ita emendabitur transgressio per capcionem
30 vadiorum. Et si quis se deuadiari non permiserit recurrendum erit ad breue
noue disseysine et cadit assisa in iuratam et duplicabitur pena transgressionis.
Et eodem modo si quis fecerit vastum vel destruccionem in tenemento quod
tenet ad vitam suam in eo quod modum excedit et racionem cum tantum ei
concedatur racionabile estouerium et non vastum facit transgressionem et si talis
35 inpediatur per aliquem cuius interfuerit parentis vel amici ille tenens assisam non
habebit. Intencio enim talem liberabit a disseysina quia in eo quod tenens
abutitur male vtendo et debitum vsum et modum debitum excedendo non

1. vel *om.* J.   4. et, Br., vt, J.   8. habuerit] habuit, J.   9. grassa, Br., *lacuna* J.
13. genus, Br., *om.* J; inuestiture] in vesture, J.   13. ignoranciam] ignoraciam, J.
19. assisam] assysam, J.   20. vt] et, J.   22. noluerit] voluerit, J.   25. statim
repetitur J.   27. diuidendo] diuidundo, Br.; dicendo, J.

much his own, as, for example, if he means to enclose for his own benefit some part which is common property or to take too much by user and thus usurp to himself what belongs to another or is common to himself and others, he commits disseisin as well as trespass in so far as [all] trespass is not disseisin: and, if perchance he enters upon another's land without an intention of usurping tenement or rights for himself, he does not commit disseisin but trespass. But because it is uncertain with what intention he does this, therefore let the plaintiff sue for himself by an assize, in which case the judge will enquire with what intention he did this, whether because he has a greater right in the property or does not have it where, for example, he was perchance misled by a plausible mistake or ignorance, but not crass ignorance, for if the whole countryside knows that the property does not belong to him and he alone does not know it, he is not excused. If, however, his ignorance were justified and the mistake was plausible and so he entered upon another's land which he believed to be his own and secretly or openly felled trees or mowed grass or other kind of crop and took it away, not because he claims seisin but by mistake or in ignor-ance, he is excused the disseisin because in this instance it is trespass rather than disseisin and, indeed, if he acknowledges the trespass, he shall make amends and, if he denies it, the assize is turned into a jury to enquire into the trespass, and by it he will stand or fall. And it will be the same if he holds in common and especially in these circumstances, unless he has done such things very frequently and customarily. For frequency changes trespass into disseisin: for example, if he often commits trespass and answers to the assize that he claims nothing in the tenement or its appurtenances, whether severally or in common, in order that he may in this way avoid the penalty of disseisin, he shall not be heard but will suffer the penalty of disseisin and redisseisin. And it will be the same if he should be taken in the act or someone else whom he avows who refuses to give a gage: the penalty of trespass will be increased by the jury if the jury should find that this is so. If, however, he says that he has a right in the property when he has no right at all, or if he says it is his severalty when it is common, the assize is to proceed forthwith in the manner of an assize and the matter will be determined by the assize, and in this case, if the property is common, there may be occasion for a judgement to divide the common property. If, however, so-and-so usurps a right for himself in another's property by felling or cutting down [boundary] trees or removing boundary stones, first of all before the assize gages must be taken and thus the trespass will be amended by the taking of gages. And if anyone does not permit gages to be taken from him, recourse must be had to a writ of novel disseisin, and the assize turns into a jury and the penalty for the trespass will be doubled. And likewise, if anyone should make waste and destruction in a tenement which he holds for the term of his life, in that he exceeds what is normal and reasonable since he is granted only reasonable est-overs and not waste, he commits a trespass and, if such a one is prevented by anyone who has an interest, a relative or a friend, the said tenant will not have an assize [against him]. For intention will free such as intervene from disseisin because, in that the tenant creates an abuse by bad user and by exceeding due

Bracton,
f. 217

poterit dicere quod disseysitus est quia tantum racionabilis vsus ei conceditur. Et si per aliquod tempus forte abusus fuerit vltra modum talis seysina nulla erit quia non est seysina quam trahit ad abusum set presumpcio iniuriosa.   Et ideo causa et intencio liberant inpedientem set hoc per assisam in modum iurate cap-
5 tam declarari oportebit scilicet vtrum sit ibi vastum vel racionabile estouerium.

Vertitur eciam assisa in iuratam propter transgressionem districcionis. Dis-triccio enim aliquando facit disseysinam et aliquando transgressionem maiorem vel minorem et secundum hoc terminabitur negocium in modum assise si ibi fuerit disseysina vel vertetur assisa in iuratam si ibi fuerit transgressio maior vel
10 minor.   Et vnde cum assisa fuerit inpetrata super iniuria districcionis si non pos-sit valere vt assisa ad terminandum disseysinam valeat tamen vt iurata ad ter-minandum transgressionem.   Transgressio enim esse poterit maior et minor. Maior vt si non sit omnino disseysina non multum tamen differens a disseysina set quasi ei proxima et vicina disseysine si ad comodum vti non potest propter
15 districcionem nimis transgressiuam vel excessiuam vltra modum et mensuram debitam.   Preterea poterit esse transgressio simplex et grauis vbi scilicet fit districcio cum nulla subicit causa distringendi vel cum non pertineat ad distrin-gentem et quo casu erit disseysina et quamuis causa subfuerit fieri non poterit ordine non obseruato et tamen simplex vt si quis distringat tenentem suum per
20 res suas dominicas cum habeat villenagium quod sufficiat vel si distringat tenen-tem tenentis sui quamuis in feodo suo cum tenens suus qui medius est sufficiens [251] habet dominicum de eodem feodo.   Ordine dico non obseruato multipliciter vt si fiat districcio per inmobilia cum sint ibi mobilia vel distringat per mobilia intrinseca cum extrinseca sufficiant vel si fiat districcio per oues vel bestias caru-
25 carum cum sint alia aueria ociosa.   Et quamuis causa subsit et ordo obseruetur adhuc poterit esse iniuriosa vt si fuit nimia cum modum excedit et mensuram. Non enim fieri debet districcio magna pro modica causa.   Aggrauari tamen poterit vt si prima teneantur et plura capiantur.   Poterit enim esse transgressio in districcione extra comitatum si aueria fuerint abducta.   Et quamuis omnia
30 bene conueniant si aueria capta replegiari vetentur vetitum illud non solum querenti iniuriosum immo regi cum sit contra pacem suam nam vbi deficiunt vadium et plegii ibi deficit pax et sic repetitis omnibus supradictis secundum quod in omnibus sit presumptuosum vel in parte aut erit transgressio simplex maior vel minor et vicina disseysine vel non erit.
35 Assisa autem noue disseysine cum sit triplex personalis propter factum penalis propter iniuriam et delictum et restitutoria.   In eo vero quod penalis est et pena suos tenere debet auctores non conpetit heredi disseysiti si disseysitus

6. districcionis *om*. J.   9. si ibi] et vbi, J.   11. disseysinam] desseysinam, J.
14. ei] ex, J; si] set, J.   15. districcionem, Br., transgressionem, J; transgressiuam, Br.,
transgressimam, J.   25. *posterius* et *om*. J.   28. si *addidimus*; teneantur] teneatur, J.
29. aueria, Br., *om*, J; fuerint] fuerit, J.   30. *post* capta *add*. et, J.

use and due means, he cannot say that he is disseised because only reasonable user is granted to him. And if he should perchance abuse [his right] beyond the limit for some time, such seisin will be void because it is not seisin which he brings into abuse but a wrongful usurpation. And therefore cause and intention free him who prevents, but it is necessary for this to be made known by the assize taken in the manner of a jury, to wit, whether there is in this instance waste or reasonable estovers.

An assize also turns into a jury on account of a trespass in distraint. For distraint sometimes causes disseisin and sometimes trespass, either serious or slight, and the matter will be accordingly determined in the manner of an assize if it is an instance of disseisin or the assize will turn into a jury if it is an instance of trespass, serious or slight. And therefore, when an assize is sued out on a wrongful distraint, if it cannot hold good as an assize to determine a disseisin, nevertheless it will hold good as a jury to determine a trespass. A trespass may be serious or slight: serious, for example, if it is not completely disseisin and yet not differing greatly from disseisin but as it were nigh to it and bordering upon it where the property cannot be profitably used on account of a distraint too transgressive or excessive, beyond the norm and proper measure. Furthermore, a trespass can be simple and serious, for example, where distraint is made when there is no underlying cause for distraint or when it is not the distrainer's business, in which case it will be disseisin. And although there is cause for distraint, it cannot be made in the wrong order, and this again is simple [trespass]: for example, if a man distrains his tenant by his demesne lands when he has villein tenements that suffice, or if he distrains his tenant's tenant, albeit in his own fee, when his tenant who is the mesne has sufficient demesne in the same fee. There are many ways, let it be said, in which the order is not observed: for example, if immovables are distrained upon when there are movables there or if distraint is made upon movables inside the house when

Bracton,
f. 217b

movables out of doors would suffice, or if distress is made upon sheep and upon plough beasts when there are other beasts not so used. And although a cause for distraint may subsist and the order be observed, yet distraint can be wrongful: for example, if it should be too great since it goes beyond the norm and proper measure. For a heavy distress should not be made for slight cause. Distraint may be aggravated: for instance, if the first beasts are retained and more are taken. And there may be trespass in distraining out of the county if the beasts should be removed. And even though everything proceeds smoothly, if there is a refusal to replevy the beasts seized, this refusal not only wrongs the plaintiff but especially the king, because it is a breach of his peace. For where gage and pledges are wanting, there peace is wanting. And so, repeating all that has been said above, according as it is a usurpation as a whole or in part, either it will be a simple trespass, grave or slight, and bordering upon disseisin, or it will not.

Bracton
f. 218b

Since the assize of novel disseisin is triple—personal on account of the act, penal on account of the wrong and delict, and restitutory—in that it is penal and the penalty ought to attach to those who did the wrong, it is not available to the

moriatur nec datur in heredes disseysitoris principalis si moriatur viuente disseysito quia pena extinguitur cum persona et heres non tenetur ex delicto antecessoris. Et eodem modo si disseysitus moriatur viuente disseysitore heredi
disseysiti non conpetit accio de iniuria facta antecessori quia inter ipsum et
5 disseysitorem nulla est obligacio quoad penam licet sit obligacio quoad restitucionem.   Conpetit tamen disseysito vel heredibus suis contra disseysitores vel
heredes suos accio per breue de ingressu non obstante eorum minori etate.   Et
si minores quoquo modo inpediantur quominus sequi possunt tunc sequentur
propinquiores amici minoris et admittantur pro minoribus et non solum in isto
10 casu verum eciam in omni alio quo minores agere poterunt et placitare.

Cum autem assisa capiatur in modum assise tunc videndum erit quantum   f. 96
querens posuerit in visu suo quia vltra id quod in iudicium reducitur non se extendit potestas iusticiarii nec eciam iuratorum sacramentum quia licet querens de
maiori quantitate disseysitus fuerit et totum in visu suo non posuerit in eo quod
15 excedit non poterit iusticiarius iudicare nec iurator iurare.   Et quamuis excessum
fuerit petenti per recognicionem iuratorum iudicandum non tamen erit locus conuiccioni set erit disseysina manifesta et locus erit assise noue disseysine contra
iuratores tantum et non contra illum iudicatum.   Si autem iudicium fecerit
pro petente de re petita vel de eius parte et ipse plus occupauerit occasione
20 iudicii locus erit certificacioni dum tamen recenter inde queratur vel assise noue
disseysine contra eum qui occupauit et hinc et inde habebit locum conuiccio.

CAP. XVIII.   DE PERTINENCIIS

Ad liberum autem tenementum pertinent iura sicut corpora.   Iura autem
siue libertates dici poterunt racione tenementorum quibus debentur seruitutes
25 vero racione tenementorum a quibus debentur.   Et semper consistunt in alieno
et non in proprio quia nemini potest seruire suus fundus proprius.   Nec potest   [252]
quis huiusmodi seruitutes constituere nisi ille qui fundum habet et tenementum
quia prediorum aliud liberum aliud seruituti suppositum.   Liberum autem dici
poterit quod in nullo tenetur vel astringitur prediis vicinorum.   Si autem
30 teneatur dicitur seruituti suppositum quod prius fuerat liberum et hoc siue teneatur predio siue tenemento alieno de voluntate et constitucione dominorum
propter seruicium certum vel propter vicinitatem.   Et talis dici poterit constitucio qua domus domui rus ruri fundus fundo tenementum tenemento subiun-
gatur et non tantum persone per se vel tenemento per se set vtrique simul.   Et

18. *post* iudicatum *lacuna in* J.   33. qua] quia, J.   33-34. subiungatur] subiungantur, J.

heir of the disseisee if the latter should die, nor is it given against the heirs of the principal disseisor if he should die during the lifetime of the disseisee, because the penalty dies with the person and an heir is not bound by a delict of his ancestor, and likewise if the disseisee should die in the lifetime of the disseisor an action is not available to the heir of the disseisee in respect of the wrong done to his ancestor, because between him and the disseisor there is no obligation involving a penalty though there is an obligation involving restitution. There is, however, available to the disseisee or his heirs an action against the disseisors or their heirs by a writ of entry, notwithstanding that they may be under age. And if minors are in any way hindered from being able to sue, then the nearest friends of the minor shall sue and they are to be admitted on behalf of the minors and not only in this case but also in every other case where minors can bring an action and plead.

When an assize is taken in the manner of an assize, then it must be seen how much the plaintiff puts in his view because the authority of the justice does not extend beyond what is brought to judgement, nor also does the oath of the jurors, because although the plaintiff may have been disseised of much more, if he does not put the whole of it in his view a judge can make no judgement and a juror swear no oath about what is in excess [of the amount in the view]. And even though the excess is adjudged to the plaintiff by the recognition of the jurors, nevertheless there will not be place for an attaint, but there will be manifest disseisin and there will be place for an assize of novel disseisin, but against the jurors only and not against him [to whom the excess] is adjudged. If, however, there should be judgement for the plaintiff with regard to the property claimed or part of it and he should seize too much by reason of the judgement, there will be place for a certification, provided complaint thereon is immediately made, or for an assize of novel disseisin against him who has seized. In both cases there will be place for an attaint.

CHAPTER 18.　OF APPURTENANCES

Bracton,
f. 220b
Rights belong to a freehold, just as corporeal things do. They can be called rights or franchises from the standpoint of the tenements to which they are due but servitudes from the standpoint of the tenements from which they are due. And servitudes are always found in another's property and not in one's own because no one may have a servitude in his own lands. Nor can anyone create such servitudes except one who has the estate and tenement. For land is either free or subject to a servitude. Land may be said to be free which is in no way bound or tied to the estates of neighbours. If, however, it is so bound, what
Bracton,
f. 221
formerly was free is said to be subjected to a servitude, and this is so whether it is bound to an estate or tenement belonging to another by the will and constitution of the owners, by reason of a specific service or by reason of vicinage. And such can be called a constitution by which a house is subordinated to a house, a field to a field, an estate to an estate, a tenement to a tenement, and not only to a

ita pertinent seruitutes fundo alicuius ex constitucione siue ex inposicione de voluntate dominorum. Item pertinere poterunt sine constitucione per longum vsum continuum et pacificum ex paciencia inter partes que trahitur ad consensum. Et vnde licet seruitus expresse non inponatur vel constituatur de
5 voluntate dominorum si quis tamen vsus fuerit per aliquod tempus pacifice sine interrupcione non tamen vi nec clam nec precario sine iudicio disseysiri non potest quia si violencia adhibeatur nunquam erit ius disseysitoris propter temporis diurnitatem nisi per negligenciam ipsius qui vim patitur ex longa pacifica et continua possessione inter presentes secus inter absentes et talis seysina
10 multipliciter poterit interrumpi. Si autem seysina fuerit clandestina vt in absencia dominorum vel illis ignorantibus quamuis hoc fiat de consensu vel dissimulacione balliuorum valere non debet. Si autem precaria fuerit id est de gracia que pro voluntate reuocari poterit non acquiritur ius ex longo tempore secus tamen in commodato. Potest tamen seruitus ita constitui in proprio ne
15 liceat domino fundi pascere in suo proprio. Et sic constituitur seruitus in fundo alieno, aliquando ab homine, aliquando ex paciencia et usu. Et eodem modo imponitur quandoque a iure et nec ab homine nec ab vsu, scilicet ne quis faciat in proprio per quod dampnum vicino eueniat vel nocumentum. Est enim nocumentum quandoque iustum et quandoque iniuriosum: iustum, vt cum de iure
20 prohiberi non possit ne faciat vt de molendino leuato in proprio fundo; iniuriosum, vt si quis fecerit aliquid in suo iniuste contra legem vel constitucionem prohibitus a iure vt ne quis stagnum suum alcius tollat per quod tenementum vicini submergatur vel ne faciat fossam in suo per quam aquam vicini diuertat vel per quam ad alueum pristinum reuerti non possit vel ne quid faciat in suo
25 quominus vicinus suus omnino vti possit seruitute inposita vel concessa vel quominus comode vtatur loco, tempore, numero, genere, qualitate vel quantitate. Et non refert vtrum hoc omnino fecerit vel quod tantumdem valeat vt si quis habuerit ius eundi per fundum alienum non solum facit disseysinam si viam obstruat set si ire non permittat omnino comode vel secundum vsum debitum
30 vel si non permittat viam reficere et eodem modo si omnino aquam non diuertat set fossam faciat vel purgare non permittat, ad aque enim ductum pertinet purgacio sicut ad viam refeccio. Vel licet omnino non inpediat si fecerit tamen quominus comode facit disseysinam vt in hiis casibus et consimilibus vt si communam habeam in certo loco cum libero et conpetenti ingressu et egressu faciat
35 quis fossatum, hayam, murum vel pallacium per quod oportebit me ire per

---

7. propter] per, J.   9. secus] sicut, J.   10. clandestina] clam destina, J.   15-18. Et
. . . proprio, Br., *om.* J.   20. non *addidimus.*   24. quid] quis, J.   27. fecerit] fecit, J.
32. refeccio] perfeccio, J.   35. per quod Br., *om.* J.

person as such or to a tenement as such but to both together.   And so servitudes are appurtenant to someone's land either by a constitution or by imposition by the will of the owners.   Again, they can be appurtenant without a constitution through long, continuous and peaceful user arising from sufferance between the parties which draws out into consent.   And in this respect, although a servitude is not expressly imposed or created by the will of the owners, yet if a man had user for some time, peacefully and without interruption, and not by force or secretly or at will, he cannot be disseised without a judgement of the court.   Because if force is used, the disseisor will never establish a right by reason of the passage of time (unless it be through the negligence of the man who suffers the violence) through long, peaceful and continuous possession between those on the spot but it is otherwise if they are absent, and such a seisin can be interrupted in many ways.   If, however, the seisin is clandestine, for example, in the absence of the owners or without their knowledge, although this occurs with the consent or through the indifference of the bailiffs, it ought not to hold good. If, however, it should be at will, that is of grace, which can be revoked at will, a right is not acquired by a long passage of time: but it is, however, otherwise in a loan.   And a servitude may be so constituted in one's own land that the owner of the soil is not allowed to graze on his own land.   And so a servitude is established in the land of another, sometimes by man's action and sometimes by sufferance and user.   And likewise it is sometimes imposed by law and not by man's action or by user: for instance, a man is not to do anything in his own land by which harm or nuisance may be caused to his neighbour.   For nuisance may sometimes be rightful and sometimes wrongful: rightful, for example, where of right a man cannot be prohibited from such acts as erecting a mill on his own land; wrongful, for example, where a man should do something unlawfully in his own land against a law or a constitution: prohibited of right, for instance, that one should not raise the level of his pond so high that the tenement of his neighbour is submerged, or make a ditch in his land whereby he diverts water from his neighbour or whereby it is prevented from returning to its original course, or do anything in his land which would prevent his neighbour from being able to use fully a servitude imposed or granted or from being able to use it with ease as regards place, time, number, kind, quality or quantity.   And it does not matter whether he does this completely or what comes to the same thing: for example, if a man has a right of way through the land of another, the latter not only commits disseisin if he obstructs the path but also if he does not allow him to pass through with complete ease or in accordance with the usual practice, or if he does not allow him to repair the path; and likewise if he does not divert the water entirely but makes a ditch or does not let it be cleaned out, for cleaning out is as essential to a watercourse as repairs are to a path.   And even though he does not completely hinder, nevertheless if he should do something whereby inconvenience is caused, he commits disseisin, as in these and similar cases: for example, if I have common in a certain place with free and easy entry and exit and someone makes a ditch, hedge, wall or paling which obliges me to go by a roundabout route where I had previously entered by a

Bracton,
f. 221b

circuitum vbi prius ingressus fui per conpendium saluo tamen vicino iure suo si
recenter ad querelam eius qui iniuriam passus est quod suum fuerit exsequatur   [253]
et propter communem vtilitatem ne quis diu iure suo inpediatur et ita si non comode.   Preterea si cui concedatur ius pascendi certo tempore et non permittat
5   eum vti aliquo tempore vel quamuis omnino non tamen permittat eum vti nisi
certis temporibus vel certis horis vel cum vti debeat vbique non permittatur vti
nisi locis certis et coartatis vel cum ius habeat pascendi ad omnia aueria et
omnimoda et cuiuscumque generis non permittit vti nisi ad quedam genera   f. 96b
aueriorum et determinata vel si constituatur ius pascendi ad certum numerum
10   non permittit tamen vti nisi ad minorem numerum et sic non debito modo et
quilibet modus habet in se debitam commoditatem.   Set non possit propter vim
competit domino fundi assisa noue disseysine.   Et in omnibus istis casibus vbi
conpetit assisa noue disseysine de communa pasture ei cui concessa est libertas
pascendi si comode vel debito modo vt predictum est vti non possit, ita conpetit
15   domino concedenti assisa noue disseysine de libero tenemento si ille cui concessum est presumptuose vel aliter quam fuerit constituta vti velit vt si per vim
vti vellet cum non esset constituta.   Et illud idem videri possit in cursu aquarum
vt si cui concedatur ius aque ducende non permittat eum ducere omnino vel
minus comode quia non permittit purgare vel si id quod continue ducere debet
20   ducere non permittit nisi certis horis vel quod integre nisi in parte et ita erit
disseysina manifesta cum nullo modo vel non comode nec debito modo permittat vti.   Si autem debitum modum excedat quis incontinenti repelli poterit post
tempus vero non nisi cum cause cognicione et sic poterit quis habere seruitutem
in fundo alieno et vti nisi ex iusta causa prohibeatur.   Iura siquidem que quis in
25   fundo alieno habere poterit sunt infinita.   Et eodem modo et eisdem de causis
quibus res corporales adquiruntur adquiruntur et iura et eodem modo quo
adquiruntur secundum rerum incorporalium adquisicionem et iuste eodem modo
amitti poterunt et iniuste.   Res vero corporales animo adquiruntur et corpore
per tradicionem res autem incorporales sicut iura et seruitutes cum loca fuerint
30   determinata solo aspectu accipientis vel sui procuratoris et possidendi voluntate
adquiruntur quia iura tradicionem non paciuntur vt ecce si vicinus fundo suo
talem inposuerit seruitutem quod liceat vicino inmittere ad pasturam aueria sua
ita poterit fundus suus licet ab inicio liber esset omnino seruire fundo vicini.   Et
ex tali constitucione et mutua vtriusque voluntate tenet seruitus dum tamen
35   interueniant accipientis voluntas et aspectus cum huiusmodi iura tradicionem

2. fuerit] fuerat, J.   5. nisi Br., non, J.   12. vbi] non, J.   21. nec *om.* J; *post* modo
add. non, J.   24. prohibeatur] prohibiatur, J.   26. quibus, Br., qui habet, J; *posterius*
adquiruntur Br., *om.* J.   27. et iuste, Br., iniuste, J.   28. amitti] admitti, J.   29. loca] loco, J.

shorter route, saving however to the neighbour his right, if immediately on the complaint of the one who has suffered the wrong, he sues for what belongs to him, and because of the common good that no one's right should be long obstructed. And so it is if inconvenience is caused. Furthermore, if a right of grazing is granted to a man for a certain time and someone does not permit him to exercise the right at any time; or, although granted for all times, nevertheless he does not permit him to exercise it except at specified times or specified hours; or, although he ought to exercise it everywhere, he is not permitted to do so except in specified and restricted places; or, although he has a right of grazing for all beasts and of all and every kind, someone does not allow him to exercise it except for certain specified kinds of beast; or, although a right of grazing is established for a certain number of animals, yet someone does not permit its exercise except for a smaller number and thus not in due measure. And each arrangement carries its own recognised advantages; and if he cannot enjoy them on account of force, an assize of novel disseisin is available to the owner of the estate. And in all those cases where an assize of novel disseisin for common of pasture is available to him to whom the franchise of grazing has been granted if he is not able to exercise it with ease or in due manner, as aforesaid, so equally there is available to the owner who grants the servitude an assize of novel disseisin in respect of his freehold if he to whom the servitude is granted seeks to usurp it or exercise it otherwise than it was constituted: for instance, if he sought to exercise it by force when it had not been constituted. And the same thing may be seen in the case of a watercourse: for example, if he to whom there is granted a right of drawing water is not permitted to draw water at all or at least not with ease because he is not permitted to clean out the watercourse; or if what he ought to draw continuously he is not permitted to draw except at specified hours; or what he should draw fully he can draw only in part; and thus there will be manifest disseisin since he is not permitted the exercise of the servitude in any way or not with ease or in a proper way. If, however, a man goes beyond what is proper, he can be repelled immediately, but not after time has elapsed except with a judicial hearing. And so a man can have a servitude in the land of another and exercise it unless for just cause it is prohibited. Indeed, the rights which a man may have in another's land are innumerable. And in the same manner and for the same causes as corporeal property is acquired, so rights are acquired; and in the same way that they are acquired according to the rules for acquiring incorporeal property and lawfully, so they may be lost, and unlawfully. Corporeal property is acquired mentally and physically by livery, but incorporeal property like rights and servitudes, once where they are to be has been settled, are acquired solely by the view of the recipient or of his agent and by the intention to possess, because rights are not capable of livery: for example, if a neighbour should impose upon his land such a servitude that his neighbour is permitted to turn his beasts in to pasture, so his land, although it was to begin with entirely free, will be subject to a servitude to his neighbour's land. And from this agreement and the mutual consent of both sides, the servitude holds good, provided the recipient has first expressed his

Bracton,
f. 222

non accipiant, quo casu statim est in seysina licet non statim inmittat aueria sua
et semper videtur vti donec seysinam suam amiserit per non vsum vel donec
disseysitus inde fuerit in toto vel in parte vt si aueria sua inmittere non possit
cum velit vel cum semel inmiserit vti non possit debito modo vel commode quo
5 casu ei subueniendum est per assisam siue vsus fuerit siue non propter solam
constitucionem cum sit quasi in possessione quia iura quasi possidentur. Et sic
adquiritur possessio seruitutis ante vsum sed sine vsu ad alium transferri non
potest nisi contineatur in constitucione seruitutis quod seruitus remaneat sibi
et heredibus suis vel cui illam dare voluerit vel assignare. Sic autem adquiritur
10 possessio seruitutis set nunquam retinetur nisi per vsum verum cum aueria sua   [254]
inmiserit vnum vel plura licet non omnia vel omnimoda inmittat que inmittere
posset per constitucionem. Et eodem modo adquiri et teneri poterit seysina sine
aliqua constitucione per pacienciam et longum vsum.

    Constitui vero potest seruitus multipliciter videlicet vt si quis habeat ius
15 pascendi in fundo alieno ius fodiendi ius hauriendi ius piscandi aquamue
ducendi et ius venandi et alia infinita poterint esse iura et secundum quod
habent sub se plures species vel non habent et secundum quod seruitutes plura
habent pertinencia et pertinencia pertinenciarum, set quoniam magis celebris
est illa seruitus per quam conceditur alicui ius pascendi ideo primo de ea
20 dicendum est que dicitur communa pasture.

CAP. XIX. DE COMMUNA PASTURE

    Communa autem nomen generale est et conuenit suis partibus sicut genus
se habet ad suas species. Communa enim ex virtute vocabuli conponitur ex
vna et cum et subintelligitur alia hoc est communa in alieno et vna cum alio et
25 non in fundo proprio quia nemini seruit suus fundus proprius. Adquiritur enim
communa modis multis sicut ex causa donacionis vt si quis dederit terram cum
communa pasture et ex causa empcionis et vendicionis vt si quis emerit in fundo
alieno vt pertineat ad tenementum suum licet sit de feodo alieno et diuersa
baronia et de diuersis comitatibus contiguis tamen ex constitucione dominorum
30 fundorum. Adquiritur eciam per seruicium et ex causa vicinitatis vt si quis cum
vicino et vicinus cum eo et ex longo vsu sine constitutione cum pacifica possessione continua ex sciencia et paciencia dominorum set non balliuorum. Et eisdem racionibus pertinere poterit communa ad liberum tenementum dum tamen

4. commode, Br., *om.* J.   7. sed *om.* J; *post* vsu *add.* cum J.   8. quod] quia, J;
remaneat] remanet, J.   11. omnia] omnino, J.   16. poterint] poterunt, J.   28. vt]
ac, J.   30. fundorum] suorum, J.   31. *ante* vicinus *add.* cum. J.   31. sine] siue, J.
32. *posterius* Et] vt, J.

agreement and had the view because rights of this kind are not capable of livery. And in this case a man is immediately in seisin although he does not turn his beasts in immediately, and he is always regarded as exercising his right until he loses his seisin by non-user or until he is disseised thereof in whole or in part: for example, if he cannot turn his beasts in when he wishes or, if when once he has turned them in, he cannot exercise his right in due manner or with ease. In this case he will be aided by an assize, whether he has exercised the right or not, solely on account of the agreement, since he is in quasi-possession because rights are quasi-possessed. And thus the possession of a servitude is acquired before user but it cannot be transferred to another without user unless it is provided in the agreement for the servitude that the servitude remain to him and his heirs or to whom he wishes to give or assign it. Thus the possession of a servitude is acquired, but it is never retained except by true user, when he turns his beasts in, whether one or several, even though he does not turn in all his beasts or every kind he could turn in under the agreement. And likewise seisin can be acquired and held irrespective of any agreement through sufferance and long user.

A servitude can be constituted in many ways: for example, where a man has a right of grazing in another's land, a right of digging, a right of drawing water, a right of fishing or leading water and a right of hunting. And there can be other rights without number, according as the servitudes include several species or do not, and according as they have several appurtenances and appurtenances of appurtenances. But since the best known is that servitude by which there is granted to someone a right of grazing, therefore first of all there must be discussed what is called common of pasture.

CHAPTER 19. OF COMMON OF PASTURE

Bracton,
f. 222
Bracton,
f. 222b
'Common' is a general noun and accommodates itself to its parts just as a genus covers its species. *Communa*, when the word is analysed, is compounded of *una* and *cum*, and the word 'alia' is understood, that is, common in another's land and together with another, and not in one's own land because no one may have a servitude in his own land. Common is acquired in many ways: for example, by cause of gift: for example, if a man were to give land with common of pasture; and by cause of purchase and sale: for example, if a man were to buy a right of common in the land of another so that it is appurtenant to his own tenement, although it belongs to another's fee and a different barony and is in different adjacent counties, still it arises out of the agreement between the owners of the estates. A right of common is acquired also by service and by cause of vicinage: for example, if a man commons with his neighbour and his neighbour with him; and from long user irrespective of an agreement but by peaceful and continuous possession with the knowledge and sufferance of the owners (but not of their bailiffs). And for the same reasons common can be appurtenant to a

a tempore in breui mortis antecessoris comprehenso vt infra alioquin si eciam
eiciantur non recuperabunt.   Constitutum est enim quod cum quis ius non
habens communicandi vsurpet communam tempore quo heredes extiterint infra
etatem vel vxores sub potestate virorum extiterint vel dum pastura fuerit in manu   f. 97
5 tenentis in dotem vel per legem Anglie vel ad terminum vite vel annorum vel per
feodum talliatum et pastura illa diu vsi fuerint quod habentes huiusmodi ingressum a tempore quo currit breue mortis antecessoris si prius communam
non habuerint si eiecti inde fuerint quamuis sine iudicio per assisam tamen noue
disseysine nullum habeant recuperare dum tamen per proprietarium in casu quo
10 possessio iuncta est iuri secus tamen erit si eiecti fuerint per ius non habentem.

In eo quod communa est nomen generale plures sub se continet species.   Est
enim communa in eo quod pastura dicitur de omni quod edi poterit vel pasci
large sumpto vocabulo vel stricte.   Large vt si quis communam habeat in alieno
scilicet communam herbagii pessone siue glandis siue nucum et quicquid sub
15 nomine pessone continetur et eciam foliorum et frondium et racionabilis estouerii
saltem ad terminum vite.   Item dici poterit communa habere ius fodiendi in
alieno aurum et argentum, lapides, cretam, arenam et alia metalla et turbam et   [255]
huiusmodi vel ius falcandi herbam vel brueram vel huiusmodi ad racionabile
estouerium vel ad secandum in alieno bosco racionabile estouerium edificandi,
20 claudendi et ardendi.

Distingui autem poterit communa pasture per tempora vt si omni tempore
vel certis temporibus vel certis horis et eciam per loca vt si vbique et per totum
sine aliqua excepcione.   Excipiuntur tamen quedam tacite et quandoque expresse sicut racionabilia defensa que exigi non poterunt racione pasture nisi
25 specialiter concedantur et non nisi post tempus.   Qualia sunt blada prata et
quedam loca specialiter custodita ad boues vel vaccas vel vitulos vel agnos vel
huiusmodi in suis temporibus.   Preterea nec in curia alicuius nec in gardinis vel
viridariis nec in parcis nec in dominicis alicuius que claudi possunt et excoli nisi
per certum modum constitucionis et certis temporibus vel certis horis et deter-
30 minatis et infra certa loca et ad certa genera aueriorum vt si ad omnimoda aueria
et sine numero vel cum coartacione et cum numero vel ad certum genus aueriorum.   Communa autem dici non debet quod quis habet in alieno siue pro precio
siue ex causa empcionis cum tenementum non habeat ad quod possit communa
pertinere set pocius herbagium cum hoc possit esse quasi personale quid siue
35 certum dederit quis pro herbagio habendo siue incertum quod si fuerit incertum
vt cum quis aliquando plus dederit aliquando minus hoc erit pocius empcio
herbagii quam pastura et pocius prediale quam personale.

1. comprehenso vt] ante comprehensum et, J.   4. extiterint *in statuto*, existencium, J.
6. et] vt, J.   14. pessone] possessone, J.   15. pessone] possessoe, J.   17. metalla]
metella, J.   33. tenementum] totum, J.

freehold, provided user is from the period included in the writ of *mort d'ancestor* (as below), otherwise if those having common are ejected they will not recover. For it has been enacted that, when any who have no right of common usurp common during the time that heirs are under age or women under the authority of their husbands, or while the pasture is in the hands of a tenant in dower or by the curtesy of England or for a term of life or of years or in fee tail, and they have used the said pasture for such a period that they had such entry [within] the time from which the writ of *mort d'ancestor* runs,[1] and if they had no common before and if they are ejected therefrom, even without a judgement of the court, they shall yet have no recovery by an assize of novel disseisin provided they are ejected by the owner in a case where possession is conjoined with right, for it will be otherwise if they were ejected by one who has no right.

Since common is a general noun it includes within itself several species. For there is common in what is called pasture of all that can be eaten or grazed, the word being used with a wide or narrow meaning. Wide: for example, if a man has common in another's land such as common of herbage, pannage, whether of acorns or nuts, and whatsoever is included under the noun 'pannage', and also of leaves and branches and reasonable estovers, at least for the term of a life. Again, it can be called common to have the right to dig in another's land for gold and silver, gems, chalk, sand and other metals and for turf and the like, or the right of mowing grass or heather or the like for reasonable estovers or of cutting in another's wood reasonable estovers for building, fencing and burning.

Rights of common of pasture may be distinguished by the times [when they are exercised]: if, for example, it is for all the time or for specified times or at specified hours; and also by the places: if, for example, it is everywhere and all over without any exception. Some things, however, are excepted tacitly and sometimes expressly, such as reasonable fenced-in portions which cannot be demanded by reason of the grazing unless they are specially granted and only then after the proper time. Such are corn-crops, meadows and certain places specially reserved for oxen or cows or calves or sheep or the like at their times. And, furthermore, [pasture does not extend] to anyone's curtilage or to gardens or orchards or to parks or to anyone's demesne lands which may be enclosed and tilled, except by express agreement and at specified times or at specified and fixed hours and within specified places and for specified kinds of beasts: for example, for beasts of every kind and without limitation of numbers or with restriction and with limitation of numbers or for beasts of a certain kind. That, however, ought not to be called common which a man has, whether for a fee or by cause of purchase, in another's estate when he has no tenement to which a right of common can be appurtenant, but rather should it be called herbage, since this may be as it were a personal thing, whether a man gives a fixed or an uncertain payment to have the herbage; and if the payment should be uncertain, as when a man sometimes gives more and sometimes less, this will be a purchase of herbage rather than [common of] pasture and be [personal rather than predial].

[1] The coronation of Henry III: Statute of Westminster I. c. 39.

CAP. XX. QUALITER DISSOLUITUR COMMUNA

Sicut autem adquiritur communa voluntate et assensu parcium ita dissolui potest ex mutua vtriusque voluntate si velint dissentire per renunciacionem remissionem et quietamclamacionem nec sufficit si vnus eorum remittere velit et
5 resilere nisi ambo in hoc consenciant. Et sicut adquiritur sine constitucione et consensu per longum vsum et pacienciam, ita amitti potest per negligenciam et non vsum in perpetuum vel ad tempus: in perpetuum vt si tempus excludat omnem accionem tam super possessione quam super proprietate vel sic in perpetuum vt excludat assisam in perpetuum super possessione et non super iure quia assisa
10 infra certum tempus limitatur et sic tempus tollit omnem accionem vel aliquam.

Dissolui eciam poterit ex toto per communem dissensum siue hoc sit inter participes et heredes vel inter vicinos dominos tenementi vel extraneos qui non nisi communam clamare poterunt in tenemento vt si ita conuenerit quod tenementum quod prius fuit communa inter partes diuidatur pro certis porcionibus
15 ita quod id quod fuit commune iam fiat omnium pro virilibus porcionibus separale secundum maius et minus et quo casu cum semel consenserint iterum non poterunt dissentire. Item potest constitucio seruitutis aliquando minui et restringi et mutari et coartari et eodem modo augeri poterunt et ampliari si non contra voluntatem contrahencium quia per hoc conpeteret domino tenementi
20 assisa noue disseysine si in contrarium per vim ageretur sicut conpeteret ei assisa noue disseysine de communa pasture cui debetur seruitus secundum modum et constitucionem seruitutis.

Est tamen quedam constitucio per quam inuito eo cui seruitus debetur [256] coartatur communa, que talis est:
25 Quia multi sunt magnates qui feoffauerunt milites et libere tenentes suos in maneriis suis de paruis tenementis et qui inpediti sunt per eosdem quod comodum suum facere non possunt de residuo maneriorum suorum sicut de vastis, boscis et magnis pasturis desicut ipsi feoffati sufficientem habere possunt pasturam quantum ad tenementa sua pertinet, prouisum est et concessum ab
30 omnibus quod cum huiusmodi feoffati a quibuscumque de cetero aramiauerint versus dominos suos assisam noue disseysine de communa pasture et de hoc quod aliquam partem predictorum tenementorum excoluerint si coram iusticiariis cognouerint quod sufficientem habeant pasturam quantum ad tenementa sua pertinet cum libero ingressu et exitu et chaciam de tenementis suis vsque ad
35 pasturam illam quod inde sint contenti et illi de quibus tales questi fuerint quieti sint de hoc quod comodum suum ita fecerunt de terris et vastis et pasturis f. 97b suis. Si autem dixerint quod sufficientem pasturam non habuerint quantum pertinet ad tenementa cum sufficienti egressu et ingressu, inquiratur inde veritas per assisam, et si per assisam recognitum fuerit quod de libero ingressu et egressu

4. remittere] mittere, J. 6. pacienciam] paciamen, J; amitti] admitti, J. 9. vt] vel, J; *posterius* super *om.* J. 10. tempus, Br., *om.* J. 12. qui] quia, J. 20. si in contriarium per vim ageretur sicut, Br.; verumtamen si per vim agetur sic, J. 29. est] fuit, J. 31. et de hoc quod aliquam, Br., *om.* J. 35. inde *in statuto,* illi, J.

CHAPTER 20. HOW RIGHTS OF COMMON ARE DISSOLVED

Bracton,
f. 222b
Bracton.
f. 223

Just as common is acquired by the will and assent of the parties, so it can be dissolved by the mutual wish of them both if they wish to withdraw their assent by a renunciation, remission and quitclaim, but it does not suffice if one of them wishes to remit and resile unless both consent to this.   And just as common is acquired, irrespective of agreement and consent, by long user and sufferance, so it can be lost by negligence and non-user, for ever or for a time: for ever, for example, if time excludes all right of action not only for possession but also for ownership, or for ever in this way, that time may exclude for ever an assize on the possession and not on the right, for an assize is subject to a period of limitation and so time takes away all or some right of action.

Bracton,
f. 227

Common can also be dissolved entirely by common withdrawal of assent, whether this is between parceners and heirs or between neighbouring owners of a tenement or third parties who can claim nothing but common in the tenement: for example, if it should be thus agreed that a tenement, which formerly was common, is to be divided between the parties in specific portions so that what was common is now made the separate property of all, by fractions, according as it is large or small.   And in this case when once the parties have expressed their consent together, they cannot thereafter dissent.   Again, the arrangements for a servitude can sometimes be lessened and restricted and altered and limited, and likewise increased and enlarged, but not against the wish of the contracting parties because thereby an assize of novel disseisin would be available to the owner of the tenement if force were used against that wish, just as an assize of novel disseisin of common of pasture is available to the man to whom a servitude is due in accordance with the terms and arrangements for the servitude.

There is, however, an enactment by which a right of common is restricted against the will of him to whom the servitude is due, and it is as follows:

St. Merton,
c. 4

Because there are many magnates, who have enfeoffed their knights and free-holders in their manors with small tenements and who are prevented by them from being able to make their profit from the rest of their manors as regards wastes, woods and large pastures, inasmuch as the said feoffees can have as much pasture as belongs to their tenements, it is provided and granted by all that, when such feoffees, by whomsoever enfeoffed, arraign an assize of novel disseisin of common of pasture against their lords on the ground that they have cultivated some part of the tenements aforesaid, if they acknowledge before the justices that they have as much pasture as belongs to their tenements with free entry and exit and a drove-way from their tenements as far as the said pasture, they shall be content therewith, and those of whom such feoffees have complained shall be quit in respect of what they have thus done for their profit in their lands, wastes and pastures.   If, however, the complainants say that they have not as much pasture as belongs to their tenements, with adequate entry and exit, let the truth thereof be enquired into by an assize, and if the assize should make known that they have

extiterint inpediti vel quod non habeant sufficientem pasturam, tunc recuperent
querentes seysinam suam per visum recognitorum ita quod per sacramentum et
discrecionem eorundem habeant querentes sufficientem pasturam cum sufficienti
et conpetenti ingressu et egressu in forma predicta, et disseysitores in miseri-
5 cordia sint et dampna reddant et de residuo liceat huiusmodi dominis comodum
suum facere et appruare.

Et quia forinceci tenentes non habent maius ius communicandi in vasto, bosco
aut pastura aliciuus domini quam sui proprii tenentes, statutum est quod predicta
constitucio de cetero locum optineat inter huiusmodi dominos et vicinos suos
10 sicut prius locum habuit inter dominos et tenentes ita quod huiusmodi dominis
vastorum boscorum et pasturarum, salua sufficienti pastura tenentibus suis et
vicinis, liceat appruare de residuo.   Et hoc obseruetur de hiis qui clamant pasturam tanquam pertinentem ad liberum tenementum suum.   Si quis autem
communam clamat per speciale factum ad certum numerum aueriorum aut alio
15 modo quam de iure communi habere deberet, cum conuencio legi deroget habeat
suum recuperare quale habere debet per formam concessionis sibi facte.
Statutum est eciam quod occasione molendini ventricii bercarie waerie vaccarie
augmentacionis curie vel curtilagii nullus grauetur per assisam noue disseysine de
communa pasture.

20 Amitti eciam poterit contra voluntatem vt si quis ita negligens fuerit quod
seysinam suam sine breui et sine iudicio resumere non possit.   Diligens enim
debet quilibet esse in vtendo cum negligencia sicut violencia possit ei esse dampnosa vt si hodie repulsus fuerit quis per vim et in crastino si possit aueria sua inmittat et vtatur et sic de die in diem et sic non amittit seysinam propter
25 diligenciam licet illam habeat contenciosam.   Si autem omnino per vim repellatur et resisti non possit vel saltem omnino non repellatur set quod comode
vti non possit nec per modum constitucionis seruitutis statim recurrendum est ad
illum qui iura tuetur et habebit remedium per assisam que super hoc prodita est   [257]
recuperande possessionis gracia.   Comode dico vt si fiat aliquid in alieno ad
30 nocumentum seruitutis per quod omnino vti non possit vel non comode vt si quis
murum fecerit vel hayam statim demolliatur vel saltem post tempus per assisam.
Item si transferri debeat communa ad alium oportet quod transferatur ad certas
personas et a certis personis vsque ad certa tenementa quibus seruitus debetur
quia huiusmodi iura sine corporibus esse non poterunt videlicet sine corporibus
35 quibus seruitur.   Et sicut incorporalia tradicionem non paciuntur nec possideri
poterunt set quasi ita nec transferri poterunt set quasi et sufficit pro tradicione aspectus loci in quo huiusmodi iura constituuntur et mutua voluntas contrahencium
et affectus possidendi et ex sola voluntate et aspectu est quis quasi in possessione

---

3. discrecionem] discrescionem, J.   12. de residuo *in statuto, om.* J.   12. *post* clamant
add. per, J.   13. pertinentem] per tenentem, J.   27. non *om.* J.   32. *prius* ad *om.* J.
38. aspectu] affectu, J.

been hindered from having free entry and exit or that they do not have sufficient pasture, then the complainants shall recover their seisin by view of the recognitors so that by their oath and discretion the plaintiffs shall have sufficient pasture with adequate and suitable entry and exit in the aforesaid form, and the disseisors shall be amerciable and pay damages.   And it is lawful for such lords to enclose and make their profit of what is left.

St. West-
minster, II.
c. 46

And because outside tenants have no more right to common in the waste, wood or pasture of any lord than his own tenants, it is ordained that the aforesaid enactment shall from henceforth apply between such lords and their neighbours just as it previously applied between lords and their tenants, so that it shall be lawful for such lords of wastes, woods and pastures, while leaving sufficient pasture for their tenants and neighbours, to enclose the rest.   And this shall be observed with respect to those who claim pasture as appurtenant to their freehold. If, however, anyone should by special deed claim common for a specified number of beasts or in any other way than he ought to have it by common right, since the covenant abrogates the law, he shall have such recovery as he ought to have by the terms of the grant made to him.   It is also ordained that on account of a windmill, sheepcote, horsepond, cowshed, the enlargement of a court or curtilage no one shall be vexed by an assize of novel disseisin of common of pasture.

Bracton,
f. 223

A right of common may also be lost unintentionally: for example, if a man is so negligent that he cannot resume his seisin without a writ and without judgement of the court.   For everyone should be diligent in exercising his right since negligence can be as harmful to him as violence: for example, if to-day a man should be repelled by force and if on the morrow, if he can, he turns his beasts in and exercises his right and does this from day to day, in this way because of his diligence he does not lose his seisin although he holds it subject to dispute.   If, however, he is completely repelled by force and can make no resistance, or at least though he is not completely repelled, he can neither exercise his right with ease nor in accordance with the terms of the agreement for the servitude, straightway there must be recourse to him who safeguards rights, and he will have a remedy by an assize which is provided in these circumstances for the sake of the recovery of possession.   I say 'with ease': for example, if anything is done in the land of another to the injury of a servitude whereby it cannot be exercised at all or not with ease, as, for instance, if a man should erect a wall or hedge, it shall be demolished immediately or at least after a time by an assize.   Again, if a right of common is to be transferred to another, it is necessary for it to be transferred by specified persons to specified persons and [from specific tenements] to specific tenements which are entitled to the servitude, for rights of this kind cannot exist without something corporeal, that is without something corporeal to which the servitude belongs.   And since incorporeal things are not capable of livery and can be no more than quasi-possessed, so they can be no more than quasi-transferred.   And in place of livery it is sufficient to have a view of the place in which such rights are established and the mutual intention of the contracting parties and the desire to possess, and a man is in quasi-possession solely from

et licet statim non fuerit vsus semper tamen vtitur vel quasi donec per non
vsum vel per vim et per negligenciam vel longam pacienciam amittat seysinam
vt si ille qui huiusmodi seruitutem alicui concesserit aliquam partem pasture sue
appruauerit vel totam et ille cui concedatur omnino teneatur extra siue prius
5 pecora sua inmiserit siue non facit disseysinam.   Si autem ille cui seruitus concessa fuerit viribus concedentis possit resistere statim cum herba pululare inceperit aueria sua inmittat et pascat siue ante vsus fuerit siue non et sic per
vsum retinebit seruitutem eciam per vnicum auerium vel per duo licet non tot
inmittat quot inmittere posset vel deberet.   Et si nullum auerium proprium habu-
10 erit sufficit si nomine suo inmittat alienum nisi in donacione contineatur quod
inmittere non liceat nisi dominicum.   Si autem proprium non habuerit nec alienum sufficit quod resistat in quantum possit et denunciet cultori opus nouum
scilicet quod excolere non sit ei licitum et sic facta contencione et re effecta
litigiosa inmittere poterit cum voluerit licet blada sint matura.   Si autem tam
15 negligens extiterit quod statim aueria non inmiserit nec alio modo contencionem
non apposuerit amittere poterit seruitutem per talem negligenciam et seysinam.
Et vnde si cum blada matura fuerint vel cum spicas emiserint et herbe naturam
mutauerint aueria tunc primo inmiserit vel contencionem fecerit, faciet domino
fundi disseysinam de tenemento suo et ita quod dominus fundi recuperare poterit
20 suum liberum tenementum propter vsurpacionem et alius amittet assisam
commune pasture et vix audiendus est inposterum super proprietate et hoc propter negligenciam siue inpotenciam cum magna negligencia trahatur ad consensum.   Set si aliquis opponere poterit sic.   Esto quod quis alienum excolat
tenementum et dominus tenementi sciens et prudens dissimulauerit quousque
25 blada matura fuerint non prius fit ei disseysina propter culturam quam quousque
blada asportauerit cultor et cum ille per tantum tempus dissimulauerit quousque
blada matura fuerint quare non amittat ille seysinam per negligentem pacienciam   f. 98
sicut et ipse pasturam?   Ad quod sciendum est quod est negligens paciencia et
paciens cautela nec fit ei in aliquo disseysina per culturam cum hoc velit quia
30 per culturam semper melioratur condicio culture secus vero est in pastura ex
quo per pacienciam nullum bladum facit suum set per culturam deterioratur   [258]
pastura et quandoque paciens meliorem suam facit condicionem et quandoque
deteriorem.   Et quamdiu fecerit iniuriam suam ex mea voluntate paciencia non
curret contra me quod si contra aliud esset.
35   Et poterit quis sic vti tam nomine proprio quam alieno vt si custos vtatur
nomine heredis qui fuerit in custodia sua vel quis alius sicut rector racione
dignitatis vel ecclesie sue, et semper vtitur talis et possidet cuius nomine vtitur et

6–7. inceperit] ceperit, J.   7. ante] autem, J.   8. non, Br., is, J.   14. tam] causa, J.
16. seruitutem per talem, Br., set per virtutem per talibus, J.   17. si] sic, J.   20. assisam
Br., seysinam, J.   26. cultor *addidimus*.   28. *posterius* est *om*. J; *posterius* et *om*. J.
34. Nota, J. *in margine*.   37. vel] vt, J.   37. Nota, J. *in margine*.

intention and the view.   And although he may not immediately have exercised the right, yet he exercises it all the time or is deemed to do so until he loses seisin by non-user or by force or by negligence or long sufferance: for example, if he who grants such a servitude to someone should enclose some part or the whole of his pasture and he who received the grant should be entirely excluded, whether he previously turned his beasts in or not, the donor commits disseisin.   If, however, he to whom the servitude was granted is able to resist the power of the donor and, as soon as the grass begins to grow, turns his beasts in to graze, whether he had exercised the right before or not, thus by user he will keep the servitude even by a single beast or two, even though he does not turn in as many as he can or should.   And if he has no beast of his own, it is sufficient if he

Bracton,
f. 223b

turns in another's beast in his own name, unless it is included in the grant that it is not permissible to turn in any beasts but those belonging to himself.   And if he has neither beasts of his own nor of another, it is sufficient for him to resist to the best of his ability, and to warn anyone tilling the soil that he was doing something abnormal, in other words, that it is not lawful for him to till the soil, and so, having raised an objection and brought the matter into dispute, he can turn his beasts in when he will, even though the corn is fully grown. If, however, he should remain so negligent that he does not turn his beasts in immediately or does not raise an objection in any way, he can by such negligence lose the servitude and seisin,   And therefore, when the corn is fully grown or when it has put forth its ears and changed from the nature of grass, if he then for the first time turns his beasts in or raises an objection, he will commit disseisin against the owner of the land in respect of his tenement with the result that the owner of the land can recover his freehold on account of usurpation and the other will lose seisin of the common of pasture, and he will thereafter hardly be heard on his property rights and this on account of negligence or lack of willpower since gross negligence draws into consent.   But where anyone can raise an objection, it is as follows: suppose that a man cultivates the tenement of another and the owner knows about it and shrewdly disregards it until the corn is fully grown, no disseisin is done to him by reason of the cultivation prior to the time when the cultivator carries away the corn.   And why does not he, who has been disregardful for so long a time until the corn is fully grown, lose his seisin by his negligent sufferance like the man who has lost his pasture?   As to this you must know that there is negligent sufferance and suffering as a device, nor is disseisin in any way done to him by cultivation, when he encourages it, since by cultivation the condition of the land cultivated is always improved; but it is different with pasture because by sufferance he does not make any corn his own and by cultivation pasture is not improved.   And sometimes he who suffers cultivation improves its condition and sometimes he makes it worse.   And so long as the cultivator commits his wrong with my assent, sufferance will not run against me, but if it is done against my will it would be a different matter.

Bracton,
f. 226b

And in this way a man can have user both in his own name and in another's: for example, if a guardian has the user in the name of an heir who is in his wardship, or anyone else like a rector by reason of his office or his church; and such a

possidetur et cum ecclesia fungatur vice minoris adquirit ecclesia per rectorem
et retinet per eundem sicut minor per tutorem et quamuis moriatur rector non
tamen cadit ecclesia de seysina sua de aliquo de quo rector seysitus moritur
nomine ecclesie sue non magis quam minor si custos moriatur et peruenerit in
5 alterius custodiam per hoc enim non mutatur status minoris. Eodem modo
fieri debet de rectore ecclesie vt videtur et quod eandem seysinam habere debeat
successor quam predecessor habuit quia ecclesia semper manet in sua possessione
quamuis rector moriatur. Et cum successor sit institutus statim nomine ecclesie
est quasi in possessione et videtur vti nomine ecclesie eciam licet pecus non
10 inmiserit et cum inpeditus fuerit cum inmittere voluerit seysinam suam et
statum predecessoris sui per assisam noue disseysine recuperabit. Si autem
tempore vacacionis ante institucionem medio tempore a possessione ceciderit
tunc fiat breue de recuperanda seysina nomine ecclesie sue quam predecessor
suus habuit die quo obiit. Set quid si ante mortem rectoris qui obiit fuerit
15 ecclesia sic disseysita? Tunc erit rectori succurendum per breue de ingressu
ad similitudinem aliarum disseysinarum licet rector heres dici non poterit set
successor.

    Si quis igitur disseysitus fuerit per vim de communa pasture sue siue in-
pediatur quominus comode et modo debito vti possit et secundum quod se
20 habet ad ea que edi possunt vel secundum quod large se habet ad alia que sunt ad
vtilitatem, si statim se non posuerit in seysinam cum possit per negligenciam vel
cum non possit propter violenciam et vim maiorem, statim recurrendum est ad
illum qui iura tuetur ad inpetrandum assisam que prodita est recuperande possessionis gracia. Plures enim constitui possunt seruitutes in vno fundo pluribus
25 et per totum sicut vni et plures possunt ibi esse seruitutes licet fundus vnus tum
racione diuersorum tenementorum ad que pertinent tum racione diuersarum
personarum quibus seruitutes debentur, et quia plures persone et diuersa
tenementa et sic diuersa iura ideo diuerse disseysine et plura breuia. Et quia
plures habere poterunt ius pascendi in vno tenemento non fiat vnum breue
30 racione tenementi in quo seruitus constituitur quod vnum est set plura. Si
autem tenementum ad quod communa pertinere dicitur commune sit inter plures
sicut inter coheredes sine particione siue omnes disseysiti fuerint siue quidam
illorum vnica erit disseysina et non plures propter vnicum ius quamuis plurium
personarum et propter vnicum tenementum ante diuisionem. Item si tene-
35 mentum in quo communa conceditur commune sit pluribus participibus
heredibus vel vicinis et vnus illorum disseysinam fecerit non erit propter hoc
super omnes inpetrandum set super illum tantum qui fecit iniuriam nisi omnes

    3. de aliquo, Br., *om.* J.   6. de rectore . . . debeat, Br., *om.* J.   21. *post* cum *add.*
non, J.   27. *prius* et] tum, J.   28. *post* iura *add.* et, J.   32. particione] participacione, J.
34. ante, Br., propter, J.

man always exercises and possesses the use in the name of him for whom it is exercised and possessed; and since a church enjoys the position of a minor, the church acquires through the rector and retains by him just as a minor does through his guardian; and although the rector dies, nevertheless the church does not fail to have its seisin of anything of which the rector dies seised in the name of his church, any more than a minor if his guardian dies and he passes into the guardianship of another, for thereby the position of a minor does not alter. And the rector of a church should be treated similarly, it seems, so that a successor ought to have the same seisin as his predecessor had because the church always remains in possession of its own rights, although the rector dies. And when a successor

Bracton,
f. 227

is instituted, he is forthwith in quasi-possession in the name of the church and is deemed to exercise his right in the name of the church, even though he does not turn a beast in and, should he be obstructed when he wishes to turn beasts in, he will recover his seisin and the position of his predecessor by an assize of novel disseisin. If, however, during a period of voidance before the institution [of a rector] there is in the mean time a lapse in possession, then a writ should be made for the recovery, in the name of his church, of the seisin which his predecessor had on the day of his death. But what if the church were thus disseised before the death of the late rector? Then the rector will be aided by a writ of entry like those for other disseisins, even though the rector cannot be called heir but successor.

Bracton,
f. 223b

If therefore a man should be disseised by force of his common of pasture or is so obstructed that he cannot exercise his right with ease or in due manner, according as it includes things which may be eaten or is taken broadly to include other things of value, if through negligence he does not put himself immediately in seisin when he can, or when he cannot on account of violence and *force majeure*, then he must have recourse at once to him who safeguards rights in order to sue out the assize which is provided for the sake of the recovery of possession. Several servitudes can be established in one estate for several persons and over the whole estate, as well as for one person, and there may be several servitudes there, even though there is a single estate, both because of the different tenements to which they are appurtenant and because of the different persons to

Bracton,
f. 224

whom the servitudes are due. And because there are several persons and different tenements and consequently different rights, therefore there are different disseisins and several writs. And because several persons can have a right of grazing in one tenement, one writ should not be made out because there is a single tenement in which the servitude is established, but several writs. If, however, the tenement to which the common is said to be appurtenant is common among several persons as among co-heirs when there is no partition, whether all of them have been disseised or some of them, there will be a single disseisin and not several disseisins, because of the single right, though belonging to several, and because there is only one tenement before it is divided. Again, if the tenement in which common is granted is common to several parceners, heirs or neighbours, and one of them commits disseisin, a writ should not on this account be sued out against them all but only against him who did the wrong, unless all or some of

vel quidam illorum ante inpetracionem hoc expresse aduocauerint. Si autem
hoc aduocauerint post inpetracionem ante capcionem assise eciam si in breui [259]
non nominentur bene se ponere poterunt in assisam ac si nominarentur si velint
sicut in aliis assisis noue disseysine vt sic terminetur negocium versus omnes quod
5 si facere noluerint nichilominus procedet assisa versus nominatos et si querens
per assisam recuperauerit recuperabit versus omnes quia si postea velint participes
iterum eum disseysire et ipse inpetrauerit super eos eciam sine iurata recuperabit
per primam assisam quia assisa super assisam de eadem re non est capienda ne
secunda contraria sit prime quia sic possent iudicia esse in incerto.

10   CAP. XXI.   DE PROCESSU

Facta autem sic inpetracione et attachiato breui statim fiat visus iuratoribus
qui communam videant et locum in quo petitur communa et eciam tenementum
ad quod communa dicitur pertinere et illud in quo petitur communa et qualitatem
et quantitatem et per quas metas et de tempore genere numero aueriorum.
15 Audito vero breui coram iusticiariis cum in partes illas venerint statim proponat
querens intencionem suam secundum formam breuis et primo confirmata persona
statim doceat racionem qualiter pertinere debeat ad tenementum suum qui si
liberum tenementum non habeat accionem non habebit.   Dicere enim poterit
quod communa pertinet ad liberum tenementum suum quia feoffatus fuit de tali
20 tenemento cum communa pasture ad tot aueria et quo casu oportet quod doceat
de qualitate pasture vtrum larga fuerit vel stricta.   Incongrue enim queritur quis
dicendo 'tot acras peto commune' cum queri debeat in quot acris.   Propterea
docere debet de quo tenemento pertinet et ad quale tenementum et eodem
modo de genere numero tempore et modo et si aliquando fuerit ampla et post-
25 modum fuerit coartata.

                CAP. XXII.   DE EXCEPCIONIBUS

Fundata igitur intencione querentis multipliciter excipi poterit a tenente vt
persona iudicis et persona sua propria et contra breue de erroribus si querela non

1. aduocauerint] aduocauerit, J.   1–2. Si . . . aduocauerint, Br., om. J.   3. nominar-
entur] nominaretur, J.   5. noluerint] voluerint, J.   13. et] vt, J.   22. commune]
communa, J.

them have expressly avowed the act before the writ was sued out. If, however, they should avow it after the writ has been sued out but before the assize is taken, even though they are not named in the writ, they may indeed, if they wish, put themselves on the assize as if they had been named, as in other assizes of novel disseisin, so that the matter may thus be determined against them all. But if they do not wish to do this, nevertheless the assize will proceed against those who are named. And if the plaintiff recovers by the assize he will recover against them all, because, if subsequently the parceners wish to disseise him again and he sues out a writ against them, he will recover even without a jury by reason of the first assize, because an assize must not be taken on an assize regarding the same thing lest the second should be at variance with the first, because judgements could thus be in a state of uncertainty.

CHAPTER 21.   OF PROCEDURE

Bracton, f. 224

When a writ has been sued out and [pledges of prosecution] taken, a view must immediately be made to the jurors, who are to see the common and the place in which common is claimed and also the tenement to which the common is said to be appurtenant and that in which common is claimed, its nature and extent and what boundaries it has and the time [when the right is exercised] and the kind and number of beasts.   And when the writ has been heard before the justices

Bracton, f. 224b

when they come to those parts, straightway the plaintiff is to put forward his claim according to the terms of the writ and, having first established his identity, he is at once to show the reason why the right of common should be appurtenant to his tenement, and, if he should not have a freehold, he will have no right of action.   For he can say that a right of common is appurtenant to his freehold because he was enfeoffed of such-and-such a tenement with common of pasture for so many beasts, and in this case it behoves him to show what kind of pasture it is, whether it is large or restricted.   His plaint is incongruous who says 'I demand

Bracton, f. 224
Bracton, f. 224b

so many acres of common' when his plaint should say in how many acres [he has common].   Furthermore, he ought to show from what tenement and to what kind of tenement his right of common is appurtenant, and likewise the kind and number [of the beasts], the season of the year and the terms arranged, and whether it was once extensive and was afterwards diminished.

CHAPTER 22.   OF EXCEPTIONS

Bracton. f. 224b₁

When therefore the plaintiff's declaration has been made, a multiplicity of exceptions can be made by the tenant: in regard, for example, to the person of

pertineat ad ipsum vel quod nunquam fuit inde seysitus et eciam contra personam
querentis vt supra de questione status excepto eo quod si libera copulata villano f. 98b
assisam arramiauerit de communa pasture pertinente ad liberum tenementum
suum cum villanus sit extra potestatem domini sui in libero tenemento recuperare
5 debet seysinam non obstante excepcione villenagii a quocumque proposita saltem
donec villanus ad villanum conuincatur et in seruitutem redigatur.   Nec eciam
tunc licitum est domino se ponere in tenementum mulieris cum hoc non sit
tenementum proprium villani quod si fecerit recuperabit villanus et vxor per
assisam noue disseysine non obstante excepcione quia nulli conpetit huiusmodi
10 excepcio nec eciam domino.   Et vnde cum aliquando proposita esset excepcio
villenagii contra villanum et vxorem liberam petentes per assisam communam
pasture vt pertinentem ad liberum tenementum ipsorum in fine consideratum
fuit quod communa pasture libero tenemento adiungeretur tanquam accessorium
principali et sic factum est per officium iudicis quod fieri debuit iure accionis.   [260]
15 Cum igitur proposita sit huiusmodi excepcio contra personas querencium
videri debet an conpetat tenenti vel non que si conpetat oportet quod tenens illam
probet sicut querens accionem.

      Continetur enim 'si talis iniuste disseysiuit' poterit enim quis esse in seysina
licet non statim vtatur et nomine alieno sicut et nomine proprio alieno sicut
20 clericus nomine ecclesie sue cum fuerit institutus et inuenerit ecclesiam suam
in seysina que nunquam fuit disseysita statim est seysitus licet non tamen vtatur.
Verumtamen si disseysitus fuerit et assisa arramiata et obiectum fuerit excipiendo
quod disseysiri non potuit quia nunquam fuit in seysina, tunc videndum est ex
qua causa dicat communam ad liberum tenementum suum pertinere vt si ex
25 causa donacionis tunc statim ex mutua voluntate contrahencium per affectum
et aspectum est quasi in seysina et sufficit pro tradicione licet non statim vtatur,
et semper videtur vti animo et voluntate presencia et aspectu ciuiliter et naturaliter donec amiserit per non vsum.   Si autem petat communam vt pertinentem
ad liberum tenementum suum ex causa successionis, tunc videndum erit vtrum
30 antecessor suus obiit inde seysitus vel non vt si ante mortem suam fuit inde
disseysitus et tunc refert quando.   Si autem inde seysitus obiit, tunc incipit statim
heres habere eandem seysinam quam antecessor suus habuit cum seysitus fuerit
de hereditate que est quasi principale et corporale et sic de accessorio sicut de
iure pascendi quod est incorporale et quod ex solo animo adquiritur et voluntate

      4. potestatem] possessionem, J.   33. accessorio] accessessorio, J.

the judge or his own person, or against the writ on the ground of errors if the plaint does not concern him, or that he was never seised thereof, and also against the person of the plaintiff (as above[1]) on a question of status, with this reservation that, if a free woman who is married to a villein arraigns an assize of common of pasture appurtenant to her freehold when the villein is living in the freehold out of the authority of his lord, she ought to recover seisin, notwithstanding the exception of villeinage by whomsoever put forward, at least until the villein is adjudged to be a villein and brought back to bondage. And even then it is not lawful for the lord to put himself in the woman's tenement since this is not the villein's own tenement and, if he should do so, the villein and his wife will have recovery by an assize of novel disseisin, notwithstanding an exception [of villeinage] because such an exception is available to no one, not even to the lord. And therefore, since the exception of villeinage had sometimes been put forward against a villein and his free wife, demanding common of pasture by an assize as appurtenant to their freehold, it was held in the end that common of pasture was to be united to the freehold as an accessory to the principal property, and thus there is done by the office of judge what should have been done by right of action. When therefore such an exception is put forward against the persons of the plaintiffs, it ought to be seen whether it is available to the tenant or not and, if it is available, it is necessary for the tenant to prove it just as a plaintiff must prove [the grounds of his] action.

Bracton,
f. 225
   For the writ also includes the words 'if so-and-so unlawfully disseised'. Now a man can be in seisin, even though he does not immediately exercise his right, and in the name of another as well as in his own name: in the name of another, like a clerk in the name of his church who, when he is instituted and finds his church in seisin which never was disseised, is immediately seised without having as yet exercised his right. Nevertheless, if a man should be disseised and an assize arraigned and an objection should be raised by excepting that he could not be disseised because he never was in seisin, then it must be seen for what cause he says that a right of common is appurtenant to his freehold: for example, if it is by cause of gift, then he is at once in quasi-seisin through the mutual intention of the contracting parties and by the desire to possess and the view, and this suffices for livery, even though he does not immediately exercise his right. And he is deemed always to exercise a right of common by intention and will, by presence and the view, [possessing] civilly and naturally, until he loses it by non-user. If, however, he demands right of common as appurtenant to his freehold by cause of succession, then it must be seen whether or not his ancestor died seised thereof: for example, if he was disseised thereof before his death; and then it is a question when. But if he died seised thereof, then the heir begins forthwith to have the same seisin as his ancestor had since he is seised of the inheritance, which is as it were the principal and corporeal thing, and consequently of the accessory such as a right of grazing, which is incorporeal and which is acquired solely by the intent and wish to possess. And although he

[1] See p. 72.

possidendi. Et licet statim vere non vtatur per inmissionem pecorum vtitur
tamen vel quasi et si postea prohibeatur ei inmittere conpetit assisa noue disseysine. Ad alium tamen transferri non potest communa per se ante verum vsum
nisi hoc forte sit cum corpore ad quod pertinuerit set non cum tenemento in quo
5 communa fuerit licet tamen cum seruitute illa. Et si forte post mortem antecessoris vti voluerit quamuis prohibitus fuerit vel inpeditus dum tamen recenter
ante mortem adhuc retinet seysinam ciuiliter licet seysinam pacificam non
habuerit et si habuerit set cum difficultate nichilominus tamen per vsum talem
retinet sibi seysinam donec omnino prohibitus fuerit quod vti non possit et tunc
10 primo ad superiorem erit recurrendum pro breui de ingressu super disseysinam
non tamen quo ad penam disseysine set quo ad restitucionem.

    Continetur eciam in breui 'de communa pasture sue pertinente ad liberum
tenementum' et ex hoc datur tenenti excepcio quod dicere poterit quod tenementum in quo communa petitur et tenementum ad quod dicitur pertinere sunt
15 de diuersis baroniis et diuersis feodis et feodum in quo communa petitur liberum
est et alteri feodo nullam debet seruitutem nec vnquam habuit talis ibi communam nec ius pascendi ex aliqua constitucione vel aliquo vsu nec pro seruicio
nec pro vicinitate. Et si vnquam habuerit seysinam vel vsum tamen nullam
habuit pacificam set contenciosam et per vadiorum capcionem cum emendacione
20 dampni et tunc doceat querens contrarium si possit. Item dicere poterit quod si
aliquam seysinam inde habuit illam habuit per vim clam vel precario et quod
tenementum ad quod communa dicitur pertinere suum liberum tenementum est   [261]
et non querentis et nisi querens doceat contrarium cadit assisa. Item excipere
poterit tenens quod querens nullam communam poterit clamare quia tenementum
25 illud est suum separale et illud includere potest et excolere pro voluntate sua et
omni tempore habere inclusum, ad quod doceat querens contrarium si possit per
assisam vel diuersum scilicet quod nullo modo includi poterit vel quod non nisi
certis horis et temporibus. Item respondere poterit tenens et dicere quod iste
qui queritur nullum omnino liberum habet tenementum vel quasi ad quod
30 aliqua communa possit pertinere nec mansiunculam, vel dicere poterit quod nulla
communa pertinet ad tale tenementum quia illud olim fuit foresta boscus et locus
vaste solitudinis et communa et iam efficitur assartum et redactum est in culturam et communa non potest pertinere ad communam presertim vbi omnes de
patria communicare solebant. Et idem dici poterit de mariscis et aliis vastitati-
35 bus in culturam redactis. Item dicere poterit contra assisam quod principalis   f. 99
disseysitor mortuus fuit ante impetracionem breuis vel ante capcionam assise,
vel dicere poterit tenens quod alias peciit tenementum cum pertinenciis et
optinuit per iudicium et illa communa ad illud tenementum pertinuit quam ideo
amisit. Item dici poterit si tenementum petatur quod ille qui modo petit tene-
40 mentum in dominico alias inde peciit communam et illam amisit per iudicium

    4. *posterius* cum, Br., tamen, J.   16. nullam, Br., villani, J.   16-17. communam, Br.,
ecclesiam, J.   33. et *om* J.

does not, in fact, exercise the right forthwith by turning beasts in, nevertheless he does as it were exercise it and, if he is subsequently forbidden to turn his beasts in, an assize of novel disseisin is available to him. A right of common as such cannot, however, be transferred to another before actual user except with the corporeal thing to which it is appurtenant, but not with the tenement in which the right of common lies, though with that servitude. And if perchance after the death of his ancestor he wishes to exercise the right, although he is prevented or hindered (provided that immediately before that death he still retains seisin civilly), though he does not have peaceful seisin or, if he has seisin, he has it with difficulty, yet nevertheless by such user he retains seisin for himself until he is completely prevented from being able to exercise the right, and then for the first time there will be recourse to the superior for a writ of entry on the disseisin, not however with regard to a penalty for disseisin but with regard to restitution.

Bracton
f. 225b
There is also included in the writ, 'of his common of pasture appurtenant to the freehold': and in consequence an exception is given to the tenant by which he can say that the tenement in which right of common is demanded and the tenement to which it is said to be appurtenant belong to different baronies and different fees, and the fee in which right of common is demanded is free and owes no servitude to the other fee, nor did so-and-so ever have common there or right of pasture by any agreement or any user, or by reason of service or of vicinage, and if ever he had seisin or user, he did not, however, have it peacefully but subject to dispute and by the taking of gages with amends for damage. And then the plaintiff should show the opposite if he can. Again, the tenant can say that, if the plaintiff had any seisin therein, he had it by force, by stealth or at will, and that the tenement to which the right of common is said to be appurtenant is his freehold and does not belong to the plaintiff, and unless the plaintiff shows the contrary the assize abates. Again, the tenant can except that the plaintiff can claim no right of common because the said tenement is his severalty and he can enclose it and cultivate it at will and have it enclosed at all times. To which it is for the plaintiff to show, if he can, the opposite by the assize or that it is otherwise: for example, that it can in no wise be enclosed or only at specified hours and seasons. Again, the tenant can answer and say that he who complains has no freehold at all or quasi-freehold, not even a hut, to which any right of common can be appurtenant. Or he can say that no right of common is appurtenant to such-and-such a tenement because it was formerly a forest, wood and uninhabited waste and common and it has now become an assart and been brought under cultivation, and a right of common cannot be appurtenant to common, particularly where all the countryside were wont to common. And the same can be said of marshes and other waste places brought under cultivation. Again, the tenant can say against the assize that the principal disseisor was dead before the writ was sued out or before the assize was taken, or he can say that on another occasion he demanded the tenement with appurtenances and obtained it by judgement of the court, and the right of common was appurtenant to that tenement and the plaintiff has therefore lost it. Again, if the tenement is demanded, he can say that he who is now claiming the tenement in demesne claimed on another occasion a

Bracton,
f. 226

et ex quo peciit communam et nemini seruit fundus proprius per hoc concessit
tacite quod nullum ius habuit petendi tenementum in dominico et talis excepcio
oritur ex presumpcione.   Et hoc quidem dici poterit siue tenementum querentis
solum sit proprium vel cum aliis commune ita quod nullus sciat suum separale.
5 Item dicere poterit contra assisam et contra breue quod die quo breue fuit inpetratum fuit querens in pacifica possessione et postea ita quod quando inpetrauit nulla subfuit causa inpetrandi et sic inpetracio nulla, et si disseysitus
fuit quando inpetrauit non habet causam querendi quia post inpetracionem sine
iudicio et iudice seysinam suam vsurpauit et quia sic iniuste et sine iudicio
10 dicere potest quod ipse iam inpetrauit breue super eum de noua disseysina de
libero tenemento vel dicere potest quod querens amisit querelam per vsurpacionem sine iudicio per iudicium subsequens de libero tenemento quia sibi vsurpauit
quod exposcere debuit per iudicium vt cum quis primo impetrauit et postea seysinam gratis oblatam receperit quam quidem sibi vsurpauerit secus esset quia
15 tunc posset querens teneri disseysito ex reconuencione vt id quod voluerit
habere pro se habeat contra se vt si vsurpator agat per assisam ad retinendum
quod vsurpauit spoliatus recuperabit per reconuencionem spoliati quia sine iudicio licet iuste seysinam sibi vsurpauit.   Nichilominus tamen si petat per assisam
id quod tenet capienda erit assisa et ille qui sic vsurpauit in misericordia pro vsur-
20 pacione remanebit restitucionem tamen non faciet per iudicium nisi ille qui ita
sine iudicio ita disseysitus est licet iuste sibi perquirere velit per assisam noue
disseysine versus vsurpantem vel agere de reconuencione.   Si quis igitur assisam
portauerit noue disseysine dum fuerit firmarius cum non conpetit ei assisa cum
teneat nomine alieno si postmodum incipiat habere in feodo et fiat dominus vbi
25 prius firmarius quero an breue inpetratum ei prodesse debeat et videtur quod non
quia tempore inpetracionis non habuit ius inpetrandi set alius et ideo spec-   [262]
tandum est tempus date.

CAP. XXIII.   DE ADMENSURACIONE PASTURE

Cum quis autem ius habeat pascendi in alieno fundo aliquando plura inmittit
30 aueria quam liceat et aliquando plura quam expediat.   Si autem plura quam

---

3. *post* tenementum *add.* et, J.   17-18. quia sine iudicio, Br., *om.* J.   19-20. pro
vsurpacione] per vsurpacionem, J.   21. iuste sibi] sibi iniuste, J.   23. dum]
cum, J.   26. Nota, J. *in margine.*

right of common therein and he lost it by judgement of the court, and since he claimed a right of common and no one has a servitude in his own land, he has, in consequence, tacitly conceded that he had no right to claim the tenement in demesne, and such an exception arises out of a presumption. And this can, indeed, be said whether the tenement is solely the plaintiff's property or held in common with others so that no one knows which is his severalty. Again, the tenant can speak against the assize and against the writ and say that, on the day when the writ was sued out and subsequently, the plaintiff was in peaceful seisin so that, when it was sued out, no cause for suing out a writ subsisted and so the suing out was null and void; that, if he was disseised at the time he sued out the writ, the plaintiff has no cause for complaint because, after he sued it out, he usurped his seisin without judgement and judge, and because he acted thus unlawfully and without judgement of the court the tenant can say that he himself has already sued out a writ against the plaintiff for novel disseisin of his freehold; or he can say that the plaintiff lost his suit on account of usurpation without judgement through a subsequent judgement regarding the freehold, because he usurped for himself what he ought to have asked for by judgement: for example, when a man first sues out a writ and afterwards receives seisin freely offered, which would be otherwise if he had usurped it, because the plaintiff would then be liable to the disseisee on a cross-claim so that what he wished to have in his favour he has to his disfavour: for example, if the usurper brings an action by an assize to retain what he has usurped, the disseisee will recover by the disseisee's cross-claim because though with justification it was without judgement of a court that he usurped seisin for himself. Nevertheless, if [a plaintiff] claims by an assize what he holds, the assize must be taken, and he who has thus usurped will remain amerciable for the usurpation, but he will not make restitution by judgement of the court unless he who has been thus disseised without judgement of the court, although justifiably, wishes to sue by an assize of novel disseisin against the usurper or proceed by cross-claim. If therefore a man, while he is fermor, should bring an assize of novel disseisin though an assize is not available to him because he holds in the name of another, if afterwards he begins to possess in fee and becomes the owner where formerly he was the fermor, it is a question whether the writ sued out should advantage him, and it seems that it will not because at the time when he acquired the writ he had no right to sue it out, but someone else had the right, and therefore regard must be had to the time in the dating clause.

Bracton,
f. 226b

CHAPTER 23. OF ADMEASUREMENT OF PASTURE

Bracton,
f. 229

When a man has a right of grazing in the land of another he sometimes turns more beasts in than is lawful and sometimes more than is advisable. If, however,

liceat vt cum concedatur ei communa ad certum numerum aueriorum vel ad
certum genus vel quantum pertinet ad tantum tenementum in eadem villa si plura
inmittat in numero vel in genere quam ei liceat contra voluntatem eius cuius
fundus fuerit si talis incontinenti resistere non possit competit ei remedium per
5 assisam pro illa parte pro qua ille qui communam habet debitum numerum
vel genus excedit eo quod in hoc contractat tenementum domini contra voluntatem suam ac sicut esse posset si omnino nullam communam haberet et aueria
sua contra voluntatem domini per violenciam inmittere vellet.   Competit eciam
ei aliud remedium vt per aliud breue id quod debitum numerum vel genus excedit
10 redigatur ad licitum numerum et ad debitam mensuram.   Admensuracio vero
nichil aliud est quam redaccio ad mensuram.   Illis autem qui communam tantum habent in fundo alicuius aliud remedium non competit nisi admensuracio.
Si autem plura quam expedit locum habet admensuracio vt si alicui concedatur
talis communa ad omnimoda aueria sua sine numero et aliis similiter successiue
15 vel ad certum numerum vel sine numero si quis tot inmiserit quot pastura omnibus non sufficiat competit ei remedium quod id quod excedit et nocet ad debitum
numerum redigatur.   De hoc autem quod dicit in breui plura scire debet numerum quot habere debet vtrum ad certum numerum vel secundum terre sue
quantitatem, et per hoc quod dicit secundum liberum tenementum quod habet
20 in predicta villa si tenens possit docere quod plura habere debeat bene licebit.
Officium vero vicecomitis in hac parte est accepto breui in propria persona
accedere ad locum in quo petitur communa et ibi conuenire faciat hundredum
et omnes quos admensuracio illa tangit et in presencia vtriusque partis si sum-
monite interesse velint et que raciones suas et responsiones pretendant per sacra-
25 mentum vicinorum per quos rei veritas melius sciri poterit et per inspeccionem
cartarum et instrumentorum diligenter inquirat quot pecora ille de quo queritur
habere debet per constitucionem seruitutis vel ex causa donacionis vel racione
tenementi sui vel ex vicinitate vel per longum vsum.   Et si sine numero et vbique
tunc inquirat ad quot aueria sufficiat pastura illa et quot sustinere possit se-
30 cundum tempus feoffamenti et secundum tempus constitucionis seruitutis vt si
communa sufficiens fuit omnibus qui ibi communicare debent et si postmodum
effecta sit insufficiens omnibus qui ibi communicare deberent per superoneracionem vel per nouum feoffamentum et per quod alii qui communicare deberent   f. 99b
racione primi feoffamenti suam amittant communam in parte vel in toto, et sic
35 omnibus examinatis procedat admensuracio et quod superfluum fuerit redigatur
ad mensuram.
Est enim modus et mensura et fines certi vltra que et citra que nequit consis-

10. numerum *om.* J.   14. aliis] alius, J.   15. numero *om.* J.   16. et, *om.* J.
23. *prius* et] vt, J.   24. que] quas, J.   27. habere] breue, J.   28. *prius* vel *et posterius*
vel *om.* J.

he turns in more than is lawful: for example, when common is granted to him for a specified number of beasts or for a specified kind or for as much as is appurtenant to such-and-such a size of tenement in the said township, if he turns in more in number or in kind than is permitted him against the will of the owner of the land and if the latter is not able to resist at once, a remedy is available to him by an assize for that surplus by which he who has a right of common exceeds the proper number or kind, because in this way he diminishes the owner's tenement against his will just as it would be if he had no right of common at all and wished to turn his beasts in by force against the owner's will. There is also another remedy available to him so that by another writ what is in excess of the proper number or kind is reduced to the permitted number and the proper measure. Admeasurement (*admensuratio*), indeed, is nothing else than reduction to measure (*ad mensuram*). To those, moreover, who have nothing but a right of common in another's land, no other remedy is available except admeasurement. If more beasts are turned in than is advisable, admeasurement is appropriate: for example, if such-and-such a right of common is granted to someone for his beasts of all kinds without limitation in numbers, and likewise to others in succession whether for a specified number or without limitation in numbers, should anyone turn so many [beasts] in that the pasture will not suffice for them all, a remedy is available to [the first] so that what is excessive and harmful will be reduced to a proper number. Inasmuch as the plaintiff says in the writ 'many' (*plura*), he ought to know how many he should have, whether up to a specified number or according to the extent of his land, and inasmuch as he says 'according to the freehold which he has in the aforesaid township', if the tenant can show that he ought to have more beasts, this will be readily allowed.

The duty of the sheriff in this matter, when the writ has been received, is to proceed in his own person to the place in which the right of common is claimed and there arrange for the hundred to assemble as well as all those affected by the admeasurement, and in the presence of both parties, if after summons they wish to be present and put forward their arguments and answers, he is diligently to enquire by the oath of neighbours by whom the truth of the matter can best be known and by the inspection of charters and instruments how many beasts he of whom complaint is made ought to have by the constitution of the servitude or by the cause of gift or by reason of his tenement or on account of vicinage or by long user. And if he may turn beasts in without restriction in number and everywhere, then the sheriff is to enquire for how many beasts the pasture is sufficient and how many it can sustain according to the time of the feoffment and of the time of the constitution of the servitude: for example, if the common was sufficient for all who ought to have common there, and if afterwards it was rendered insufficient for all who ought to have common there by surcharging or by a new feoffment whereby the others who ought to have common there by reason of the first feoffment lose their common in part or in whole. And thus when everything has been examined the admeasurement is to proceed and what is in excess is to be reduced to its proper measure.

There is indeed a mode and a measure and specific limits, beyond and below

Bracton,
f. 229*b*

tere rectum.   Et notandum quod communicantibus contra dominum tenementi
duo conpetunt remedia de superoneracione vel admensuracio vel assisa noue   [263]
disseisine de communa pasture si communa per superoneracionem amittatur in
toto vel in parte.   Eodem modo sicut domino conpetit contra eos de superone-
5 racione contra voluntatem suam et eodem modo plures communicantes eadem
habent remedia inter se si quis eorum superonerauerit.   Plures eciam heredes et
participes qui aliquam partem tenementi sui reliquerint ad pasturam in communi et vnus vel quidam superonerauerit quod locum habeat admensuracio vel
assisa noue disseysine non tamen de communa pasture set de libero tenemento
10 ac si vnus sine aliis aliquid sibi vellet appropriare.   Et si sit quis qui pasturam
velit superonerare aliter quam liceat vel expediat vel aliter quam pater vel alius
antecessor fecerit fiat admensuracio per breue.   Et sedita contencione sic
superoneracionis si iterum contingat aliquem ipsam superonerare tunc fiat secundum processum huius constitucionis:

15   Cum placitum fuerit motum per breue de admensuracione pasture et pastura
fuerit admensurata aliquando coram iusticiariis et aliquando in comitatu multociens contingat quod post huiusmodi admensuracionem factam iterum ponat ille
qui superonerauit pasturam plura aueria quam ad ipsum pertineret habendi,
statutum est quod de secunda superoneracione fiat remedium querenti sub hac
20 forma quod querens habeat breue de iudicio de superoneracione secunda si coram
iusticiariis admensuracio fuerit pasture quod vicecomes in presencia parcium
premunitarum si interesse voluerint inquirat de superoneracione que si inuenta
fuerit mandetur iusticiariis sub sigillo vicecomitis et sigillis iuratorum.   Et
iusticiarii adiudicent querenti dampna sua et ponant in extractis valorem ani-
25 malium que superonerans post admensuracionem factam posuit in pasturam
vltra numerum quem debuit et extractas liberent baronibus de scaccario de
quibus oneretur vicecomes in extractis de scaccario.   Si autem in comitatu facta
fuerit admensuracio tunc ad instanciam querentis exeat breue de cancellaria
vicecomiti quod inquirat super huiusmodi superoneracione et de aueriis positis
30 in pastura vltra debitum numerum vel de precio et vicecomes de precio illo
respondeat regi ad scaccarium suum.

CAP. XXIV.   QUO IURE

Non semper autem debetur seruitus prediis vicinorum ex consensu et constitucione dominorum vt si quis habeat communam pasture et ius pascendi in fun-

1. communicantibus] comunicantibus, J.   4. de] et, J.   7. reliquerint] reliquerit, J.
10. sine aliis] siue alius, J.   16. in comitatu *in statuto, om.* J.   21. vicecomes] tunc, J.
23. sigillis *in statuto, om.* J.   29. superoneracione] oneracione, J.

which right cannot exist.　And it is to be noted that two remedies are available to commoners against the owner of a tenement for surcharging: either admeasurement or an assize of novel disseisin of common of pasture if by surcharging common is lost in whole or in part.　And similarly, just as a remedy is available to the owner against the commoners for surcharging against his will, likewise several commoners have the same remedies as between themselves if any one of them surcharges.　Where also there are several heirs and parceners who leave some part of their tenement for pasture in common and one or some of them surcharge, admeasurement or an assize of novel disseisin is appropriate, not, however, in respect of the common of pasture but of the freehold, as if one should wish to appropriate something for oneself without the others.　And if there is anyone who means to surcharge the pasture otherwise than is permitted or is advisable or otherwise than his father or other ancestor has done, an admeasurement is to be made by writ.　And when the dispute regarding surcharge has thus been settled, if it again should happen that any one surcharges the same common, then let the procedure be according to this enactment:

St. Westminster, II. c. 8　　When a plea has been moved by a writ of admeasurement of pasture and the pasture has been admeasured, sometimes before the justices and sometimes in the county court, it often happens that, after such admeasurement has been made, he who first surcharged the pasture again turns more beasts in than he ought to have, it is ordained that upon the second surcharge redress is to be given to the plaintiff in this manner: if the pasture was admeasured before the justices the plaintiff is to have a judicial writ with regard to the second surcharge to the effect that the sheriff, in the presence of the parties after summons if they wish to be present, is to enquire about the surcharge and, if it is found to exist, the justices are to be informed under the seal of the sheriff and the seals of the jurors.　And the justices shall adjudge his damages to the plaintiff and place in the estreats the value of the beasts which the man who surcharges turned on the pasture beyond the number which he ought to put there after the admeasurement was made, and they shall deliver to the barons of the exchequer the estreats with which the sheriff will be charged in the estreats of the exchequer.　If, however, the admeasurement has been made in the county court, then, at the instance of the plaintiff, a writ is to issue out of the chancery to the sheriff that he shall enquire about such surcharge and about the beasts turned on the pasture beyond the proper number and about their value, and the sheriff shall answer for the said value to the king at his exchequer.

CHAPTER 24.　OF THE PLEA: BY WHAT RIGHT

Bracton, f. 229b　　A servitude, however, is not always due from the lands of neighbours by consent and agreement of the owners: as where a man has common of pasture

do alieno set ex negligencia et dissimulacione vicini per vsum tantum et talis
seysina magis habet substanciam ex tempore quam ex iure.   Et ideo absurdum
erit omnino quod cum tali remaneat possessio cum semel per assisam fuerit
adquisita nisi doceat de iure suo.   Set prius videndum est cui conpetat accio.
5 Non enim poterit quis alium inplacitare per hoc breue quo iure nisi sit capitalis
dominus tocius manerii vel ville in qua petitur communa vel saltem alicuius
partis et quod sint de diuersis baroniis vel diuersis feodis vel diuersis feoffamentis
ita quod dominus qui petit et ille versus quem petitur iura sua habeant separata
sicut tenementa diuersa et pasturas diuersas secundum quod pastura large se
10 habeat vel stricte.   Si autem plures feoffati fuerint ab vno domino in vno   [264]
manerio vel in vna villa non conpetit eis tale breue vel talis accio cum inter
vicinos recte loquendo de eadem baronia et eodem feodo pocius debet dici vicinitas quam communa debita secundum quod dicitur si vnus communicet cum vicino
et vicinus cum eo et aliter non.   Cum igitur quis per iudicium seysinam suam
15 recuperauerit propter vsum amittere debet illam nisi doceat quo iure illam
exigat.   Et poterit vnus dominus capitalis vel plures placitare versus vnum dominum capitalem vel versus plures siue tenementa habeant in diuersis villis siue in
vna villa dum tamen ibi sunt diuerse baronie vel diuersa feoda.

Ad summonicionem vero huiusmodi breuis potest summonitus essoniari pri-
20 mo die et eodem modo querens si voluerit.   Si autem summonitus non venerit
nec se essoniauerit attachietur sicut in personali accione quia hic non petitur
pastura sicut per breue de recto.   Cum autem post omnes districciones semel
comparuerit, tunc statim inquiratur si inplacitatus communam petat et clamet
et si respondeat quod sic tunc inquiratur qualem et ipsa specificata procedatur
25 sicut per breue de recto, et si ex tunc defaltam fecerit capiatur pastura in
manum regis per paruum cape donec comparuerit et sic amittere poterit de facili
et hoc ita si nulla precessit assisa noue disseysine set si precesserit recenter tunc
per assisam videri poterit que et qualis fuerit communa que petitur.   Inquiratur
eciam si tale seruicium fecerit et tale et si talis a tali tempore cuius non existat
30 memoria semper communam habuerit et si taliter feoffatus fuerit vt dicit cum
communa pasture vel si illam emit et huiusmodi et secundum quod probatum
fuerit per patriam retinebitur communa vel amittetur.   Si autem venerit tunc
docere poterit quo iure communam petit vt si ipse simul communicauerit cum
aliis de communi consensu ab antiquo vel quod facit ei certum seruicium tale vel   f. 100
35 tale.   Seruicium enim multiplex est vt in denariis, mensuris, falcacionibus,
aruris, operibus, consuetudinibus et prestacionibus variis dum tamen certis et
determinatis temporibus et terminis non tamen ad voluntatem accipientis inde-
terminate, aliquando plus et aliquando minus, quod si ita esset pocius precium

15. *post* illam *add.* pro quo iure, J.   22–23. semel comparuerit] simul operuerint, J.
29. fecerit] fecerint, J.   32. venerit] venerint, J.   35. in] si, J; mensuris, Br., messuris, J.

and right of grazing in another's land by the negligence and indifference of a neighbour through user only. Such seisin has substance rather through [the passage of] time than of right. And therefore it will be altogether absurd that possession should remain with such a one when once it has been acquired through an assize, if he does not show what his right is. But first it must be seen to whom an action is available. For a man cannot implead another by this writ of *quo jure* unless he is the chief lord of the whole manor or township in which common is claimed or at least of some part of it and unless they belong to different baronies or different fees or different feoffments so that the lord who claims and he against whom he claims have their rights in severalty, such as different tenements and different pastures, depending on whether the pasture is had at large or restricted. If, however, there should be several enfeoffed by one lord in one manor or in one township, such a writ or such an action is not available to them since, strictly speaking, between neighbours of the same barony and the same fee one ought to speak of vicinage as due rather than common, just as one speaks when a man commons with his neighbour and the neighbour commons with him: and not otherwise. When therefore a man recovers his seisin by judgement of the court by reason of user, he ought to lose it unless he shows by what right he claims it. And one chief lord or several can implead one chief lord or several, whether they have tenements in different townships or in one township, provided there are different baronies or different fees involved.

Bracton,
f. 230

When a man is summoned by such a writ he can be essoined on the first day, and so can the plaintiff if he wishes. If, however, he who is summoned neither appears nor essoins himself, he shall be attached as in a personal action because pasture is not claimed here as by a writ of right. When, however, after all distraints he once appears, then enquiry will forthwith be made whether he who is impleaded is demanding and claiming a right of common, and if he replies that he is, then enquiry will be made about what kind and, when this has been specified, the action will proceed as if by a writ of right, and if thereafter he makes default, the pasture is to be taken into the king's hand by the little *cape* until he appears, and thus he can easily lose the right. So it is if no assize of novel disseisin has previously been held, but if an assize has been recently held, then it can be seen from the assize what common he claimed and of what kind. Enquiry will also be made whether he rendered this or that service and whether so-and-so always had a right of common from time immemorial and whether he was so enfeoffed, as he says, with common of pasture or if he purchased it, and so on, and according to what is proved by the jury the right of common will be retained or lost. If, however, he appears, then he can show by what right he claims right of common: for example, if he has commoned together with others by common consent from times of old, or because he renders for it a specific service such as this or that. Service, indeed, takes many forms, such as money, mowing, reaping, ploughing, works, customs and various renders, provided they are rendered at specific and fixed times and terms, not indeterminately at the will of the recipient, sometimes more and sometimes less, and, if it was that, it should be

pro herbagio diceretur quam communa.   Si autem cum ius non habeat pascendi
herbam pauerit per escapium vel cum warda facta et propterea denarios dederit
vel seruicium fecerit hoc pocius erit emenda pro transgressione quam seruicium
pro communa.   Si autem vicinitas vel seruicium non interuenerit docere
5 oportet interuenisse donacionem et titulum vel longum tempus et longum
vsum qui memoriam hominum excedat.   Tale enim tempus sufficit pro iure non
quia ius deficit set quia accio deficit vel probacio.   Et sufficit pro iure si ille de
quo queritur docere possit quod aliquando simul communicauerint licet nunc
non communicent vt si querens per neglicenciam suam vel suorum communam
10 suam amiserit vt si vicinus partem suam excoluerit et appropriauerit hoc vicinus
sibi et negligencie sue poterit imputare.   Et cum querens ad obiecta re-
sponderit contrarium vel diuersum hoc per patriam in modum inquisicionis
declarabitur scilicet per verba hec: si talis querens et homines sui de tali villa et   [265]
ille de quo queritur et homines sui de alia villa semper simul communicare solent
15 in tali loco et tali.   Si autem tenementa talium sint de eadem baronia et de eodem
feodo et in vna villa non poterit quis communam dedicere inter vicinos propter
vicinitatem nisi hoc fecerit aliquid speciale.   Et si recognitum sit in iudicio ab eo
qui communam clamat quod tenens terram in qua communa petitur illam includere possit et arare et in ea edificare vel aliud facere pro voluntate sua cadit
20 breue quo iure.   Tenens autem inplicatus ponere se poterit in magnam assisam
ad recognoscendum vtrum ipse maius ius habeat tenendi terram siue tenementum
sine communam quam idem petens ibi habere vel clamare possit quam ille qui
petit habendi communam pasture in eadem sicut illam petit vel e conuerso.

In hoc autem breui duo sunt verba que non tangunt ipsum ius hominem tamen
25 ab accione repellunt desicut ipse non communicat in terris ipsius nec seruicium sibi
fecit per quod communicare debeat in terris suis.   Poterit eciam peti iudicium
contra querentem et desicut ille capit redditum pro communa de eisdem de-
forciantibus si communam habere debeat.   Item docere poterit qualiter tenementum sit separale tenentis quare communam habere non debet.   Item potest
30 dici quod omnes qui communam habent in pastura illa non sunt in breui nominati
nec ille sine parcennariis debet respondere.   Item sicut inplacitatus ponere se
poterit in magnam assisam ita proferre poterit in hoc breui duellum.   Item
desicut ille petens est peti poterit iudicium si ponere se possit in magnam assisam.
Item defendere debet seysinam sui antecessoris vel monstrare per quam racionem
35 clamant communam habere.

Et sciendum quod si quis de communa pasture sue disseysitus fuerit et perquisierit per breue de noua disseisine, et ille disseisitor incontinenti sibi perquisiuerit sibi per breue de quo iure, semper precedet assisa noue disseysine sicut
in aliis placitis et secundum quod seysina querenti remanserit vel non procedet.
40 Et eodem modo fieri poterit vt predictum est de omni genere commune que in

1. herbagio] homagio, J; cum om. J.   2 escapium] escambium, J.   4. docere] dicere non, J.
6–7. non quia . . . pro iure, J. in margine.   9. communicent] communicet, J.   10. post suam
add amiserit vel, J, om. Br.   13. si om. J.   22. sine] siue, J.; posterius quam] quia, J.
31. debet] debent, J.   37–38. de noua . . . breue de, Br., om. J.; procedet] procedat, J.

called a payment for herbage rather than common. But if, when he has no
right of grazing he has grazed the grass with his straying beasts or made fine
for watch duty, and for that has given money or rendered service, this is amends
for a trespass rather than service for a right of common. If, however, vicinage
or service do not arise, then it is necessary to show that a gift and a title have
intervened or a long passage of time and long user stretching beyond the memory
of man. For such a passage of time suffices for right, not because right is
Bracton,
f. 230b
wanting but because an action or a proof fails. And it suffices for a right if he
of whom complaint is made can show that at one time they commoned together
although now they do not: for example, if the plaintiff by his own negligence or
that of his men loses his right of common, when a neighbour cultivates his
portion and encloses it, he should blame this on himself and his negligence.
And when the plaintiff has replied to objections by asserting the opposite or that
the facts are otherwise, this will be made known by the country in the manner of
an inquisition, for instance, in these words: if so-and-so, the plaintiff, and his
men of such-and-such a township and he of whom complaint is made and his
men of another township were wont always to common together in this place or
that. If, however, the tenements of these men are of the same barony and of the
same fee and in one township, no one can deny a right of common between
neighbours by reason of vicinage unless some special [deed] denies it. And,
if it is admitted in court by him who claims a right of common that the tenant of
the land in which common is claimed can enclose it and plough it and build on it
or do anything else he wishes, the writ of *quo jure* abates. However, the tenant
who is impleaded can put himself on the grand assize to make recognition
whether he has a greater right to hold the land or tenement, without any common
which the said demandant may have or claim to have there, than he who claims to
have common of pasture therein as he claims it, or conversely.

In this writ there are two words which do not touch the right itself, yet they
exclude a man from an action: inasmuch as he does not common in his lands nor
render him service for which he should have a right of common in his lands.
Judgement can also be sought against the plaintiff: inasmuch as he takes rent for
common from the said deforciants, whether he should have common. Again,
the tenant can show how the tenement is his severalty, for which reason the
plaintiff ought not to have a right of common. Again, it can be said that all
who have a right of common in the said pasture are not named in the writ, nor
ought he [who is named] to answer without his parceners. Again, just as he who
is impleaded can put himself on the grand assize, so can the tenant offer battle
in this writ, and again, inasmuch as he is the demandant, he can pray judgement
if he may put himself on the grand assize. Again, he ought to deny the seisin of
his ancestor or show the reason for their claim to right of common.

And be it known that, if a man is disseised of his common of pasture and sues
out a writ of novel disseisin, and the disseisor immediately aids himself with a
writ of *quo jure*, the assize of novel disseisin will always proceed first as in other
pleas, and according to whether seisin rests with the plaintiff or not, [the *quo jure*]
will proceed. And it can be done in the same way, as aforesaid, with respect to

alieno haberi potest si hoc esset in vsu quod amittere possit quis possessionem
nisi posset docere de iure. Cum autem recognitum sit vel conuictum per iuratam
vel alio modo quod summonitus nullam communam habere debeat tunc habebit
querens pacem per tale breue:

5   Rex vicecomiti salutem. Scias quod cum A. summonitus esset in curia
nostra ad respondendum B. quo iure ipse communam clamauit in terra ipsius B.
in tali villa desicut idem A. nullam communam habuit in terra ipsius B. in eadem
villa vel in alia nec idem A. ei seruicium fecit quare communam habere debuit,
idem A. venit in eadem curia nostra et auditis hinc inde interrogacionibus et
10   responsis tandem consideratum est quod predictus A. nullam communam
habere poterit vel exigere in terra ipsius B. et ideo tibi precipimus quod eidem
B. terram suam in predicta villa de N. in pace habere facias ita quod predictus
A. nullam communam sine voluntate ipsius B. habeat ibidem.

CAP. XXV. DE RACIONABILI ESTOUERIO

15   Est autem alia communa secundum quod large se habet vna cum alio non
tamen ad pastum set ad aliam commoditatem vt si quis habere debeat in fundo   [266]
alieno ius secandi vel falcandi in foresta vel in alicuius bosco vel aliis vastatibus
ad racionabile estouerium suum edificandi, ardendi siue claudendi et alia quedam
faciendi que necessaria sunt secundum constitucionem seruitutis in plus vel
20   minus in qua quidem constitucione oportet modum attendere vt estouerium sit
racionabile secundum quantitatem bosci vel vasti in quo fuerit seruitus constituta secundum quod fuerit ampla vel parua eciam et quantitas tenementi ad
quod debetur illa seruitus et sic oportet omnia ponderare quod non excedat
modum nec minuatur set quod omnia permaneant in mensura. Et si aliquis ip-
25   sorum modum excedere velit vel minuere ille scilicet ad quem seruitus pertinet
plus capiendo quam racio permittat vel quam liceat et sic vastum faciat et f. 100b
destruccionem dominus ille cuius fundus fuerit procuret admensuracionem vel
agat de transgressione vel de disseysina, et eodem modo ille cui seruitus debetur
si per dominum fundi minuatur agat per breue ad hoc quod liceat ei vti plene vel
30   saltem comode. Si autem turbaria vel brueria herbagium pascua boscus vel
vastitas communis sit inter participes vel coheredes et aliquis eorum in estouerio
capiendo modum excedat et vastum faciat vel destruccionem tunc non erit locus
admensuracioni nec noue disseysine set quod partes conpellantur ad diuisionem
per communi diuidendo iudicium. Et eodem modo fiat de iure fodiendi,
35   falcandi et de aliis quibuscumque seruitutibus secundum quod statutum est.

2–3. vel . . . communam, Br., *om.* J.   4. per] vel, J.   17. vastatibus] vastitatibus, J.
20. attendere] pretendere, J.   26. sic] si, J.   27. admensuracionem] mensuracionem, J.
34. per, Br., pro, J.

every kind of common that can be had in the soil of another: if it has been enjoyed, a man may lose possession unless he can show his right. When, however, it is made known or found by a jury or in some other way that the one who has been summoned ought not to have common, then will the plaintiff have peace by a writ as follows:

The king to the sheriff, greeting. Know ye that, whereas A. was summoned to our court to answer B. by what right he claimed a right of common in the land of the said B. in such and such a township, inasmuch as the said [B] had no right of common in the said [A's] land in the said township or in any other, nor did the said A. do him service for which he ought to have common, the said A. came into our court and, after the questions and answers on one side and the other had been heard, it was at last adjudged that the aforesaid A. could not have or demand common in the land of the said B., and therefore we command you to let the said B. have his land in the aforesaid township of N. in peace so that the aforesaid A. shall have no common there against the will of the said B.

CHAPTER 25. OF REASONABLE ESTOVERS

Bracton,
f. 231
There is another right of common according as the words 'together with another' are taken broadly, to mean not only for pasture but for some other advantage: for example, if a man should have in another's land the right to cut or scythe in a forest or in someone's wood or in other wastes for his reasonable estovers, and to build, burn or fence and do other essential things according to the constitution of the servitude, whether much or little, in which constitution it is necessary to settle the amount so that the estovers may be reasonable in accordance with the extent of the wood or waste in which the servitude has been established, depending on whether it is large or small, and also the extent of the tenement to which the servitude is due. And thus all things must be so weighed that the servitude does not go beyond or fall short of the proper amount but that everything remains in proportion. And if any one of them wishes to exceed or diminish that proportion, that is to say, the man to whom the servitude belongs, in taking more than reason allows or than is permitted, and so causes waste and destruction, the owner of the land may obtain an admeasurement or bring an action of trespass or of disseisin; and likewise he to whom the servitude is due, if the servitude is diminished by the owner of the land, may bring an action by writ to the effect that he may be permitted to exercise his right fully or at least with ease. If, however, turbary, heath, herbage, pasture, wood or waste is common between parceners or coheirs, and any one of them, in taking estovers, exceeds the proper amount and causes waste and destruction, neither admeasurement nor an action of novel disseisin will be appropriate but the parties will be forced to a partition by a judgement for the division of common.
Bracton,
f. 231b
And the same procedure is to be followed in regard to a right of digging, mowing and all other servitudes in accordance with what has been agreed.

CAP. XXVI. DE NOCUMENTIS SERUITUTIBUS INIURIOSIS

Potest eciam quis habere seruitutem sicut ius aque ducende ex fundo alieno et per fundum alienum vsque ad fundum proprium ad irrigandum agrum suum vel aliud comodum inde faciendum et quo casu inpediri non debet quominus du-
5 cere possit omnino vel saltem comode et modo debito secundum constitucionem seruitutis vt si ducere debeat omni tempore et non permittat nisi aliquo tempore vel si certis temporibus non permittat aliquo tempore vel non in debita quantitate vel si non permittat alueum purgare per quod aque ductus inpeditur et tenementa vicinorum submerguntur. In omnibus istis casibus fit disseysina
10 et consulitur disseysitis per breue quare talis diuertit cursum aque ad nocumentum liberi tenementi sui.

Nocumentorum aliud iniuriosum et dampnosum et aliud dampnosum et non iniuriosum et vnde cum fiat querela de nocumento queri oportet ad quod dampnum aliquid fiat et vtrum sit dampnosum et iniuriosum et quo casu omnino
15 erit tollendum. Si autem non iniuriosum licet dampnosum tunc erit sustinendum vt si quis seruitutem habeat et ius pascendi in alieno conpetit ei liber ingressus et egressus. Si autem ille cuius fundus fuerit aliquid faciat in ingressu quominus omnino ingredi possit vel minus comode vt si murum, fossatum vel hayam fecerit, nocumentum facit iniuriosum et quod ita factum est statim flagrante facto
20 tolli poterit et demolliri et sine breui post tempus tamen non nisi cum breui. Et eodem modo fieri debet si cui concedatur ius eundi per fundum alienum si via quocunque modo obstruatur vel coartatur quominus ire possit omnino vel minus comode vel si aque ductus concedatur et diuertatur ad nocumentum in parte vel in toto. Item poterit quis habere communam cum alio et ius fodiendi
25 sicut ius pascendi et ius venandi, piscandi, potandi, hauriendi et alia plura que   [267] infinita sunt faciendi cum earum pertinenciis sicut cum libero accessu et recessu secundum quod ad dictam communam pasture pertinet liber ingressus et conpetens egressus. In omnibus predictis et aliis casibus multis iacet assisa noue disseysine eodem modo sicut de communa pasture et eciam eodem modo quo
30 iure si hoc esset in vsu.

Item si seruitus fundo alieno inponatur a iure licet non ab homine per quod prohibetur ne quis faciat in suo quod nocere possit vicino vt si stagnum exaltauit in suo vel se nouo fecerit per quod noceat vicino si per hoc fundus vicini submergeretur hoc erit ad nocumentum liberi tenementi vicini iniuriosum nisi
35 hoc a vicino permissum sit quod liceat. Et sicut poterit quis habere seruitutem in fundo vicini si constituatur ita eciam poterit per longum vsum sine constitucione ex paciencia dominorum et sciencia quia longa paciencia trahitur ad con-

5–6 constitucionem, Br., consuetudinem, J.   6 vt] et, J.   7. tempore, *om.* J.
14. iniuriosum] iuriosum, J.   15. iniuriosum] iuriosum, J.   19. flagrante *om.* J.
20. demolliri] demolliari, J.   34. submergeretur] submergeratur, J.

CHAPTER 26.   OF NUISANCES PREJUDICIAL TO SERVITUDES

Bracton,
f. 231b

A man may also have a servitude such as the right to lead water from an-other's land and through another's land to his own land to irrigate his field or to profit thereby in some other way, and in this case he ought not to be impeded so that he cannot lead water at all or at least not conveniently and in the usual way according to the constitution of the servitude: for example, if he ought to lead water all the time and [the other] only permits it sometimes; or if at prescribed times and he does not allow it at any time or not in the proper amount; or if he does not allow him to clean out the channel so that the watercourse is obstructed and the tenements of neighbours are submerged.   In all these cases disseisin is committed and those disseised are assisted by the writ 'why does so-and-so divert a watercourse to the nuisance of his freehold'.

Some nuisances are wrongful and hurtful and some hurtful but not wrongful, and hence, when a plaint is made about a nuisance, it is necessary to ask what damage is done and whether it is hurtful and wrongful, in which case it must be entirely removed (if, however, it is not wrongful though hurtful, then it must be borne): for example, if a man should have a servitude and the right of grazing in another's land he is entitled to free entry and exit, but if he to whom the land belongs does anything affecting entry whereby the other cannot enter at all or not with ease—for instance, if he makes a wall, ditch or hedge—he commits a wrongful nuisance and what is so done can be removed and demolished immedi-ately while the facts are fresh and without a writ: but not without a writ, after a lapse of time.   And similar steps should be taken where a man is granted a right of way over another's land if the path should be in any way obstructed or nar-rowed so that he cannot pass at all or not with ease, or if a watercourse is granted and it is diverted to his nuisance in part or in whole.   Again, a man can have a right of common with another and a right of digging as well as a right of grazing and a right of hunting, fishing, watering [his cattle], drawing water, and doing many other things without number, together with their appurtenances such as free access and departure in the way that free entry and suitable exit are appur-tenant to the said common of pasture.   In all the aforesaid cases and many others

Bracton.
f. 232

an assize of novel disseisin lies in the same way as it does for common of pasture, and also and in the same way quo jure if it was being enjoyed.

Again, if a servitude should be imposed upon another's land by law though not by man, whereby it is unlawful for a man to do anything in his own land which can harm a neighbour: for example, if he has raised the level of a pond in his own land or if he makes a new one to his neighbour's hurt, if his land is thereby submerged, this will be a wrongful nuisance to his neighbour's freehold unless he should be permitted by his neighbour to do this.   And just as a man can have a servitude in his neighbour's land if one is constituted, so also he can have it by long user without any constitution through the sufferance of the owners with their knowledge, because long sufferance draws into consent,

sensum sicut in communibus pasturis et huiusmodi.   Id eciam quod ab inicio
non fuit nocumentum iniuriosum ex post facto et constitucione fieri poterit iniuriosum vt si cui ab inicio facere licuit in suo, ex constitucione seruitutis
conuenerit ne facere liceat vel e conuerso si cui ab inicio facere non liceat
5 postmodum facere liceat ex constitucione.

CAP. XXVII. DE NOCUMENTIS PERTINENCIARUM

Omnia autem iura prenominata omnesque seruitutes sunt de pertinenciis
tenementorum et a tenementis pertinent ad tenementa et habent huiusmodi pertinencie suas pertinencias sicut ius pascendi ad quod pertinet via et liber ingressus
10 et egressus et eodem modo ad ius fodiendi, falcandi, secandi, hauriendi, potandi,
venandi, piscandi, pascendi et huiusmodi pertinet liber accessus et recessus sicut
via iter et actus racione vsuum diuersorum.   Ad ius eciam aque ducende
pertinet purgacio et ad iter secundum quod est de pertinenciis per se vel pertinenciis pertinenciarum vt si via per se concedatur sine alia seruitute tunc per-
15 tinet refeccio sicut ad aque ductum pertinet purgacio.   Et sicut possunt huiusmodi iura et seruitutes auferri per disseysinam, ita fieri poterunt nocumenta
iniuriosa in pertinenciis pertinenciarum videlicet quod quis comode vti non
possit vt si quis omnino viam obstruat vel chaciam per quam ingredi solet
in pasturam fossato, muro vel haya vel pallacio tale nocumentum non multum
20 differt a disseysina et ideo tolli debet per assisam cum sit iniuriosum ad custum
eius qui opus illud fecerit si hoc fuerit in suo.   Si autem in alieno conpetit ei   f. 101
assisa noue disseysine de libero tenemento cuius fuerit fundus in quo opus illud
factum fuerit et secundum quod assisa noue disseysine sub se continet nocumentum quia omnis disseysina nocet per hoc tolli poterit nocumentum et querenti
25 restitui dampnum tam de disseysina tenementi quam de nocumento, quod quidem
non esset si tantum de nocumento ageretur.   Item si minus comode ire possit ad
locum seruitutis et ad pasturam vt si viam coartauerit vel vbi ire solebat per
conpendium conpellat eum ire per circulum et si permittat eum ire non tamen
permittit eum ire ad vsum debitum in seruitute constitutum vt si debeat quis
30 habere viam ad carectam et carrum non permittit eum habere nisi iter et actum
et ingressum strictum, per assisam tollatur iniuriosum nocumentum per breue   [268]
quare obstruxit vel coartauit aliquo modorum supradictorum.   Et si fossatum
non fecerit neque murum per quod obstruat per opus manifestum, sufficit tamen
si faciat quod tantumdem valet vt si ire non permittat et hec locum habent cum

2–3. fieri . . . constitucione, Br., *om.* J.   4. conuenerit ne, Br., conuertitur ve, J; *post*
conuerso *add.* et, J.   5. constitucione, Br., consuetudine, J.   7. sunt] sicut, J.   8. *prius*
et *om.* J.   19. *posterius* vel] et, J.   22. fundus *om.* J.   24. per hoc . . . nocumentum et,
Br., *om.* J.   25. de disseysina] disseysinam, J.   26. ire] non, J.   30. *prius* et] ad, J.
33. manifestum *vel* manufactum *in nonnullis textis*, Br., manuficum, J.

as in the case of common pasture and the like. That, too, which at the beginning was not a wrongful nuisance can become wrongful from what is afterwards done. It may be made wrongful by a constitution: for example, if someone was originally allowed to do something in his land and by the constitution of a servitude it is agreed that he is not to be permitted to do it, or conversely, if at the beginning a man is not allowed to do something and subsequently is allowed to do it by virtue of a constitution.

CHAPTER 27. OF NUISANCES TO APPURTENANCES

Bracton,
f. 232

All the rights mentioned above and all the servitudes are appurtenances of tenements and pertain from tenements to tenements. Such appurtenances have their own appurtenances, like the right of grazing to which appertain a right of way and free entry and exit; and in the same way to a right of digging, mowing, cutting, drawing water, watering [cattle], hunting, fishing, grazing and the like there pertains free access and departure, such as roadways, footpaths and bridle-paths in respect of different uses. To the right also of conveying water pertains the right to clean out the watercourse. And as for a right of way, according as it is an appurtenance of itself or an appurtenance of an appurtenance: for example, if a right of way is granted by itself without any other servitude, then the right of repair pertains to it just as cleaning out pertains to the right to convey water. And just as such rights and servitudes may be taken away by disseisin, so can wrongful nuisances be committed in the appurtenances of appurtenances so that, indeed, a man cannot have convenient user: for example, if a man completely obstructs a path or drove-way, by which entry is wont to be had into a pasture, by a ditch, wall, hedge or paling, such a nuisance does not greatly differ from a disseisin, and therefore, since it is wrongful, it ought to be removed by an assize at the cost of him who did the work, if it was done on his own land. But if it was done on another's land, an assize of novel disseisin of freehold is available to him who owns the land in which the work was done, and just as the assize of novel disseisin covers nuisance because every disseisin is a nuisance, in consequence the nuisance may be removed and the damage made good to the plaintiff, both for the disseisin of the tenement and for the nuisance, but this would not be so if an action was brought only for the nuisance. Again, if he cannot go with ease to the place where the servitude is and to the pasture: for example, if the owner has narrowed the path or, where he was wont to go by a short route, the owner compels him to go round about, or if he allows him to go, does not allow him to go for the use laid down in the servitude: for example, if a man ought to have a roadway for a cart and waggon

Bracton,
f. 232b

and he lets him have only a footpath and bridlepath and narrow entry, the wrongful nuisance will be removed by an assize [or] by a writ 'why did he obstruct' or 'narrow' in any of the aforesaid ways. And even if he does not make a ditch or a wall whereby he creates an obstruction by some visible work, nevertheless it

facta fuerint extra loca deputata seruitutibus. Si autem infra tunc locum
habebit assisa noue disseysine de pastura. Ad constitucionem hominum eciam
inponitur seruitus quod quis habeat aque ducende per fundum alienum et sic est
constitucio hominis. Est eciam constitucio iuris ne quis faciat in suo iniuriose
5 videlicet ne stagnum faciat vel exaltet vel prosternat per quod nocere possit
vicino vt si per refullum aque submergat tenementum vicini, et eodem modo quod
nec domum nec pontem nec stagnum gurgitem exclusam nec molendinum per
quod vicino iniuste noceatur et sic ne faciat nocumentum iniuriosum vicino in
construendo in proprio vel alieno nec eodem modo in prosternendo vel demol-
10 liendo vel destruendo omnino iniuriose quod iuste factum est ab inicio et
leuatum vt si murum prosternauerit quis fossatum piscariam stagnum pontem
vel exclusam vel huiusmodi. Eodem modo facere poterit quis nocumentum
iniuriosum et pocius disseysinam si quis in reficiendo vel demolliendo vel ad-
mensurando cum hoc ei liceat iuste, si modum debitum excedat. Et sicut potest
15 quis facere nocumentum iniuriosum in faciendo ita poterit in non faciendo in
proprio vel alieno vt si teneatur ex constitucione obstruere claudere purgare et
reficere et non fecerit cum ad hoc teneatur. Et sicut potest quis nocere in non
faciendo ita nocere poterit in non permittendo, vt si quis non permittat alium
qui tenetur obstruere, claudere, purgare vel reficere cum ad hoc teneatur ex
20 constitucione vel ex longa consuetudine. Poterit eciam esse nocumentum
iniuriosum propter communem et publicam vtilitatem quod quidem non esset
propter vtilitatem priuatam vt si quis firmauerit piscariam vel stagnum habens
predia ex vtraque parte aque cum fundus liber sit ex omni parte quod nichil
debeat fundo vicino subtus nec supra per hoc licet faciat dampnum vicinis non
25 tamen facit iniuriam, verumtamen propter vtilitatem publicam que priuate prefertur sustinenda sunt hec ad publicum dampnum tollendum. Et multa alia fieri
poterunt nocumenta iniuriosa.

Item si quis aliquid fecerit quominus ad fontem lacum puteum piscinam iri
possit vel hauriri vel de fontanea aqua non tantum aquam ducere vel haurire
30 tales cadere possunt in assisam set discrete sunt seruitutes aque ductus et
haustus, vel si quis prohibetur aqua vti vel haurire siue pecus ad aquam apellere
similiter cadit in assisam set hoc non est de cisterna, quia cisterna non habet
aquam perpetuam nec aquam viuam quia cisterna in imbribus concipitur set lacus,
puteus, piscina aliquando viuam aquam non habent. Item si quis ire ad fontem
35 prohibeatur habet accionem quare quis obstruxerit viam ei cui conceditur
haustus. Cuicumque enim conceditur haustus ei conceditur iter ad fontem et
accessus et licet quis vti possit nouas tamen venas querere vel aperire non potest

9. construendo] constituendo, J.   14. cum] tum, J; ei . . . excedat, Br., om. J.
15. *posterius* in] et, J.   17. reficere] deficere, J.   21. propter] cum, J.   23. aque om. J.
26. hec] hoc, J.   27. nocumenta] nocumentum, J.   29. tantum] tantam, J. et Br.
31. quis] cui, J; pecus] penis, J.   32. quia] de, J.   32. habet] habent, J.   34. non om. J.

suffices if he does what amounts to the same thing: for example, if he will not allow him passage. And these things are relevant if they are done outside the places assigned for the servitudes. If, however, they are done within them, then an assize of novel disseisin of pasture will hold good. By a constitution of man a servitude is also imposed that a man may lead water through another's land, and such is a constitution of man. There is also a constitution of law that no one shall act wrongfully in his own land, namely, that he shall not make a pond or raise or lower its level whereby he may injure his neighbour: for example, if he should submerge his neighbour's tenement by the overflow of water; and similarly he shall not make any house, bridge, pond, weir, sluice or mill whereby his neighbour is unlawfully harmed; and so he may not commit an unlawful nuisance to his neighbour by building on his own land or another's land nor also by levelling or demolishing or completely destroying wrongfully what was rightfully done and erected at the beginning: for example, if a man should destroy a wall, ditch, fishery, pond, bridge, sluice or the like. Likewise a man can commit a wrongful nuisance or rather disseisin if, in repairing or demolishing or admeasuring, although he is lawfully allowed to do this, he should go beyond the proper limits. And just as a man can commit wrongful nuisance in doing, so he can in not doing, in his own or another's land: for example, if he is bound by a constitution to stop up, enclose, clean out and repair and he does not do this although he is under an obligation. And just as a man can commit a nuisance in not doing, so he can in not permitting: for example, if a man will not permit another who is under obligation to stop up, enclose, clean out or repair, although he is bound to do this by a constitution or by long custom. There can also be a wrongful nuisance because of the common and public welfare, which would not be such by reason of private welfare: for example, if a man should establish a fishery or pool having fields on both sides of the water; since the estate is free in every part so that it has no obligations to a neighbouring estate below him or above him, although he may thereby do damage to his neighbours, nevertheless he does no wrong. Still, because of the public welfare which is given preference over private welfare, these things are to be restrained in order to remove public damage. And many other things can become wrongful nuisances.

Bracton.
f. 233
Again, if a man should do anything whereby it is made impossible to go to a spring, lake, well or pond or to draw water, such persons may fall into an assize. Not only to lead water from a spring or draw it, for the servitudes of leading water and drawing it are separate, but if one is forbidden to use water or to draw it or drive his cattle to the water, he likewise falls into the assize. But this is not the case with a tank, because a tank does not have water all the time or running water, because a tank has rain water as its source. But a lake, well or pond sometimes do not have running water. Again, if anyone is prevented from going to a spring, he has an action 'why someone has obstructed' the path of him to whom a right of drawing water is granted. To everyone, indeed, to whom is granted the right of drawing water there is granted a right of way and access to the spring, and although a man may exercise this right, yet he cannot look for and

quia aliter vti non potest quam alio anno vti solet. Riuus autem est locus per longitudinem depressus quo aqua decurrit. Specus vero est locus ex quo despicitur et inde dicta sunt spectacula. Reficere autem est id quod corruptum est in pristinum statum restaurare. Ei vero permittitur reficere et purgare riuum [269]
5 qui ius habet seruitutis et qui aque ducende causa hoc fecit. Ad pristinum statum dico quia si quis riuum deprimit vel atollit dilatat vel extendit aperit apertum vel coartat per excessum delinquit. Item aque ductus quandoque debetur et datur prediis et quandoque personis. Quod vero prediis datur persona extincta non extinguitur: quod autem datur personis cum personis amittitur et
10 ideo ad nullum transit successorem. Si diurnarum vel nocturnarum horarum aque ductum habeam non possum alia hora ducere quam qua ius habeam. Item diuidi poterit aqua non solum temporibus set mensuris.

 Ea autem que subleuata sunt ad nocumentum iniuriosum prostrata vel demollita statim flagrante maleficio sicut de aliis disseysinis demolliri poterunt et
15 prosterni vel releuari et reparari si querens ad hoc sufficiat, si autem non f. 101b recurrendum est ad eum qui iura tuetur. Si quis autem in vno comitatu fecerit quod noceat in alio semper impetretur breue ad vicecomitem illius comitatus in quo nocumentum illud factum fuerit. Et sic pertinet quandoque huiusmodi emendacio ad vicecomitem sicut de via obstructa per breue quod iusticiet propter
20 communem vtilitatem ne transeuntes ire diu inpediantur quia hoc esset commune dampnum. Et in hoc est vicecomes iusticiarius sicut super detencione aueriorum contra vadium et plegios propter communem vtilitatem ne animalia diu inclusa pereant et eodem modo de pastura et de piscaria et de racionabili estouerio in bosco vel brueria habendo et in quibus non habet potestatem
25 cognoscendi sine waranto nisi tantum de via dum tamen hoc fecerit recenter flagrante delicto. Ad querelam post longum tamen interuallum se intromittere non debet sine waranto vel sine breui nec licitum erit vicecomiti se intromittere sine breui vltra tempus disseysito concessum et hoc non nisi cum consensu et querela eius cui iniuriatum est. Cum autem contingat aliquando quod aliquis
30 ius habens appruandi se fossatum aut sepem leuauerit ad aliquorum nocumentum et illi ad quorum nocumentum noctanter vel alio tali tempore quod non credant factum eorum sciri fossatum huiusmodi aut sepem prostrauerint nec sciri poterit per veredictum alicuius inquisicionis aut iuratorum qui fossatum eius aut sepem prostrauerint nec velint homines de vicinis villatis indictare de
35 huiusmodi facto culpabiles statutum est quod villate propinque superadiacentes distringantur leuare huiusmodi fossatum vel hayam propriis custubus et ad dampna restituenda conpellantur querenti.

 Cum autem breue de justicies vicecomiti liberetur de communa pasture vel

---

2. locus] litus, J. 4. Ei] Et, J. 11. possum] possunt, J. 11. qua ius] quamuis, J. 19. propter] per, J. 24. *prius* in] et, J. 31. alio *in statuto, om.* J. 32. credant] credat, J. 34. indictare *in statuto*; iudicare, J.

open up new outlets because the right cannot be otherwise used than it was wont to be used in the preceding years. A canal is a longitudinal depression along which water flows. And a cavity (*specus*) is a place from which one is looked down on, from which the word 'public show' (*spectaculum*) derives. And to repair is to restore to its original state what has been broken. Indeed, he is allowed to repair and clean a canal who has the right of the servitude and has made it in order to lead water. I say 'its original state' because a man is at fault for excess if he depresses or raises the canal, widens or extends it, makes an opening bigger or narrows it. Again, the right of leading water is sometimes due and given to estates and sometimes to persons. What is given to estates is not extinguished though the person die; what, however, is given to persons is lost with those persons and therefore passes to no successor. If I have the right to convey water during the daytime or during the night I cannot convey it at any other hour than that for which I have the right. Again, water can be reckoned not only in terms of time but of amount.

Those things which are erected (or rased or destroyed) as a wrongful nuisance can be immediately knocked down and demolished (or re-erected and repaired) while the wrongdoing is fresh, as in the case of other disseisins, if the plaintiff has sufficient resources to do this but, if not, there must be recourse to him who safeguards rights. If, however, a man does something in one county which causes nuisance in another, a writ is always to be sued out to the sheriff of that county in which the said nuisance has been committed. And thus such redress sometimes pertains to the sheriff, as in the case of the obstruction of a road, by a writ of *justicies* on behalf of the public welfare lest travellers should be for long prevented from going on their journeys, for this would be a public mischief. And in this matter the sheriff is a justice, just as in regard to the detinue of beasts against gage and pledges, because of the public welfare lest animals that are impounded for long should perish, and likewise in regard to pasture and fishery and having reasonable estovers and wood or heath, but of these matters the sheriff is not empowered to take cognizance without a warrant except only in regard to [the obstruction of a] road, provided he takes action immediately while the offence is fresh. A sheriff should not, however, meddle with a plaint after a long interval of time without a warrant or a writ, nor will it be permitted to a sheriff to meddle without a writ beyond the period of time allowed to a disseisee, and then only with the consent and at the complaint of the injured party. Since, however, it sometimes happens that someone who has the right to enclose his land raises a dyke or a hedge to the nuisance of some others, and those to whose nuisance it is, either by night or at such other time when they suppose their deed would not be known, knock down such dyke or hedge, and it cannot be known by verdict of any inquest or jurors who knocked down his dyke or hedge, nor do the men of the neighbouring townships wish to indict those guilty of such a deed, it is enacted that the nearest adjacent townships shall be distrained to erect such dyke or hedge at their own cost and be compelled to make good his damages to the plaintiff.

When, however, a writ of *justicies* is delivered to a sheriff in regard to common

Bracton,
f. 233*b*

St. Westminster, II.
c. 46

Bracton,
f. 233*b*

de via vel huiusmodi statim in presencia parcium conuenire debet hundredum.
Et inprimis videat in cuius fundo siue tenemento illud nouum opus factum
fuerit, et si in fundo illius de quo queritur inueniatur factum iniuste et ad
nocumentum liberi tenementi querentis si hoc constiterit per iuratam vicecomes
5 amouere faciat per visum recognitorum id quod nocet ad custum delinquentis
et illud reparari faciat sicut esse debet et solet. Si autem coram iusticiariis
debent huiusmodi nocumenta per breue noue disseysine terminari, tunc fiat de
officio vicecomitis in omnibus sicut in communi breui noue disseysine preterquam
de visu iuratoribus faciendo et quo casu querens faciat visum iuratoribus de eo
10 quod nocet qualecumque sit illud vel quantum vel per quas metas vt certa res in   [270]
iudicium deducatur et vt sciri possit vtrum plus posuerit in visu suo vel minus
vel eciam nichil et inde certificare possint iusticiariis cum fuerint requisiti et
eciam vtrum nocumentum iustum sit vel iniuriosum magnum vel minimum vel
omnino nullum licet dampnosum vt per hoc sciri possit vtrum querela pertineat
15 ad querentem vel non. Item videre oportet tenementum cui nocitum est
iniuriose quia si querens tenementum non habeat cui nocere possit nichil valebit
querela vel si ille de quo queritur nullum tenementum habeat quod noceat.

CAP. XXVIII.   DE EXCEPCIONIBUS

In aduentu vero iusticiariorum plures sunt faciende interrogaciones vt sciri
20 possit vtrum ad querentem pertineat accio vel non et quo casu cum querens suam
fundauerit intencionem excipere poterit ille de quo queritur contra intencionem
querentis multis modis.   Continetur in breui Questus est nobis talis quod talis,
et vnde eadem fit responsio vt supra de libero tenemento vt si dicat quod
fossatum non leuauerit vel quid aliud set alius non procedat assisa maxime quoad
25 penam et per hoc breue, quia heredes et succedentes non tenentur ad penam ex
delicto aliorum licet teneantur ad restitucionem status quod res ad pristinum
statum reducatur eciam sine pena non tamen quia iniuriam fecerint set quia tenent rem que nocet ad similitudinem eius quod dicitur de tigno iniuncto quod
quis teneatur actioni de tigno iniuncto non solum qui tignum iniunxit set eciam
30 ille qui habet tignum iniunctum.   Et eodem modo dicendum est de eo qui fossatum stagnum vel alia queque prostrauerit vel leuauerit cum illa habeat prostrata
vel leuata. Et illud idem erit dicendum si tempore nocumenti facti non habuit
querens tenementum cui noceri poterit et ideo non fuit ei iniuriatum et de iniuria

2. inprimis] primis, J.   11. deducatur] reducatur, J.   15. Item videre oportet, Br.,
om. J.   17. nullum *addidimus.*   20. vtrum *dupplicatur in* J.   24. *post* quid *add.* si, J.
25. tenentur] tenent, J.   26. teneantur] teneatur, J.   28–29. quod . . . iniuncto, Br., *om.* J
33. altero] alii, J.

of pasture or a right of way or the like, he should forthwith call a meeting of the hundred court in the presence of the parties.   And in the first place he should see in whose land or tenement the change has been made and, if it is found that it was done unlawfully on the land of the man of whom complaint is made and to the nuisance of the plaintiff's freehold, and if this is found by a jury, the sheriff shall cause what is harmful to be removed by view of the recognitors at the cost of the offender and cause everything to be restored as it should and was wont to be.   If, however, such actions of nuisance ought to be determined by a writ of novel disseisin before the justices, then the duty of the sheriff will be in all respects as in the ordinary writ of novel disseisin, except as regards the view to be presented to the jurors.   And in this case the plaintiff is to let the jurors view what is harmful: what kind it is, or how much, or by what metes, so that a specific matter may be brought to trial and so that it may be known whether the plaintiff put too much or too little in his view or even nothing, and the jurors can certify the

Bracton,
f. 234

justices thereof when they are asked, and also whether the nuisance is rightful or wrongful, great or small, or no nuisance at all, even though hurtful, so that by this means it may be known whether or not a plaint is available to the plaintiff. Again, it is necessary to view the tenement which has been wrongfully harmed because, if the plaintiff has no tenement which can be harmed, his plaint will avail him nothing, nor if the man of whom complaint is made has no tenement which may cause harm.

CHAPTER 28.   OF EXCEPTIONS

Bracton,
f. 234

At the coming of the justices many enquiries have to be made so that it can be known whether or not a right of action is available to the plaintiff, and in this case, when the plaintiff has made his declaration, he of whom complaint is made can except against the plaintiff's declaration in many ways. It is contained in the writ: 'So-and-so has complained to us that so-and-so', and the same answer is made thereon, as above, with regard to a freehold: for example, if he says that he did not raise a dyke or anything else but another did it, the assize will not proceed, especially as regards a penalty, nor by means of this writ, because heirs and successors are not liable to a penalty for an offence done by others although they are liable, without a penalty, to restore the condition of a property so that it is returned to its original state; not because they have done a wrong but because they hold the property which is causing the harm, like what is said about a tied beam: that the man who is liable to an action concerning a tied beam is not only he who tied the beam but also the man who possesses the tied beam.   The same must be said of him who has knocked down or erected a dyke, a pool or anything else so long as he has what has been knocked down or erected. And the same must be said if at the time when the nuisance was committed, the plaintiff did not have a tenement which could be harmed, and therefore no injury was done him, and from an injury done to another no one ought to advantage

altero illata nemo adquirere sibi debet.   Item continetur iniuste et sine iudicio
leuauit exaltauit siue prostrauit et quo casu responderi poterit quod ipse non
leuauit set cum alius sine iudicio prostrauit ille refecit et reparauit.   Item de hoc
quod dicitur ad nocumentum, responderi poterit quod nullum est ibi nocumentum
5 et quamuis sit ibi nocumentum non tamen est iniuriosum nec querens ius habet
prohibendi ne fiat sicut videri poterit in molendino leuato vbi vicinus prohibere
non poterit ne fiat licet dampnum senciat quod est ideo non iniuriosum licet
dampnosum et sic dici poterit de aliis nocumentis que dampnosa sunt et non
iniuriosa.
10   Si autem nichil sit quod dici poterit quare assisa debeat remanere procedat
assisa et si fiat pro querente amoueatur id quod nocet et in pristinum statum
redigatur ad custum eius qui deliquit et per omnia fiat sicut esse solet et debet   f. 102
siue fieri debeat prostracio demollicio refeccio siue reparacio apericio vel admensuracio.   Et vnde si per iudicium fieri debeant aliqua istorum ad veterem
15 formam conformentur secundum altitudinem latitudinem longitudinem pro-
funditatem et strictitatem.   Restitui enim debet primus status et refici reficit enim
qui reparat qui aperit et qui purgat quia purgare refeccionis est porcio set non
potest quis tamen sub specie refeccionis aliquid facere deterius neque alcius neque
latius neque humilius neque longius neque aque ductum sic purgare per quod
20 aqua aliter fluat quam solet.   Et si quis conuictus fuerit per assisam quod aquam   [271]
diuerterit vel aliquid fecerit vel inmiserit per quod aqua fluat vel pressior alcior
rarior vel rapidior vel per quod in aliquo minuatur vel per quod alueum
fluminis mutetur ad incomodum vicini ad pristinum statum per assisam re-
formetur.   Item non solum tenetur qui aquam diuertet set eciam ille qui
25 denegat vt aliter aqua fluat cum ius non habuerit et is qui dolo fecerit quo magis
aqua fluat aliter quam solet vel minus solito vt si fossam in suo fecerit vel ita
aque ductum fecerit vel purgauerit quod modum excedat et per hoc aquam
vicini auferat in toto vel in parte.   Set si quis, cum sibi per assisam perquirere
debeat vel cum perquisiuerit, propria auctoritate spreto iudicio seysinam suam
30 vsurpauerit quod per iudicem reposcere deberet et quod sic sibi presumpserit
per iudicem restituerit vix in posterum super proprietate audietur.
    Ad hoc autem quod dicitur iniuste si nocumentum sit iniuriosum et damp-
nosum erit ad hoc demolliendum et si non iniuriosum licet dampnosum cadit
accio quantum ad illum querentem licet non quantum ad alios vel quamuis
35 iniuriosum ei qui queritur amittit tamen accionem si propria auctoritate et sine
iudicio prostrauerit post longum tempus vbi conqueri deberet licet recenter
prosternere possit secundum quod tunc presens esset vel absens ille cui nocitum
est.   Item poterit nocumentum esse iniuriosum et dampnosum quantum ad vnum

3. cum] quod, J.   7. *posterius* non *om.* J.   14. si per] super, J.   16. reficit, Br.,
desicut, J.   18. aliquid, Br., porcionem aliquam, J.   19. latius] laicius, J.   21. *post
fluat* J. *add.* aliter quam solet *per incuriam.*   22. rapidior] lapidior, J; *posterius* vel *om.* J;
ulterius vel] illis, J.   25. habuerit] habuerat, J.   26. in] et, J.   30. iudicem] iudicium, J.
33. ad hoc *scripsimus,* adhuc, J.   37. cui nocitum] qui nactum, J.

himself. Again, the writ contains the words 'unlawfully and without a judgement' he set up, heightened or knocked down, and in this case answer can be made that he did not set up but, when someone else without a judgement knocked down, he remade and restored. Again, in that it is said 'to the nuisance', answer can be made that in this instance there is no nuisance and, even though there may be a nuisance there, nevertheless it is not wrongful and the plaintiff has no right to forbid its being done, as may be seen in the case of the erection of a mill which a neighbour cannot forbid to be done although he may have damage, which is therefore not wrongful although damaging. And thus it can be said of other nuisances which cause damage but are not wrongful.

If, however, there is nothing that can be said why the assize should be stayed, it is to proceed and, if it finds for the plaintiff, the nuisance is to be removed and everything brought back to its original state at the cost of him who commits the offence, and in all respects let it be done as it used and ought to be, whether it should be to knock down or to demolish, to remake or to repair, to open up or to admeasure. And therefore, if by judgement of the court any one of these things ought to be done, they are to be brought into conformity with the old form in height, width, length, depth and narrowness. For the pristine state ought to be restored and remade, for he remakes who restores, who opens up and who cleans out, because cleaning out is part and parcel of remaking. But no one can, however, under the appearance of remaking make anything lower or higher or broader or deeper or longer, nor can he so clean out a watercourse that the water flows otherwise than it is wont to do. And if anyone should be found by the assize to have diverted water or made or installed anything whereby water flows either too violently, too high, too meagrely or too rapidly or whereby it is in any way diminished, or whereby the bed of a stream is changed, to the inconvenience of a neighbour, it is to be restored by the assize to its pristine state. Further, not only is he held liable who diverts the water but also he who refuses to let the water flow in another way when he has no right to do so, and he who craftily causes more water to flow than is wont or less than is usual: for example, if he should make a ditch in his property or should so construct a watercourse or clean it out that he goes beyond his limits and thereby takes away his neighbour's water, in whole or in part. But if a man, when he ought to sue by an assize or when he has sued, should scorn the judgement of the court and of his own authority usurp his seisin, what he ought to have claimed through a judge and what he has thus arrogated to himself is to be restored [to the other party] by a judge: with difficulty will he be heard in future on the matter of ownership.

In that the writ says 'unlawfully', if the nuisance is wrongful and damaging, it must for this reason be demolished; and, if not wrongful although damaging, the action fails as regards the plaintiff, though not as regards others; or even though it is harmful to him who complains, he yet loses the action if of his own authority and without a judgement of the court he has knocked something down after a long time has elapsed, for there he ought to have entered a complaint: though he can knock down immediately, depending on whether he who is injured is present or absent. Again, a nuisance can be wrongful and damaging as regards one

Bracton,
f. 234b

Bracton,
f. 234

vel pluras personas priuatas et quantum ad priuatum nocumentum. Poterit
esse nocumentum contra communem vtilitatem que semper et in omni casu
preferenda est priuate.

Item de stagno et gurgite leuato vel prostrato ad nocumentum iniuriosum
5 videndum erit vtrum leuatum sit omnino in tenemento ipsius querentis cum
habeat tenementum ex vtraque parte ripe et quo casu pocius erit disseysina de
libero tenemento quam assisa de nocumento. Si autem leuatum sit vel prostra-
tum omnino in tenemento illius de quo queritur pocius erit assisa de nocumento
quam de libero tenemento cum hoc totum sit in alieno. Si autem pars quedam
10 in proprio et quedam in alieno vt si aqua diuidatur in medium tunc pro ea parte
que fuerit in proprio locum habebit assisa noue disseysine de libero tenemento
et pro ea parte que fuerit in alieno locum habebit assisa de nocumento et sic
erunt due assise de vno facto. Et cum onerosum sit vtramque consequi videndum erit que illarum debet preferri ad iniuriam ex toto tollendam ne pro vna
15 parte procedat et pro alia infecta remaneat. Et si velis corrigere per assisam
noue disseysine totum quod actum est de libero tenemento hoc esse non
poterit quia assisa illa non conprehendit assisam de nocumento quod factum est
in alieno. Melius est ergo quod per assisam de nocumento per quam poterit
vtraque terminari quia assisa de nocumento extendit se ad fundum alienum et
20 assisa noue disseysine de libero tenemento extendit se ad fundum alienum in
eo quod nociua est et iniuriosa licet se non extendat quantum ad liberum
tenementum. Et sic assisa de nocumento terminabit vtramque scilicet quod
nocumentum tollatur et quod res ad pristinum statum reducatur. Item ex vno
facto plures possunt esse disseysine de libero tenemento et plura nocumenta
25 iniuriosa eodem modo. Plures disseysine de libero tenemento vt si quis fossatum leuauerit in fundo alieno inuito domino per hoc facit disseysinam de
libero tenemento ei qui dominus est et obstruccionem vie et diuersionem aque
que sunt quasi nocumenta iniusta licet in alieno. Set omnes terminari poterunt
per vnicam assisam de libero tenemento cum surgant ex vno facto per facti　　[272]
30 emendacionem. Si autem vna vel ambe emendantur que nocent adhuc poterit
iniuria remanere pro parte et ideo melius est quod vna assumatur que totum
terminat negocium. Et eodem modo potest quis facere in suo ex vno facto per
quod plura iminere nocumenta possunt vicino vt si viam obstruat fossato per
quam ingredi solet pasturam facit disseysinam de communa et similiter nocu-
35 mentum in via et si diuertat aquam sic facit vnam disseysinam de communa in
proprio et duo nocumenta ex vno facto. Item potest vnus ex vno facto pluribus
obligari et teneri ex disseysina et nocumento vt si quis alterius tenementum incluserit vel commune et in quo vnus liberum tenementum habeat et alius communam pasture, vnus vel plures, tercius iter et actum et quartus adaquacionem

4. vel *om.* J.　　11. de] in, J.　　18–19. per quam . . . de nocumento, Br., *om.* J.　　25. *post*
iniuriosa *add.* et, J.　　30. emendacionem] commendacionem, J.; emendantur *scripsimus*,
erigantur, Br. *et* J.　　30. nocent] nocet, J.　　31. assumatur] assimiletur, J.　　35. et] vt, J.
36. J; proprio] propria, J.　　38. *prius* et] vt, J.

person or several private persons and [constitute] a private nuisance. A
nuisance can be against the public welfare, which always and in every case is to
be given preference over private welfare.

Bracton,
f. 234b

Again, as regards a pool and weir raised or lowered to a wrongful nuisance, it
must be seen whether it was raised entirely in the tenement of the plaintiff, should
he have a tenement along each side of the bank, in which case it will be disseisin
of a freehold rather than an assize of nuisance. If, however, it is raised or lowered
entirely in the tenement of him of whom complaint is made, it will be an assize
of nuisance rather than of freehold since it is wholly in the property of someone
else. If, however, a certain part of it is in one's own property and a certain part
in someone else's property—for example, if the water is divided in midstream—
then for that part which is in one's own property an assize of novel disseisin of
freehold will be appropriate, and for that part which is in someone else's property
an assize of nuisance will be appropriate, and so there will be two assizes in
respect of one act. And since it is burdensome to prosecute both actions, it
must be seen which of them ought to be given preference in order to remove the
wrong as a whole lest an action should proceed in respect of one part and remain
unfinished in respect of the other. And if you wish to remedy by an assize of
novel disseisin all that has been done in respect of a freehold, this cannot be
because the said assize does not include an assize of nuisance done in another's
land. It is better therefore [to proceed] by an assize of nuisance by which both
can be determined because an assize of nuisance extends to the land of another;
and an assize of novel disseisin of freehold extends to another's land to the extent
that it is harmful and wrongful, though it does not extend so far as the freehold.
And thus an assize of nuisance will determine both matters, namely that the
nuisance be abated and that the property be brought back to its original state.

Bracton,
f. 235

Further, arising out of one act there can be several disseisins of freehold and,
similarly, several wrongful nuisances. There may be several disseisins of freehold: for example, if a man raises a dyke in another's land against the will of the
owner, he thereby commits disseisin of freehold against him who is the owner
and obstruction of a right of way and diversion of a watercourse, which are as
it were unlawful nuisances although in another's land. But since they arise from
one act, all can be determined by a single assize of freehold by the rectification
of that act. For if one or two are rectified which are harmful, yet the wrong
can still in part remain. And therefore it is better that one assize be used which
settles the whole business. And likewise a man can do something in his own
property by a single act whereby several nuisances can befall a neighbour:
for example, if he obstructs with a dyke the road by which entry is wont to be
made to a pasture, he commits disseisin of common and likewise a nuisance as
regards a right of way, and should he divert the water, so by a single act he commits one disseisin of common in his own property and two nuisances. Further,
by a single act one man can be put under obligation and made liable to several
others for disseisin and nuisance: for example, if a man encloses the tenement of
another or a tenement held in common and in it one has a freehold and another
has common of pasture (there may be one or several) and a third has a right of

in aliqua parte et sic in infinitum, plures erunt hic disseysine et plura nocumenta
et vnde prius recurrendum erit ad remedium quod totum terminat si dominus
tenementi voluerit alioquin quilibet agat pro se et per se. Item si quis diuertit
cursum aque refert in quo comitatu vel in qua villa vel in quo loco factum   f. 102*b*
5 fuerit id quod nocet sicut in stagno, gurgite et huiusmodi. Item refert vtrum
aqua in qua id factum est quod nocet sit propria eius de quo queritur vel communis vel in parte propria sicut vsque ad filum aque et partim aliena. Si autem
omnino propria eius qui diuertit et in eadem villa, et tenementum cui nocitum
est in eadem villa tunc stet breue cum dicatur quod talis diuertit cursum aque in
10 tali villa ad nocumentum liberi tenementi talis in eadem villa. Si aqua autem sit
communis plurium vel propria alicuius quamuis non ad vsum piscandi tantum
tunc refert quis.

Poterit libertatem concedere ad nocumentum libertatis prius concesse vt si
cui concedatur libertas habendi mercatum aliquo loco certo ita quod non sit ad
15 nocumentum alicuius mercati vicini. Et vnde in primis videndum est quale
mercatum dici debeat vicinum et quale non vicinum siue remotum et quale sit
nocumentum ad hoc quod sufficiat ad tollendum id quod nocet vtrum videlicet
dampnosum et iniuriosum vel tantum dampnosum et non iniuriosum quia remotum vel iniuriosum et dampnosum quia vicinum vel si vicinum non iniuriosum
20 quia non ad dampnum set ad comodum.   Vicinum autem dici poterit mercatum
et nocumentum iniuriosum quia dampnosum quandoque vt si nouum mercatum
leuatum sit infra sex leucas et dimidiam et terciam partem dimidie. Et est racio
secundum dicta seniorum quia omnes racionabiles diete constant ex viginti
miliaribus. Diuidatur ergo dieta in tres partes. Prima autem matutina detur
25 euntibus versus mercatum, secunda detur ad emendum et vendendum, que
quidem sufficere debet omnibus, nisi sint forte mercatores stallarii, qui merces
deposuerint et exposuerint venales, quibus necessaria erit prolixior mora in
mercato, et tercia pars relinquitur redeuntibus de mercato ad propria, et que
quidem omnia necesse erit facere de die et non de nocte propter insidias et incur-
30 sum latronum vt omnia sint in tuto. Cum igitur infra talem terminum in-
petretur mercatum erit prosternendum per assisam quia nocumentum dampnosum est et iniuriosum quia sic vicinum. Si autem vltra talem terminum licet
dampnosum non erit tamen iniuriosum quia remotum et non vicinum. Item   [273]
poterit mercatum esse vicinum et infra predictos terminos et non iniuriosum
35 quia non dampnosum set pocius ad comodum vt si illud de nouo leuatum sit

5. stagno] stango, J.   6. in qua, Br., *om*. J.   8–9. et in . . . nocitum est, Br., *om*. J.
9. dicatur] dicat, J.   19. *prius* vel] et, J; et] vel, J; *posterius* vel] et, J; *post* vicinum *add*. et, J.
21. si *om*. J.

way and a bridlepath and a fourth has the right of watering cattle in some part, and so on endlessly, there will be here several disseisins and several nuisances. And therefore recourse must first be had to the remedy which will settle the whole business if the owner of the tenement agrees [to be the plaintiff]; otherwise everyone is to bring an action for himself and by himself. Further, if a man diverts a watercourse, it is important in which county or in which township or in which place that was done which causes harm, as in a pool, a weir or the like. It is also important whether the water in which that was done which causes harm is the property of him of whom complaint is made or is held in common or is in part his property, for example, up to midstream and in part another's. If, however, the watercourse is entirely the property of him who diverts it and it is in the same township as the tenement to which harm is caused, then the writ will stand since it is said that so-and-so diverts the watercourse in such-and-such a township to the nuisance of the freehold of so-and-so in the same township. But if the water is the common property of several or someone's private property, and not simply the fishing rights, it is then important to know whose it is.

A franchise can be granted to the nuisance of a franchise already granted: for example, if a franchise of holding a market is granted to someone in some particular place on condition that it will not be a nuisance to any neighbouring market. It must therefore first be seen which kind of market should be described as neighbouring and which should be described as not neighbouring but remote, and what kind of nuisance it is that is regarded as sufficient for abating what is harmful: namely, whether the nuisance is damaging and wrongful, or only damaging and not wrongful because the market is remote, or wrongful and damaging because the market is neighbouring or, if it is neighbouring, not wrongful because not hurtful but advantageous. The market can, however, be

Bracton, f. 235b

described as neighbouring and the nuisance as wrongful because sometimes it is damaging: for example, if a new market is established within six and a half miles and a third of half a mile. And according to the sayings of our elders the reason is because all reasonable day's journeys consist of twenty miles. A day's journey is therefore divided into three parts: the first part, in the morning, is allowed for those going to market; the second for buying and selling, which ought to be sufficient for everybody unless perhaps for merchants with stalls who arrange and expose merchandise for sale, to whom a longer stay in the market will be necessary; and the third part is given over to those returning from market to their homes; and it will be necessary to do all these things by day, and not by night because of the ambushes and the attacks of thieves, so that everything may be safe. When therefore a market is obtained within such a limit, it must be suppressed by an assize in that the nuisance is both damaging and wrongful because the market is so neighbouring [upon another]. If, however, the market is outside such a limit, although it may be damaging, yet it will not be wrongful because it is remote and not neighbouring. Further, a market can be neighbouring and within the limits aforesaid and not wrongful because it is not damaging but rather advantageous: for example, if the market, newly established, is on the

secundo die vel tercio ad plus post diem alterius mercati.   Si autem ante secundo die vel tercio erit iniuriosum quia dampnosum et vnde si mercatum non sit vicinum non erit demolliendum quia non iniuriosum licet dampnosum.   Si autem vicinum et infra terminum predictum, si fuerit ad comodum erit sustinendum
5 propter verba nisi sit ad nocumentum.   Item si eleuacio vnius sit ad nocumentum alterius, tunc videndum erit quod ipsorum prius fuerit eleuatum et ideo licet ad nocumentum non tamen iniuriosum quia primum.   Item quamuis dampnosum non erit iniuriosum si de licencia querentis fuerit eleuatum.

   In assisa autem noue disseysine de communa pasture vel de alia que seruitutes
10 dici possunt et iura si contingat quod vna parcium moriatur vel ambe, recuperare poterunt heredes disseysiti versus disseysitores vel eorum heredes cuiuscumque fuerint etatis petentes vel deforciantes per breue de ingressu super disseysinam et eodem modo successores eorum qui nomine pecierint alieno sicut ecclesiastice persone.   Et si visus petatur faciat petens visum tenementi sicut
15 faceret disseysitus si viueret iuratoribus de tenementis ad que dicuntur huiusmodi iura pertinere vt sciri possit in quibus locis et infra quas metas contineantur sicut fit tota die de communa pasture per breue de recto et per breue quo iure. De iure vero aduocacionis ecclesie sufficit quod videatur corpus cui illud ius inest si visus inde petatur: vnum tamen est videre ius aduocacionis et aliud ecclesiam.
20 Quod autem dicitur superius de breui de ingressu et assisis et seruitutibus dici poterit de nocumentis id idem vt si aliquis in suo faceret iniuriose quod fundo vicino noceret et super hoc aramiata esset assisa et ante capcionem assise moreretur vna pars vel ambe quod propter minorem etatem heredum non cessaret repeticio.

25   CAP. XXIX.   DE REDISSEYSINIS

   Si quis autem fuerit disseysitus de tenemento suo vel aliquo quod pertineat ad tenementum et per curiam regis ad assisam, recognicionem, iuratam, iudicium, reddicionem, concordiam, defaltam vel alio quocunque modo seysinam suam recuperauerit et seysinam suam habuerit, si illi qui seysinam sic amiserint illos
30 qui sic recuperauerint postmodum eiecerint, si inde per inquisicionem coram vicecomite et custodibus placitorum corone captam conuictum fuerit, statim per constitucionem de Marleberge capiantur et saluo in prisona custodiantur

   4–5. erit . . . verba, Br., *om.* J.   7–8. quia . . . iniuriosum, Br., *om.* J.   10. *post* ambe *add.* et, J.   11. *post* poterunt *add.* dicti, J; versus *dupplicatur in* J.   12. Nota J. *in margine.*   14. tenementi] tenenti, J.   16. iura] tenementa, J.   20. prius et] in J. 31. conuictum] conuictus, J.

second day or the third at most after the day of the other market; but if it is two or three days before, it will be wrongful because it is damaging.　And hence, if a market is not neighbouring, it must not be suppressed, because it is not wrongful, albeit damaging.　If, however, it is neighbouring and within the limit aforesaid, it will be sustained if it should be advantageous because of the words 'unless it be to the nuisance.'　Further, if the setting up of one market should be to the nuisance of another, then it must be seen which of them was first set up and therefore, although causing a nuisance, is nevertheless not wrongful because it is the first [established].　Further, even though it is damaging, it will not be wrongful if it is set up by leave of the plaintiff.

　　　In an assize of novel disseisin of common of pasture or of another common which can be called servitudes and rights, if it happens that one or both of the parties should die, the heirs of the disseisee can recover against the disseisors or their heirs whatever the age of the demandants or deforciants, by a writ of entry upon disseisin, and likewise the successors of those who claim in the name of another, as do ecclesiastics.　And if a view is demanded, the demandant shall make a view to the jurors, just as the disseisee would have made it if he had been living, of the tenements to which such rights are said to be appurtenant so that it can be known in which places and between which metes they are contained, as is done every day in the case of common of pasture by a writ of right and by a writ of *quo jure*.　As regards the right to the advowson of a church it suffices that there be viewed the corporeal thing where the said right inheres if a view thereof should be demanded: yet it is one thing to view a right of advowson and another to view a church.　What is said above regarding a writ of entry and assizes and servitudes can be said also regarding nuisances: for example, if someone should do something unlawfully in his own property which should harm his neighbour's land and an assize thereon should be arraigned and before the assize is taken one or both of the parties should die, the recovery would not be stayed because of the minority of heirs.

Bracton,
f. 236

CHAPTER 29.　OF REDISSEISINS

St. Merton,
c. 3
St. West-
minster, II.
c. 26

Bracton,
f. 236b

St. Marl-
borough,
c. 8

　　　Should a man have been disseised of his tenement or of anything which is appurtenant to a tenement, and should he have recovered his seisin in the king's court by way of an assize, recognition, jury, judgement, surrender, concord, default or in any other way whatsoever, and should he have his seisin, if those who so lost seisin should subsequently eject those who have so recovered it and are convicted thereof by an inquest held before the sheriff and the keepers of the pleas of the crown, then by the Constitution of Marlborough they shall be at

donec inde redimantur et per plegios non dimittantur, set si vicecomes tales f. 103
replegiari temere permiserit, grauiter eo ipso puniendus erit et conuictus nichilominus dampna reddet in duplo propter duplex delictum suum, quia facit disseysinam contra pacem et quia ausu temerario irritat ea que in curia regis rite
5 acta sunt.

CAP. XXX.   DE INTRUSIONE

Possessionum autem quedam nudi pedis posicio quedam intrusio.   Intrusio
vero est vbi quis cui nullum ius conpetit nec scintilla iuris possessionem vacuam
ingreditur que nec corpore nec animo possidetur, sicut hereditatem persedentem [274]
10 antequam adita fuerit ab herede vel saltem a domino capitali custodie racione
vel escaete si heredes non existant, vel si post mortem alicuius per finem factum
vel per modum donacionis vbi successio locum sibi vendicare non possit, vel si
post mortem alicuius qui tenuerit ad vitam debeat tenementum reuerti ad proprietarium ponat quis se in seysinam antequam tenementum perueniat ad eum
15 ad quem peruenire deberet ex causis predictis.   Cum igitur quis ita se intruserit
cum nichil iuris habeat, et heredem venientem vel capitalem dominum vel eum
ad quem tenementum reuerti deberet, per finem factum vel per modum donacionis vel vt escaeta pro defectu, pro delicto vel alio quocumque modo, non admiserit, succurritur petenti pluribus modis secundum diuersitatem casuum.   Si
20 reuerti namque debeat ad capitalem dominum tanquam escaeta sua eo quod feoffatus sibi et heredibus suis de corpore suo prouenientibus obierit sine herede de
se, tunc fiat tale breue:

Pone per vadium et saluos plegios A. quod sit coram etc. ad respondendum
B. quare intrusit se in tantam terram cum pertinenciis in tali villa quam C.
25 tenuit de predicto B. et vnde idem C. seysitus fuit die quo obiit et que ad ipsum
B. reuerti debuit tanquam ad capitalem dominum illius feodi eo quod predictus
C. obiit sine herede de se.

Et cum quis se intruserit in terram aliquam quasi heres, cum non sit, super
seysinam capitalis domini que in manu sua remanere debet donec rectus heres
30 veniat, facturus domino quod de iure facere debet, tunc sic:

ad respondendum B. quo waranto se intrusit in tantam terram que est de
feodo ipsius B. et quam predictus B. ceperat in manum suam donec rectus heres
veniret ad faciendum ei quod de iure facere deberet, vt dicit.

7. quedam, Br.; que dicitur, J.   9. persedentem *scripsimus*: possidentem, J, iacentem, Br.
14. seysinam] seisina, J.   29. seysinam] seysina, J.   30. sic] sit, J.   31. se *om.* J.
32. ceperat] ceperit, J.

once arrested and kept safely in prison until they are redeemed therefor and they shall not be released by giving pledges; if the sheriff should rashly permit such men to be replevied, he shall incur heavy punishment on that account; and, furthermore, upon conviction [they] shall pay double damages because of [their] double offence, because [they] commit a disseisin against the peace and because, rashly daring, [they] set at nought matters properly done in the king's court.

St. West-
minster, II.
c. 26

CHAPTER 30.   OF INTRUSION

Bracton,
f. 159b

Bracton,
f. 160

Possession sometimes arises out of the placing of the bare foot [upon the soil] and sometimes out of intrusion.   Intrusion is where one to whom no right or particle of right belongs enters into a vacant possession, which is possessed neither physically nor mentally, such as an inheritance lying long [unoccupied] before it is entered upon by the heir, or at least by the chief lord by reason of wardship or of escheat if there are no heirs; or where after the death of anyone [it should revert to another] by fine levied or by form of gift where a right of succession can claim no place for itself, or where after the death of someone who held for life, the tenement ought to revert to the owner and a man puts himself in seisin before the tenement reached him to whom it ought to come for the reasons aforesaid.   When therefore a man intrudes himself in this fashion when he has no right and will not admit the incoming heir or the chief lord or him to whom the tenement should revert by fine levied or by form of gift or by way of escheat through failure [of heirs] or for felony or in any other way whatever, the plaintiff

Bracton,
f. 160b

has a remedy of several sorts according to the difference in the cases.   For if the tenement ought to revert to the chief lord as his escheat because one enfeoffed to himself and the heirs of his body died without a direct heir, then a writ will issue as follows:

Place A. under gage and safe pledges that he will be before etc. to answer B. why he has intruded himself in such-and-such an amount of land with appurtenances in such-and-such a township which C. held of the aforesaid B. and whereof the said C. was seised on the day when he died and which ought to revert to the said B. as the chief lord of the said fee, because the aforesaid C. died without direct heir.

And if a man should intrude himself in some land as if he were the heir when he is not, [entering] upon the seisin of the chief lord which ought to remain in his hand until the true heir comes, prepared to perform that which is due to the lord as of right, then thus:

to answer B. by what warrant he has intruded himself in such-and-such an amount of land which belongs to the fee of the said B. and which the aforesaid B. had taken into his hand until the true heir should come to perform that which he ought of right to perform to him, as he says.

intrusione per se, et vbi culpabiles esse poterunt de intrusione tam illi qui ius f. 103b
habent in re quam illi qui non habent. Et si intrusor cum recenter eiectus
fuerit recuperare non poterit per assisam similiter nec per conuiccionem recuperabit. Nulli eciam conceditur excepcio cui denegatur accio vt si in causa
5 spoliacionis vbi nichil ad querentem pertineat de seysina, vt si intrusor dicat
forte quod disseysitus seruus sit vel bastardus vel quod nichil iuris habeat in
tenemento vel huiusmodi nichil ad eum quia si petere deberet nulla sibi conpeteret
accio, et quo casu semper poterit tenens in possessione remanere quamuis nichil
iuris habeat in re possessa quia cum neuter ius habeat, melior est causa possi-
10 dentis. Et ideo, si ille qui ius non habeat talem eiciat, eiector excepcionem contra
eum non habebit quia si peteret accionem non haberet. Item agere poterit quis
de intrusione vbi quis racione alicuius carte vel homagii se posuerit in seysinam
de aliquo tenemento de quo nullam habuit seysinam in vita donatoris. Item
vbi quis se posuerit in seysinam sine breui, procuracione vel waranto. Item si
15 cum duobus facta fuerit donacio et alteri eorum tradicio ac vnus propria auctoritate racione nude carte se posuerit in seysinam. Breue vero de intrusione
secundum generalem formam tale est:

Ostensurus quare intrusit se in tantam terram quam B. qui nuper obiit
tenuit de eodem A. ad vitam suam tantum et que post mortem eiusdem B. ad
20 eum reuerti debuit, vt idem A. dicit.

CAP. XXXI. DE FIRMIS ET RERUM ACCIONIBUS

Poterit autem quis in vno et eodem tenemento liberum habere tenementum
et alius vsumfructum et vsum et habitacionem. Solent enim aliquando tales cum
eiecti fuerint infra terminum suum perquirere sibi per breue de conuencione, set
25 quia tale breue locum habere non potuit inter aliquas personas nisi tantum inter
illum qui ad firmam tradidit ad terminum et illum qui ceperit nec alios ligare
poterit obligacio conuencionis et eciam quia inter tales personas vix potuit
terminari negocium, ideo de consilio curie prouisum fuit firmario remedium
contra quoscumque deiectores per tale breue:
30 Precipe A. quod reddat B. tantum terre cum pertinenciis in tali villa per
quam idem A. dimisit scilicet.
Et si alius eiecerit quam ille qui dimisit, tunc sic:
quam C. de N. ei dimisit ad terminum qui nondum preteriit, infra quem [276]
predictus A. vel predictus C. ipsum B. de eadem terra vel firma sua iniuste
35 eiecit, vt dicit. Et nisi fecerit etc.

3. per om. J.   5. pertineat scripsimus, om. J.   7. conpeteret] conpetet, J.   9. cum
om. J.   12. seysinam] seysina, J.   14. seysinam] seysina, J; procuratore, Br., procuracione, J.   15. facta] causa, J.   25. personas om. J.

intrusion [as subsidiary] but only with the intrusion by itself, and since both those who have right in the property as well as those who have none can be guilty of intrusion.   And if an intruder, when he has been immediately ejected, cannot recover by an assize, so he will not recover by an attaint.   To no one, moreover, is an exception allowed to whom an action is denied: for example, in an action of dispossession where the plaintiff has no seisin: for example, if the intruder happen to say that the disseised is a villein or a bastard or that he has no right in the tenement or the like, for this is nothing to him because, if he should claim, he would have no action, and in this case the tenant can always remain in possession even though he has no right in the property possessed, for when neither has a right, the possessor has the better case.   And so, if he who has no right should eject such a one, the ejector will have no exception against him because, if he were to claim, he would have no action.   Furthermore, a man can bring an action of intrusion where, by virtue of some charter or homage, someone puts himself in seisin of some tenement whereof he had no seisin in the lifetime of the donor; or, again, where a man puts himself in seisin without a writ, proxy or warrant; or, again, where a gift has been made to two men, and the livery has been made to one of them while the other, of his own authority, by virtue of the bare charter, puts himself in seisin.   The writ of intrusion is generally in the form that follows:

To show why he intruded himself in such-and-such an amount of land which B., who lately died, held of the said A. for his life only and which after the death of the said B. should revert to him, as the said A. says.

CHAPTER 31.   OF FERMS AND REAL ACTIONS

Bracton,
f. 220
In one and the same tenement one man may have the freehold and another the usufruct, user and right to dwell.   Such persons, when they were ejected within their term, used to aid themselves by a writ of covenant, but because such a writ could not apply between any persons save only between him who let to ferm for a term and him who took [the lease], nor could the obligations of the agreement bind others, and also because the business could rarely be settled between such persons, therefore by advice of the court a remedy was provided for the fermor against any ejectors whatsoever by a writ as follows:

Command A. that he render to B. such-and-such an amount of land with its appurtenances in such-and-such a township [which] the said A. demised [etc.] (and if the ejector were other than he who demised, then thus: which C. of N. demised to him) for a term which has not yet expired, and within which the aforesaid A. (or the aforesaid C.) unlawfully ejected the said B. from the said
Bracton,
f. 220b
land (or from his ferm), as he says.   And unless he do so etc.

Vel sic:

Si A. fecerit te securum etc., tunc summone B. quod sit etc. ad respondendum
eidem A. quare iniuste eiecit eundem de tanto terre quam idem A. vel alius ei
dimisit ad terminum qui nondum preteriit infra quem, vt supra.

5   Prima tamen forma magis conpetens est et conpendiosa propter capcionem
terre in manum regis ad vitandum attachiamenta et dilaciones.   Non enim poterit
aliquis firmarium eicere de firma sua magis quam tenentem aliquem de libero
tenemento suo, et vnde si quis firmarium a firma eiecerit seysinam restituet cum
dampnis quia talis spoliacio non multum differt a disseysina.   Domino tamen
10 proprietatis conpetit assisa noue disseysine versus extraneum eiectorem et
firmario competit remedium per hoc breue:

Si B. fecerit te securum etc., tunc summone A. quod sit coram etc. ostensurus
quare deforciat prefato B. tantum terre cum pertinenciis in N. quod A. ei dimisit
ad terminum qui nondum preteriit infra quem terminum idem A. prefato C.
15 terram illam vendidit occasione cuius vendicionis idem C. prefatum B. de terra
illa eiecit, vt dicit.

Et si tale breue conpetat versus extraneum propter vendicionem multo
forcius conpetit contra ipsum dominum qui dimisit et sine causa eiecit quam
contra extraneum qui autem causam habuit qualem, videlicet causa vendicionis
20 ei facte per quam venditor ipsum firmarium eiecit.

Fiunt eciam breuia remedialia in hoc casu, vt si A. dimiserit B. vnam acram
terre ad terminum annorum et idem A. durante termino illo eandem terram
vendiderit C. in feodo, occasione cuius vendicionis idem C. prefatum B. de
predicta terra eiciat ac predictus A. nichil sibi retinuerit vnde conuencionem
25 tenere possit B. nec waranciam vel escambium ei facere.   Et quia fraus et
dolus nemini debet patrocinari prouisa fuerunt breuia:

Si A. fecerit te securum etc. summone B. etc. ostensurus quare deforciat
predicto A. tantum terre cum pertinenciis in N. quam C. dimisit predicto A. vel
D. patri predicti A. cuius heres ipse est ad terminum qui nondum preteriit infra
30 quem terminum idem C. prefato B. terram illam vendidit.

Vel sic:

infra quem terminum idem C. terram illam vendidit occasione cuius vendicionis idem B. prefatum A. de terra illa eiecit.

Vel sic:

35   Ostensurus quare deforciat predictis A. et B. centum acras terre cum pertinenciis in N. quam C. de D. dimisit E. et prefate B. quondam vxori eiusdem
E. ad terminum xl. annorum qui nondum preteriit, infra quem terminum prefatus
E. illam dimisit predicto tali ad terminum viginti annorum iam preteritorum post
quem quidem terminum terra illa ad prefatam B. reuerti debuit, vt dicunt.

40   Et sic rehabebit firmarius terminum suum cum dampnis suis.   Domino vero

Or thus:

if [B.] give you security etc., then summon [A.] to be etc. to answer the said
[B.] why he has unlawfully ejected him from such-and-such an amount of land
which the said A. (or another) demised to him for a term which has not yet expired, within which (as above).

The first form of writ is, however, more suitable and quicker on account of the
seizure into the king's hand to the avoiding of attachments and delays.   No one
may eject any fermor from his ferm any more than any tenant from his freehold.
Wherefore, if anyone should eject a fermor from his ferm, he shall restore his
seisin with damages, for spoliation of this kind does not greatly differ from disseisin.   But the assize of novel disseisin lies for the owner against a third party
who ejects [the fermor], and to the fermor there is available a remedy by this
writ:

Bracton,
f. 220

If B. give you security etc., then summon [C.] to be before etc. to show why
he deforces the aforesaid B. of such-and-such an amount of land with its appurtenances in N. which A. demised to him for a term which has not yet expired,
within which term the said A. sold the said land to the aforesaid C., by reason of
which sale the said C. has ejected the aforesaid B. from the said land, as he says.

If such a writ is available against a third party by reason of a sale, much more
is it available against the owner himself who demised and has ejected without
cause than against the third party who has some kind of cause, to wit, the cause
of sale made to him, in consequence of which the [buyer] has ejected the fermor.

Remedial writs are also provided in this case, for example, where A. has demised to B. an acre of land for a term of years and the said A. has sold the said
land to C. in fee during that term, and by virtue of that sale the said C. ejects the
aforesaid B. from the aforesaid land, and the aforesaid A. has retained nothing
for himself whence he can keep his covenant with B. or give him warranty or
exchange.   And because fraud and guile should give no one protection, these
writs have been provided:

If A. give you security etc., summon B. etc. to show why he deforces the aforesaid A. of such-and-such an amount of land with its appurtenances in N. which C.
demised to the aforesaid A. (or D., father of the aforesaid A., whose heir he is)
for a term which has not yet expired, within which term the said C. sold the said
land to the aforesaid B.

Or thus:

within which term the said C. sold the said land, by virtue of which sale the
said B. has ejected the aforesaid A. from the said land.

Or thus:

to show why he deforces the aforesaid A. and B. of a hundred acres of land
with appurtenances in N., which C. of D. demised to E. and the aforesaid B.,
formerly the wife of the said E., for the term of forty years which has not yet expired, within which term the aforesaid E. demised the said land to the aforesaid
so-and-so for a term of twenty years now past, after which term the said land
ought to revert to the aforesaid B., as they say.

Bracton,
f. 220b

And so the fermor will recover his term with his damages.   To the owner of the

proprietatis competit remedium versus eiectorem per assisam noue disseysine et
per inde recuperabit tenementum, dampna vero minime. Si autem dominus
proprietatis tenementum ad firmam traditum alicui dederit in dominico tenen-   f. 104
dum, seysinam ei facere poterit saluo firmario termino suo. Poterit enim eum
5   inducere in seysinam vacuam quantum ad ipsum et suos et attornare ei firmarium et seruicium suum dum tamen non vtatur feoffatus nec explecia capiat   [277]
nec firmarium inpediat vti nec ipsum eiciat. Poterit enim quilibet eorum sine
preiudicio alterius in seysina esse eiusdem tenementi, vnus vt de termino alius vt
de feodo vel libero tenemento. Et datur ista accio heredibus et conpetit contra
10   heredes, quia recte dicimus totum fundum nostrum esse eciam cum vsus fructus
alienus sit, quia non dominii pars est vsusfructus set seruitutis, vt via et iter, nec
falso dicitur meum esse cuius non potest vlla pars dici alterius esse.

4. suo] su, J.   6. non om. J.   12. vlla Br., et vna, J.

property there is available a remedy against the ejector by the assize of novel disseisin, and thereby he will recover the tenement, but not damages. If, however, the owner of the property should grant a tenement subject to a lease to someone to hold in demesne, he can give him seisin, saving his fermor's term. He may, indeed, put the feoffee in vacant seisin, so far as he and his are concerned, and attorn to him the fermor and the fermor's service, provided that the feoffee does not himself use the land or take the profits or obstruct the fermor's use of the land or eject him. Each of them may, in fact, be in seisin of the same tenement without prejudice to the other, the one as to the term and the other as to the fee or freehold. And this right of action is given to heirs and is available against heirs, because we rightly speak of an estate as wholly ours, even though the usufruct belongs to another, because the usufruct does not partake of ownership but of servitude, like a right of way or passage, nor do I wrongly call that mine of which no part can be said to belong to another.